I asked my editor if we could start a chapter with a splash page even though it wasn't going to be in color in the magazine. All he said was "no." Whaa? Why not?! All the other manga series are doing it! We even did it in chapter 4 already!

—Tsugumi Ohba

The seasons keep changing, but personally I like working in winter the best.

—Takeshi Obata

Tsugumi Ohba
Born in Tokyo, Tsugumi Ohba is the author of the hit series *Death Note*. His current series *Bakuman.* is serialized in *Weekly Shonen Jump*.

Takeshi Obata
Takeshi Obata was born in 1969 in Niigata, Japan, and is the artist of the wildly popular SHONEN JUMP title *Hikaru no Go*, which won the 2003 Tezuka Osamu Cultural Prize: Shinsei "New Hope" award and the 2000 Shogakukan Manga award. Obata is also the artist of *Arabian Majin Bokentan Lamp Lamp*, *Ayatsuri Sakon*, *Cyborg Jichan G.*, and the smash hit manga *Death Note*. His current series *Bakuman.* is serialized in *Weekly Shonen Jump*.

Volume 13

SHONEN JUMP Manga Edition

Story by **TSUGUMI OHBA**
Art by **TAKESHI OBATA**

Translation | **Tetsuichiro Miyaki**
English Adaptation | **Julie Lutz**
Touch-up Art & Lettering | **James Gaubatz**
Design | **Fawn Lau, Chii Maene**
Editor | **Alexis Kirsch**

BAKUMAN. © 2008 by Tsugumi Ohba, Takeshi Obata
All rights reserved.
First published in Japan in 2008 by SHUEISHA Inc., Tokyo.
English translation rights arranged by SHUEISHA Inc.

The rights of the author(s) of the work(s) in this publication to be
so identified have been asserted in accordance with the Copyright,
Designs and Patents Act 1988. A CIP catalogue record for this book
is available from the British Library.

The stories, characters and incidents mentioned in this publication are
entirely fictional.

Printed in the U.S.A.

Published by VIZ Media, LLC
P.O. Box 77010
San Francisco, CA 94107

10 9 8 7 6 5 4 3 2 1
First printing, August 2012

BAKUMAN.
13

FANS
and
LOVE
AT FIRST
SIGHT

STORY BY
TSUGUMI OHBA

ART BY
TAKESHI OBATA

SHONEN JUMP MANGA

BAKUMAN。

バクマン。

vol. 13

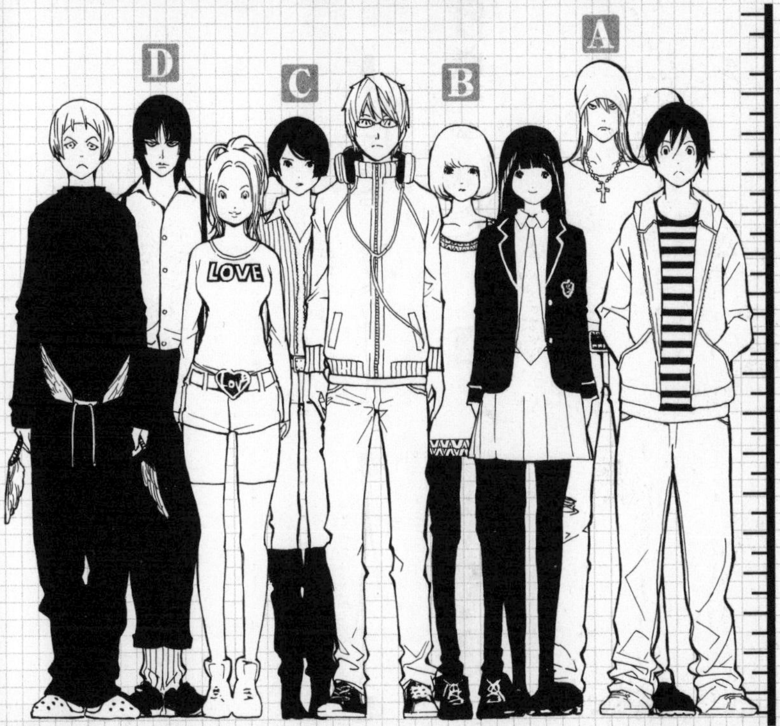
D
C
B
A
LOVE
LOVE

EIJI
Nizuma

A manga prodigy and Tezuka Award winner at the age of 15. One of the most popular creators in *Jump*.

Age: 21

KAYA
Takagi

Miho's friend and Akito's wife. A nice girl who actively works as the interceder between Moritaka and Azuki.

Age: 21

AKITO
Takagi

Manga writer. An extremely smart guy who gets the best grades in his class. A cool guy who becomes very passionate when it comes to manga.

Age: 20

MIHO
Azuki

A girl who dreams of becoming a voice actress. She promised to marry Moritaka under the condition that they not see each other until their dreams come true.

Age: 21

MORITAKA
Mashiro

Manga artist. An extreme romantic who believes that he will marry Miho Azuki once their dreams come true.

Age: 20

*These ages are from December 2014.

STORY In order to attain the glory that only a handful of people can, two young men decide to walk the rough "path of manga" and become professional manga creators. This is the story of a great artist, Moritaka Mashiro, a talented writer, Akito Takagi, and their quest to become manga legends!

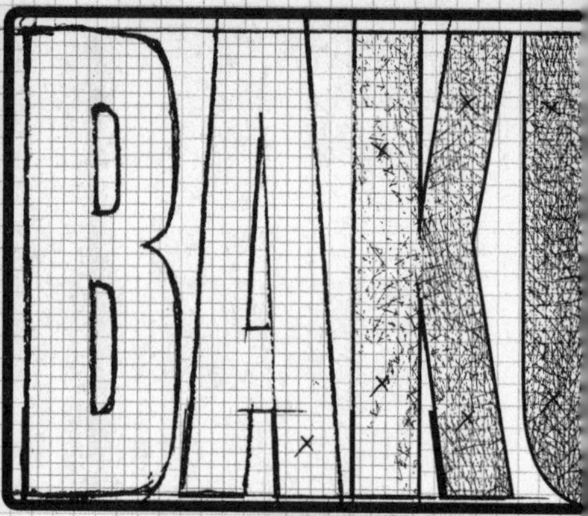

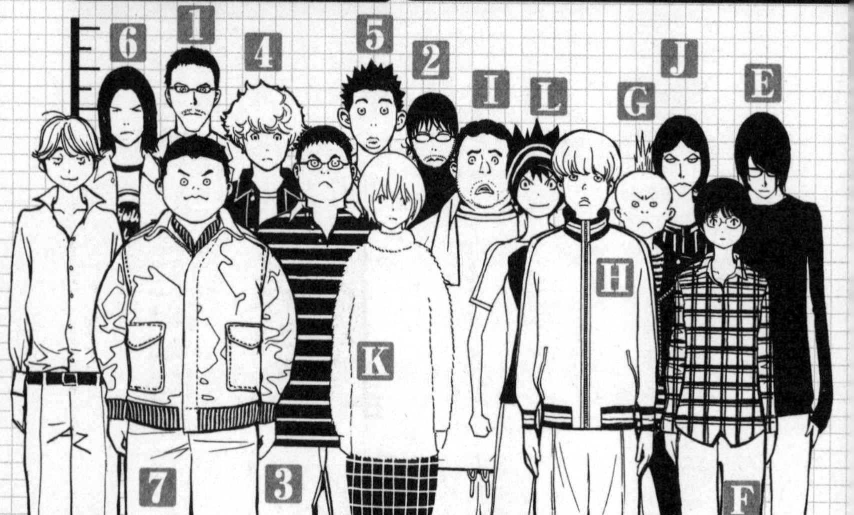

6
1
4
5
2
I
L
G
J
E
H
K
7
3
F
8

WEEKLY SHONEN JUMP Editorial Department

1 Editor in Chief Sasaki
2 Deputy Editor in Chief Heishi
3 Soichi Aida
4 Yujiro Hattori
5 Akira Hattori
6 Koji Yoshida
7 Goro Miura
8 Masakazu Yamahisa

The MANGA ARTISTS and ASSISTANTS

A SHINTA FUKUDA
B KO AOKI
C AIKO IWASE
D KAZUYA HIRAMARU
E RYU SHIZUKA
F NATSUMI KATO
G YASUOKA
H SHOYO TAKAHAMA
I TAKURO NAKAI
J SHUICHI MORIYA
K SHUN SHIRATORI
L ICHIRIKI ORIHARA

BAKUMAN。

vol.13

CONTENTS

(FANS AND LOVE
AT FIRST SIGHT)

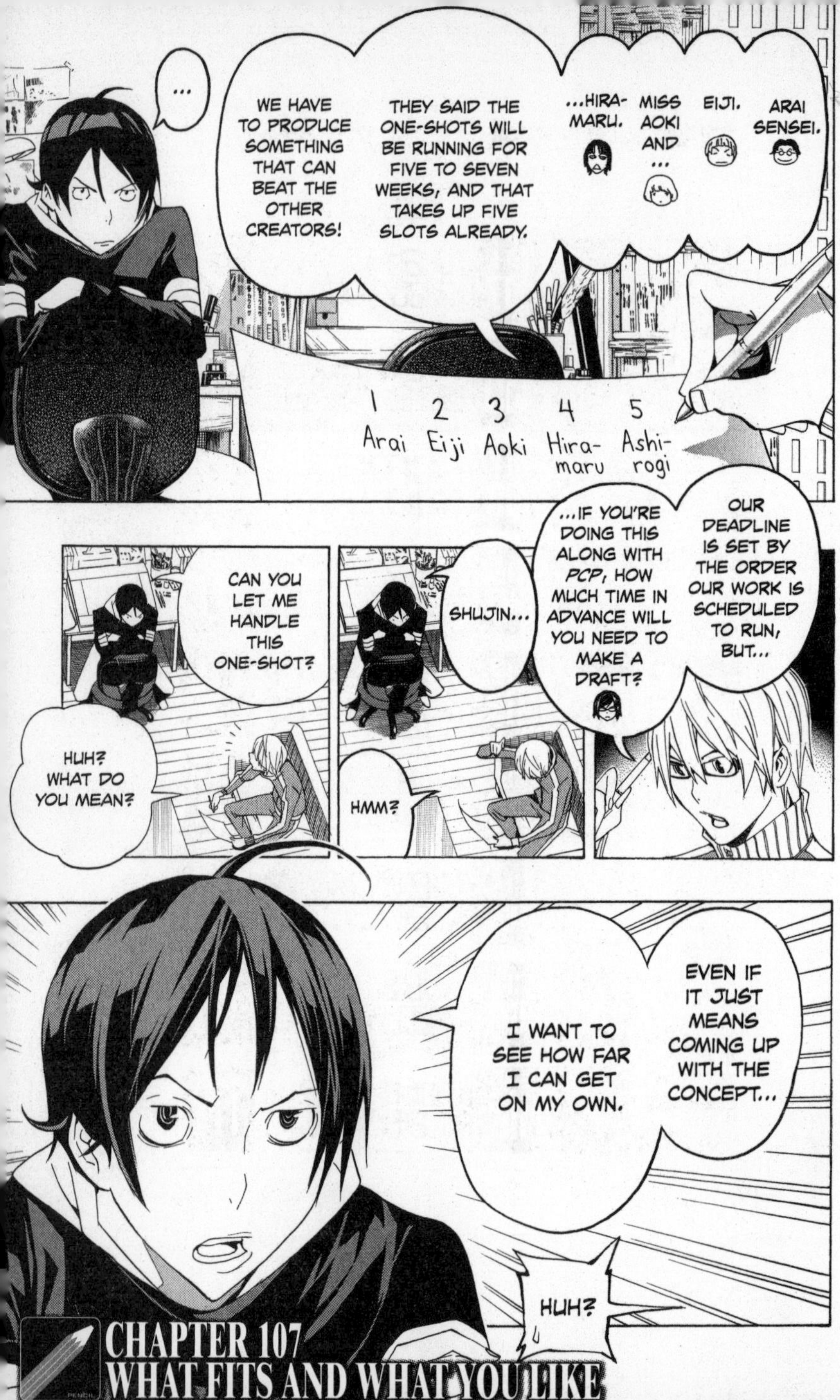

ARAI SENSEI.
EIJI.
MISS AOKI AND ...
...HIRA-MARU.
THEY SAID THE ONE-SHOTS WILL BE RUNNING FOR FIVE TO SEVEN WEEKS, AND THAT TAKES UP FIVE SLOTS ALREADY.
WE HAVE TO PRODUCE SOMETHING THAT CAN BEAT THE OTHER CREATORS!
...
1 Arai 2 Eiji 3 Aoki 4 Hira-maru 5 Ashi-rogi
OUR DEADLINE IS SET BY THE ORDER OUR WORK IS SCHEDULED TO RUN, BUT...
...IF YOU'RE DOING THIS ALONG WITH *PCP*, HOW MUCH TIME IN ADVANCE WILL YOU NEED TO MAKE A DRAFT?
SHUJIN...
HMM?
CAN YOU LET ME HANDLE THIS ONE-SHOT?
HUH? WHAT DO YOU MEAN?
EVEN IF IT JUST MEANS COMING UP WITH THE CONCEPT...
I WANT TO SEE HOW FAR I CAN GET ON MY OWN.
HUH?

CHAPTER 107
WHAT FITS AND WHAT YOU LIKE

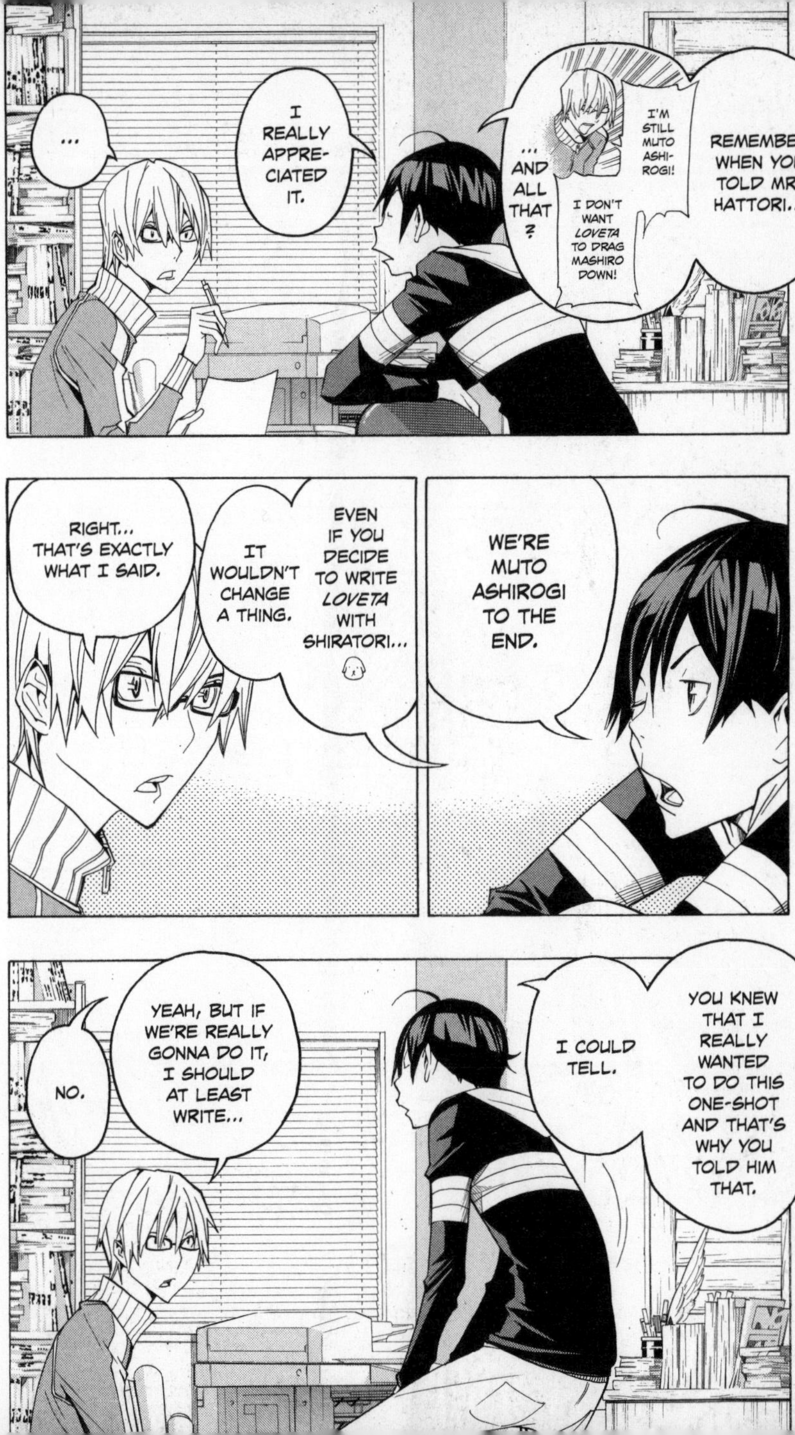

REMEMBER WHEN YOU TOLD MR. HATTORI...
I'M STILL MUTO ASHIROGI!
I DON'T WANT *LOVETA* TO DRAG MASHIRO DOWN!
...AND ALL THAT?
I REALLY APPRECIATED IT.
...
WE'RE MUTO ASHIROGI TO THE END.
EVEN IF YOU DECIDE TO WRITE *LOVETA* WITH SHIRATORI...
IT WOULDN'T CHANGE A THING.
RIGHT... THAT'S EXACTLY WHAT I SAID.
YOU KNEW THAT I REALLY WANTED TO DO THIS ONE-SHOT AND THAT'S WHY YOU TOLD HIM THAT.
I COULD TELL.
YEAH, BUT IF WE'RE REALLY GONNA DO IT, I SHOULD AT LEAST WRITE...
NO.

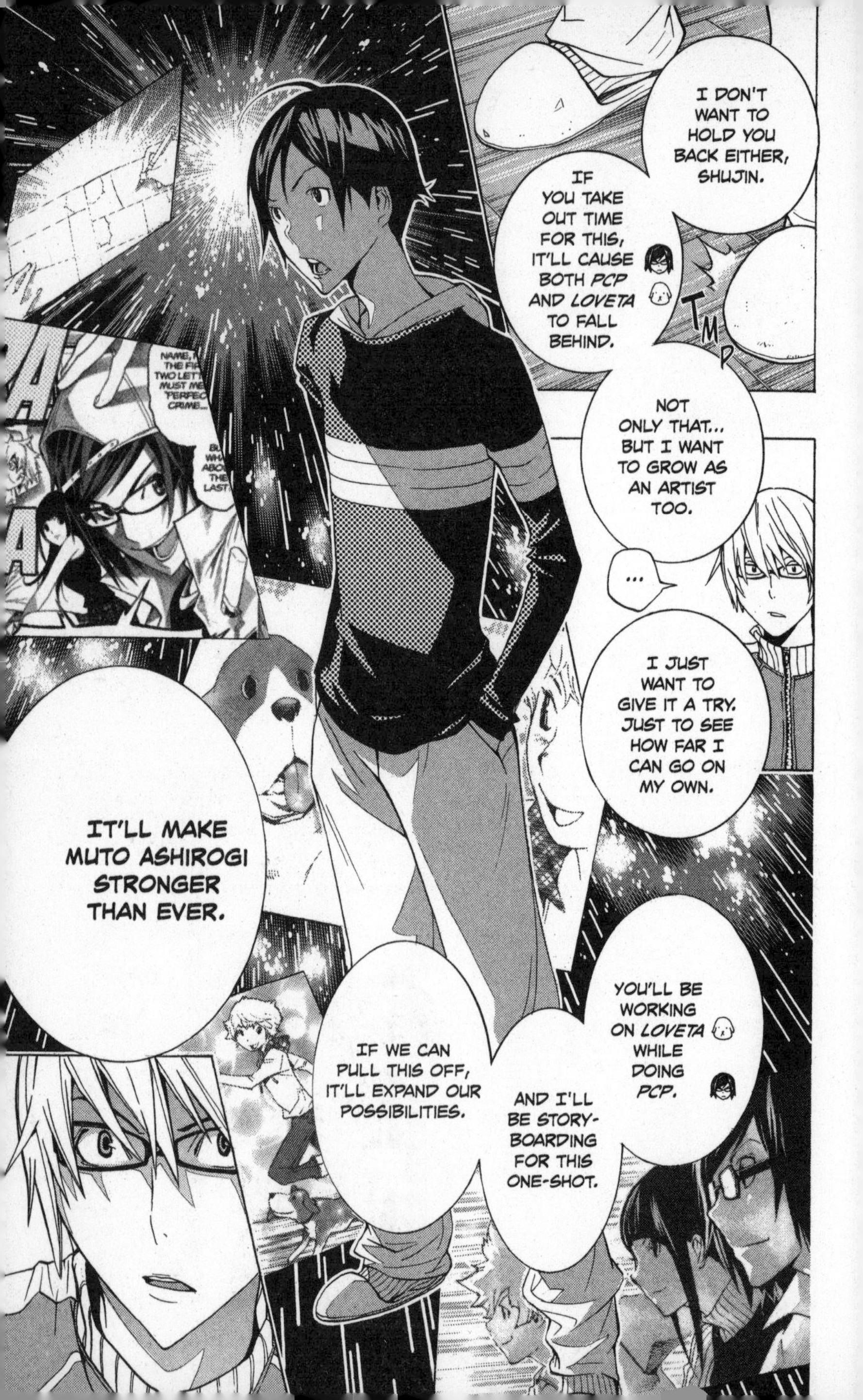
I DON'T WANT TO HOLD YOU BACK EITHER, SHUJIN.
IF YOU TAKE OUT TIME FOR THIS, IT'LL CAUSE BOTH *PCP* AND *LOVETA* TO FALL BEHIND.
TMP
NOT ONLY THAT... BUT I WANT TO GROW AS AN ARTIST TOO.
...
I JUST WANT TO GIVE IT A TRY. JUST TO SEE HOW FAR I CAN GO ON MY OWN.
YOU'LL BE WORKING ON *LOVETA* WHILE DOING *PCP*.
AND I'LL BE STORY-BOARDING FOR THIS ONE-SHOT.
IF WE CAN PULL THIS OFF, IT'LL EXPAND OUR POSSIBILITIES.
IT'LL MAKE MUTO ASHIROGI STRONGER THAN EVER.

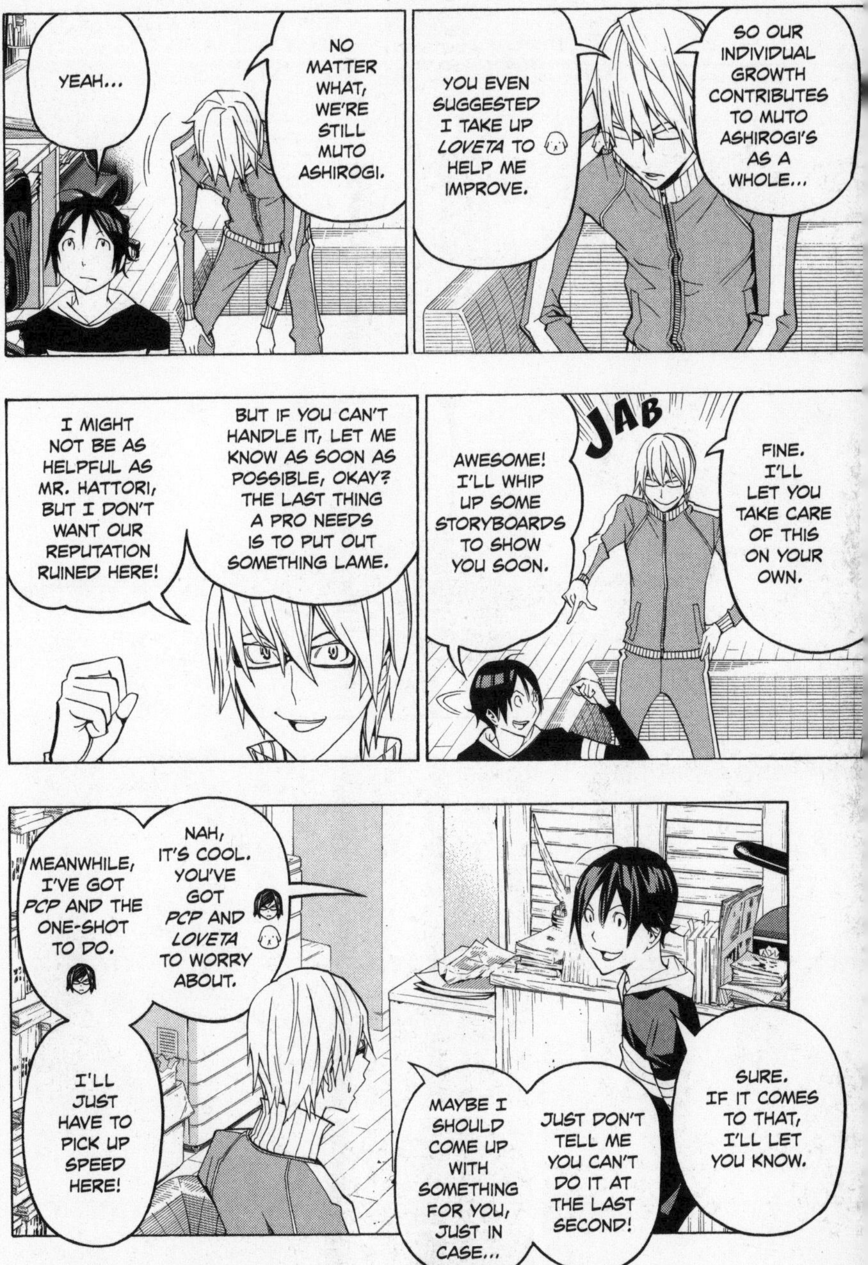
SO OUR INDIVIDUAL GROWTH CONTRIBUTES TO MUTO ASHIROGI'S AS A WHOLE...
YOU EVEN SUGGESTED I TAKE UP *LOVETA* TO HELP ME IMPROVE.
NO MATTER WHAT, WE'RE STILL MUTO ASHIROGI.
YEAH...
FINE. I'LL LET YOU TAKE CARE OF THIS ON YOUR OWN.
JAB
AWESOME! I'LL WHIP UP SOME STORYBOARDS TO SHOW YOU SOON.
BUT IF YOU CAN'T HANDLE IT, LET ME KNOW AS SOON AS POSSIBLE, OKAY? THE LAST THING A PRO NEEDS IS TO PUT OUT SOMETHING LAME.
I MIGHT NOT BE AS HELPFUL AS MR. HATTORI, BUT I DON'T WANT OUR REPUTATION RUINED HERE!
SURE. IF IT COMES TO THAT, I'LL LET YOU KNOW.
JUST DON'T TELL ME YOU CAN'T DO IT AT THE LAST SECOND!
MAYBE I SHOULD COME UP WITH SOMETHING FOR YOU, JUST IN CASE...
NAH, IT'S COOL. YOU'VE GOT *PCP* AND *LOVETA* TO WORRY ABOUT.
MEANWHILE, I'VE GOT *PCP* AND THE ONE-SHOT TO DO.
I'LL JUST HAVE TO PICK UP SPEED HERE!

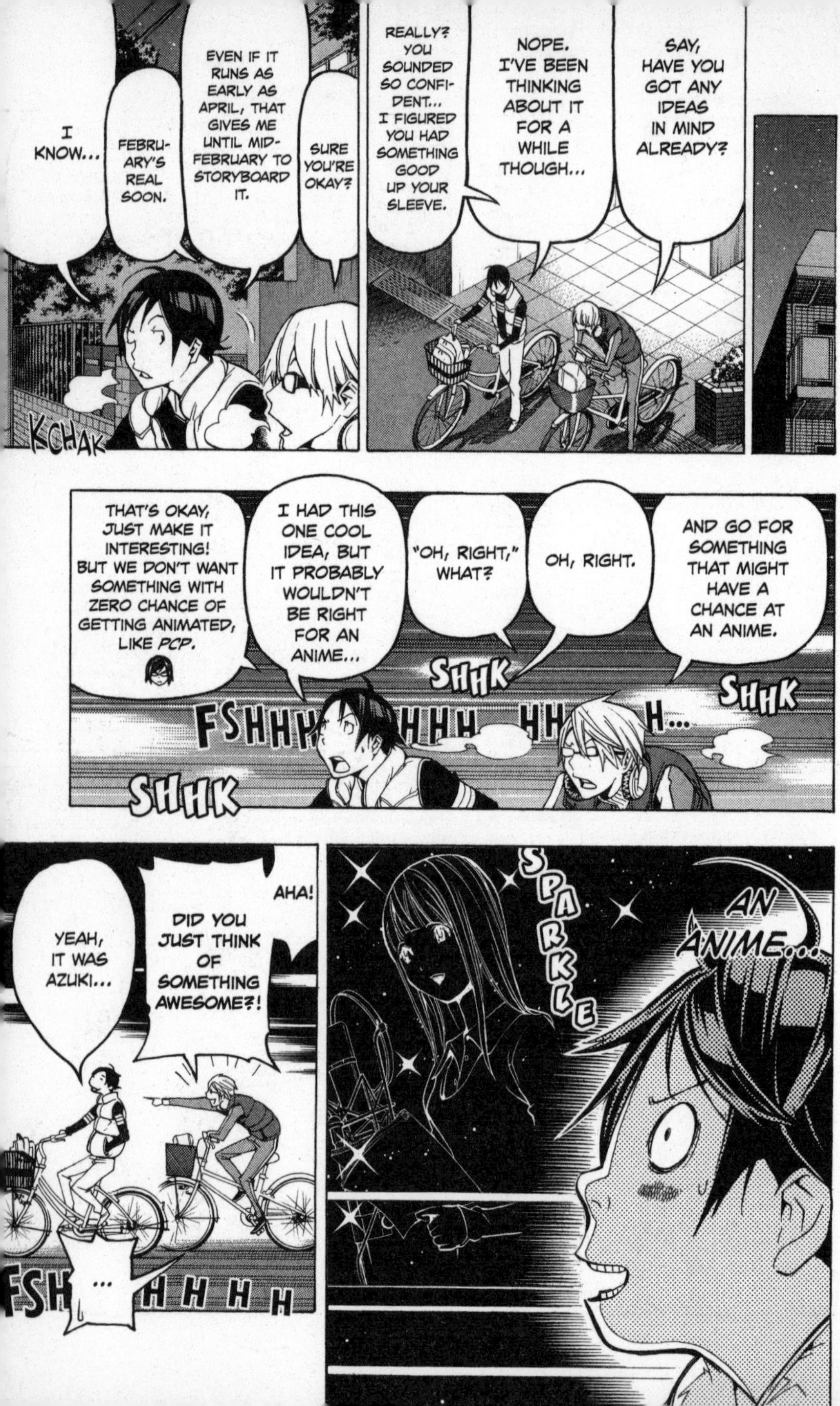
SAY, HAVE YOU GOT ANY IDEAS IN MIND ALREADY?
NOPE. I'VE BEEN THINKING ABOUT IT FOR A WHILE THOUGH...
REALLY? YOU SOUNDED SO CONFI-DENT... I FIGURED YOU HAD SOMETHING GOOD UP YOUR SLEEVE.
SURE YOU'RE OKAY?
EVEN IF IT RUNS AS EARLY AS APRIL, THAT GIVES ME UNTIL MID-FEBRUARY TO STORYBOARD IT.
FEBRU-ARY'S REAL SOON.
I KNOW...
KCHAK
AND GO FOR SOMETHING THAT MIGHT HAVE A CHANCE AT AN ANIME.
OH, RIGHT.
"OH, RIGHT," WHAT?
I HAD THIS ONE COOL IDEA, BUT IT PROBABLY WOULDN'T BE RIGHT FOR AN ANIME...
THAT'S OKAY, JUST MAKE IT INTERESTING! BUT WE DON'T WANT SOMETHING WITH ZERO CHANCE OF GETTING ANIMATED, LIKE *PCP*.
SHHK
SHHK
FSHHHHHHH HHH...
SHHK
AN ANIME...
SPARKLE
AHA! DID YOU JUST THINK OF SOMETHING AWESOME?!
YEAH, IT WAS AZUKI...
...
FSHHHHHH

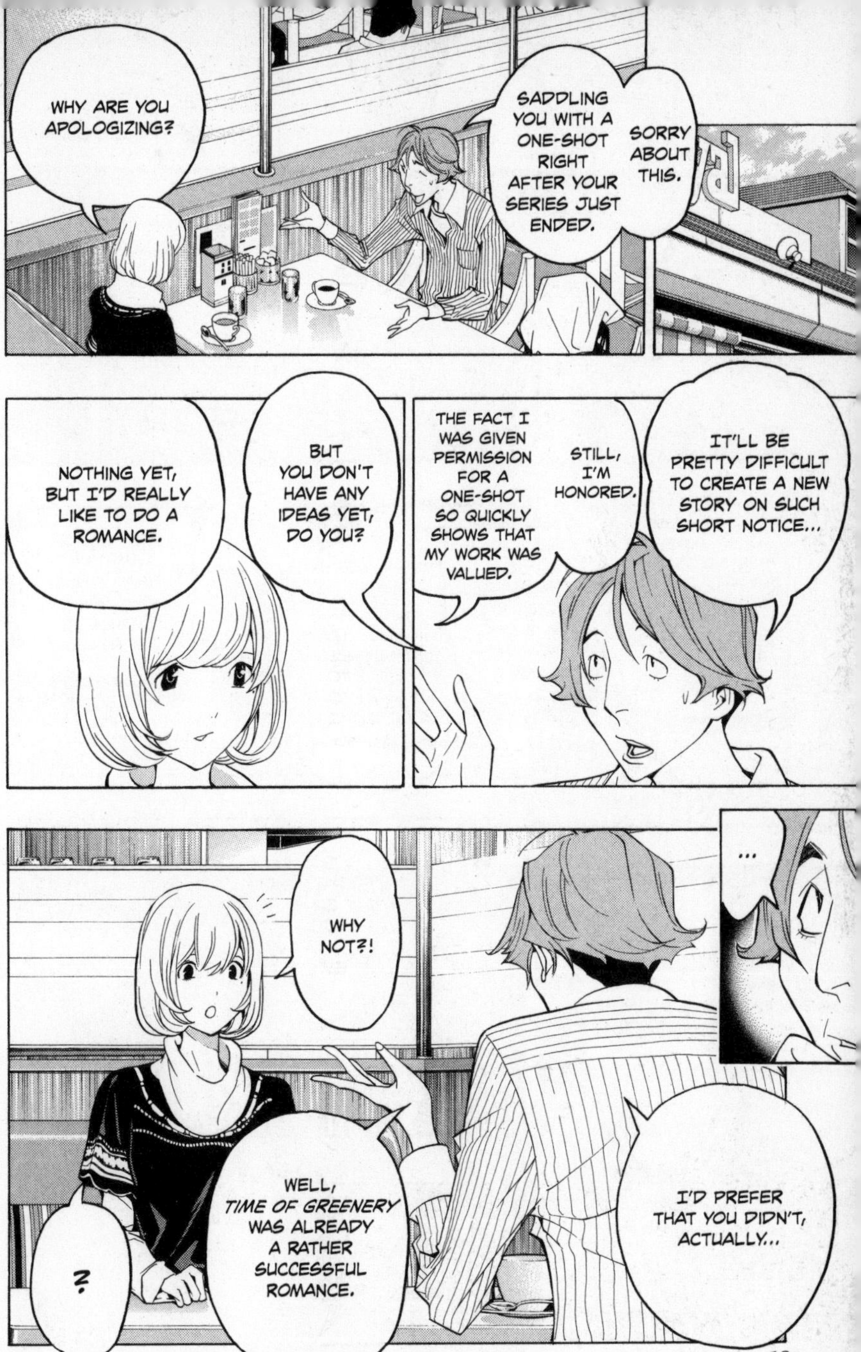
SORRY ABOUT THIS.
SADDLING YOU WITH A ONE-SHOT RIGHT AFTER YOUR SERIES JUST ENDED.
WHY ARE YOU APOLOGIZING?
IT'LL BE PRETTY DIFFICULT TO CREATE A NEW STORY ON SUCH SHORT NOTICE...
STILL, I'M HONORED.
THE FACT I WAS GIVEN PERMISSION FOR A ONE-SHOT SO QUICKLY SHOWS THAT MY WORK WAS VALUED.
BUT YOU DON'T HAVE ANY IDEAS YET, DO YOU?
NOTHING YET, BUT I'D REALLY LIKE TO DO A ROMANCE.
...
I'D PREFER THAT YOU DIDN'T, ACTUALLY...
WHY NOT?!
WELL, *TIME OF GREENERY* WAS ALREADY A RATHER SUCCESSFUL ROMANCE.
?

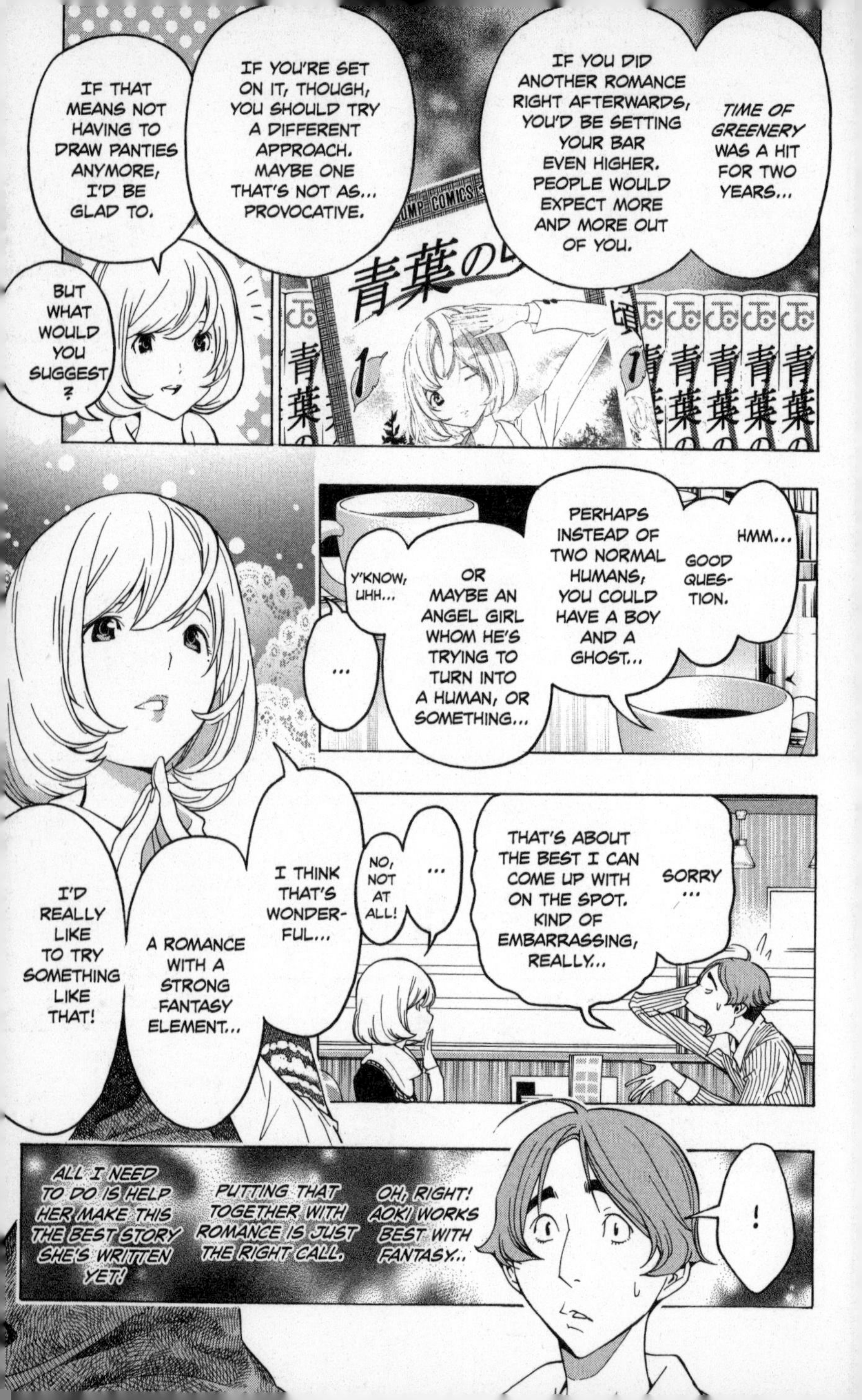

TIME OF GREENERY WAS A HIT FOR TWO YEARS...
IF YOU DID ANOTHER ROMANCE RIGHT AFTERWARDS, YOU'D BE SETTING YOUR BAR EVEN HIGHER. PEOPLE WOULD EXPECT MORE AND MORE OUT OF YOU.
IF YOU'RE SET ON IT, THOUGH, YOU SHOULD TRY A DIFFERENT APPROACH. MAYBE ONE THAT'S NOT AS... PROVOCATIVE.
IF THAT MEANS NOT HAVING TO DRAW PANTIES ANYMORE, I'D BE GLAD TO.
BUT WHAT WOULD YOU SUGGEST?
HMM...
GOOD QUES-TION.
PERHAPS INSTEAD OF TWO NORMAL HUMANS, YOU COULD HAVE A BOY AND A GHOST...
OR MAYBE AN ANGEL GIRL WHOM HE'S TRYING TO TURN INTO A HUMAN, OR SOMETHING...
Y'KNOW, UHH...
...
SORRY...
THAT'S ABOUT THE BEST I CAN COME UP WITH ON THE SPOT. KIND OF EMBARRASSING, REALLY...
...
NO, NOT AT ALL!
I THINK THAT'S WONDER-FUL...
A ROMANCE WITH A STRONG FANTASY ELEMENT...
I'D REALLY LIKE TO TRY SOMETHING LIKE THAT!
!
OH, RIGHT! AOKI WORKS BEST WITH FANTASY...
PUTTING THAT TOGETHER WITH ROMANCE IS JUST THE RIGHT CALL.
ALL I NEED TO DO IS HELP HER MAKE THIS THE BEST STORY SHE'S WRITTEN YET!

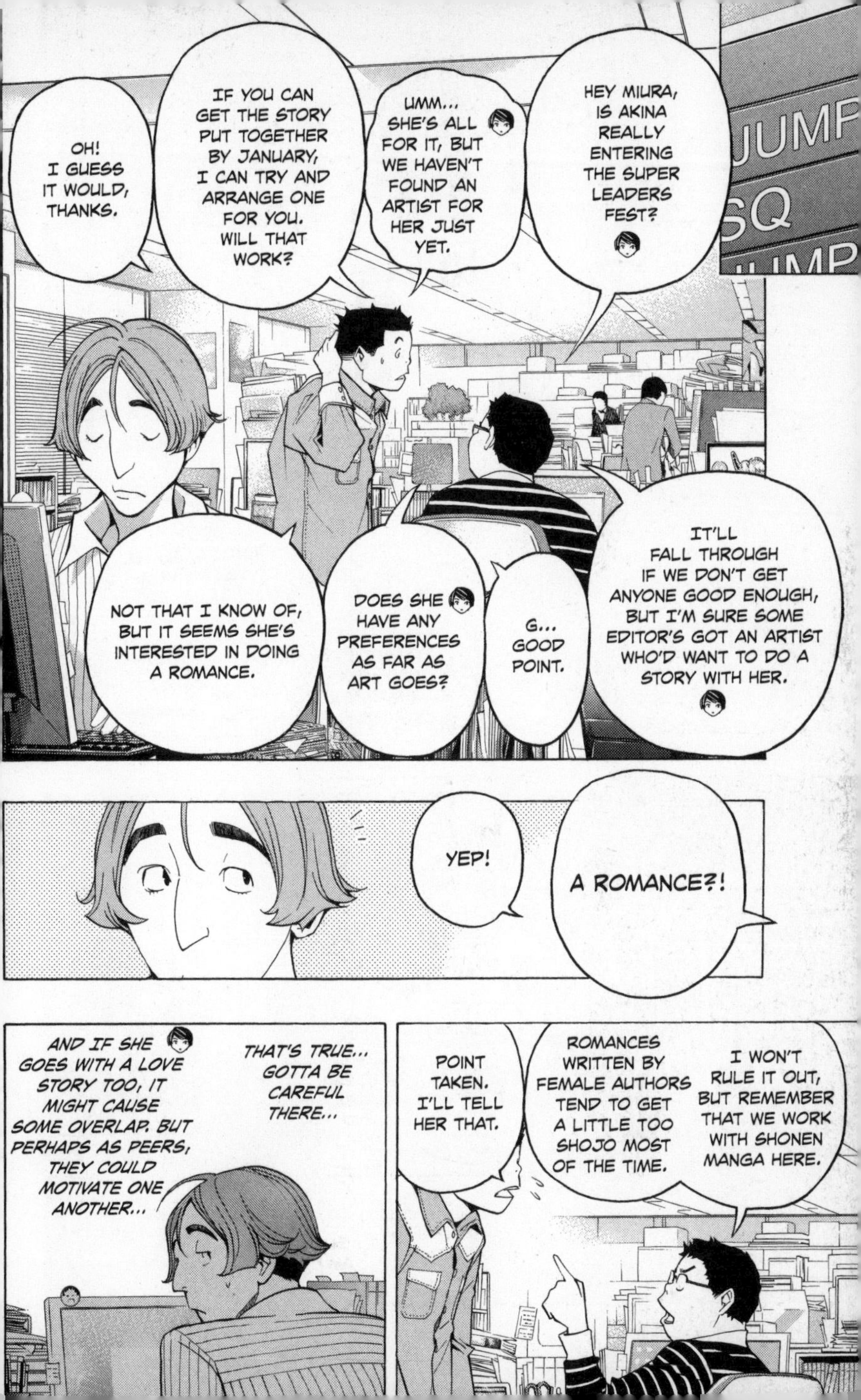
HEY MIURA, IS AKINA REALLY ENTERING THE SUPER LEADERS FEST?
UMM... SHE'S ALL FOR IT, BUT WE HAVEN'T FOUND AN ARTIST FOR HER JUST YET.
IF YOU CAN GET THE STORY PUT TOGETHER BY JANUARY, I CAN TRY AND ARRANGE ONE FOR YOU. WILL THAT WORK?
OH! I GUESS IT WOULD, THANKS.
IT'LL FALL THROUGH IF WE DON'T GET ANYONE GOOD ENOUGH, BUT I'M SURE SOME EDITOR'S GOT AN ARTIST WHO'D WANT TO DO A STORY WITH HER.
G... GOOD POINT.
DOES SHE HAVE ANY PREFERENCES AS FAR AS ART GOES?
NOT THAT I KNOW OF, BUT IT SEEMS SHE'S INTERESTED IN DOING A ROMANCE.
A ROMANCE?!
YEP!
I WON'T RULE IT OUT, BUT REMEMBER THAT WE WORK WITH SHONEN MANGA HERE.
ROMANCES WRITTEN BY FEMALE AUTHORS TEND TO GET A LITTLE TOO SHOJO MOST OF THE TIME.
POINT TAKEN. I'LL TELL HER THAT.
THAT'S TRUE... GOTTA BE CAREFUL THERE...
AND IF SHE GOES WITH A LOVE STORY TOO, IT MIGHT CAUSE SOME OVERLAP. BUT PERHAPS AS PEERS, THEY COULD MOTIVATE ONE ANOTHER...

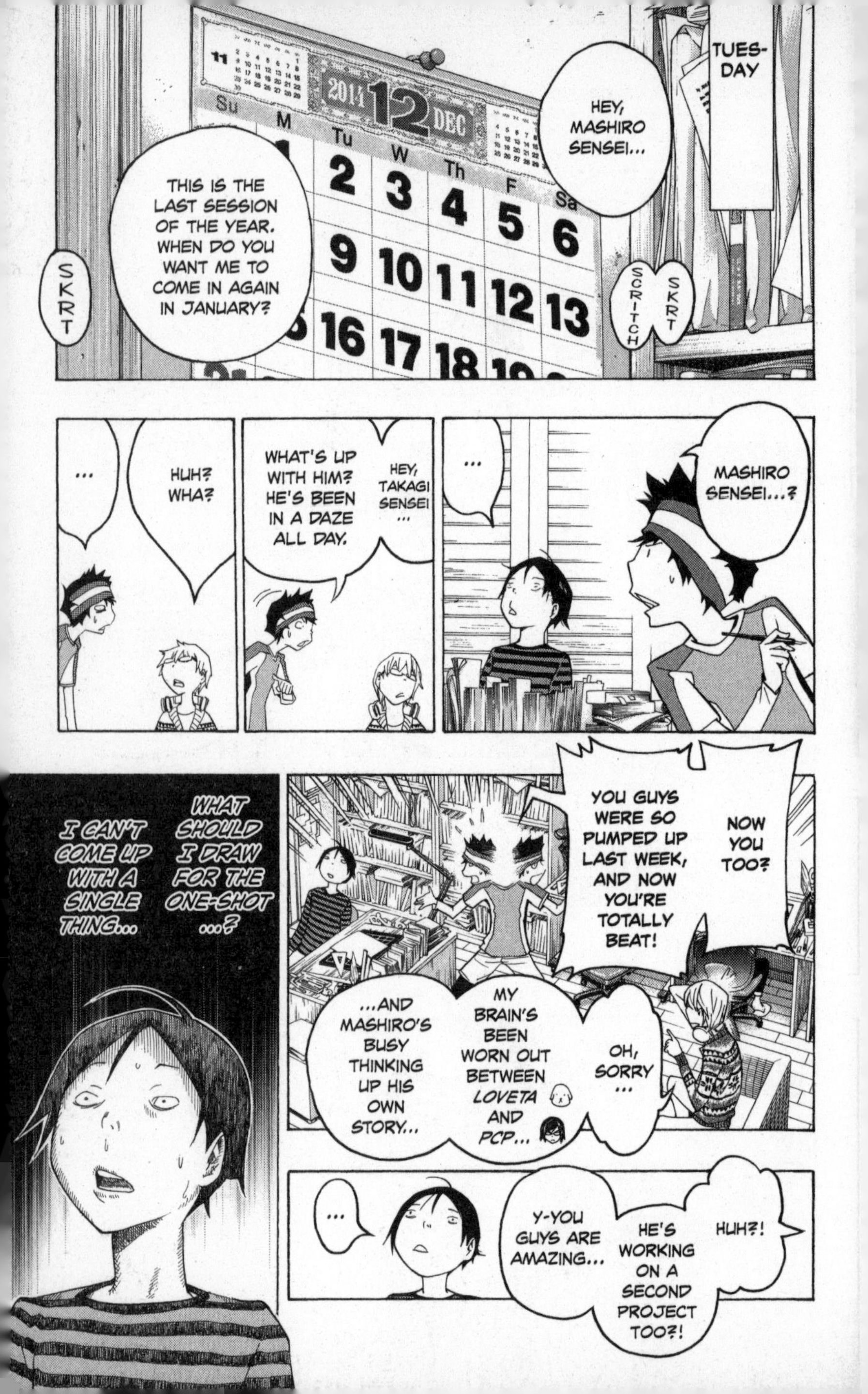
TUES-DAY
HEY, MASHIRO SENSEI...
SKRT
SCRITCH
2014 12 DEC
THIS IS THE LAST SESSION OF THE YEAR. WHEN DO YOU WANT ME TO COME IN AGAIN IN JANUARY?
SKRT
MASHIRO SENSEI...?
...
HEY, TAKAGI SENSEI...
WHAT'S UP WITH HIM? HE'S BEEN IN A DAZE ALL DAY.
HUH? WHA?
...
NOW YOU TOO?
YOU GUYS WERE SO PUMPED UP LAST WEEK, AND NOW YOU'RE TOTALLY BEAT!
OH, SORRY...
MY BRAIN'S BEEN WORN OUT BETWEEN *LOVETA* AND *PCP*...
...AND MASHIRO'S BUSY THINKING UP HIS OWN STORY...
HUH?!
HE'S WORKING ON A SECOND PROJECT TOO?!
Y-YOU GUYS ARE AMAZING...
...
WHAT SHOULD I DRAW FOR THE ONE-SHOT...?
I CAN'T COME UP WITH A SINGLE THING...

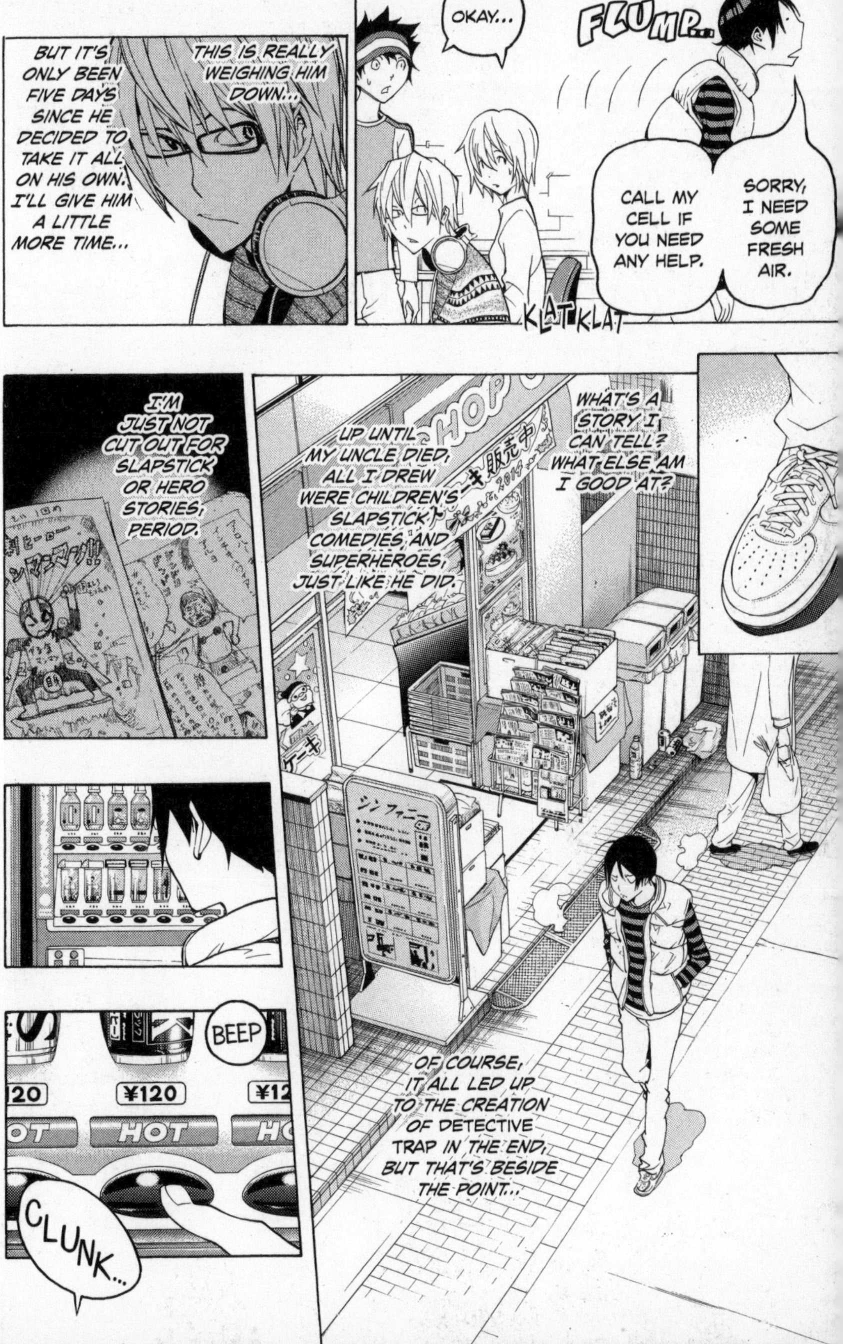
FLUMP...
SORRY, I NEED SOME FRESH AIR.
CALL MY CELL IF YOU NEED ANY HELP.
OKAY...
KLAT KLAT
THIS IS REALLY WEIGHING HIM DOWN...
BUT IT'S ONLY BEEN FIVE DAYS SINCE HE DECIDED TO TAKE IT ALL ON HIS OWN. I'LL GIVE HIM A LITTLE MORE TIME...
WHAT'S A STORY I CAN TELL? WHAT ELSE AM I GOOD AT?
UP UNTIL MY UNCLE DIED, ALL I DREW WERE CHILDREN'S SLAPSTICK COMEDIES AND SUPERHEROES, JUST LIKE HE DID.
OF COURSE, IT ALL LED UP TO THE CREATION OF DETECTIVE TRAP IN THE END, BUT THAT'S BESIDE THE POINT...
I'M JUST NOT CUT OUT FOR SLAPSTICK OR HERO STORIES, PERIOD.
BEEP
¥120
HOT
CLUNK...

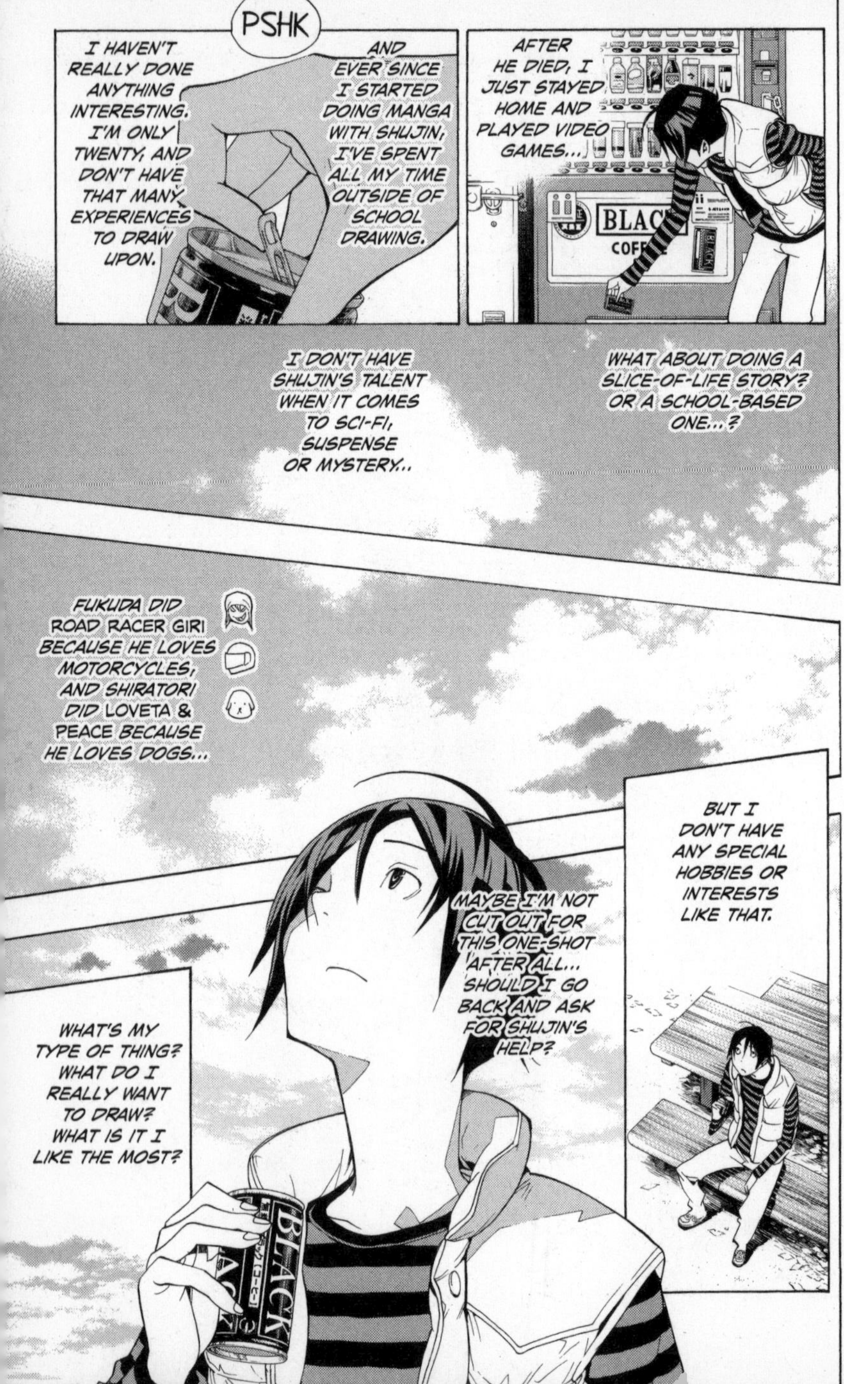
AFTER HE DIED, I JUST STAYED HOME AND PLAYED VIDEO GAMES...
PSHK
AND EVER SINCE I STARTED DOING MANGA WITH SHUJIN, I'VE SPENT ALL MY TIME OUTSIDE OF SCHOOL DRAWING.
I HAVEN'T REALLY DONE ANYTHING INTERESTING. I'M ONLY TWENTY, AND DON'T HAVE THAT MANY EXPERIENCES TO DRAW UPON.
WHAT ABOUT DOING A SLICE-OF-LIFE STORY? OR A SCHOOL-BASED ONE...?
I DON'T HAVE SHUJIN'S TALENT WHEN IT COMES TO SCI-FI, SUSPENSE OR MYSTERY...
FUKUDA DID ROAD RACER GIRI BECAUSE HE LOVES MOTORCYCLES, AND SHIRATORI DID LOVETA & PEACE BECAUSE HE LOVES DOGS...
BUT I DON'T HAVE ANY SPECIAL HOBBIES OR INTERESTS LIKE THAT.
MAYBE I'M NOT CUT OUT FOR THIS ONE-SHOT AFTER ALL... SHOULD I GO BACK AND ASK FOR SHUJIN'S HELP?
WHAT'S MY TYPE OF THING? WHAT DO I REALLY WANT TO DRAW? WHAT IS IT I LIKE THE MOST?

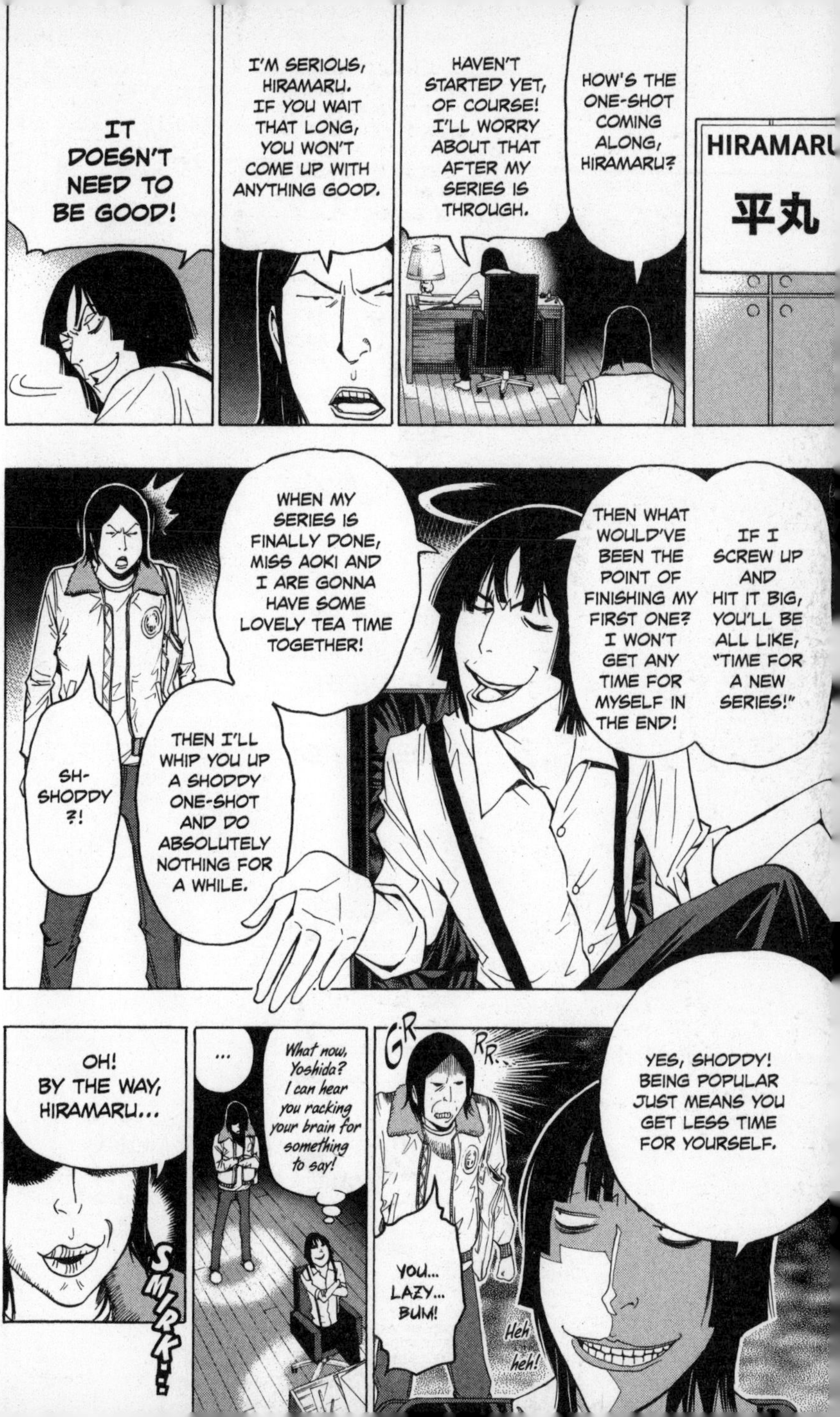
HIRAMARU
平丸
HOW'S THE ONE-SHOT COMING ALONG, HIRAMARU?
HAVEN'T STARTED YET, OF COURSE! I'LL WORRY ABOUT THAT AFTER MY SERIES IS THROUGH.
I'M SERIOUS, HIRAMARU. IF YOU WAIT THAT LONG, YOU WON'T COME UP WITH ANYTHING GOOD.
IT DOESN'T NEED TO BE GOOD!
IF I SCREW UP AND HIT IT BIG, YOU'LL BE ALL LIKE, "TIME FOR A NEW SERIES!"
THEN WHAT WOULD'VE BEEN THE POINT OF FINISHING MY FIRST ONE? I WON'T GET ANY TIME FOR MYSELF IN THE END!
WHEN MY SERIES IS FINALLY DONE, MISS AOKI AND I ARE GONNA HAVE SOME LOVELY TEA TIME TOGETHER!
THEN I'LL WHIP YOU UP A SHODDY ONE-SHOT AND DO ABSOLUTELY NOTHING FOR A WHILE.
SH-SHODDY?!
YES, SHODDY! BEING POPULAR JUST MEANS YOU GET LESS TIME FOR YOURSELF.
Heh heh!
GRRR...
YOU... LAZY... BUM!
What now, Yoshida? I can hear you racking your brain for something to say!
...
OH! BY THE WAY, HIRAMARU...
SMIRK...

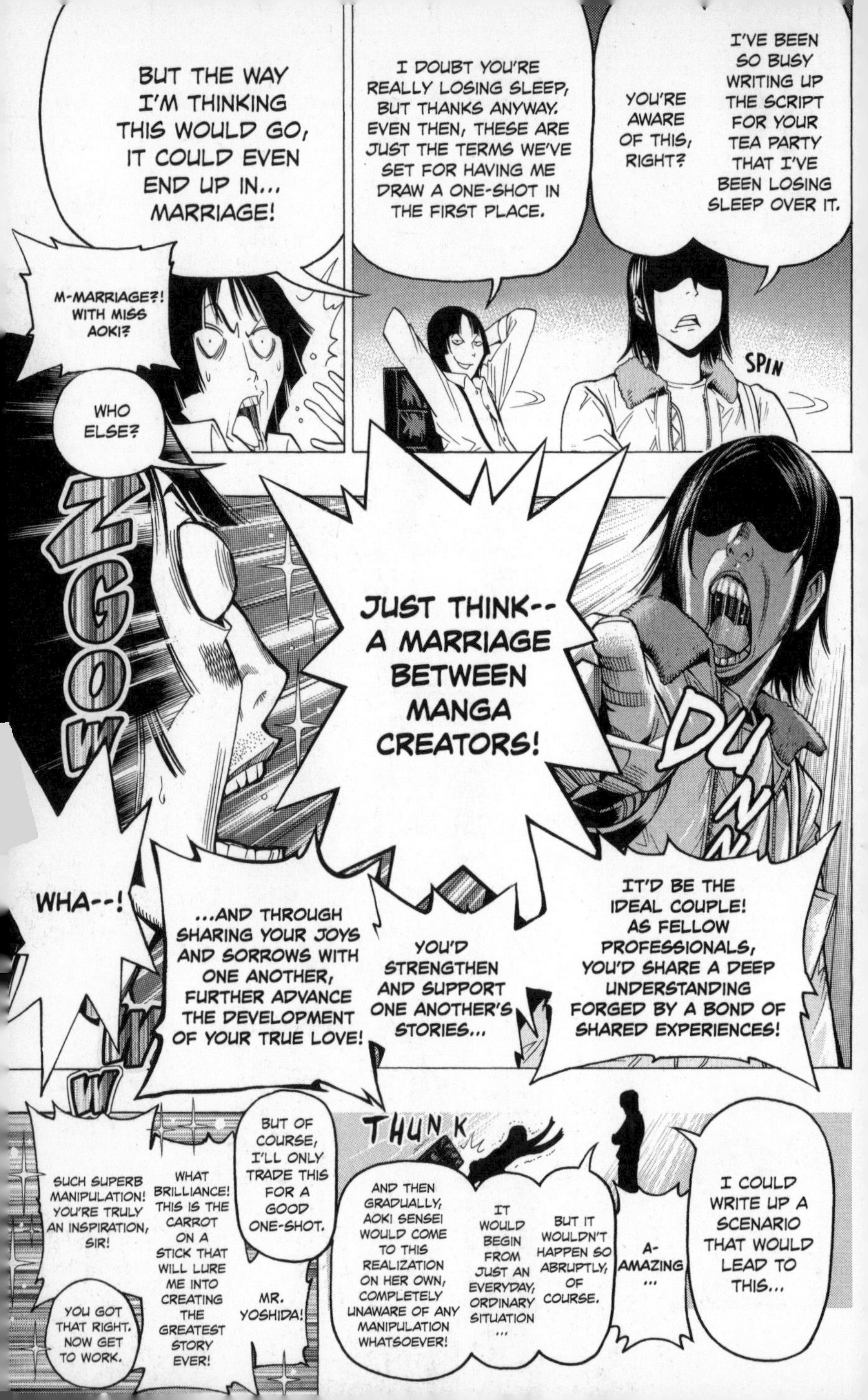
I'VE BEEN SO BUSY WRITING UP THE SCRIPT FOR YOUR TEA PARTY THAT I'VE BEEN LOSING SLEEP OVER IT.
YOU'RE AWARE OF THIS, RIGHT?
SPIN
I DOUBT YOU'RE REALLY LOSING SLEEP, BUT THANKS ANYWAY. EVEN THEN, THESE ARE JUST THE TERMS WE'VE SET FOR HAVING ME DRAW A ONE-SHOT IN THE FIRST PLACE.
BUT THE WAY I'M THINKING THIS WOULD GO, IT COULD EVEN END UP IN... MARRIAGE!
M-MARRIAGE?! WITH MISS AOKI?
WHO ELSE?
DUNN
JUST THINK--A MARRIAGE BETWEEN MANGA CREATORS!
IT'D BE THE IDEAL COUPLE! AS FELLOW PROFESSIONALS, YOU'D SHARE A DEEP UNDERSTANDING FORGED BY A BOND OF SHARED EXPERIENCES!
YOU'D STRENGTHEN AND SUPPORT ONE ANOTHER'S STORIES...
...AND THROUGH SHARING YOUR JOYS AND SORROWS WITH ONE ANOTHER, FURTHER ADVANCE THE DEVELOPMENT OF YOUR TRUE LOVE!
ZGOW
WHA--!
I COULD WRITE UP A SCENARIO THAT WOULD LEAD TO THIS...
A-AMAZING...
BUT IT WOULDN'T HAPPEN SO ABRUPTLY, OF COURSE.
IT WOULD BEGIN FROM JUST AN EVERYDAY, ORDINARY SITUATION...
AND THEN GRADUALLY, AOKI SENSEI WOULD COME TO THIS REALIZATION ON HER OWN, COMPLETELY UNAWARE OF ANY MANIPULATION WHATSOEVER!
THUNK
BUT OF COURSE, I'LL ONLY TRADE THIS FOR A GOOD ONE-SHOT.
MR. YOSHIDA!
WHAT BRILLIANCE! THIS IS THE CARROT ON A STICK THAT WILL LURE ME INTO CREATING THE GREATEST STORY EVER!
SUCH SUPERB MANIPULATION! YOU'RE TRULY AN INSPIRATION, SIR!
YOU GOT THAT RIGHT. NOW GET TO WORK.

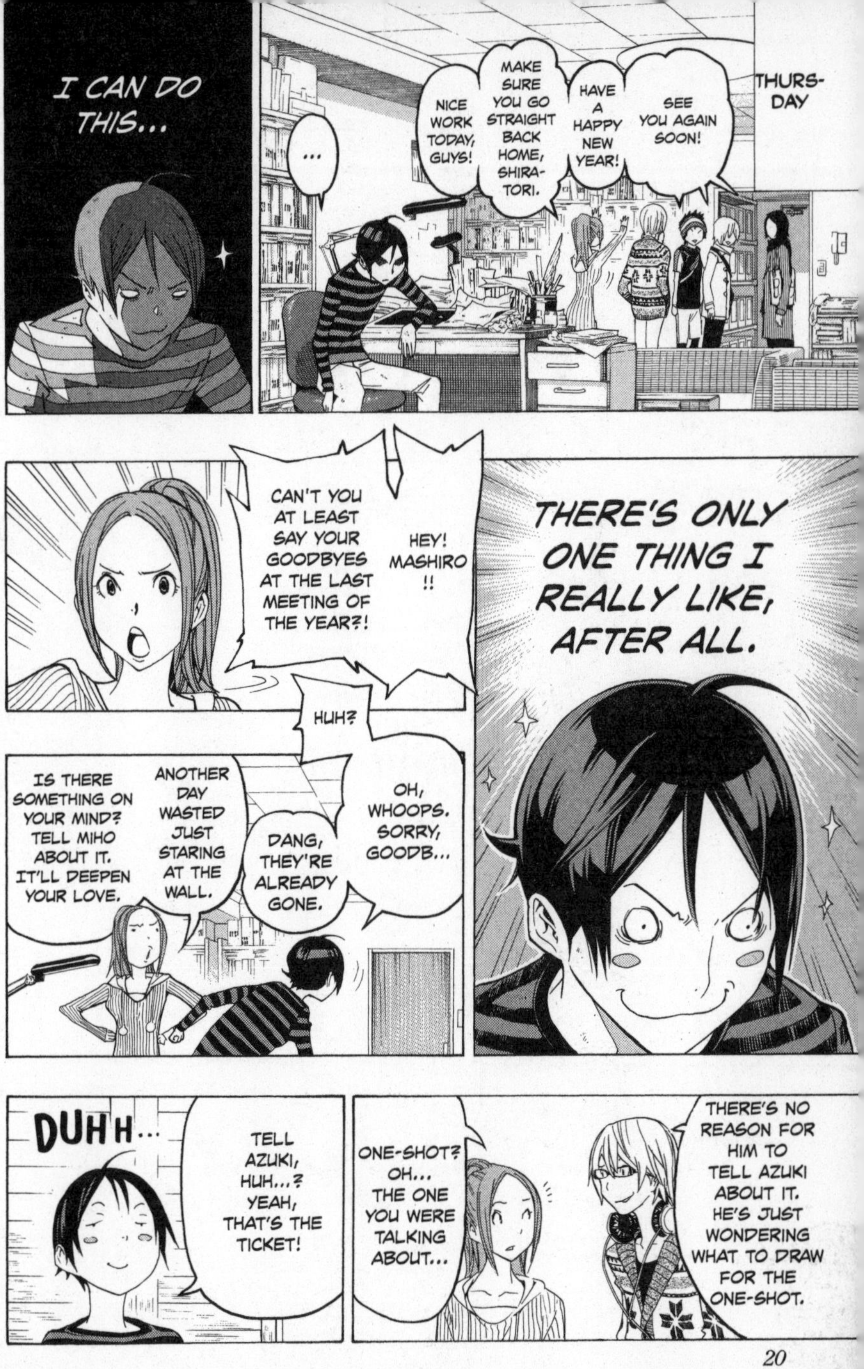
THURS-DAY
SEE YOU AGAIN SOON!
HAVE A HAPPY NEW YEAR!
MAKE SURE YOU GO STRAIGHT BACK HOME, SHIRATORI.
NICE WORK TODAY, GUYS!
...
I CAN DO THIS...
THERE'S ONLY ONE THING I REALLY LIKE, AFTER ALL.
HEY! MASHIRO !!
CAN'T YOU AT LEAST SAY YOUR GOODBYES AT THE LAST MEETING OF THE YEAR?!
HUH?
OH, WHOOPS. SORRY, GOODB...
DANG, THEY'RE ALREADY GONE.
ANOTHER DAY WASTED JUST STARING AT THE WALL.
IS THERE SOMETHING ON YOUR MIND? TELL MIHO ABOUT IT. IT'LL DEEPEN YOUR LOVE.
THERE'S NO REASON FOR HIM TO TELL AZUKI ABOUT IT. HE'S JUST WONDERING WHAT TO DRAW FOR THE ONE-SHOT.
ONE-SHOT? OH... THE ONE YOU WERE TALKING ABOUT...
TELL AZUKI, HUH...? YEAH, THAT'S THE TICKET!
DUHH...

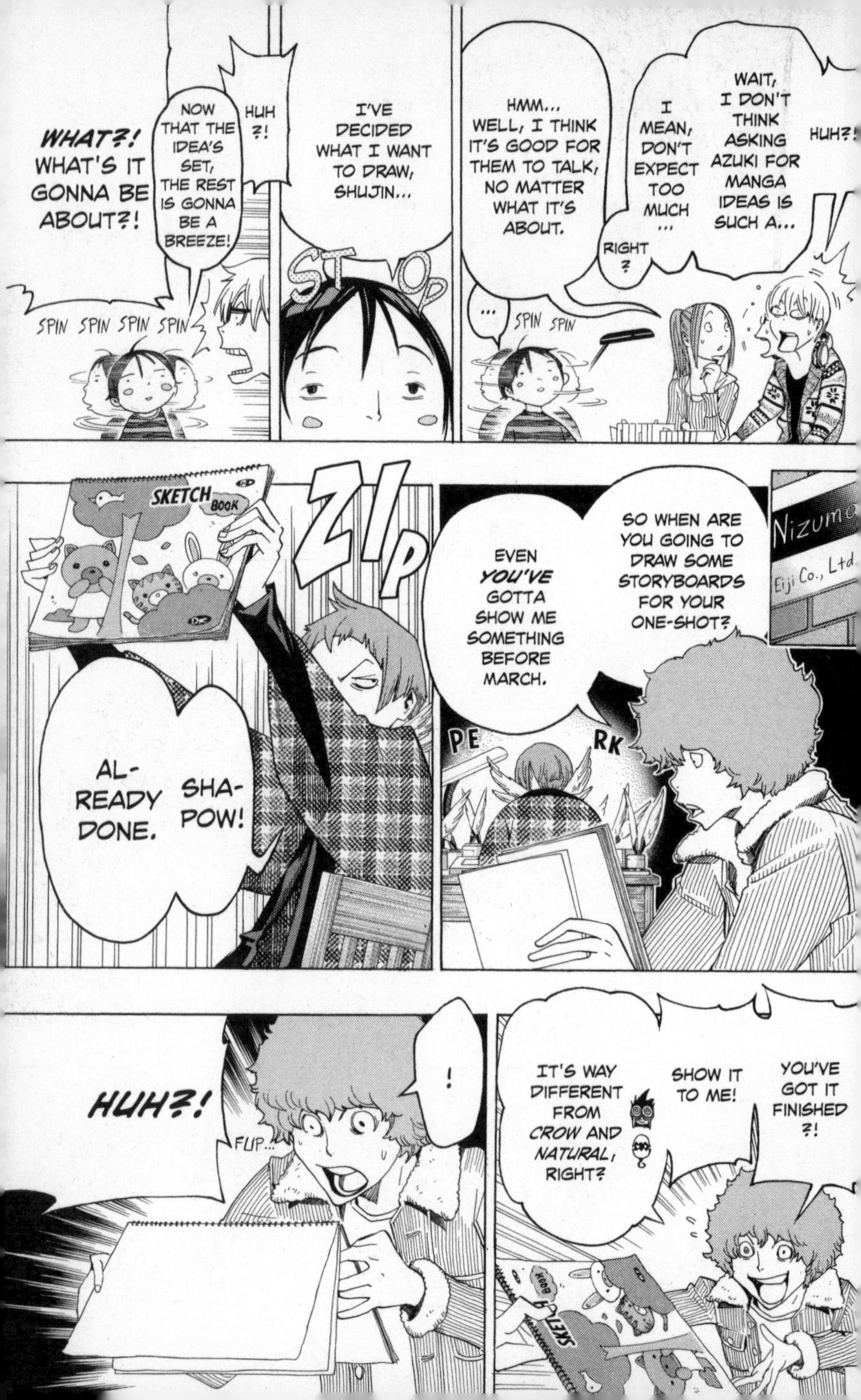
HUH?!
WAIT, I DON'T THINK ASKING AZUKI FOR MANGA IDEAS IS SUCH A...
I MEAN, DON'T EXPECT TOO MUCH...
RIGHT?
HMM... WELL, I THINK IT'S GOOD FOR THEM TO TALK, NO MATTER WHAT IT'S ABOUT.
...
SPIN SPIN
STOP
I'VE DECIDED WHAT I WANT TO DRAW, SHUJIN...
HUH?!
NOW THAT THE IDEA'S SET, THE REST IS GONNA BE A BREEZE!
WHAT?! WHAT'S IT GONNA BE ABOUT?!
SPIN SPIN SPIN SPIN
Nizumo Eiji Co., Ltd.
SO WHEN ARE YOU GOING TO DRAW SOME STORYBOARDS FOR YOUR ONE-SHOT?
EVEN YOU'VE GOTTA SHOW ME SOMETHING BEFORE MARCH.
PERK
ZIP
SKETCH BOOK
SHA-POW!
AL-READY DONE.
YOU'VE GOT IT FINISHED?!
SHOW IT TO ME!
IT'S WAY DIFFERENT FROM CROW AND NATURAL, RIGHT?
!
HUH?!
FLIP...

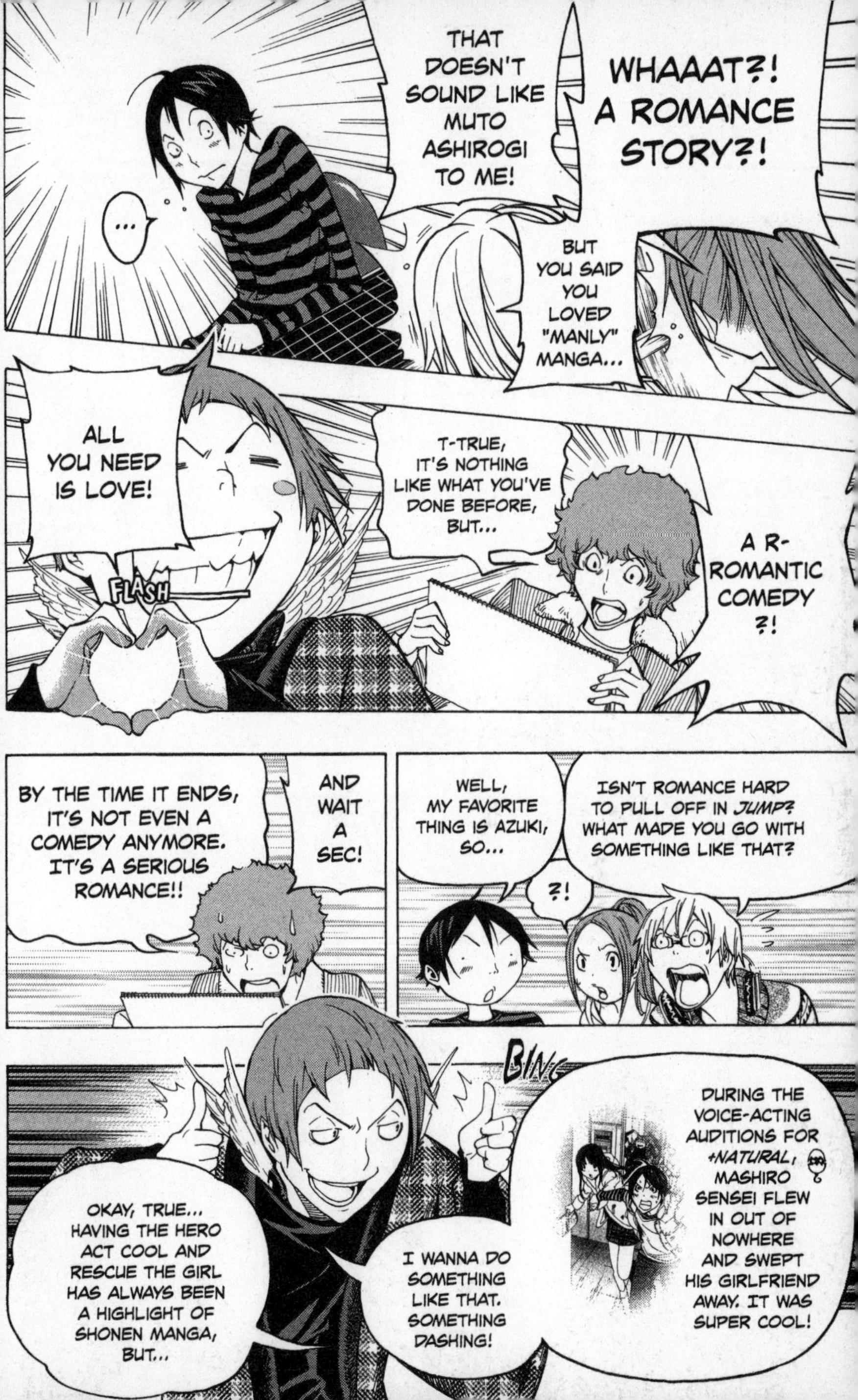
WHAAAT?! A ROMANCE STORY?!
THAT DOESN'T SOUND LIKE MUTO ASHIROGI TO ME!
BUT YOU SAID YOU LOVED "MANLY" MANGA...
...
A R- ROMANTIC COMEDY ?!
T-TRUE, IT'S NOTHING LIKE WHAT YOU'VE DONE BEFORE, BUT...
ALL YOU NEED IS LOVE!
FLASH
ISN'T ROMANCE HARD TO PULL OFF IN *JUMP*? WHAT MADE YOU GO WITH SOMETHING LIKE THAT?
?!
WELL, MY FAVORITE THING IS AZUKI, SO...
AND WAIT A SEC!
BY THE TIME IT ENDS, IT'S NOT EVEN A COMEDY ANYMORE. IT'S A SERIOUS ROMANCE!!
BING
DURING THE VOICE-ACTING AUDITIONS FOR *+NATURAL*, MASHIRO SENSEI FLEW IN OUT OF NOWHERE AND SWEPT HIS GIRLFRIEND AWAY. IT WAS SUPER COOL!
I WANNA DO SOMETHING LIKE THAT. SOMETHING DASHING!
OKAY, TRUE... HAVING THE HERO ACT COOL AND RESCUE THE GIRL HAS ALWAYS BEEN A HIGHLIGHT OF SHONEN MANGA, BUT...

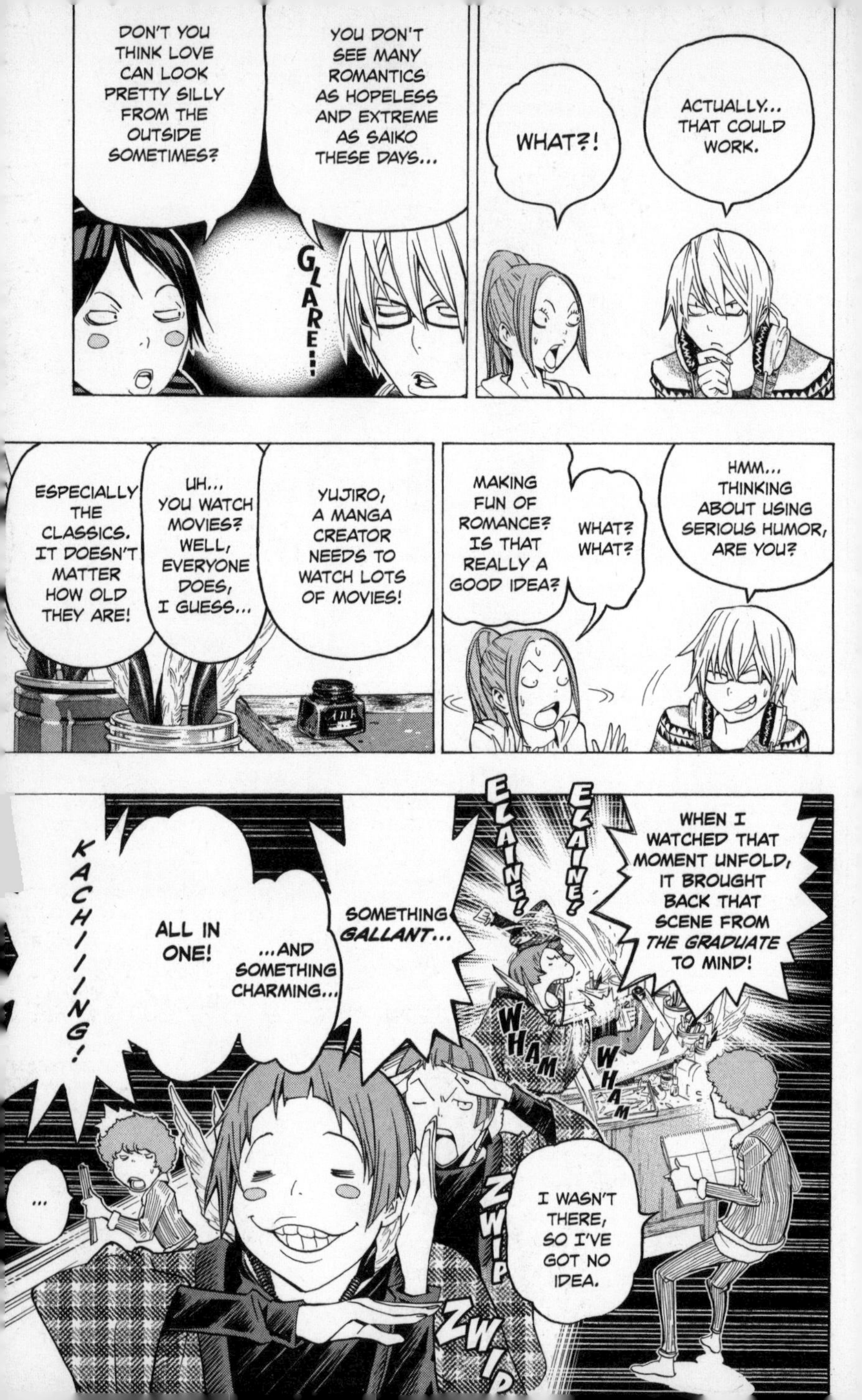

ACTUALLY... THAT COULD WORK.
WHAT?!
YOU DON'T SEE MANY ROMANTICS AS HOPELESS AND EXTREME AS SAIKO THESE DAYS...
GLARE!!
DON'T YOU THINK LOVE CAN LOOK PRETTY SILLY FROM THE OUTSIDE SOMETIMES?
HMM... THINKING ABOUT USING SERIOUS HUMOR, ARE YOU?
WHAT? WHAT?
MAKING FUN OF ROMANCE? IS THAT REALLY A GOOD IDEA?
YUJIRO, A MANGA CREATOR NEEDS TO WATCH LOTS OF MOVIES!
UH... YOU WATCH MOVIES? WELL, EVERYONE DOES, I GUESS...
ESPECIALLY THE CLASSICS. IT DOESN'T MATTER HOW OLD THEY ARE!
WHEN I WATCHED THAT MOMENT UNFOLD, IT BROUGHT BACK THAT SCENE FROM *THE GRADUATE* TO MIND!
ELAINE!
ELAINE!
SOMETHING *GALLANT*...
...AND SOMETHING CHARMING...
ALL IN ONE!
KACHIIIING!
WHAM
WHAM
I WASN'T THERE, SO I'VE GOT NO IDEA.
ZWIP
ZWIP
...

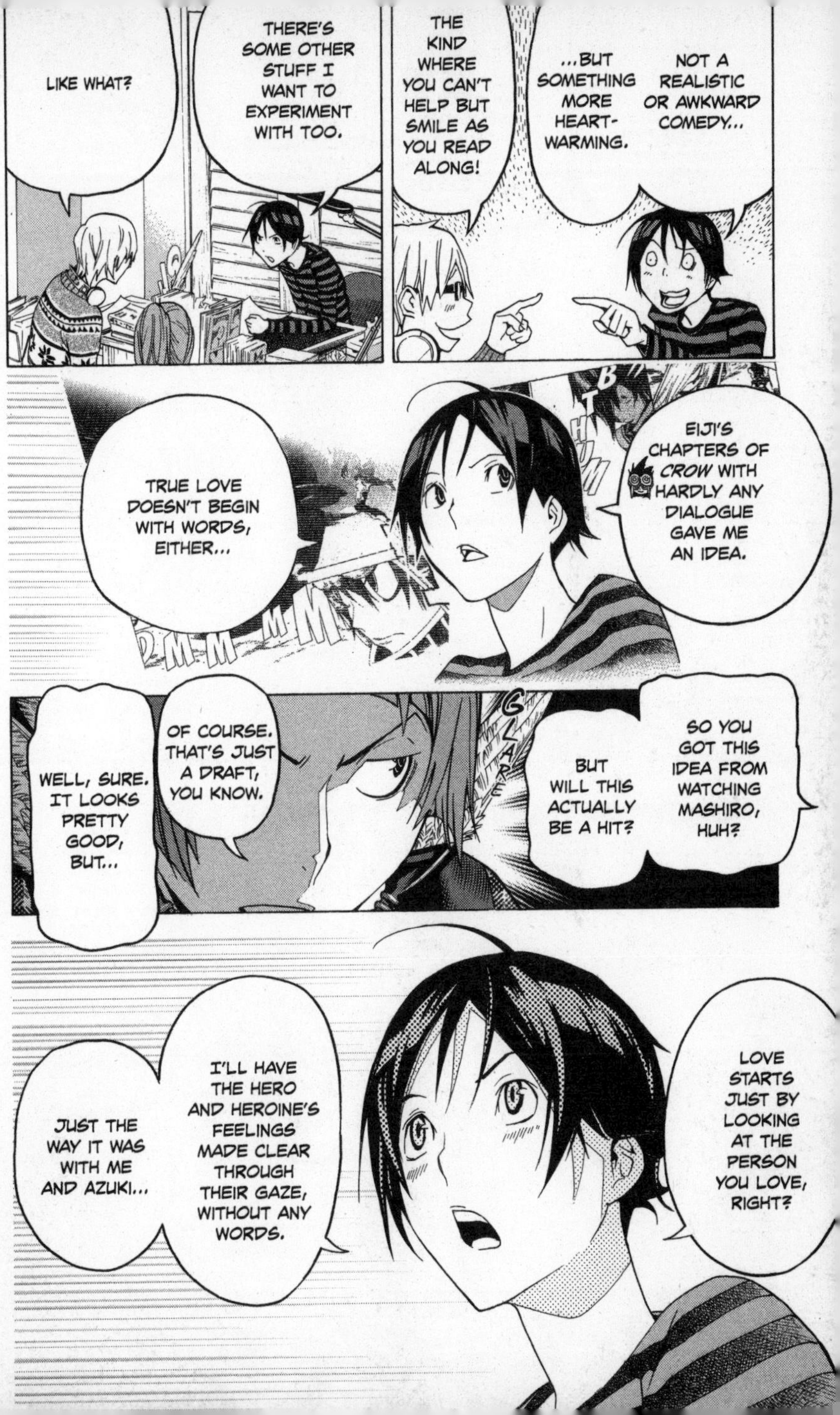
NOT A REALISTIC OR AWKWARD COMEDY...
...BUT SOMETHING MORE HEART-WARMING.
THE KIND WHERE YOU CAN'T HELP BUT SMILE AS YOU READ ALONG!
THERE'S SOME OTHER STUFF I WANT TO EXPERIMENT WITH TOO.
LIKE WHAT?
EIJI'S CHAPTERS OF *CROW* WITH HARDLY ANY DIALOGUE GAVE ME AN IDEA.
TRUE LOVE DOESN'T BEGIN WITH WORDS, EITHER...
SO YOU GOT THIS IDEA FROM WATCHING MASHIRO, HUH?
BUT WILL THIS ACTUALLY BE A HIT?
GLARE
OF COURSE. THAT'S JUST A DRAFT, YOU KNOW.
WELL, SURE. IT LOOKS PRETTY GOOD, BUT...
LOVE STARTS JUST BY LOOKING AT THE PERSON YOU LOVE, RIGHT?
I'LL HAVE THE HERO AND HEROINE'S FEELINGS MADE CLEAR THROUGH THEIR GAZE, WITHOUT ANY WORDS.
JUST THE WAY IT WAS WITH ME AND AZUKI...

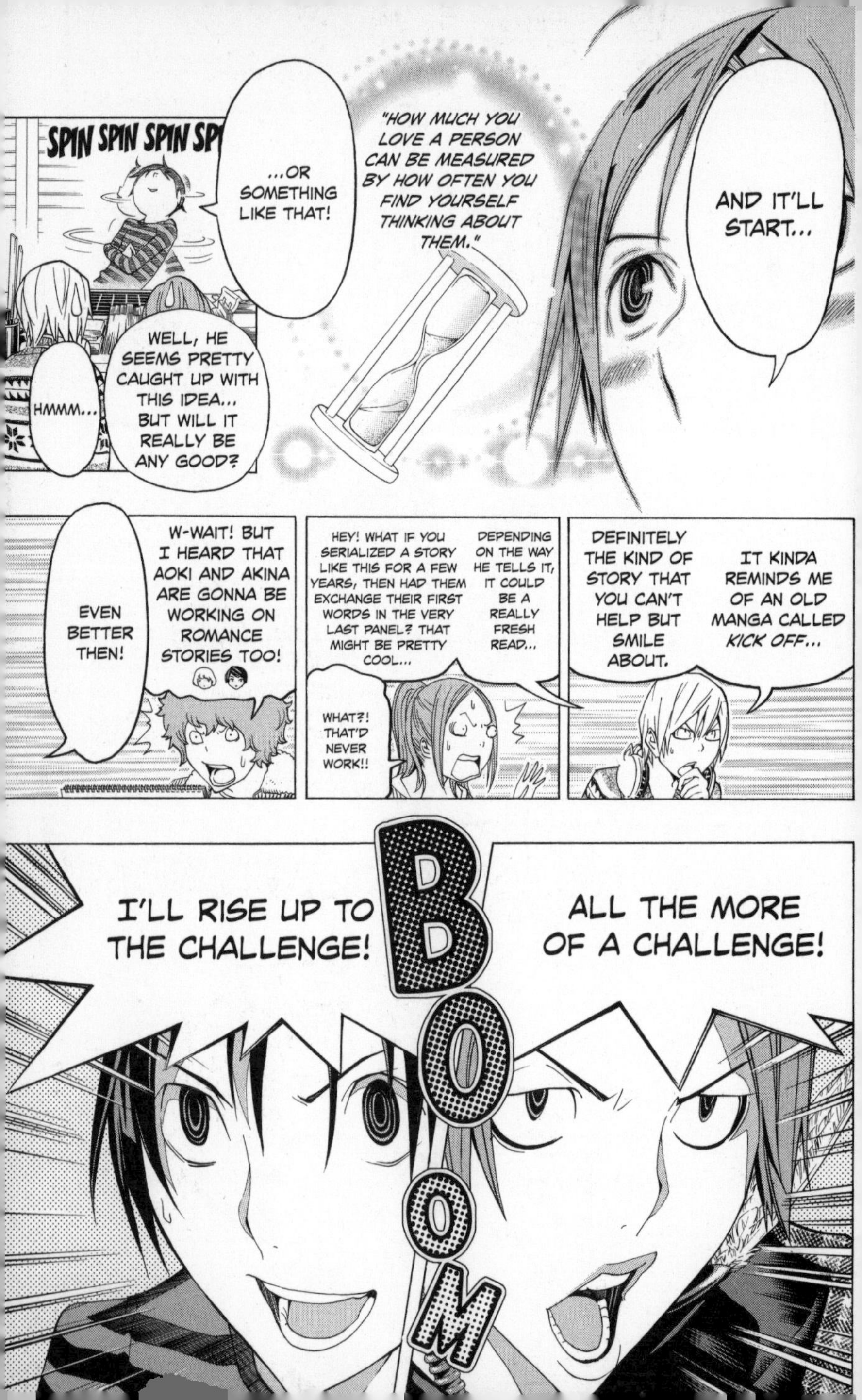
AND IT'LL START...
"HOW MUCH YOU LOVE A PERSON CAN BE MEASURED BY HOW OFTEN YOU FIND YOURSELF THINKING ABOUT THEM."
...OR SOMETHING LIKE THAT!
SPIN SPIN SPIN SP
WELL, HE SEEMS PRETTY CAUGHT UP WITH THIS IDEA... BUT WILL IT REALLY BE ANY GOOD?
HMMM...
IT KINDA REMINDS ME OF AN OLD MANGA CALLED *KICK OFF*...
DEFINITELY THE KIND OF STORY THAT YOU CAN'T HELP BUT SMILE ABOUT.
DEPENDING ON THE WAY HE TELLS IT, IT COULD BE A REALLY FRESH READ...
HEY! WHAT IF YOU SERIALIZED A STORY LIKE THIS FOR A FEW YEARS, THEN HAD THEM EXCHANGE THEIR FIRST WORDS IN THE VERY LAST PANEL? THAT MIGHT BE PRETTY COOL...
WHAT?! THAT'D NEVER WORK!!
W-WAIT! BUT I HEARD THAT AOKI AND AKINA ARE GONNA BE WORKING ON ROMANCE STORIES TOO!
EVEN BETTER THEN!
ALL THE MORE OF A CHALLENGE!
BOOOOM
I'LL RISE UP TO THE CHALLENGE!

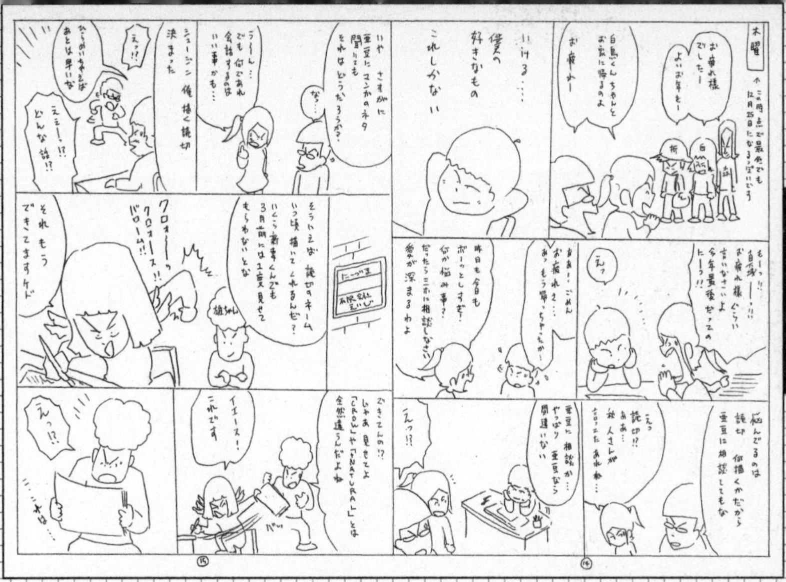
木曜
←この時点で最低でも12月25日になる筈です
お疲れ様でした一 よいお年を一
白鳥くんちゃんとお家に帰るのよ
お疲れ一
いける…
僕の好きなもの
これしかない
もーっ!! お疲れ様ぐらい言いなさいよ 今年最後だってのにーっ!!
えっ
あっ… ごめん お疲れさま… あっもう帰っちゃったか
昨日も今日もボーっとしすぎ! 何か悩み事? だったらミホに相談しなさい! 愛が深まるわよ
悩んでるのは 読切 何描くかだから 亜豆に相談してもな
えっ 読切!? ああ… 秋人さんが言ってたあれね…
亜豆に相談か… やっぱり亜豆なら間違いない
えっ!?
な…
いや さすがに亜豆にマンガのネタ聞いても それはどうだろうか…
うーん… でも何であれ会話するのはいい事かも…
シュージン 俺 描く読切 決まった
えっ!?
ひらめいちゃえば あとは早いな
ええー!? どんな話!?
そういえば 読切のネーム いつ頃描いてくれるんだ? いくら新妻くんでも 3月前には1度見せてもらわないとな
クロォーーッ クロォーース!! バロームッ!!
それもう できてますケド
できてんの!? じゃあ見せてよ 「CROW」や「NATURAL」とは 全然違うんだよね
イエース! これです
バッ
えっ!?
…これは…

OHBA'S STORYBOARD

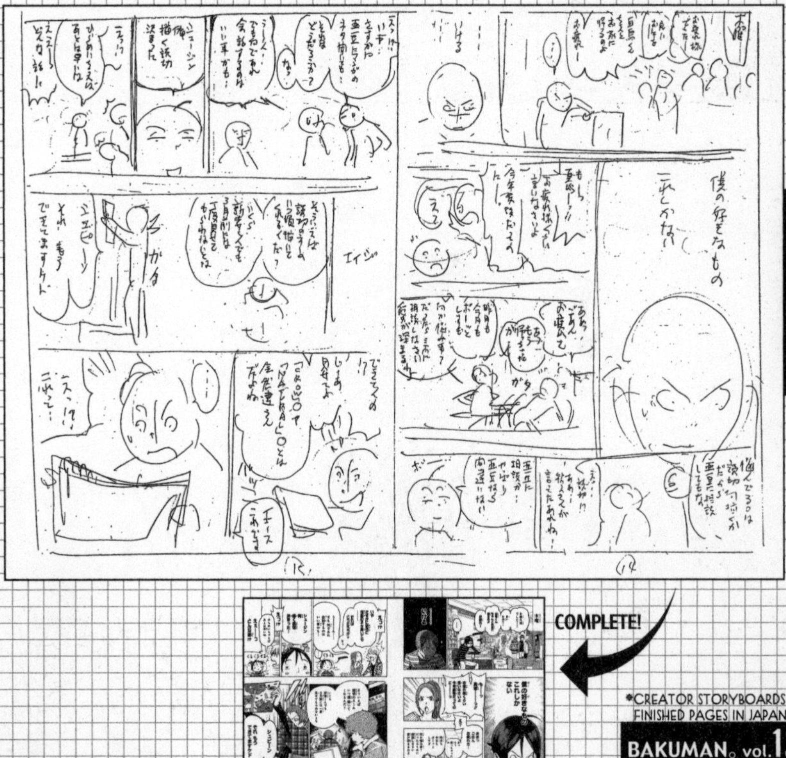

OBATA'S STORYBOARD

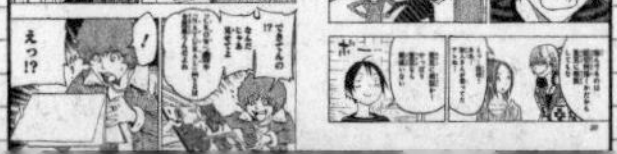

COMPLETE!

*CREATOR STORYBOARDS AND FINISHED PAGES IN JAPANESE

BAKUMAN。 vol.13

"Until the Final Draft Is Complete"

Chapter 107, pp. 20-21

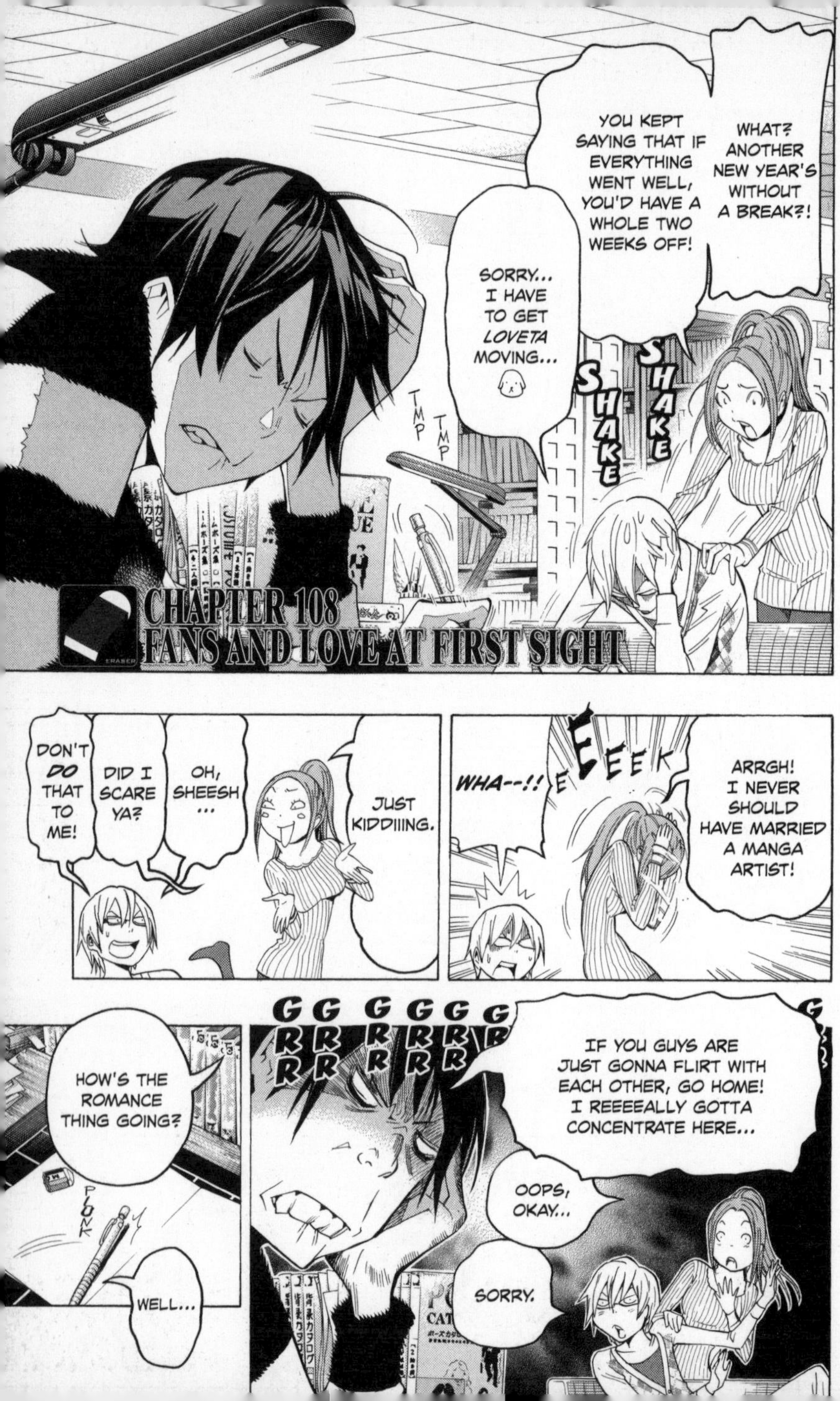
WHAT? ANOTHER NEW YEAR'S WITHOUT A BREAK?!
YOU KEPT SAYING THAT IF EVERYTHING WENT WELL, YOU'D HAVE A WHOLE TWO WEEKS OFF!
SHAKE
SHAKE
SORRY... I HAVE TO GET *LOVETA* MOVING...
TMP TMP
CHAPTER 108
FANS AND LOVE AT FIRST SIGHT
ARRGH! I NEVER SHOULD HAVE MARRIED A MANGA ARTIST!
EEEEK
WHA--!!
JUST KIDDIIING.
OH, SHEESH...
DID I SCARE YA?
DON'T *DO* THAT TO ME!
GRRR
IF YOU GUYS ARE JUST GONNA FLIRT WITH EACH OTHER, GO HOME! I REEEEALLY GOTTA CONCENTRATE HERE...
OOPS, OKAY...
SORRY.
HOW'S THE ROMANCE THING GOING?
PLONK
WELL...

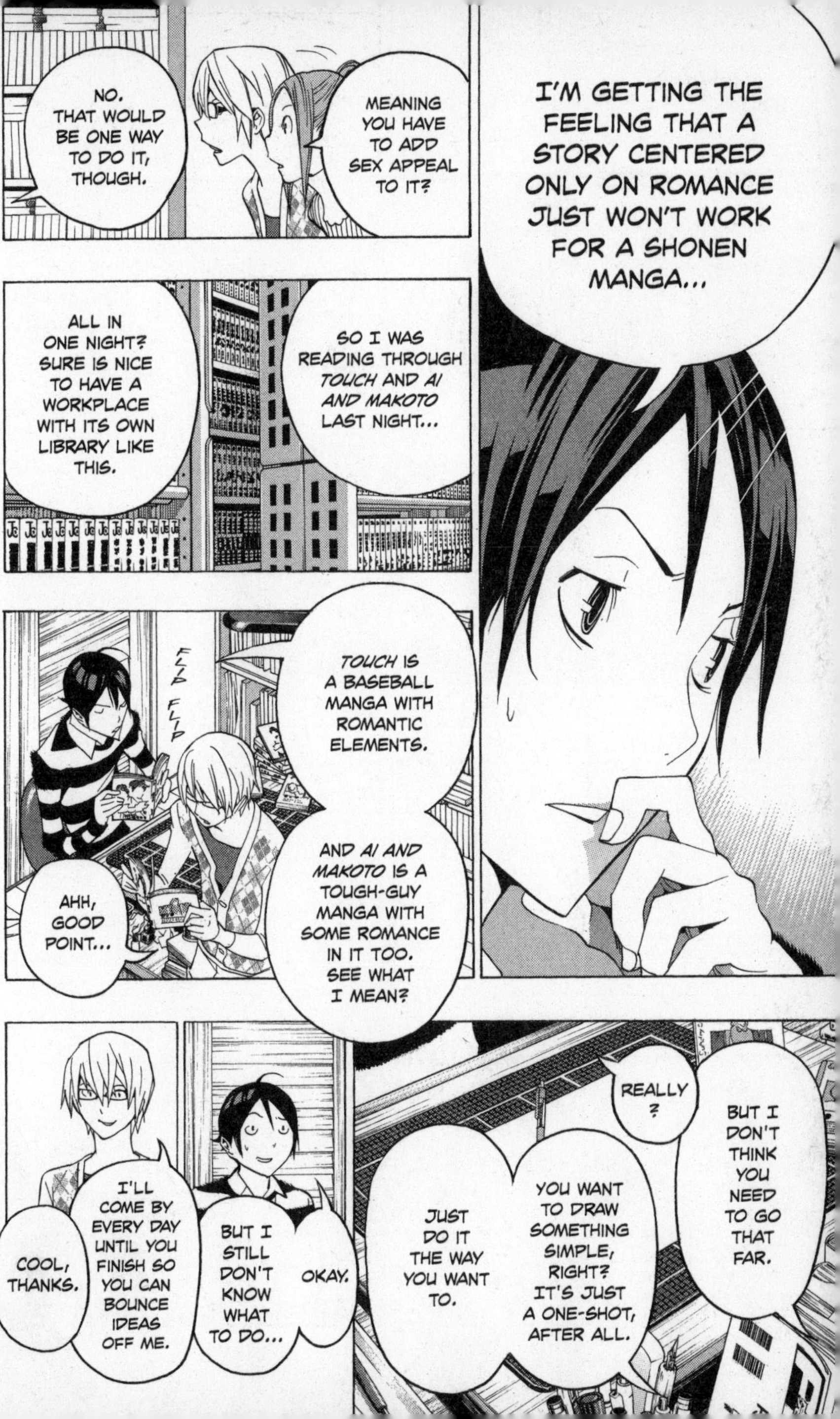
I'M GETTING THE FEELING THAT A STORY CENTERED ONLY ON ROMANCE JUST WON'T WORK FOR A SHONEN MANGA...
MEANING YOU HAVE TO ADD SEX APPEAL TO IT?
NO. THAT WOULD BE ONE WAY TO DO IT, THOUGH.
SO I WAS READING THROUGH *TOUCH* AND *AI AND MAKOTO* LAST NIGHT...
ALL IN ONE NIGHT? SURE IS NICE TO HAVE A WORKPLACE WITH ITS OWN LIBRARY LIKE THIS.
TOUCH IS A BASEBALL MANGA WITH ROMANTIC ELEMENTS.
AND *AI AND MAKOTO* IS A TOUGH-GUY MANGA WITH SOME ROMANCE IN IT TOO. SEE WHAT I MEAN?
FLIP FLIP
AHH, GOOD POINT...
REALLY?
BUT I DON'T THINK YOU NEED TO GO THAT FAR.
YOU WANT TO DRAW SOMETHING SIMPLE, RIGHT? IT'S JUST A ONE-SHOT, AFTER ALL.
JUST DO IT THE WAY YOU WANT TO.
OKAY.
BUT I STILL DON'T KNOW WHAT TO DO...
I'LL COME BY EVERY DAY UNTIL YOU FINISH SO YOU CAN BOUNCE IDEAS OFF ME.
COOL, THANKS.

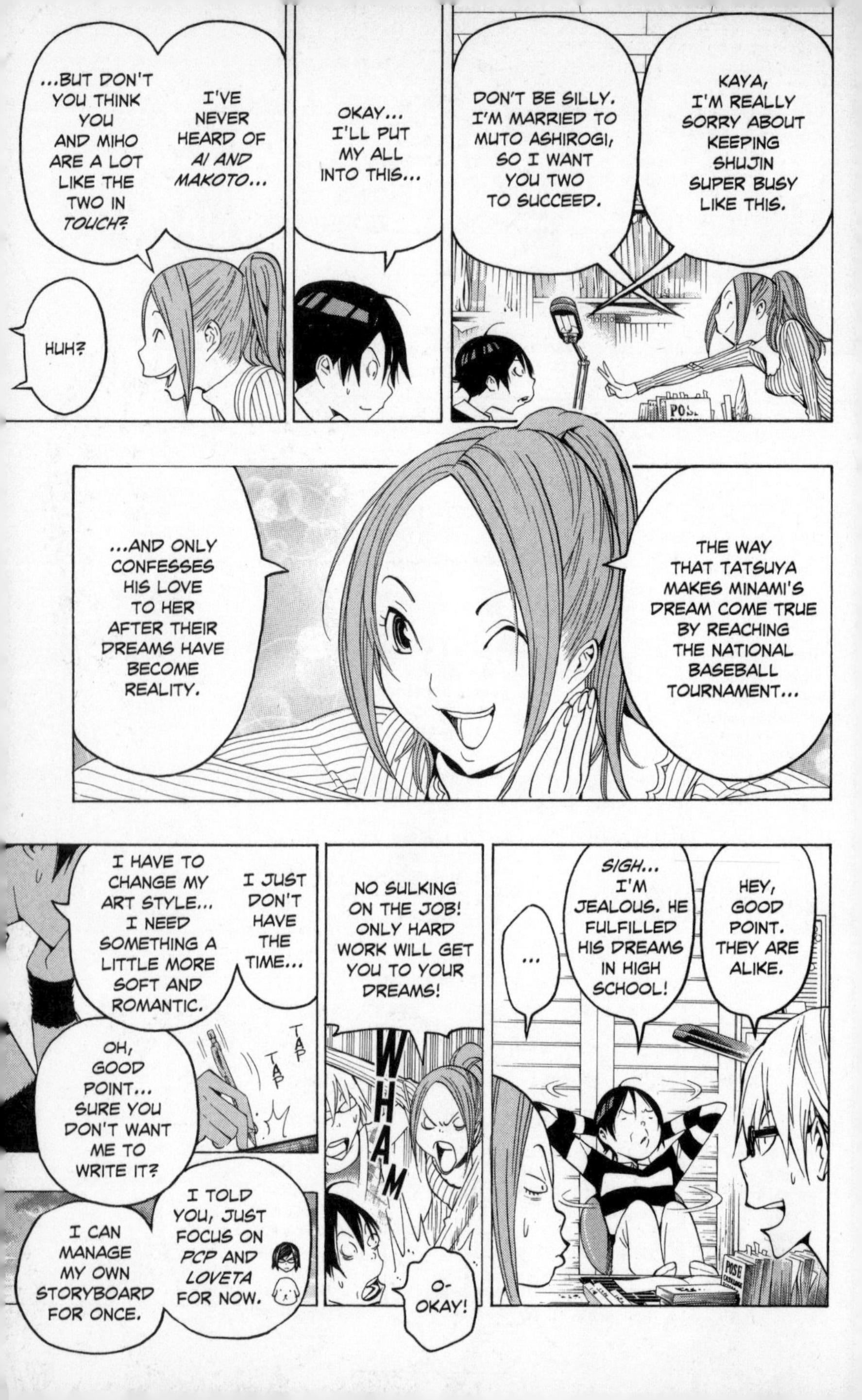
KAYA, I'M REALLY SORRY ABOUT KEEPING SHUJIN SUPER BUSY LIKE THIS.
DON'T BE SILLY. I'M MARRIED TO MUTO ASHIROGI, SO I WANT YOU TWO TO SUCCEED.
OKAY... I'LL PUT MY ALL INTO THIS...
I'VE NEVER HEARD OF *AI AND MAKOTO*...
...BUT DON'T YOU THINK YOU AND MIHO ARE A LOT LIKE THE TWO IN *TOUCH*?
HUH?
THE WAY THAT TATSUYA MAKES MINAMI'S DREAM COME TRUE BY REACHING THE NATIONAL BASEBALL TOURNAMENT...
...AND ONLY CONFESSES HIS LOVE TO HER AFTER THEIR DREAMS HAVE BECOME REALITY.
HEY, GOOD POINT. THEY ARE ALIKE.
SIGH... I'M JEALOUS. HE FULFILLED HIS DREAMS IN HIGH SCHOOL!
...
NO SULKING ON THE JOB! ONLY HARD WORK WILL GET YOU TO YOUR DREAMS!
WHAM
O-OKAY!
I JUST DON'T HAVE THE TIME...
I HAVE TO CHANGE MY ART STYLE... I NEED SOMETHING A LITTLE MORE SOFT AND ROMANTIC.
TAP TAP
OH, GOOD POINT... SURE YOU DON'T WANT ME TO WRITE IT?
I TOLD YOU, JUST FOCUS ON *PCP* AND *LOVETA* FOR NOW.
I CAN MANAGE MY OWN STORYBOARD FOR ONCE.

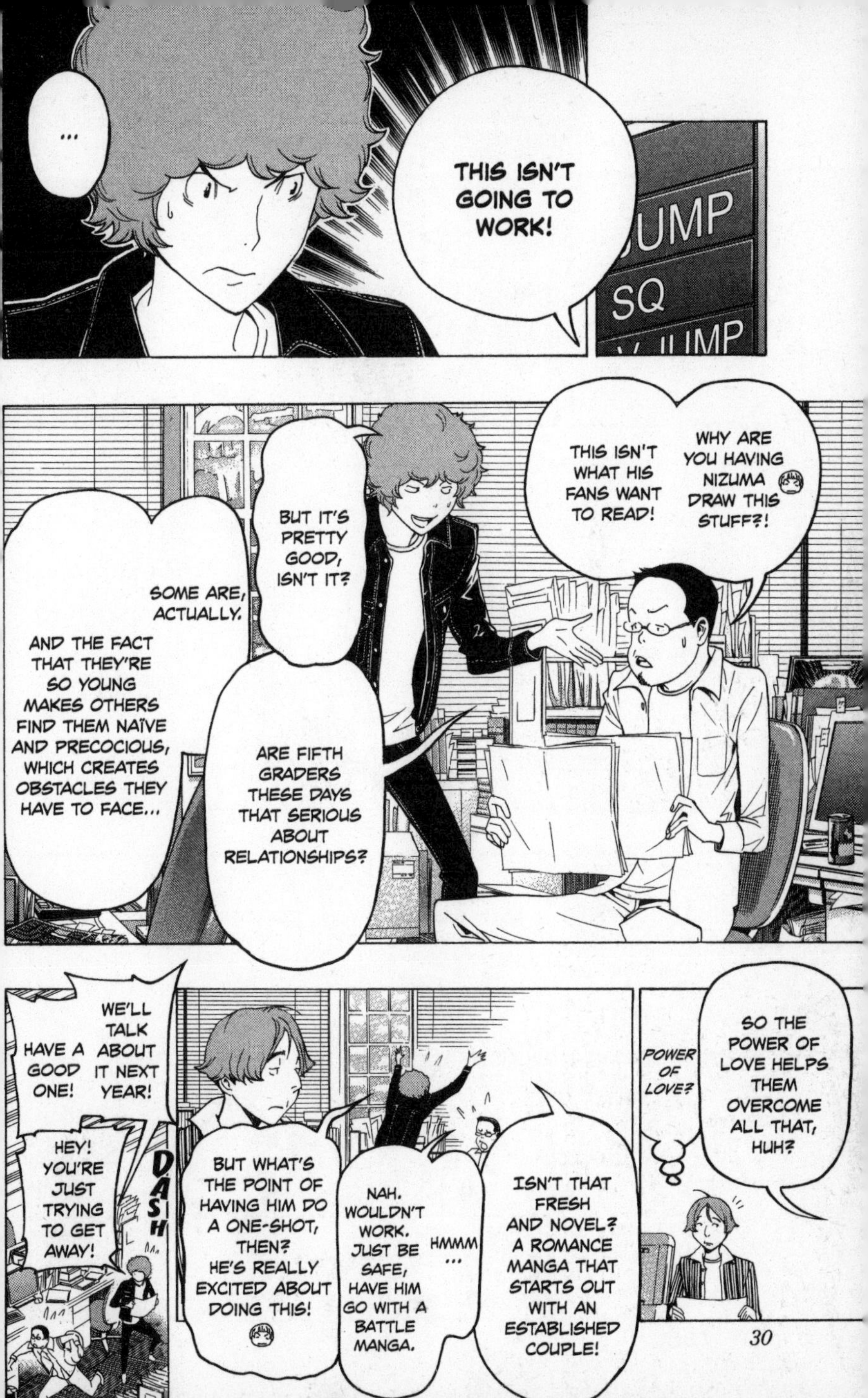
THIS ISN'T GOING TO WORK!
...
WHY ARE YOU HAVING NIZUMA DRAW THIS STUFF?!
THIS ISN'T WHAT HIS FANS WANT TO READ!
BUT IT'S PRETTY GOOD, ISN'T IT?
ARE FIFTH GRADERS THESE DAYS THAT SERIOUS ABOUT RELATIONSHIPS?
SOME ARE, ACTUALLY.
AND THE FACT THAT THEY'RE SO YOUNG MAKES OTHERS FIND THEM NAÏVE AND PRECOCIOUS, WHICH CREATES OBSTACLES THEY HAVE TO FACE...
SO THE POWER OF LOVE HELPS THEM OVERCOME ALL THAT, HUH?
POWER OF LOVE?
ISN'T THAT FRESH AND NOVEL? A ROMANCE MANGA THAT STARTS OUT WITH AN ESTABLISHED COUPLE!
HMMM...
NAH. WOULDN'T WORK. JUST BE SAFE, HAVE HIM GO WITH A BATTLE MANGA.
BUT WHAT'S THE POINT OF HAVING HIM DO A ONE-SHOT, THEN? HE'S REALLY EXCITED ABOUT DOING THIS!
WE'LL TALK ABOUT IT NEXT YEAR!
HAVE A GOOD ONE!
DASH
HEY! YOU'RE JUST TRYING TO GET AWAY!

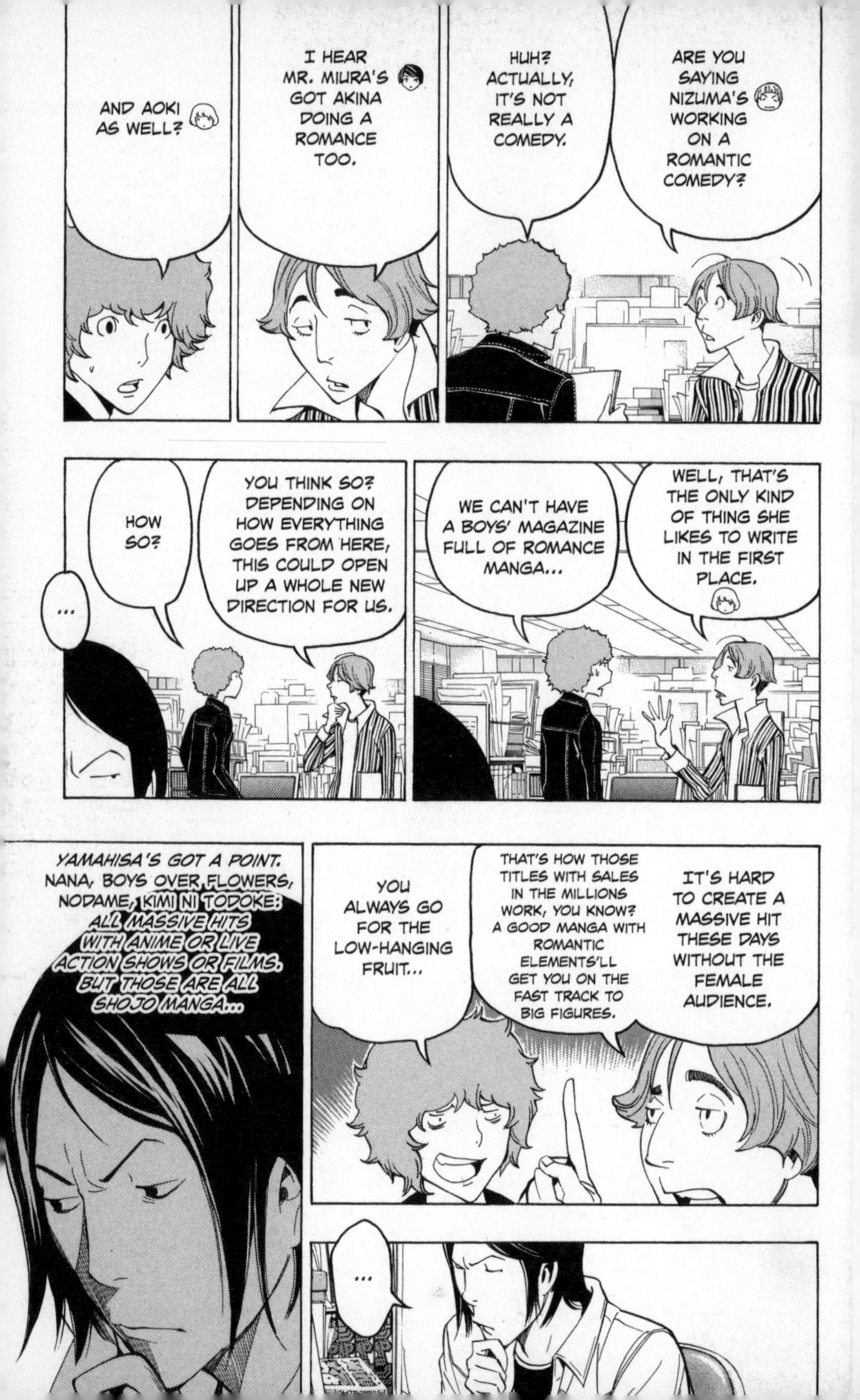
ARE YOU SAYING NIZUMA'S WORKING ON A ROMANTIC COMEDY?
HUH? ACTUALLY, IT'S NOT REALLY A COMEDY.
I HEAR MR. MIURA'S GOT AKINA DOING A ROMANCE TOO.
AND AOKI AS WELL?
WELL, THAT'S THE ONLY KIND OF THING SHE LIKES TO WRITE IN THE FIRST PLACE.
WE CAN'T HAVE A BOYS' MAGAZINE FULL OF ROMANCE MANGA...
YOU THINK SO? DEPENDING ON HOW EVERYTHING GOES FROM HERE, THIS COULD OPEN UP A WHOLE NEW DIRECTION FOR US.
HOW SO?
...
IT'S HARD TO CREATE A MASSIVE HIT THESE DAYS WITHOUT THE FEMALE AUDIENCE.
THAT'S HOW THOSE TITLES WITH SALES IN THE MILLIONS WORK, YOU KNOW? A GOOD MANGA WITH ROMANTIC ELEMENTS'LL GET YOU ON THE FAST TRACK TO BIG FIGURES.
YOU ALWAYS GO FOR THE LOW-HANGING FRUIT...
...
YAMAHISA'S GOT A POINT. NANA, BOYS OVER FLOWERS, NODAME, KIMI NI TODOKE: ALL MASSIVE HITS WITH ANIME OR LIVE ACTION SHOWS OR FILMS. BUT THOSE ARE ALL SHOJO MANGA...

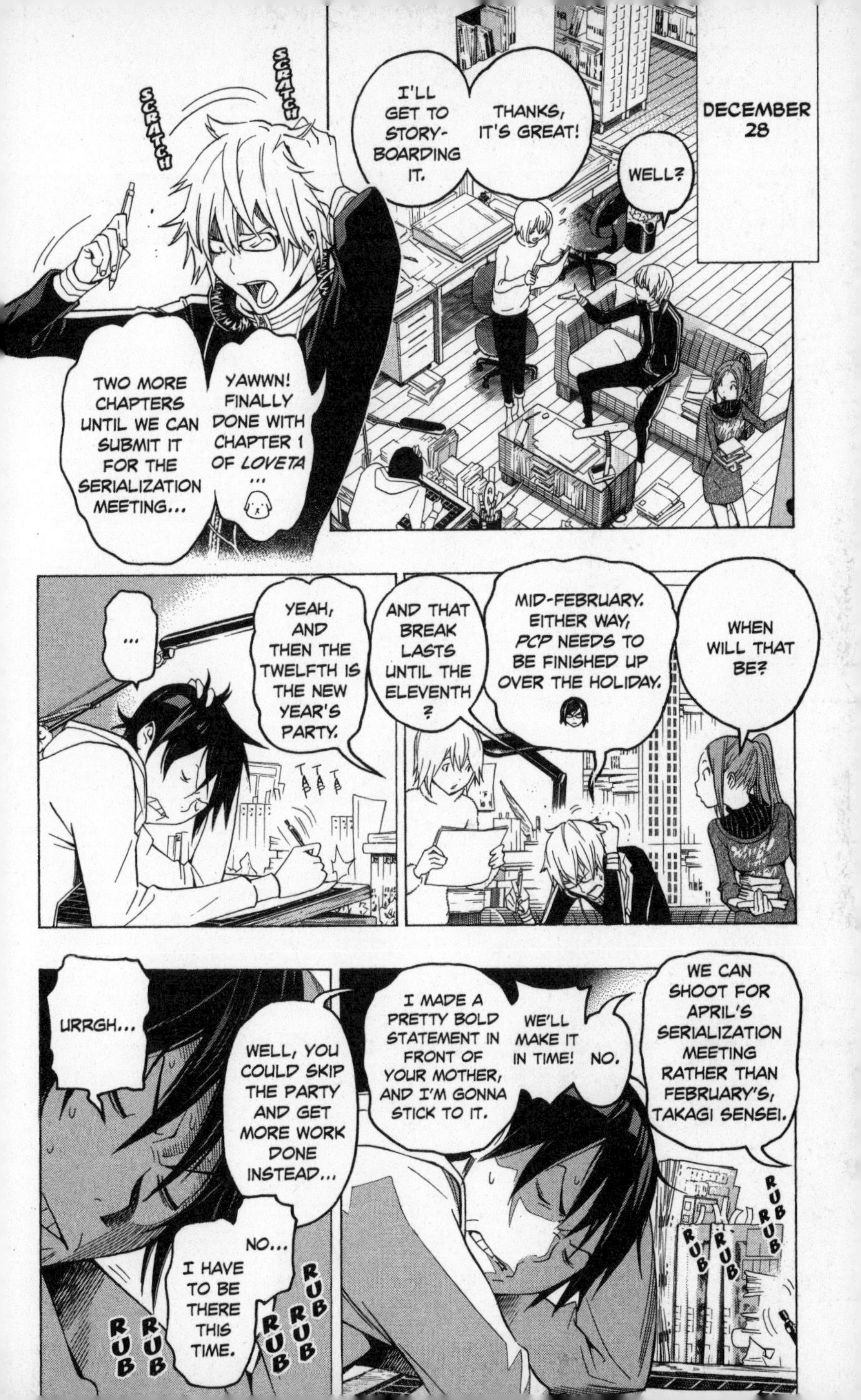
DECEMBER 28
WELL?
THANKS, IT'S GREAT!
I'LL GET TO STORY-BOARDING IT.
SCRATCH
SCRATCH
YAWWN! FINALLY DONE WITH CHAPTER 1 OF *LOVETA*...
TWO MORE CHAPTERS UNTIL WE CAN SUBMIT IT FOR THE SERIALIZATION MEETING...
WHEN WILL THAT BE?
MID-FEBRUARY. EITHER WAY, *PCP* NEEDS TO BE FINISHED UP OVER THE HOLIDAY.
AND THAT BREAK LASTS UNTIL THE ELEVENTH?
YEAH, AND THEN THE TWELFTH IS THE NEW YEAR'S PARTY.
...
WE CAN SHOOT FOR APRIL'S SERIALIZATION MEETING RATHER THAN FEBRUARY'S, TAKAGI SENSEI.
NO.
WE'LL MAKE IT IN TIME!
I MADE A PRETTY BOLD STATEMENT IN FRONT OF YOUR MOTHER, AND I'M GONNA STICK TO IT.
RUB RUB RUB RUB
WELL, YOU COULD SKIP THE PARTY AND GET MORE WORK DONE INSTEAD...
URRGH...
NO... I HAVE TO BE THERE THIS TIME.
RUB RUB RUB RUB

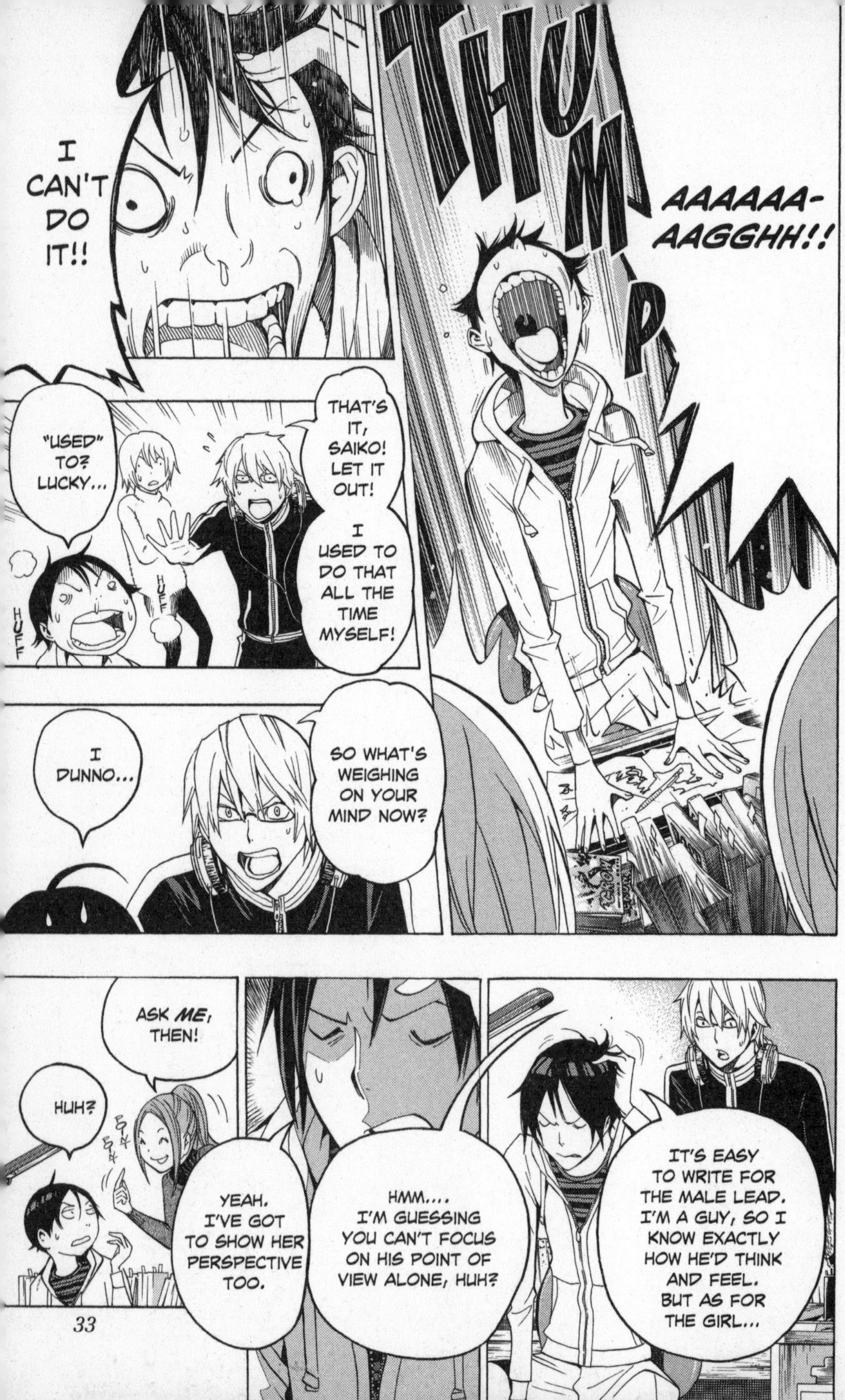
THUMP
AAAAAA-AAGGHH!!
I CAN'T DO IT!!
THAT'S IT, SAIKO! LET IT OUT!
I USED TO DO THAT ALL THE TIME MYSELF!
"USED" TO? LUCKY...
HUFF
HUFF
SO WHAT'S WEIGHING ON YOUR MIND NOW?
I DUNNO...
IT'S EASY TO WRITE FOR THE MALE LEAD. I'M A GUY, SO I KNOW EXACTLY HOW HE'D THINK AND FEEL. BUT AS FOR THE GIRL...
HMM.... I'M GUESSING YOU CAN'T FOCUS ON HIS POINT OF VIEW ALONE, HUH?
YEAH. I'VE GOT TO SHOW HER PERSPECTIVE TOO.
ASK *ME*, THEN!
HUH?

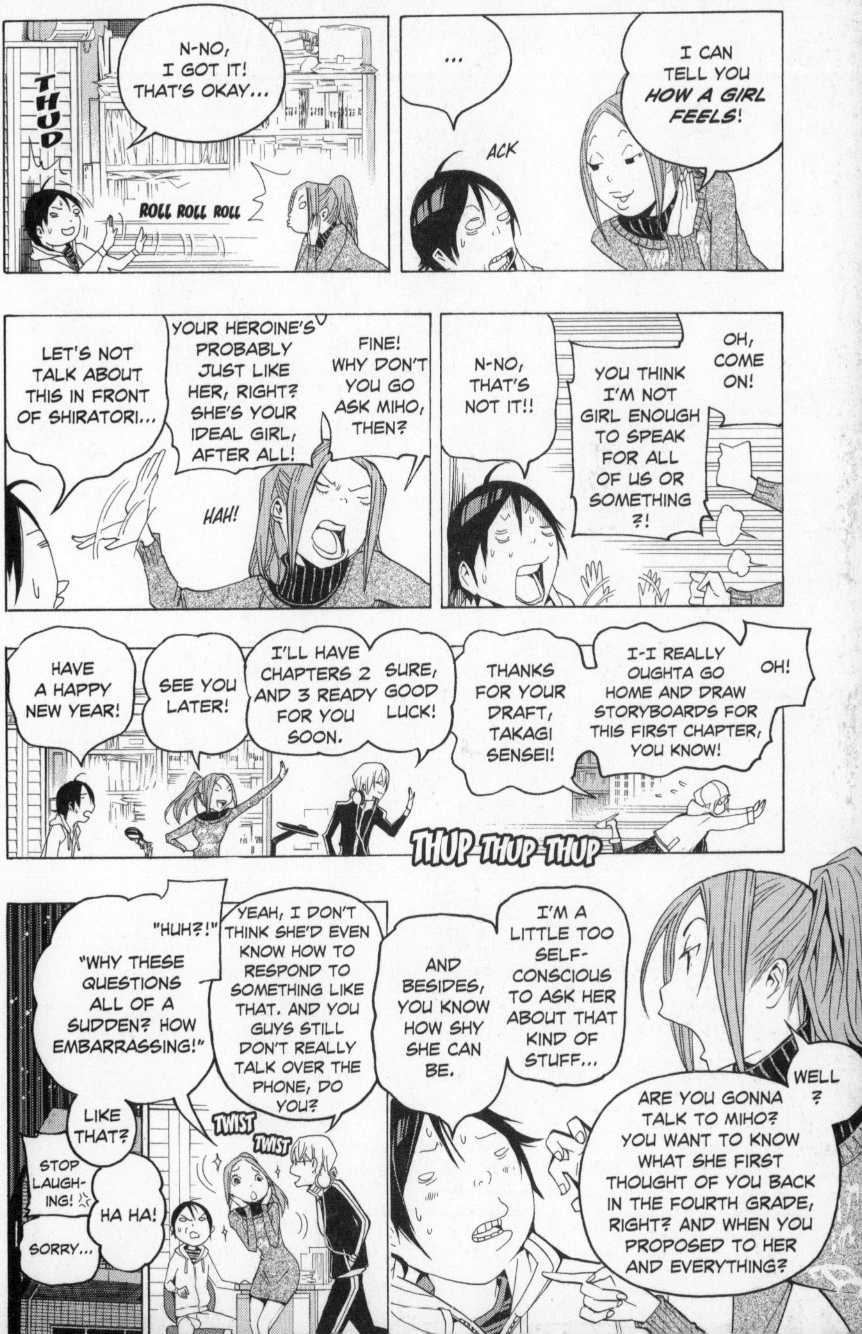
I CAN TELL YOU HOW A GIRL FEELS!
ACK
...
N-NO, I GOT IT! THAT'S OKAY...
THUD
ROLL ROLL ROLL
OH, COME ON!
YOU THINK I'M NOT GIRL ENOUGH TO SPEAK FOR ALL OF US OR SOMETHING?!
N-NO, THAT'S NOT IT!!
FINE! WHY DON'T YOU GO ASK MIHO, THEN?
YOUR HEROINE'S PROBABLY JUST LIKE HER, RIGHT? SHE'S YOUR IDEAL GIRL, AFTER ALL!
HAH!
LET'S NOT TALK ABOUT THIS IN FRONT OF SHIRATORI...
OH!
I-I REALLY OUGHTA GO HOME AND DRAW STORYBOARDS FOR THIS FIRST CHAPTER, YOU KNOW!
THANKS FOR YOUR DRAFT, TAKAGI SENSEI!
SURE, GOOD LUCK!
I'LL HAVE CHAPTERS 2 AND 3 READY FOR YOU SOON.
SEE YOU LATER!
HAVE A HAPPY NEW YEAR!
THUP THUP THUP
WELL?
ARE YOU GONNA TALK TO MIHO? YOU WANT TO KNOW WHAT SHE FIRST THOUGHT OF YOU BACK IN THE FOURTH GRADE, RIGHT? AND WHEN YOU PROPOSED TO HER AND EVERYTHING?
I'M A LITTLE TOO SELF-CONSCIOUS TO ASK HER ABOUT THAT KIND OF STUFF...
AND BESIDES, YOU KNOW HOW SHY SHE CAN BE.
YEAH, I DON'T THINK SHE'D EVEN KNOW HOW TO RESPOND TO SOMETHING LIKE THAT. AND YOU GUYS STILL DON'T REALLY TALK OVER THE PHONE, DO YOU?
"HUH?!"
"WHY THESE QUESTIONS ALL OF A SUDDEN? HOW EMBARRASSING!"
LIKE THAT?
TWIST
TWIST
STOP LAUGHING!
HA HA!
SORRY...

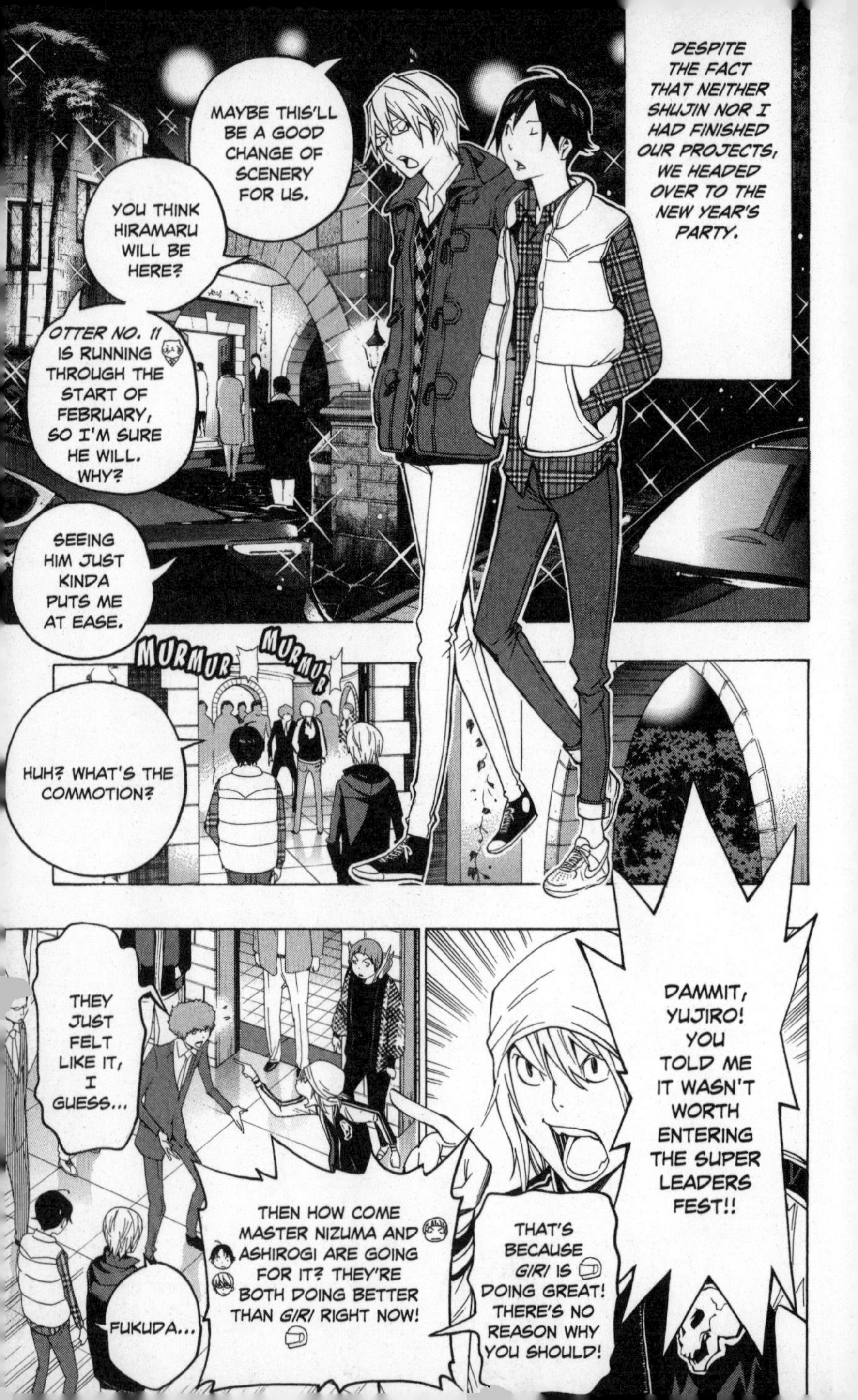
DESPITE THE FACT THAT NEITHER SHUJIN NOR I HAD FINISHED OUR PROJECTS, WE HEADED OVER TO THE NEW YEAR'S PARTY.
MAYBE THIS'LL BE A GOOD CHANGE OF SCENERY FOR US.
YOU THINK HIRAMARU WILL BE HERE?
OTTER NO. 11 IS RUNNING THROUGH THE START OF FEBRUARY, SO I'M SURE HE WILL. WHY?
SEEING HIM JUST KINDA PUTS ME AT EASE.
MURMUR
MURMUR
HUH? WHAT'S THE COMMOTION?
DAMMIT, YUJIRO! YOU TOLD ME IT WASN'T WORTH ENTERING THE SUPER LEADERS FEST!!
THEN HOW COME MASTER NIZUMA AND ASHIROGI ARE GOING FOR IT? THEY'RE BOTH DOING BETTER THAN *GIRI* RIGHT NOW!
THAT'S BECAUSE *GIRI* IS DOING GREAT! THERE'S NO REASON WHY YOU SHOULD!
THEY JUST FELT LIKE IT, I GUESS...
FUKUDA...

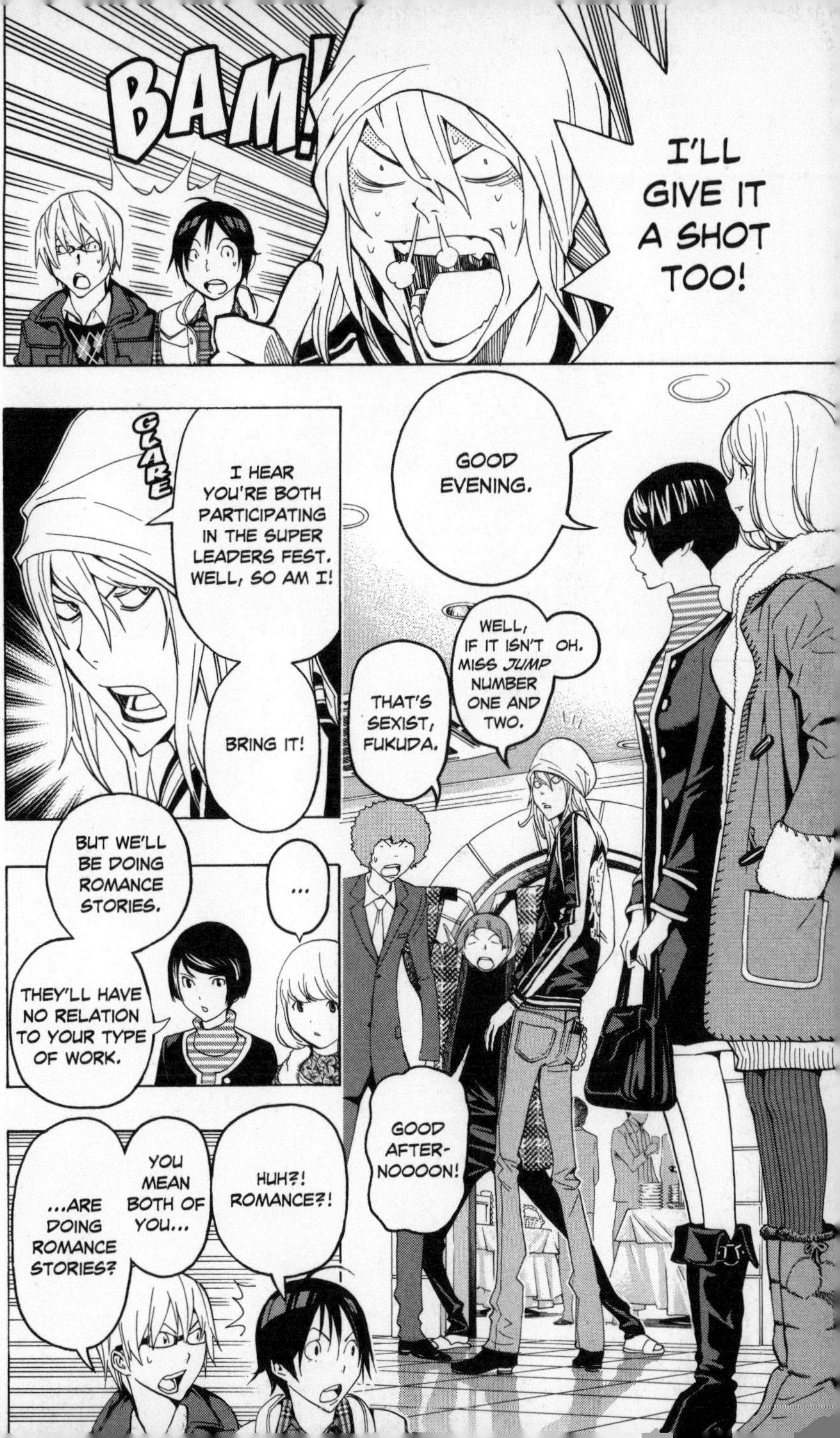
I'LL GIVE IT A SHOT TOO!
BAM!
GOOD EVENING.
OH. WELL, IF IT ISN'T MISS JUMP NUMBER ONE AND TWO.
THAT'S SEXIST, FUKUDA.
GOOD AFTER-NOOOON!
GLARE
I HEAR YOU'RE BOTH PARTICIPATING IN THE SUPER LEADERS FEST. WELL, SO AM I!
BRING IT!
...
BUT WE'LL BE DOING ROMANCE STORIES.
THEY'LL HAVE NO RELATION TO YOUR TYPE OF WORK.
HUH?! ROMANCE?!
YOU MEAN BOTH OF YOU...
...ARE DOING ROMANCE STORIES?

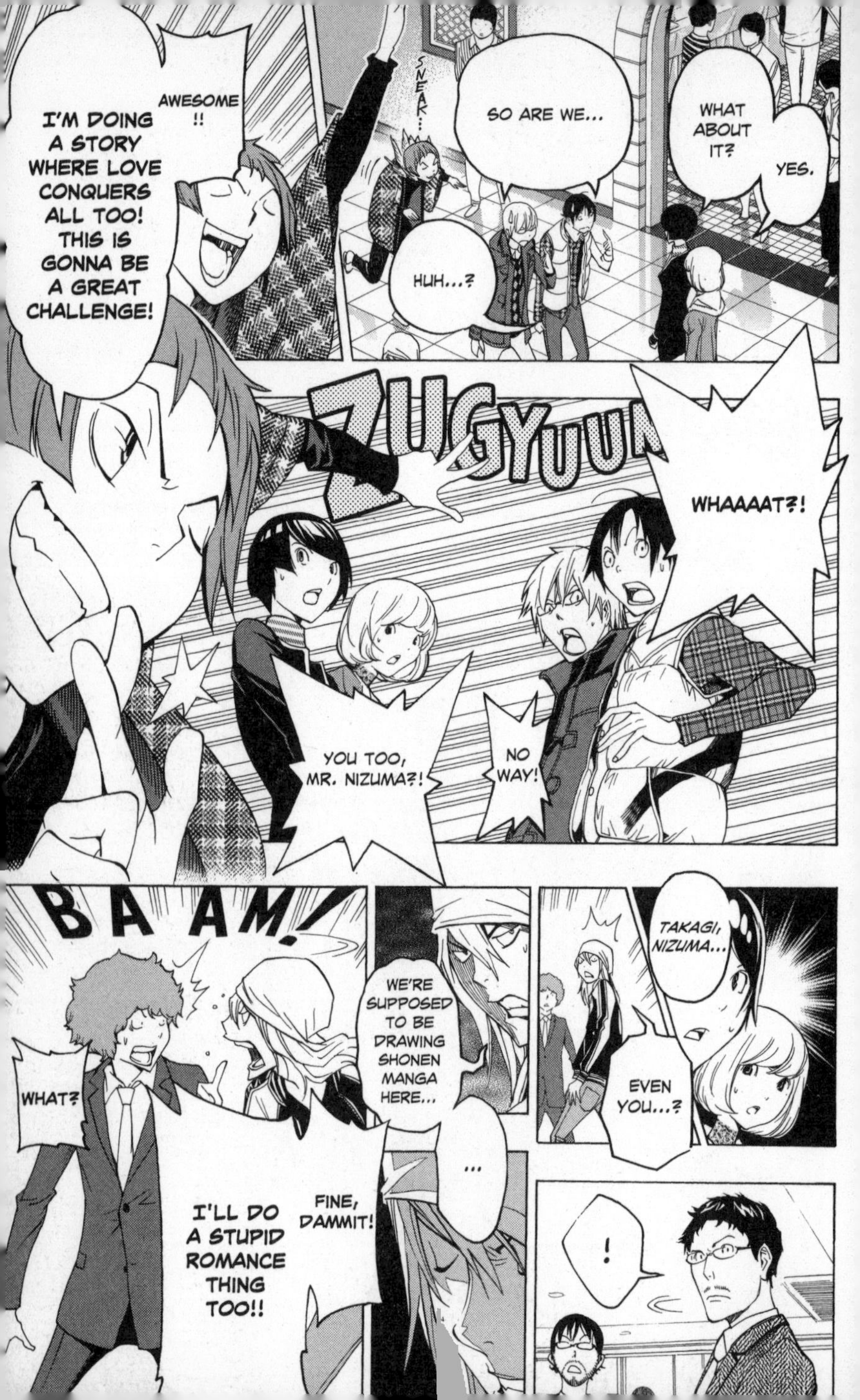
WHAT ABOUT IT?
YES.
SO ARE WE...
SNEAK...
HUH...?
AWESOME!!
I'M DOING A STORY WHERE LOVE CONQUERS ALL TOO! THIS IS GONNA BE A GREAT CHALLENGE!
ZUGYUUN
WHAAAAT?!
NO WAY!
YOU TOO, MR. NIZUMA?!
TAKAGI, NIZUMA...
EVEN YOU...?
WE'RE SUPPOSED TO BE DRAWING SHONEN MANGA HERE...
BAAM!
WHAT?
!
...
FINE, DAMMIT!
I'LL DO A STUPID ROMANCE THING TOO!!

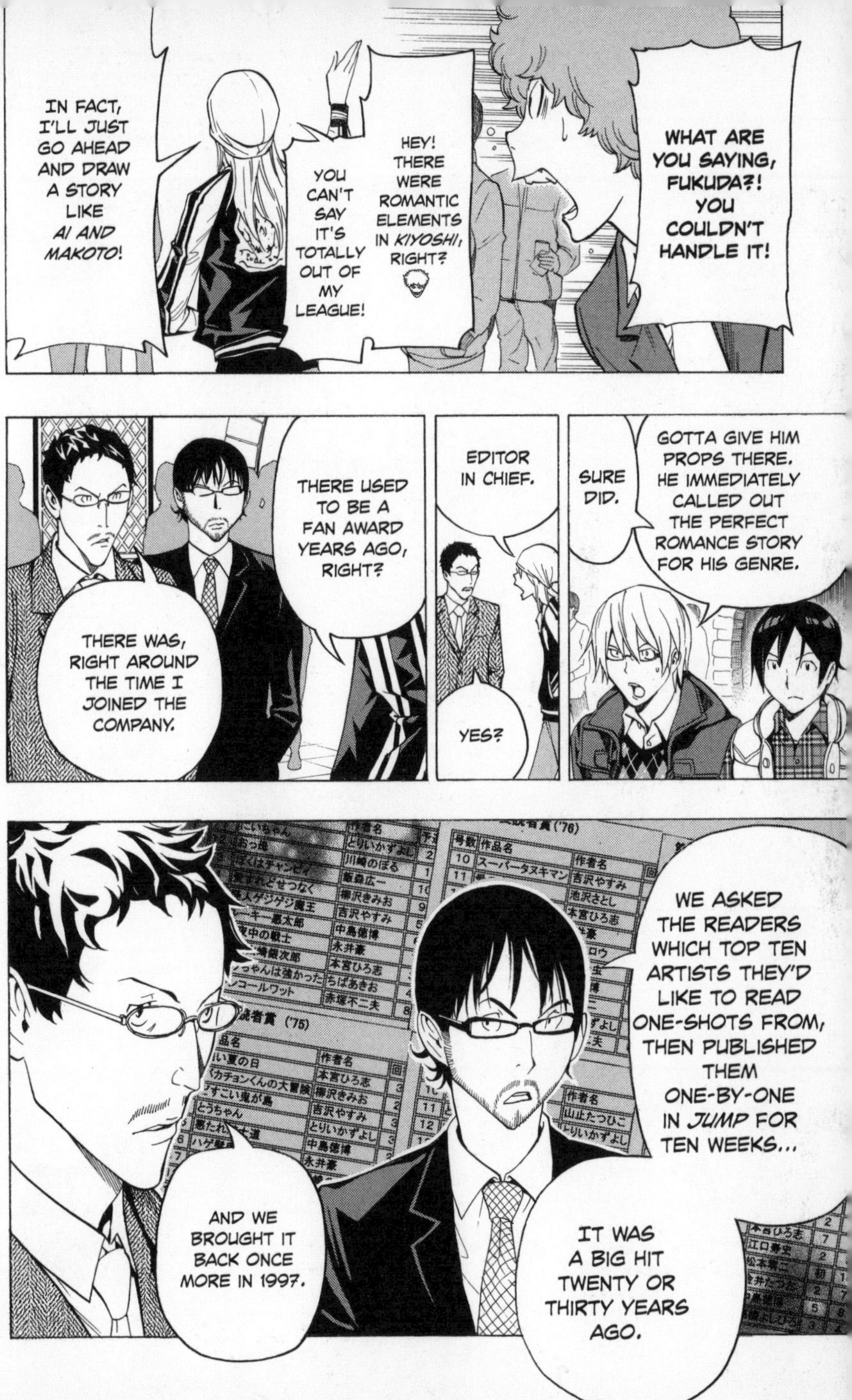
WHAT ARE YOU SAYING, FUKUDA?! YOU COULDN'T HANDLE IT!
HEY! THERE WERE ROMANTIC ELEMENTS IN *KIYOSHI*, RIGHT?
YOU CAN'T SAY IT'S TOTALLY OUT OF MY LEAGUE!
IN FACT, I'LL JUST GO AHEAD AND DRAW A STORY LIKE *AI AND MAKOTO*!
GOTTA GIVE HIM PROPS THERE. HE IMMEDIATELY CALLED OUT THE PERFECT ROMANCE STORY FOR HIS GENRE.
SURE DID.
EDITOR IN CHIEF.
YES?
THERE USED TO BE A FAN AWARD YEARS AGO, RIGHT?
THERE WAS, RIGHT AROUND THE TIME I JOINED THE COMPANY.
WE ASKED THE READERS WHICH TOP TEN ARTISTS THEY'D LIKE TO READ ONE-SHOTS FROM, THEN PUBLISHED THEM ONE-BY-ONE IN *JUMP* FOR TEN WEEKS...
IT WAS A BIG HIT TWENTY OR THIRTY YEARS AGO.
AND WE BROUGHT IT BACK ONCE MORE IN 1997.

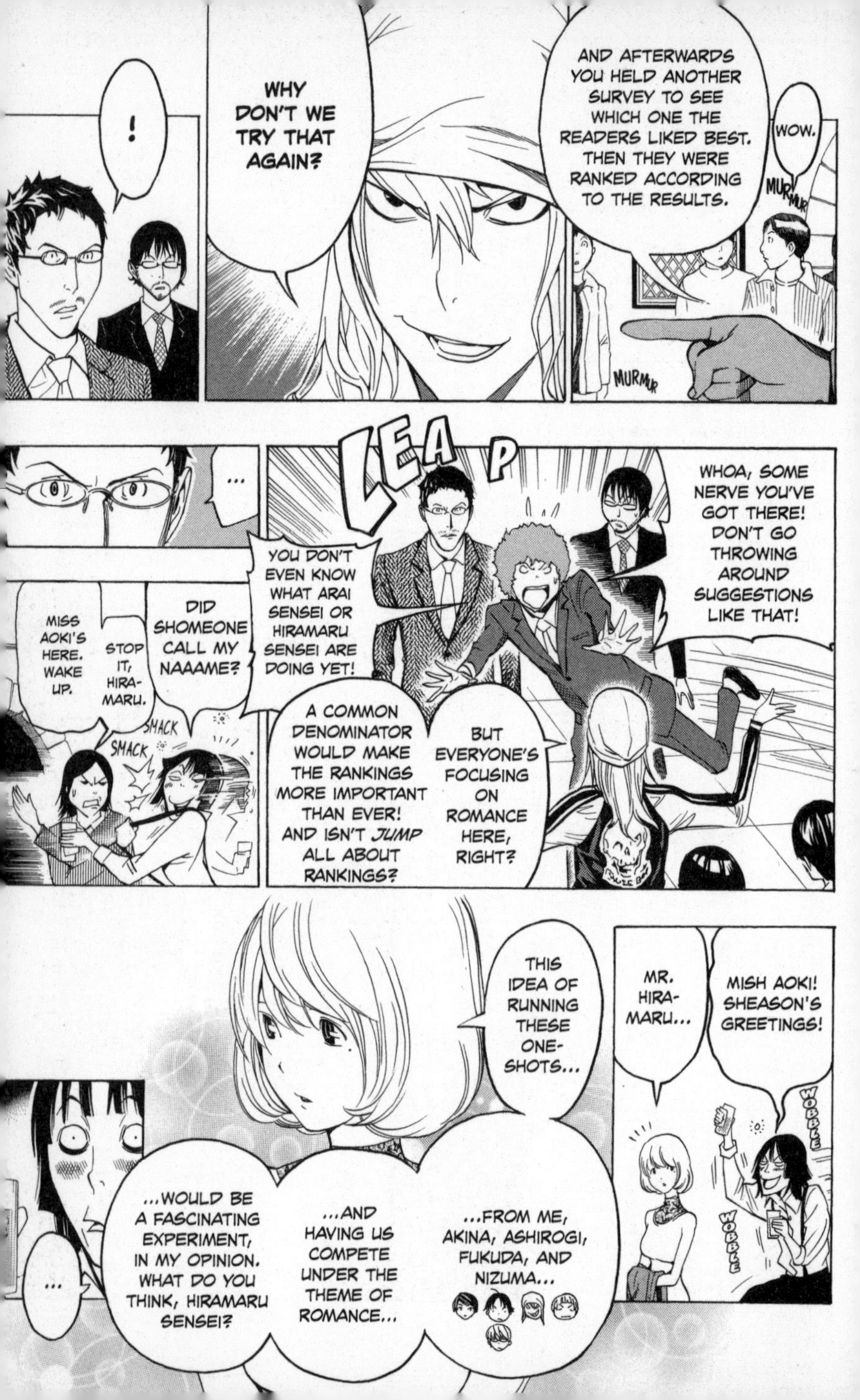
AND AFTERWARDS YOU HELD ANOTHER SURVEY TO SEE WHICH ONE THE READERS LIKED BEST. THEN THEY WERE RANKED ACCORDING TO THE RESULTS.
WOW.
MURMUR
MURMUR
WHY DON'T WE TRY THAT AGAIN?
!
LEAP
WHOA, SOME NERVE YOU'VE GOT THERE! DON'T GO THROWING AROUND SUGGESTIONS LIKE THAT!
YOU DON'T EVEN KNOW WHAT ARAI SENSEI OR HIRAMARU SENSEI ARE DOING YET!
BUT EVERYONE'S FOCUSING ON ROMANCE HERE, RIGHT?
A COMMON DENOMINATOR WOULD MAKE THE RANKINGS MORE IMPORTANT THAN EVER! AND ISN'T *JUMP* ALL ABOUT RANKINGS?
...
DID SHOMEONE CALL MY NAAAME?
STOP IT, HIRA-MARU.
MISS AOKI'S HERE. WAKE UP.
SMACK
SMACK
MISH AOKI! SHEASON'S GREETINGS!
MR. HIRA-MARU...
WOBBLE
WOBBLE
THIS IDEA OF RUNNING THESE ONE-SHOTS...
...FROM ME, AKINA, ASHIROGI, FUKUDA, AND NIZUMA...
...AND HAVING US COMPETE UNDER THE THEME OF ROMANCE...
...WOULD BE A FASCINATING EXPERIMENT, IN MY OPINION. WHAT DO YOU THINK, HIRAMARU SENSEI?
...

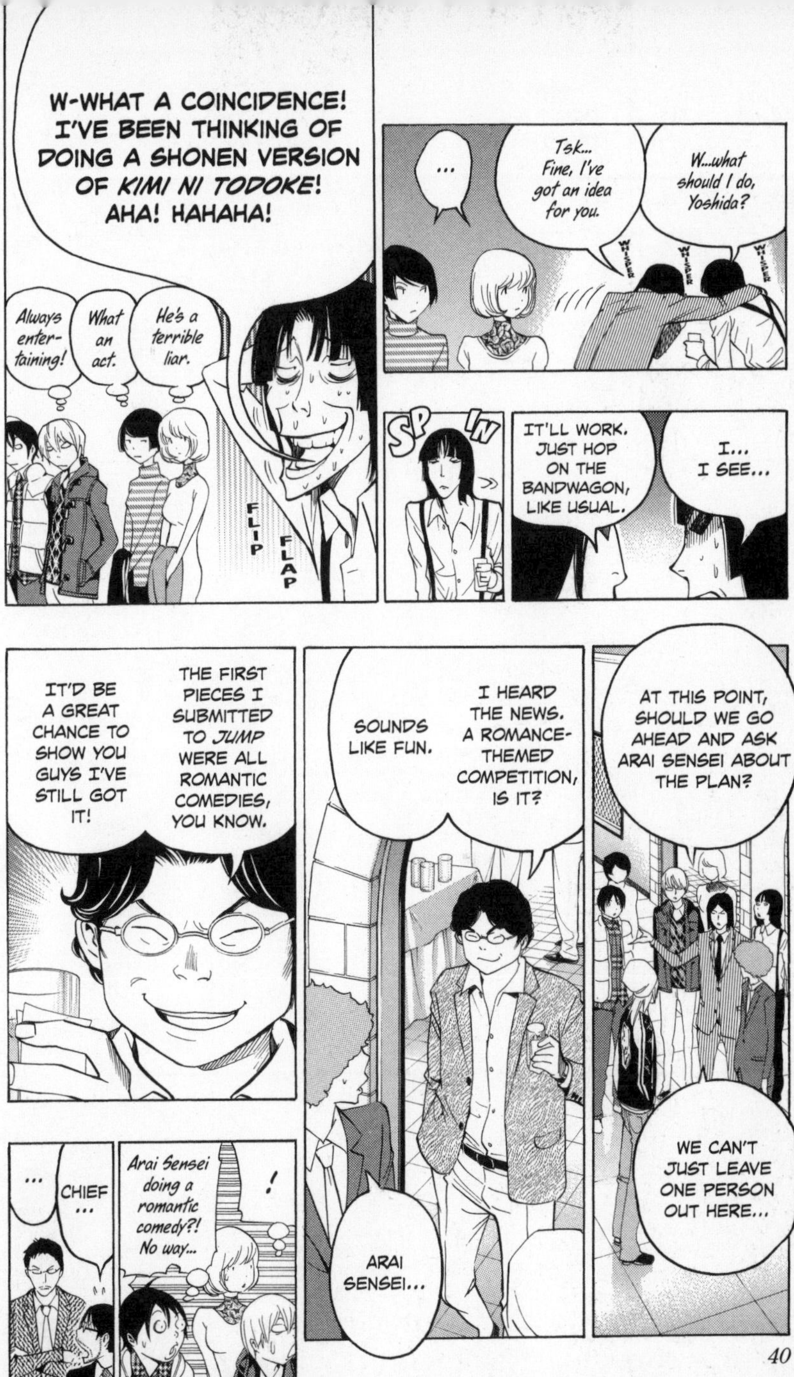
W...what should I do, Yoshida?
WHISPER
Tsk... Fine, I've got an idea for you.
WHISPER
WHISPER
...
I... I SEE...
IT'LL WORK. JUST HOP ON THE BANDWAGON, LIKE USUAL.
SPIN
W-WHAT A COINCIDENCE! I'VE BEEN THINKING OF DOING A SHONEN VERSION OF *KIMI NI TODOKE*! AHA! HAHAHA!
FLIP
FLAP
He's a terrible liar.
What an act.
Always enter-taining!
AT THIS POINT, SHOULD WE GO AHEAD AND ASK ARAI SENSEI ABOUT THE PLAN?
WE CAN'T JUST LEAVE ONE PERSON OUT HERE...
I HEARD THE NEWS. A ROMANCE-THEMED COMPETITION, IS IT?
SOUNDS LIKE FUN.
ARAI SENSEI...
THE FIRST PIECES I SUBMITTED TO *JUMP* WERE ALL ROMANTIC COMEDIES, YOU KNOW.
IT'D BE A GREAT CHANCE TO SHOW YOU GUYS I'VE STILL GOT IT!
!
Arai Sensei doing a romantic comedy?! No way...
CHIEF...
...

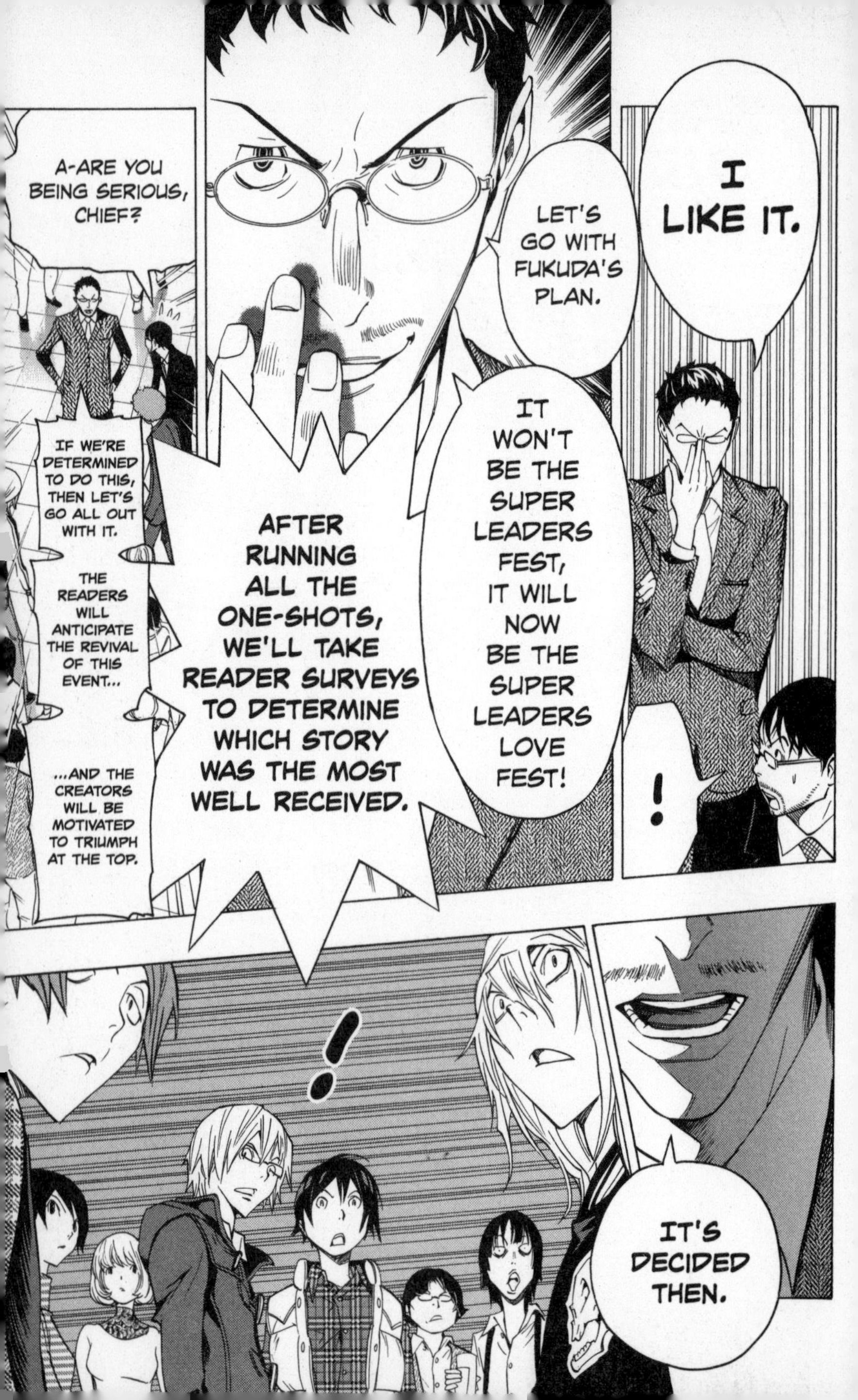
I LIKE IT.
LET'S GO WITH FUKUDA'S PLAN.
!
IT WON'T BE THE SUPER LEADERS FEST, IT WILL NOW BE THE SUPER LEADERS LOVE FEST!
AFTER RUNNING ALL THE ONE-SHOTS, WE'LL TAKE READER SURVEYS TO DETERMINE WHICH STORY WAS THE MOST WELL RECEIVED.
A-ARE YOU BEING SERIOUS, CHIEF?
IF WE'RE DETERMINED TO DO THIS, THEN LET'S GO ALL OUT WITH IT.
THE READERS WILL ANTICIPATE THE REVIVAL OF THIS EVENT...
...AND THE CREATORS WILL BE MOTIVATED TO TRIUMPH AT THE TOP.
IT'S DECIDED THEN.
!

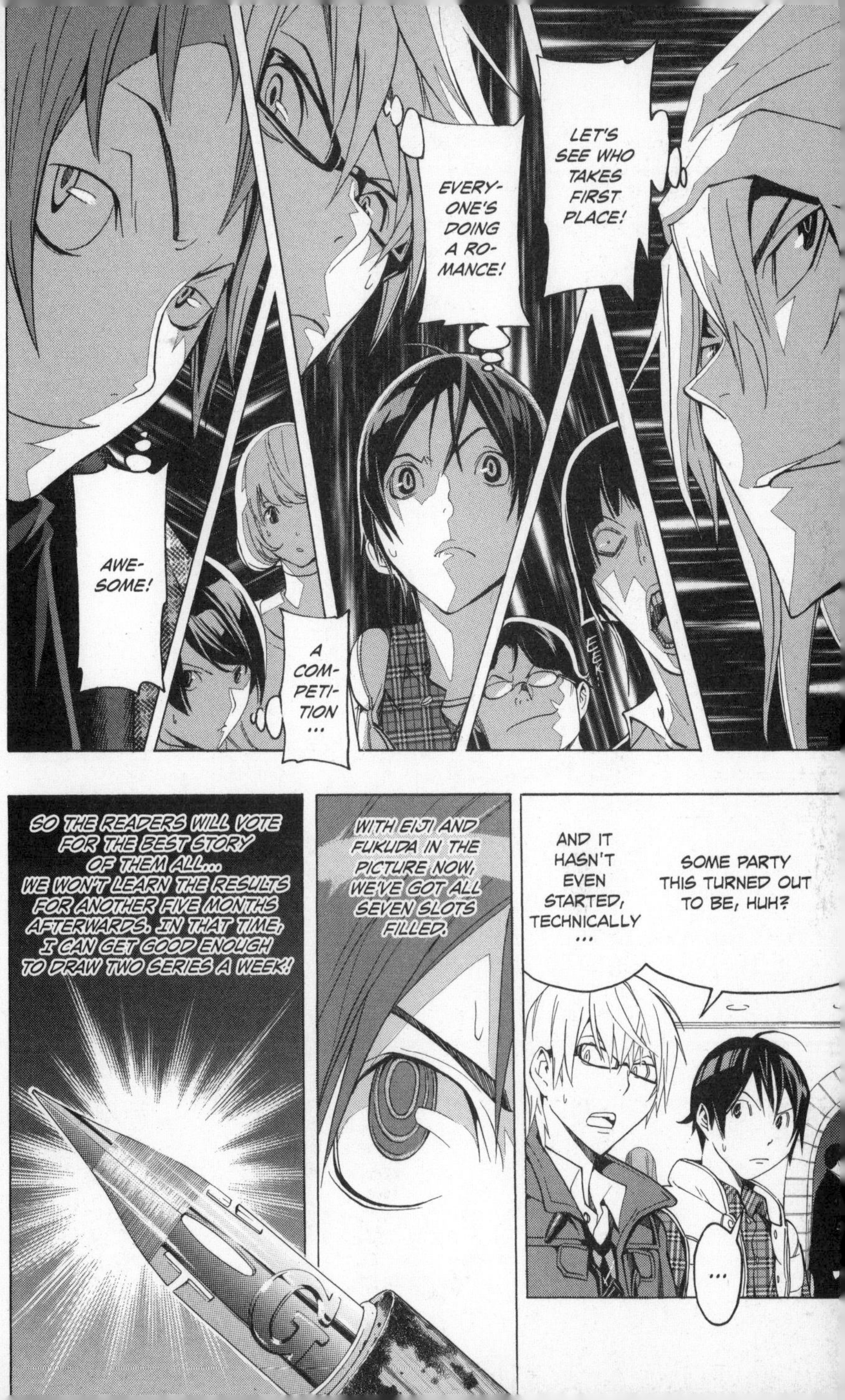
LET'S SEE WHO TAKES FIRST PLACE!
EVERY-ONE'S DOING A RO-MANCE!
A COM-PETI-TION...
AWE-SOME!
SOME PARTY THIS TURNED OUT TO BE, HUH?
AND IT HASN'T EVEN STARTED, TECHNICALLY...
...
WITH EIJI AND FUKUDA IN THE PICTURE NOW, WE'VE GOT ALL SEVEN SLOTS FILLED.
SO THE READERS WILL VOTE FOR THE BEST STORY OF THEM ALL... WE WON'T LEARN THE RESULTS FOR ANOTHER FIVE MONTHS AFTERWARDS. IN THAT TIME, I CAN GET GOOD ENOUGH TO DRAW TWO SERIES A WEEK!

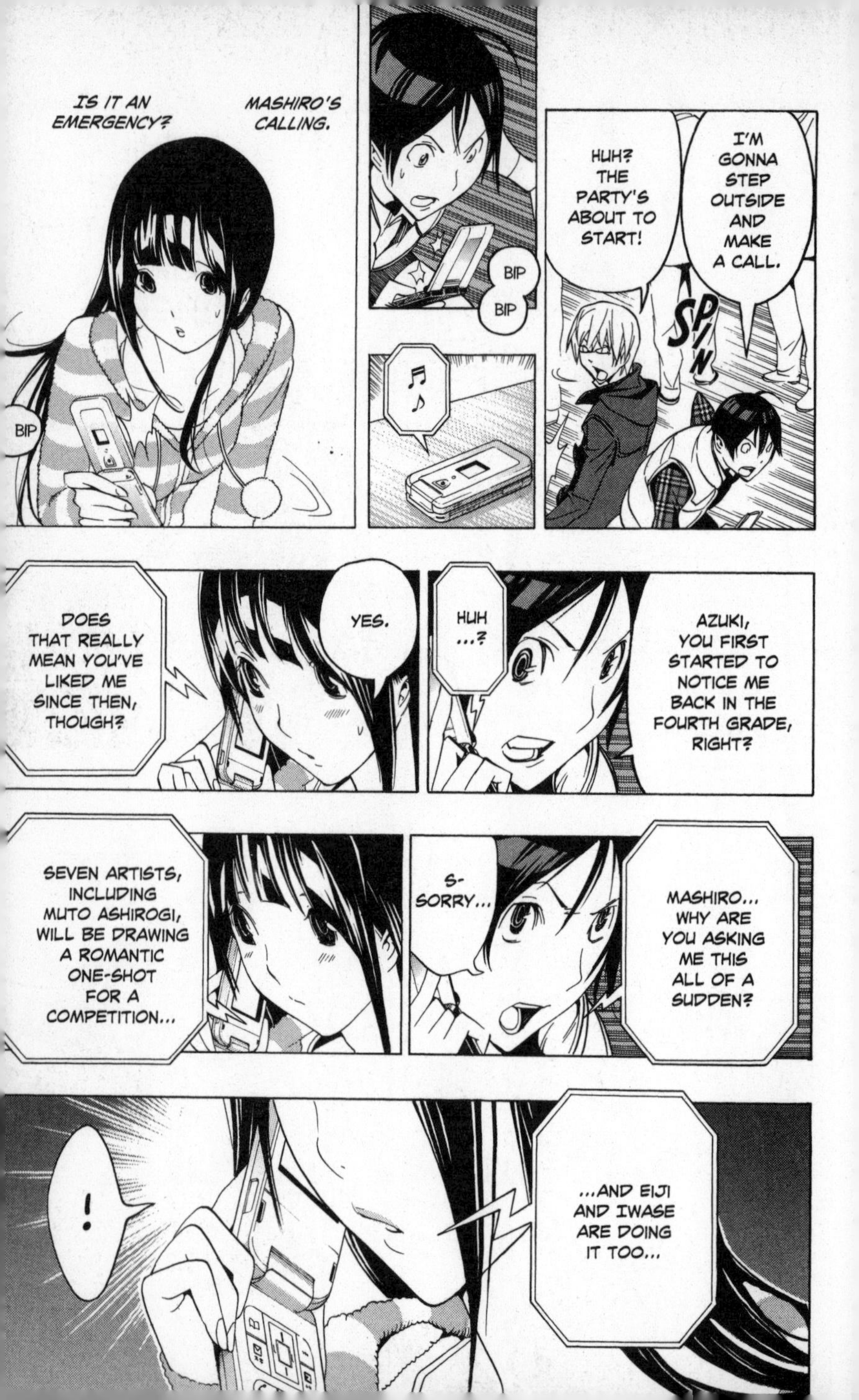
I'M GONNA STEP OUTSIDE AND MAKE A CALL.
HUH? THE PARTY'S ABOUT TO START!
SPIN
BIP
BIP
♪ ♪
MASHIRO'S CALLING.
IS IT AN EMERGENCY?
BIP
AZUKI, YOU FIRST STARTED TO NOTICE ME BACK IN THE FOURTH GRADE, RIGHT?
HUH ...?
YES.
DOES THAT REALLY MEAN YOU'VE LIKED ME SINCE THEN, THOUGH?
MASHIRO... WHY ARE YOU ASKING ME THIS ALL OF A SUDDEN?
S-SORRY...
SEVEN ARTISTS, INCLUDING MUTO ASHIROGI, WILL BE DRAWING A ROMANTIC ONE-SHOT FOR A COMPETITION...
...AND EIJI AND IWASE ARE DOING IT TOO...
!

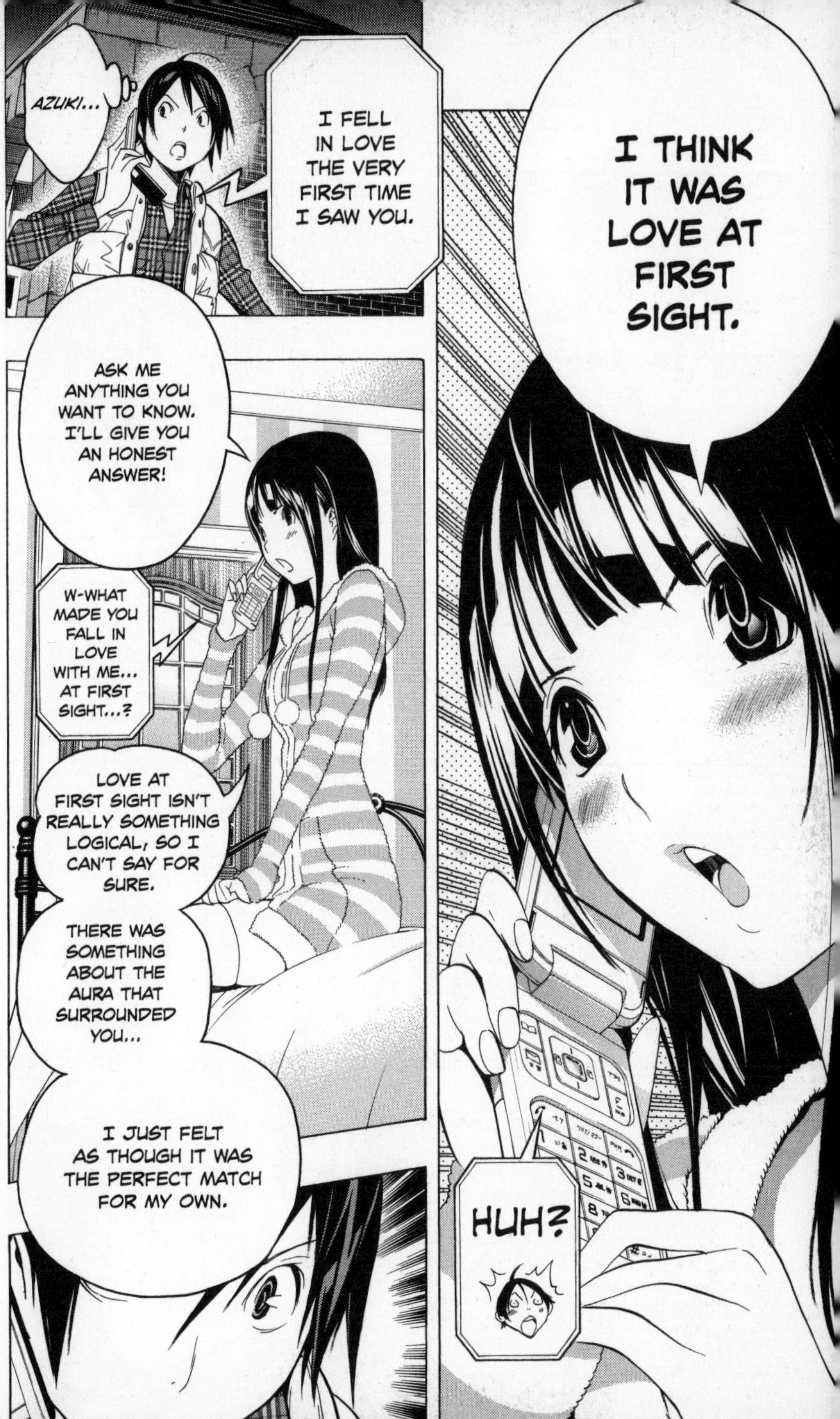
I THINK IT WAS LOVE AT FIRST SIGHT.
HUH?
AZUKI...
I FELL IN LOVE THE VERY FIRST TIME I SAW YOU.
ASK ME ANYTHING YOU WANT TO KNOW. I'LL GIVE YOU AN HONEST ANSWER!
W-WHAT MADE YOU FALL IN LOVE WITH ME... AT FIRST SIGHT...?
LOVE AT FIRST SIGHT ISN'T REALLY SOMETHING LOGICAL, SO I CAN'T SAY FOR SURE.
THERE WAS SOMETHING ABOUT THE AURA THAT SURROUNDED YOU...
I JUST FELT AS THOUGH IT WAS THE PERFECT MATCH FOR MY OWN.

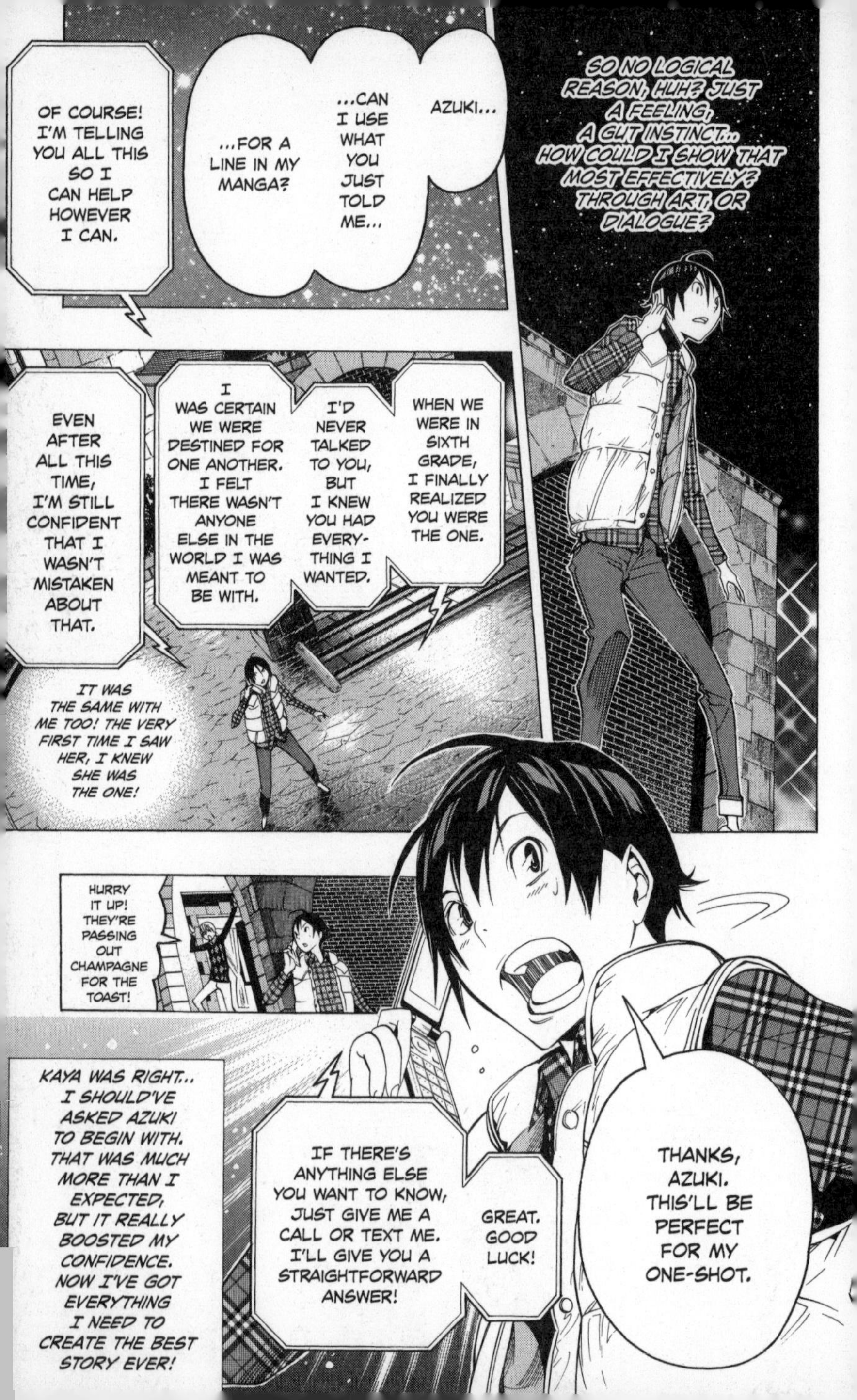
SO NO LOGICAL REASON, HUH? JUST A FEELING, A GUT INSTINCT... HOW COULD I SHOW THAT MOST EFFECTIVELY? THROUGH ART OR DIALOGUE?
AZUKI...
...CAN I USE WHAT YOU JUST TOLD ME...
...FOR A LINE IN MY MANGA?
OF COURSE! I'M TELLING YOU ALL THIS SO I CAN HELP HOWEVER I CAN.
WHEN WE WERE IN SIXTH GRADE, I FINALLY REALIZED YOU WERE THE ONE.
I'D NEVER TALKED TO YOU, BUT I KNEW YOU HAD EVERYTHING I WANTED.
I WAS CERTAIN WE WERE DESTINED FOR ONE ANOTHER. I FELT THERE WASN'T ANYONE ELSE IN THE WORLD I WAS MEANT TO BE WITH.
EVEN AFTER ALL THIS TIME, I'M STILL CONFIDENT THAT I WASN'T MISTAKEN ABOUT THAT.
IT WAS THE SAME WITH ME TOO! THE VERY FIRST TIME I SAW HER, I KNEW SHE WAS THE ONE!
THANKS, AZUKI. THIS'LL BE PERFECT FOR MY ONE-SHOT.
GREAT. GOOD LUCK!
IF THERE'S ANYTHING ELSE YOU WANT TO KNOW, JUST GIVE ME A CALL OR TEXT ME. I'LL GIVE YOU A STRAIGHTFORWARD ANSWER!
HURRY IT UP! THEY'RE PASSING OUT CHAMPAGNE FOR THE TOAST!
KAYA WAS RIGHT... I SHOULD'VE ASKED AZUKI TO BEGIN WITH. THAT WAS MUCH MORE THAN I EXPECTED, BUT IT REALLY BOOSTED MY CONFIDENCE. NOW I'VE GOT EVERYTHING I NEED TO CREATE THE BEST STORY EVER!

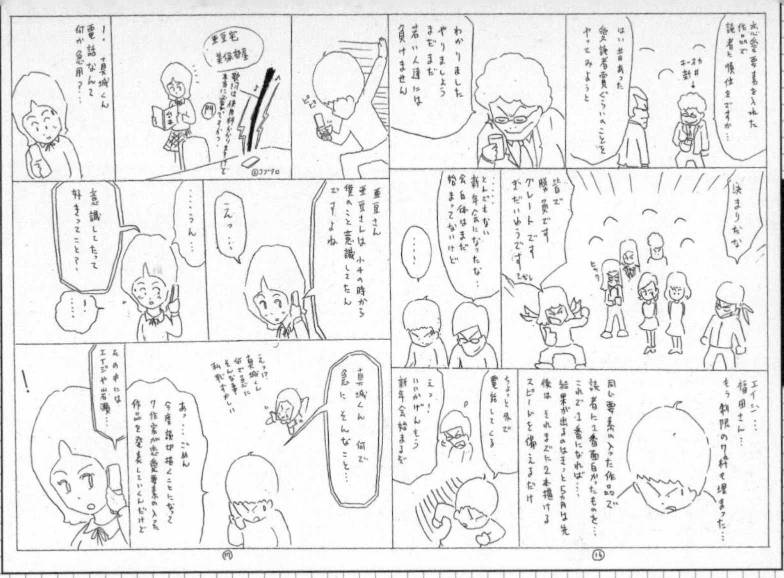
恋愛要素を入れた作品で読者と順位をですか…
はい 昔あった愛読者賞ぐらいのことをやってみようと
わかりました やりましょう まだまだ若い人達には負けません
決まりだな
皆で勝負です グレートです
とんでもない新年会になったな… 会自体はまだ始まってないけど
……
エイジ… 福田さん… もう制限の7枠も埋まった…
同じ要素の入った作品で読者に1番面白かったものを… これで1番になれば… 結果が出るのはきっと5カ月は先 僕はそれまでに2本描けるスピードを備えるだけ
ちょっと外で電話してくる
えっ! いいかげんもう新年会始まるぞ
ピピ
亜豆宅
美保部屋
! 真城くん 電話なんて何か急用?…
亜豆さん 亜豆さんは小4の時から僕のこと意識してたんですよね
えっ…
…うん…
意識してたって好きってこと?…
!……
真城くん 何で急にそんなこと…
えっ!? 真城くん 何で急にそんな事 私恥ずかしい
あっ… ごめん 今度読切描くことになって 7作家が恋愛要素の入った作品を発表していくんだけど
その中にはエイジや岩瀬…
!
⑰
⑯

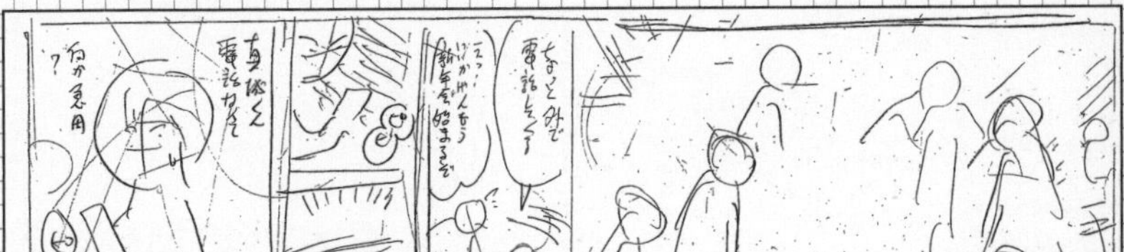

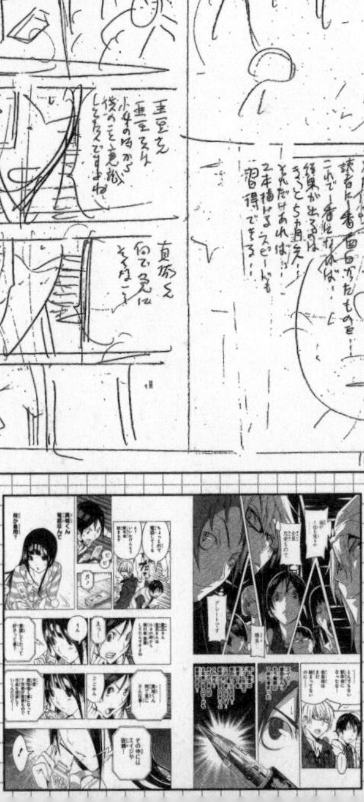

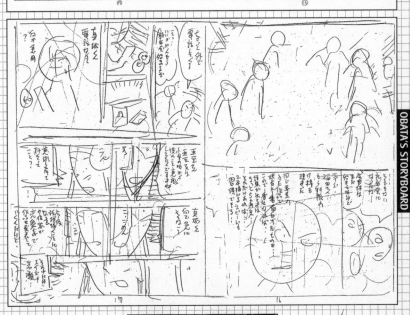

COMPLETE!

*CREATOR STORYBOARDS AND FINISHED PAGES IN JAPANESE

BAKUMAN。 vol.13

"Until the Final Draft Is Complete"

Chapter 108, pp. 42-43

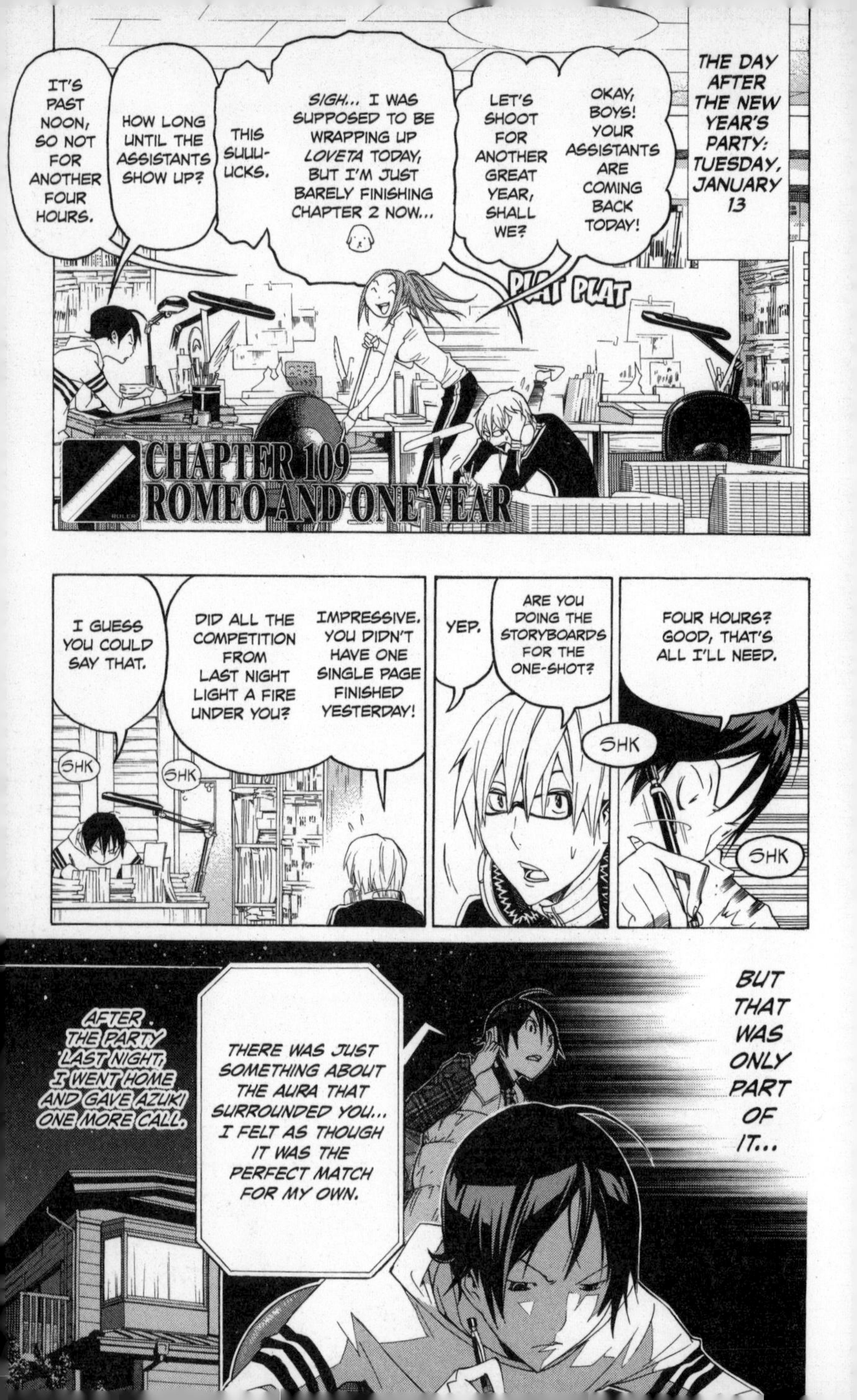
THE DAY AFTER THE NEW YEAR'S PARTY: TUESDAY, JANUARY 13
OKAY, BOYS! YOUR ASSISTANTS ARE COMING BACK TODAY!
LET'S SHOOT FOR ANOTHER GREAT YEAR, SHALL WE?
PLAT PLAT
SIGH... I WAS SUPPOSED TO BE WRAPPING UP LOVETA TODAY, BUT I'M JUST BARELY FINISHING CHAPTER 2 NOW...
THIS SUUUUCKS.
HOW LONG UNTIL THE ASSISTANTS SHOW UP?
IT'S PAST NOON, SO NOT FOR ANOTHER FOUR HOURS.
CHAPTER 109 ROMEO AND ONE YEAR
FOUR HOURS? GOOD, THAT'S ALL I'LL NEED.
SHK
ARE YOU DOING THE STORYBOARDS FOR THE ONE-SHOT?
SHK
YEP.
IMPRESSIVE. YOU DIDN'T HAVE ONE SINGLE PAGE FINISHED YESTERDAY!
DID ALL THE COMPETITION FROM LAST NIGHT LIGHT A FIRE UNDER YOU?
I GUESS YOU COULD SAY THAT.
SHK
SHK
BUT THAT WAS ONLY PART OF IT...
THERE WAS JUST SOMETHING ABOUT THE AURA THAT SURROUNDED YOU... I FELT AS THOUGH IT WAS THE PERFECT MATCH FOR MY OWN.
AFTER THE PARTY LAST NIGHT, I WENT HOME AND GAVE AZUKI ONE MORE CALL.

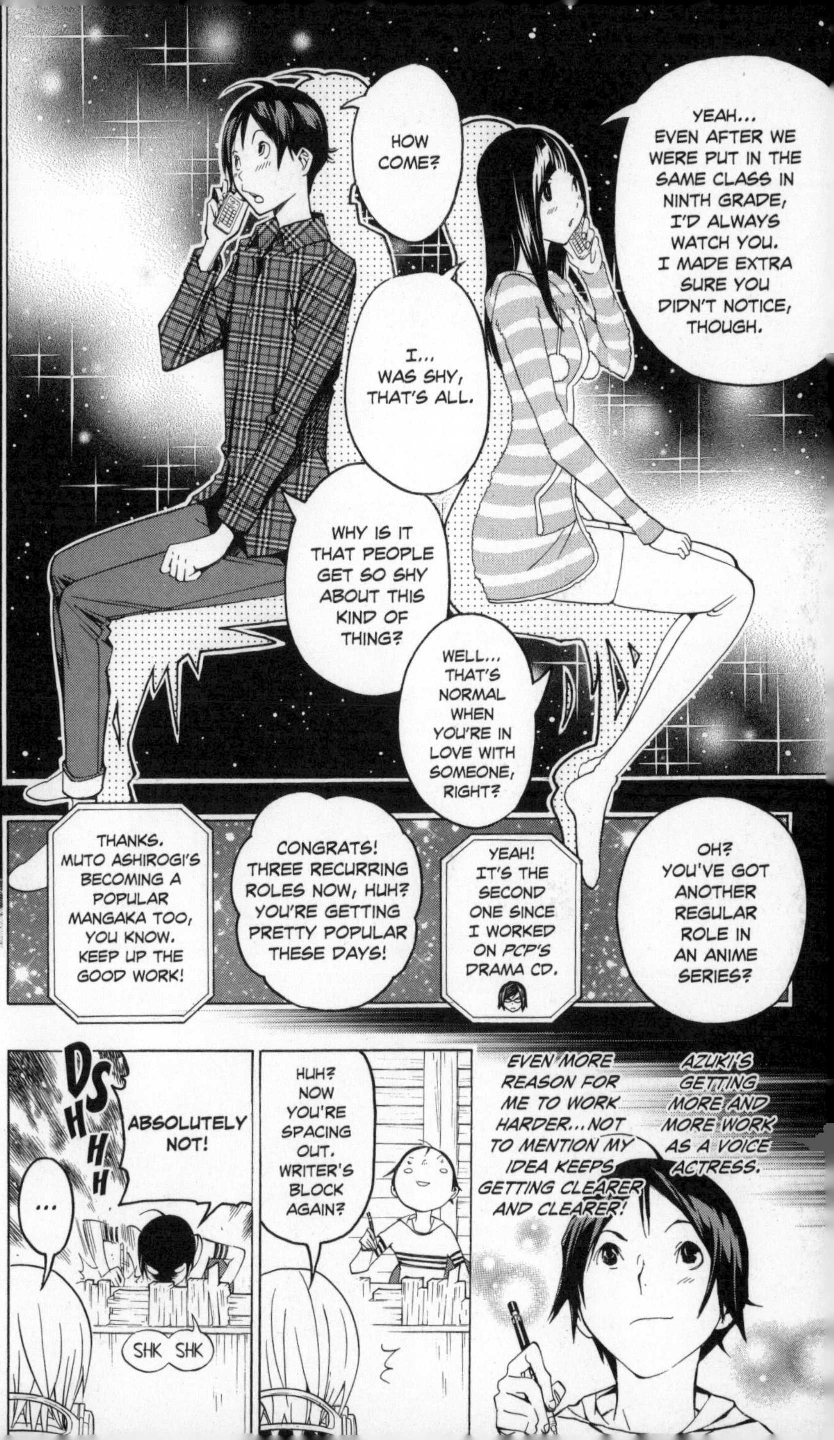
YEAH... EVEN AFTER WE WERE PUT IN THE SAME CLASS IN NINTH GRADE, I'D ALWAYS WATCH YOU. I MADE EXTRA SURE YOU DIDN'T NOTICE, THOUGH.
HOW COME?
I... WAS SHY, THAT'S ALL.
WHY IS IT THAT PEOPLE GET SO SHY ABOUT THIS KIND OF THING?
WELL... THAT'S NORMAL WHEN YOU'RE IN LOVE WITH SOMEONE, RIGHT?
OH? YOU'VE GOT ANOTHER REGULAR ROLE IN AN ANIME SERIES?
YEAH! IT'S THE SECOND ONE SINCE I WORKED ON *PCP'S* DRAMA CD.
CONGRATS! THREE RECURRING ROLES NOW, HUH? YOU'RE GETTING PRETTY POPULAR THESE DAYS!
THANKS. MUTO ASHIROGI'S BECOMING A POPULAR MANGAKA TOO, YOU KNOW. KEEP UP THE GOOD WORK!
AZUKI'S GETTING MORE AND MORE WORK AS A VOICE ACTRESS.
EVEN MORE REASON FOR ME TO WORK HARDER... NOT TO MENTION MY IDEA KEEPS GETTING CLEARER AND CLEARER!
HUH? NOW YOU'RE SPACING OUT. WRITER'S BLOCK AGAIN?
DSHHH
ABSOLUTELY NOT!
...
SHK SHK

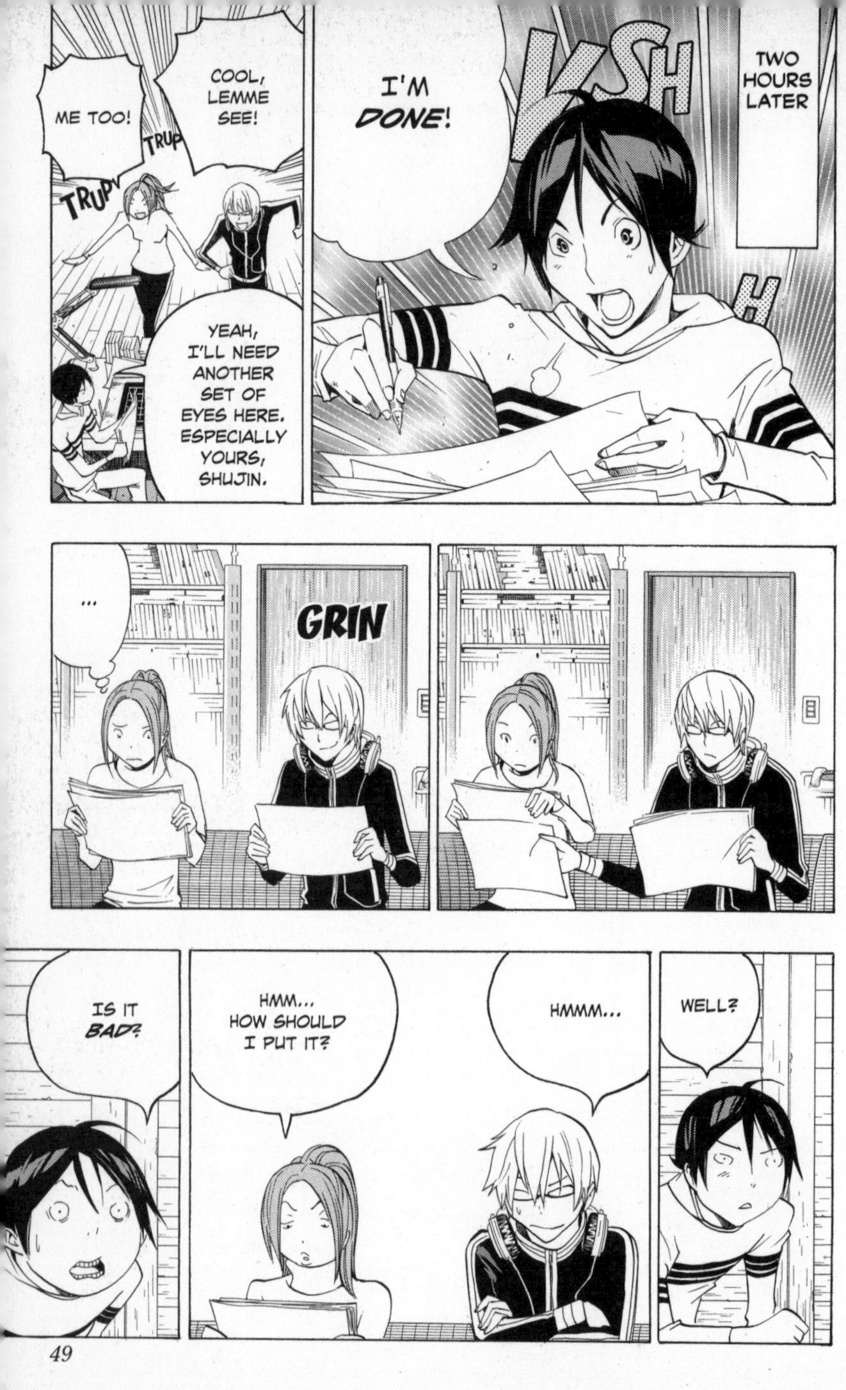
TWO HOURS LATER
KSH
H
I'M DONE!
COOL, LEMME SEE!
ME TOO!
TRUP
TRUP
YEAH, I'LL NEED ANOTHER SET OF EYES HERE. ESPECIALLY YOURS, SHUJIN.
GRIN
...
WELL?
HMMM...
HMM... HOW SHOULD I PUT IT?
IS IT BAD?

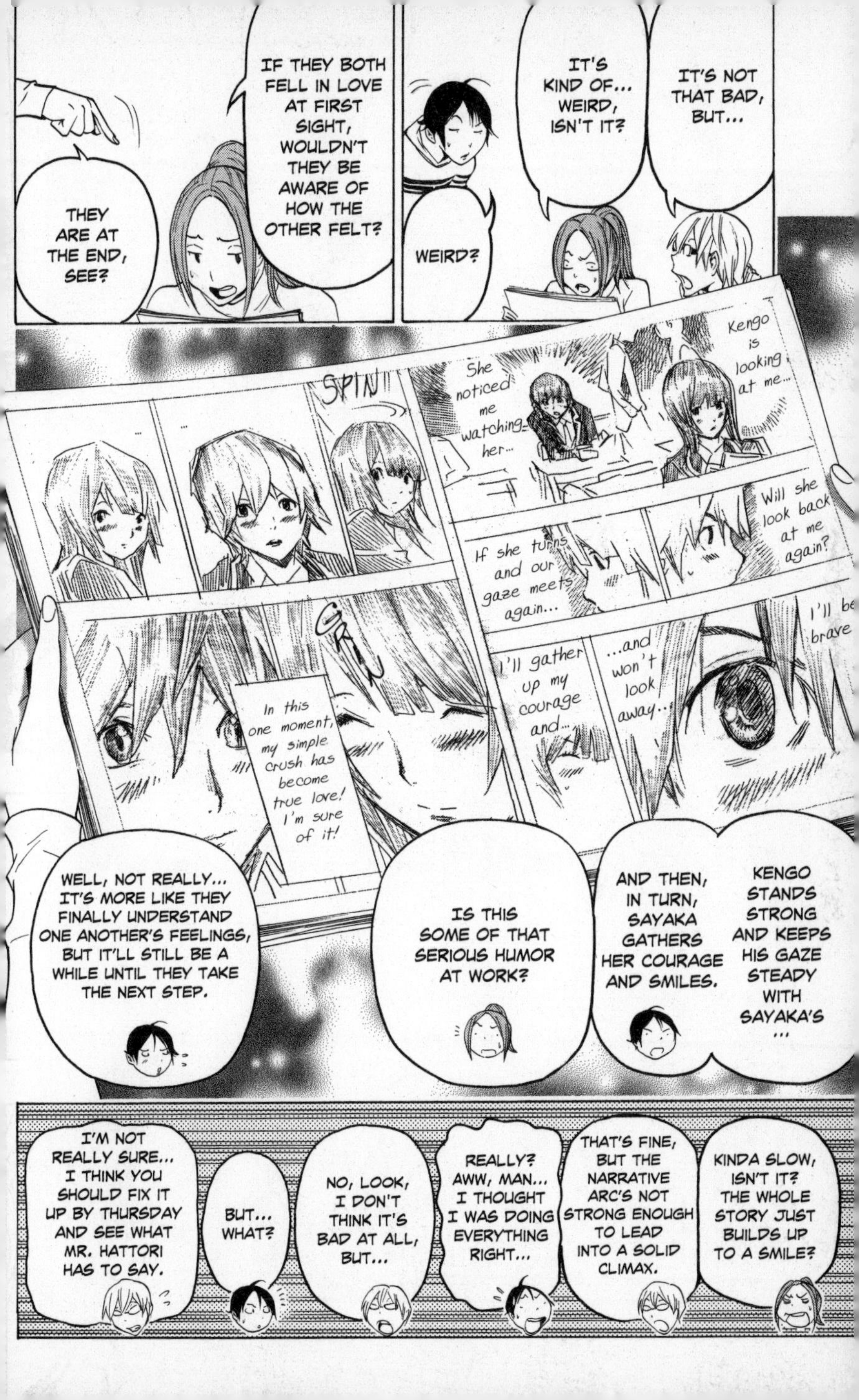
IT'S NOT THAT BAD, BUT...
IT'S KIND OF... WEIRD, ISN'T IT?
WEIRD?
IF THEY BOTH FELL IN LOVE AT FIRST SIGHT, WOULDN'T THEY BE AWARE OF HOW THE OTHER FELT?
THEY ARE AT THE END, SEE?
Kengo is looking at me...
She noticed me watching her...
SPIN
Will she look back at me again?
If she turns and our gaze meets again...
I'll be brave
...and won't look away...
I'll gather up my courage and...
In this one moment, my simple crush has become true love! I'm sure of it!
KENGO STANDS STRONG AND KEEPS HIS GAZE STEADY WITH SAYAKA'S...
AND THEN, IN TURN, SAYAKA GATHERS HER COURAGE AND SMILES.
IS THIS SOME OF THAT SERIOUS HUMOR AT WORK?
WELL, NOT REALLY... IT'S MORE LIKE THEY FINALLY UNDERSTAND ONE ANOTHER'S FEELINGS, BUT IT'LL STILL BE A WHILE UNTIL THEY TAKE THE NEXT STEP.
KINDA SLOW, ISN'T IT? THE WHOLE STORY JUST BUILDS UP TO A SMILE?
THAT'S FINE, BUT THE NARRATIVE ARC'S NOT STRONG ENOUGH TO LEAD INTO A SOLID CLIMAX.
REALLY? AWW, MAN... I THOUGHT I WAS DOING EVERYTHING RIGHT...
NO, LOOK, I DON'T THINK IT'S BAD AT ALL, BUT...
BUT... WHAT?
I'M NOT REALLY SURE... I THINK YOU SHOULD FIX IT UP BY THURSDAY AND SEE WHAT MR. HATTORI HAS TO SAY.

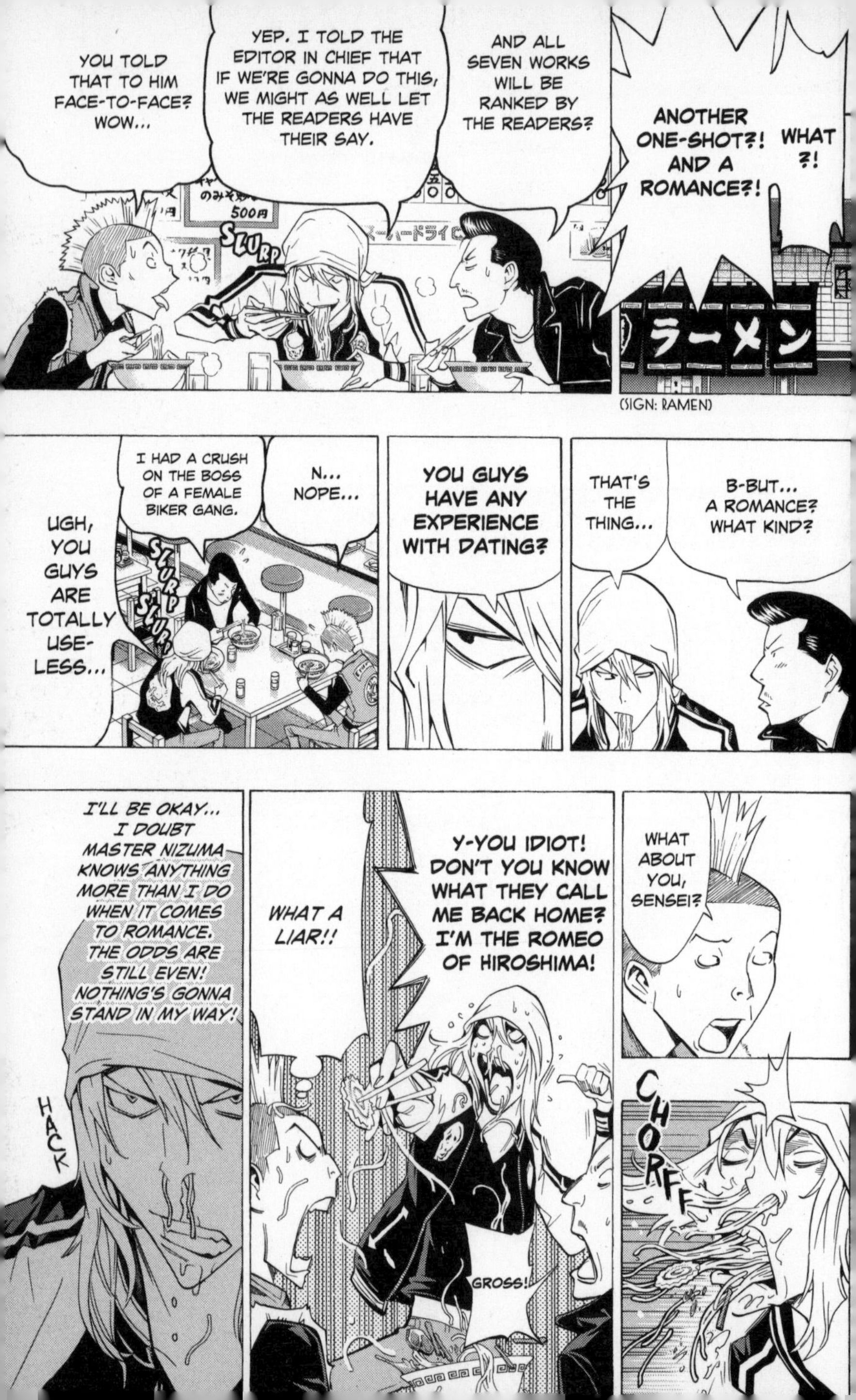
WHAT ?!
ANOTHER ONE-SHOT?! AND A ROMANCE?!
(SIGN: RAMEN)
AND ALL SEVEN WORKS WILL BE RANKED BY THE READERS?
YEP. I TOLD THE EDITOR IN CHIEF THAT IF WE'RE GONNA DO THIS, WE MIGHT AS WELL LET THE READERS HAVE THEIR SAY.
YOU TOLD THAT TO HIM FACE-TO-FACE? WOW...
SLURP
B-BUT... A ROMANCE? WHAT KIND?
THAT'S THE THING...
YOU GUYS HAVE ANY EXPERIENCE WITH DATING?
N... NOPE...
I HAD A CRUSH ON THE BOSS OF A FEMALE BIKER GANG.
UGH, YOU GUYS ARE TOTALLY USE-LESS...
SLURP
SLURP
WHAT ABOUT YOU, SENSEI?
CHORFF
Y-YOU IDIOT! DON'T YOU KNOW WHAT THEY CALL ME BACK HOME? I'M THE ROMEO OF HIROSHIMA!
WHAT A LIAR!!
GROSS!
I'LL BE OKAY... I DOUBT MASTER NIZUMA KNOWS ANYTHING MORE THAN I DO WHEN IT COMES TO ROMANCE. THE ODDS ARE STILL EVEN! NOTHING'S GONNA STAND IN MY WAY!
HACK

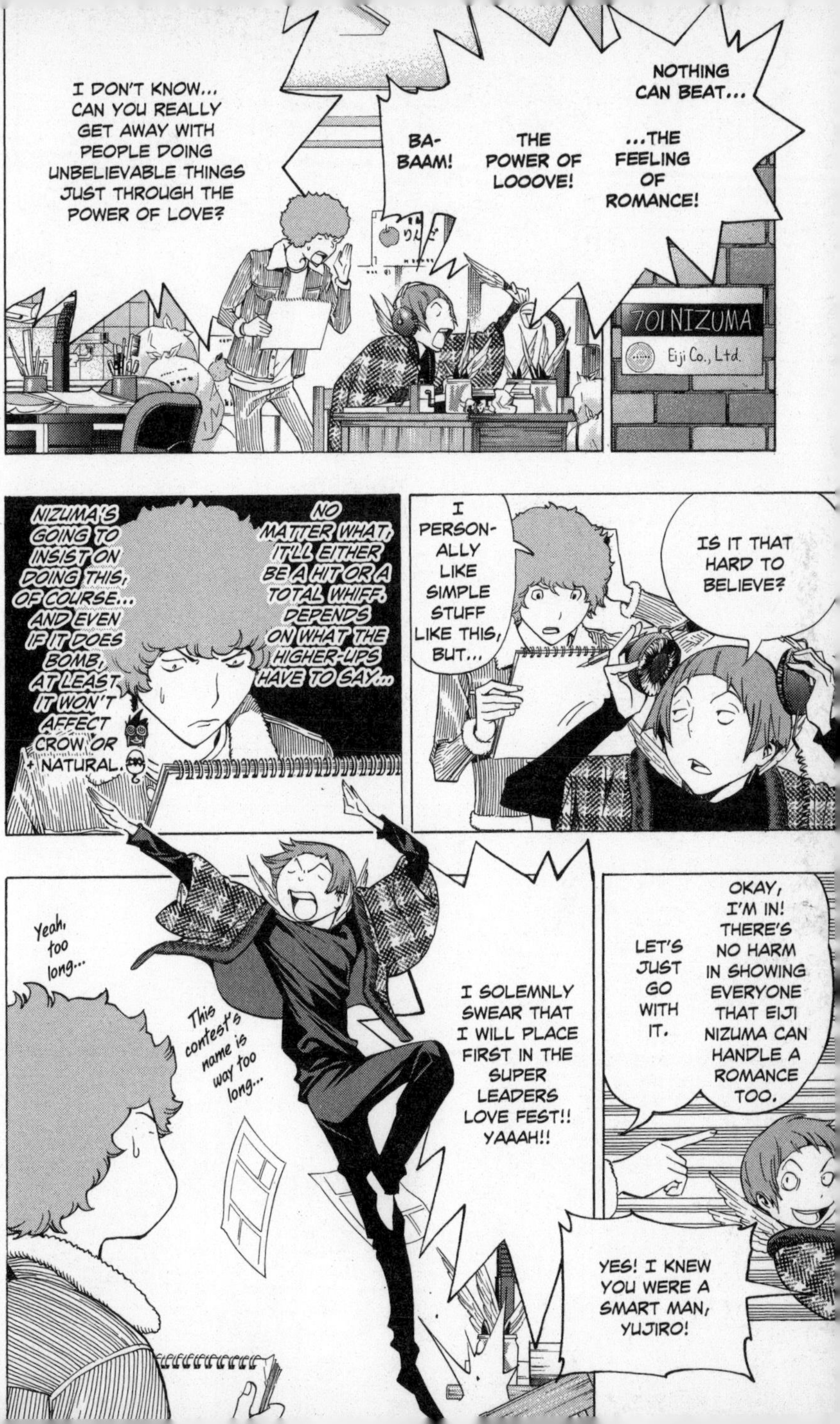
NOTHING CAN BEAT...
...THE FEELING OF ROMANCE!
THE POWER OF LOOOVE!
BA-BAAM!
I DON'T KNOW... CAN YOU REALLY GET AWAY WITH PEOPLE DOING UNBELIEVABLE THINGS JUST THROUGH THE POWER OF LOVE?
701 NIZUMA
Eiji Co., Ltd.
IS IT THAT HARD TO BELIEVE?
I PERSONALLY LIKE SIMPLE STUFF LIKE THIS, BUT...
NO MATTER WHAT, IT'LL EITHER BE A HIT OR A TOTAL WHIFF. DEPENDS ON WHAT THE HIGHER-UPS HAVE TO SAY...
NIZUMA'S GOING TO INSIST ON DOING THIS, OF COURSE... AND EVEN IF IT DOES BOMB, AT LEAST IT WON'T AFFECT CROW OR NATURAL.
OKAY, I'M IN! THERE'S NO HARM IN SHOWING EVERYONE THAT EIJI NIZUMA CAN HANDLE A ROMANCE TOO.
LET'S JUST GO WITH IT.
YES! I KNEW YOU WERE A SMART MAN, YUJIRO!
I SOLEMNLY SWEAR THAT I WILL PLACE FIRST IN THE SUPER LEADERS LOVE FEST!! YAAAH!!
This contest's name is way too long...
Yeah, too long...

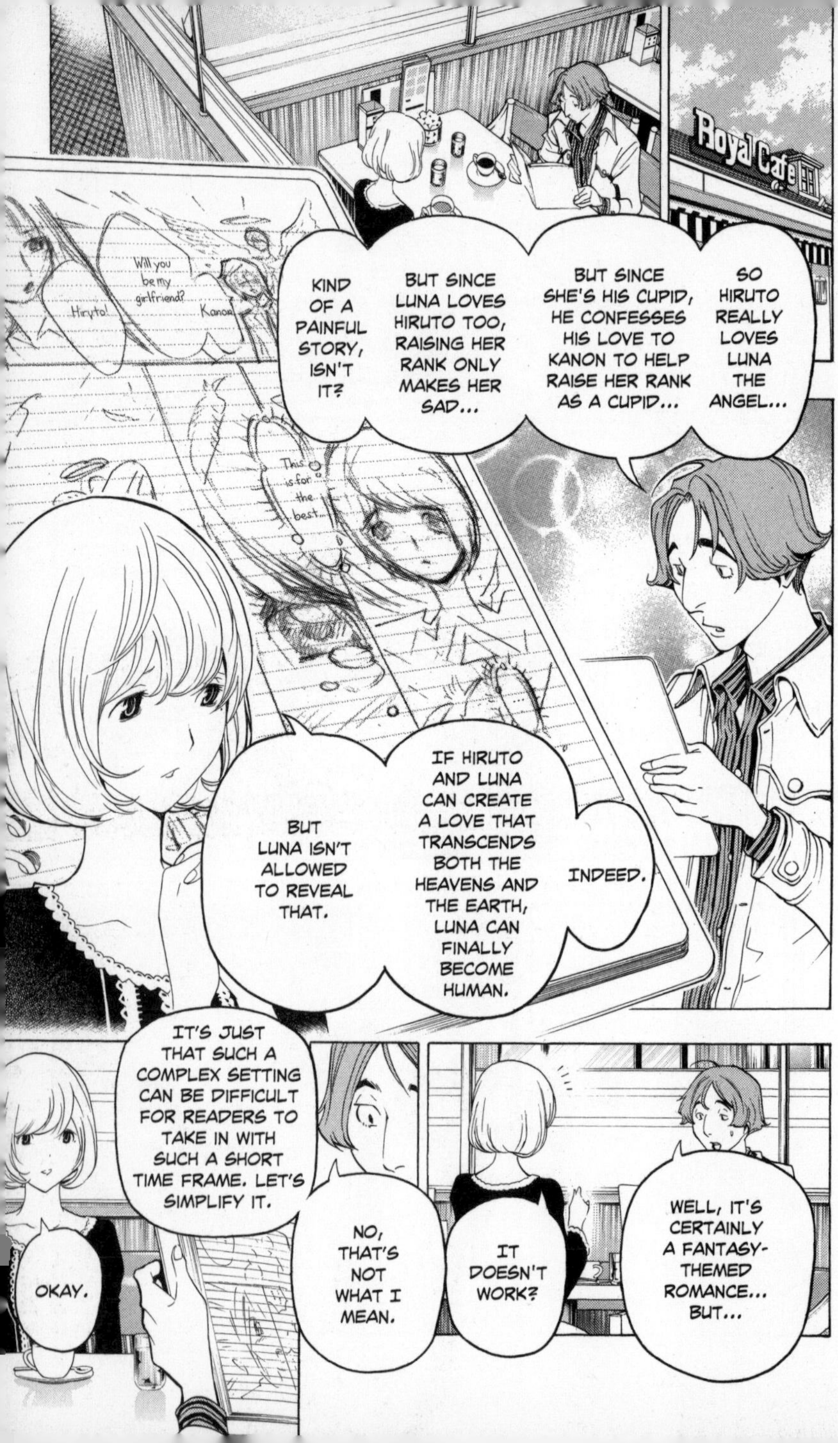
Royal Cafe
SO HIRUTO REALLY LOVES LUNA THE ANGEL...
BUT SINCE SHE'S HIS CUPID, HE CONFESSES HIS LOVE TO KANON TO HELP RAISE HER RANK AS A CUPID...
BUT SINCE LUNA LOVES HIRUTO TOO, RAISING HER RANK ONLY MAKES HER SAD...
KIND OF A PAINFUL STORY, ISN'T IT?
Will you be my girlfriend?
Kanon
Hiryto!
This is for the best...
INDEED.
IF HIRUTO AND LUNA CAN CREATE A LOVE THAT TRANSCENDS BOTH THE HEAVENS AND THE EARTH, LUNA CAN FINALLY BECOME HUMAN.
BUT LUNA ISN'T ALLOWED TO REVEAL THAT.
WELL, IT'S CERTAINLY A FANTASY-THEMED ROMANCE... BUT...
IT DOESN'T WORK?
NO, THAT'S NOT WHAT I MEAN.
IT'S JUST THAT SUCH A COMPLEX SETTING CAN BE DIFFICULT FOR READERS TO TAKE IN WITH SUCH A SHORT TIME FRAME. LET'S SIMPLIFY IT.
OKAY.

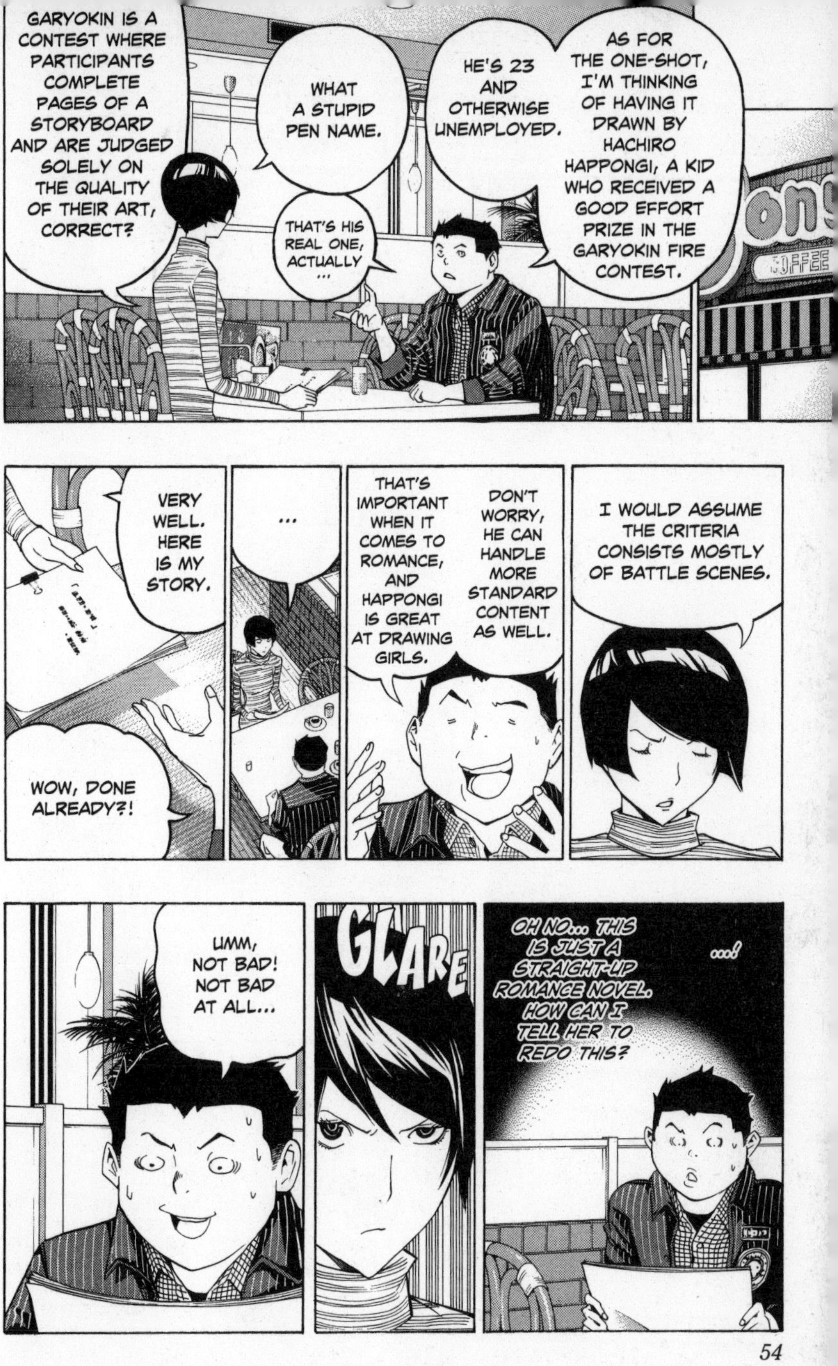
AS FOR THE ONE-SHOT, I'M THINKING OF HAVING IT DRAWN BY HACHIRO HAPPONGI, A KID WHO RECEIVED A GOOD EFFORT PRIZE IN THE GARYOKIN FIRE CONTEST.
HE'S 23 AND OTHERWISE UNEMPLOYED.
WHAT A STUPID PEN NAME.
THAT'S HIS REAL ONE, ACTUALLY ...
GARYOKIN IS A CONTEST WHERE PARTICIPANTS COMPLETE PAGES OF A STORYBOARD AND ARE JUDGED SOLELY ON THE QUALITY OF THEIR ART, CORRECT?
COFFEE
I WOULD ASSUME THE CRITERIA CONSISTS MOSTLY OF BATTLE SCENES.
DON'T WORRY, HE CAN HANDLE MORE STANDARD CONTENT AS WELL.
THAT'S IMPORTANT WHEN IT COMES TO ROMANCE, AND HAPPONGI IS GREAT AT DRAWING GIRLS.
...
VERY WELL. HERE IS MY STORY.
WOW, DONE ALREADY?!
OH NO... THIS IS JUST A STRAIGHT-UP ROMANCE NOVEL. HOW CAN I TELL HER TO REDO THIS?
...!
GLARE
UMM, NOT BAD! NOT BAD AT ALL...

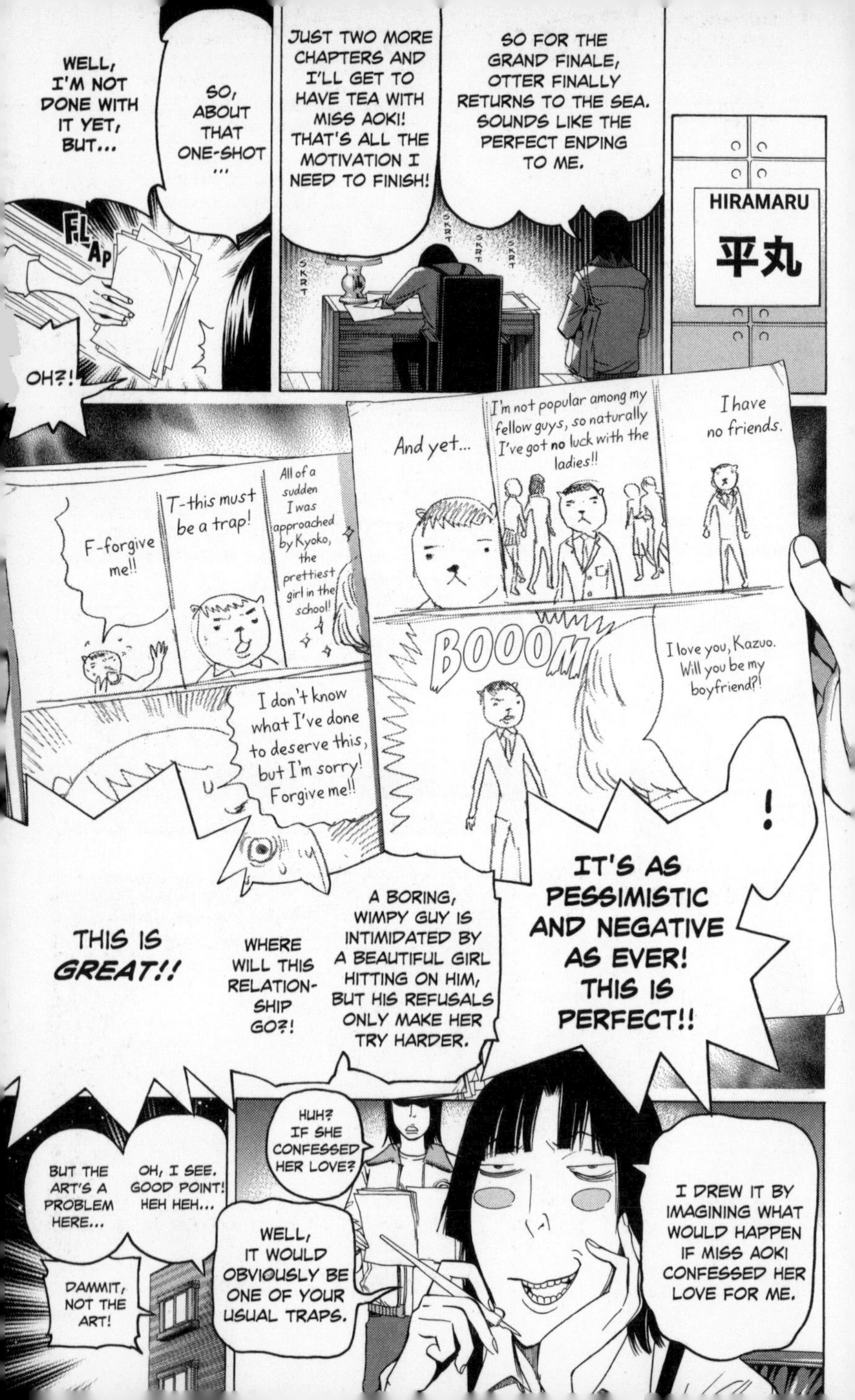
HIRAMARU
平丸
SO FOR THE GRAND FINALE, OTTER FINALLY RETURNS TO THE SEA. SOUNDS LIKE THE PERFECT ENDING TO ME.
JUST TWO MORE CHAPTERS AND I'LL GET TO HAVE TEA WITH MISS AOKI! THAT'S ALL THE MOTIVATION I NEED TO FINISH!
SKRT SKRT SKRT SKRT
SO, ABOUT THAT ONE-SHOT...
WELL, I'M NOT DONE WITH IT YET, BUT...
FLAP
OH?!
I have no friends.
I'm not popular among my fellow guys, so naturally I've got no luck with the ladies!!
And yet...
I love you, Kazuo. Will you be my boyfriend?!
BOOOM
All of a sudden I was approached by Kyoko, the prettiest girl in the school!
T-this must be a trap!
F-forgive me!!
I don't know what I've done to deserve this, but I'm sorry! Forgive me!!
!
IT'S AS PESSIMISTIC AND NEGATIVE AS EVER! THIS IS PERFECT!!
A BORING, WIMPY GUY IS INTIMIDATED BY A BEAUTIFUL GIRL HITTING ON HIM, BUT HIS REFUSALS ONLY MAKE HER TRY HARDER.
WHERE WILL THIS RELATIONSHIP GO?!
THIS IS GREAT!!
I DREW IT BY IMAGINING WHAT WOULD HAPPEN IF MISS AOKI CONFESSED HER LOVE FOR ME.
HUH? IF SHE CONFESSED HER LOVE?
WELL, IT WOULD OBVIOUSLY BE ONE OF YOUR USUAL TRAPS.
OH, I SEE. GOOD POINT! HEH HEH...
BUT THE ART'S A PROBLEM HERE...
DAMMIT, NOT THE ART!

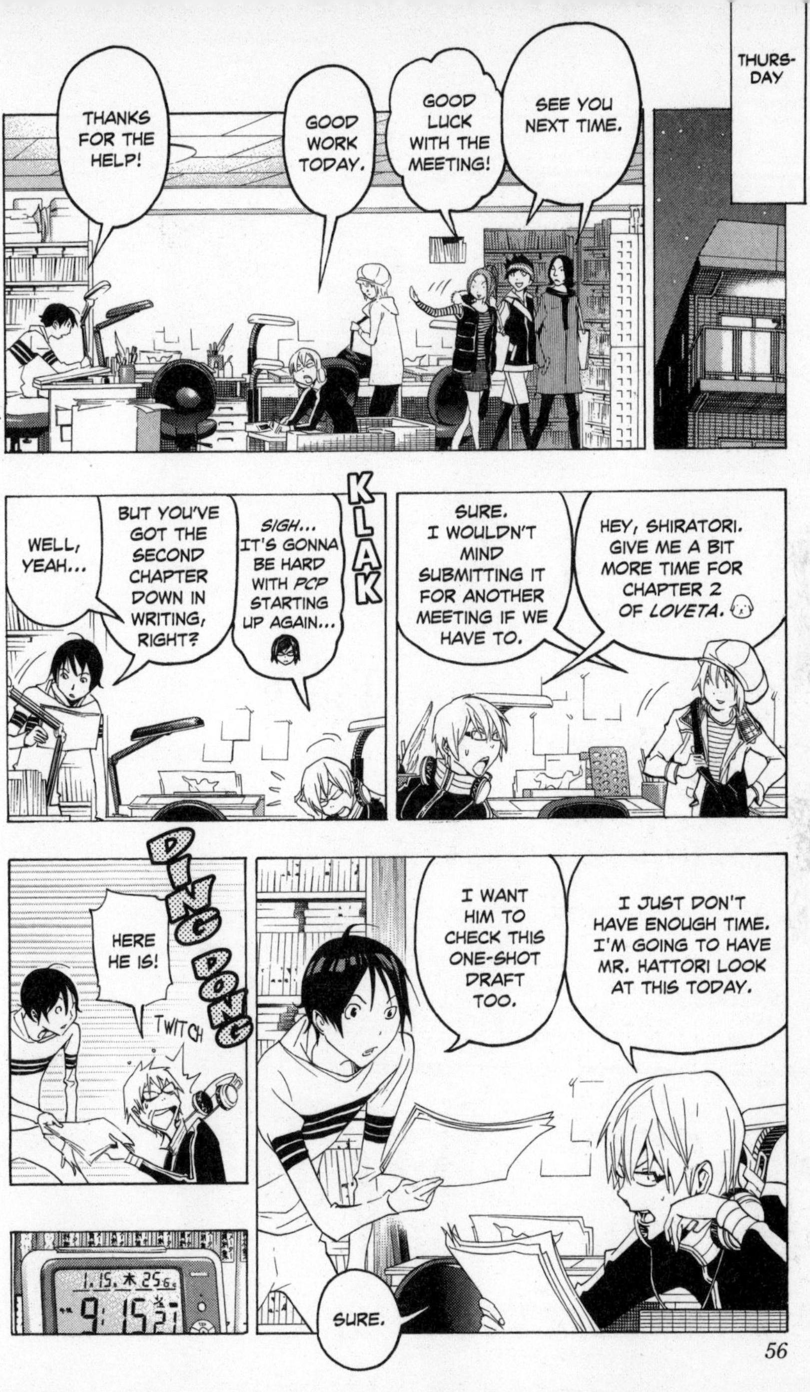
THURS-DAY
SEE YOU NEXT TIME.
GOOD LUCK WITH THE MEETING!
GOOD WORK TODAY.
THANKS FOR THE HELP!
HEY, SHIRATORI. GIVE ME A BIT MORE TIME FOR CHAPTER 2 OF *LOVETA*.
SURE. I WOULDN'T MIND SUBMITTING IT FOR ANOTHER MEETING IF WE HAVE TO.
KLAK
SIGH... IT'S GONNA BE HARD WITH *PCP* STARTING UP AGAIN...
BUT YOU'VE GOT THE SECOND CHAPTER DOWN IN WRITING, RIGHT?
WELL, YEAH...
I JUST DON'T HAVE ENOUGH TIME. I'M GOING TO HAVE MR. HATTORI LOOK AT THIS TODAY.
I WANT HIM TO CHECK THIS ONE-SHOT DRAFT TOO.
SURE.
DING DONG
HERE HE IS!
TWITCH

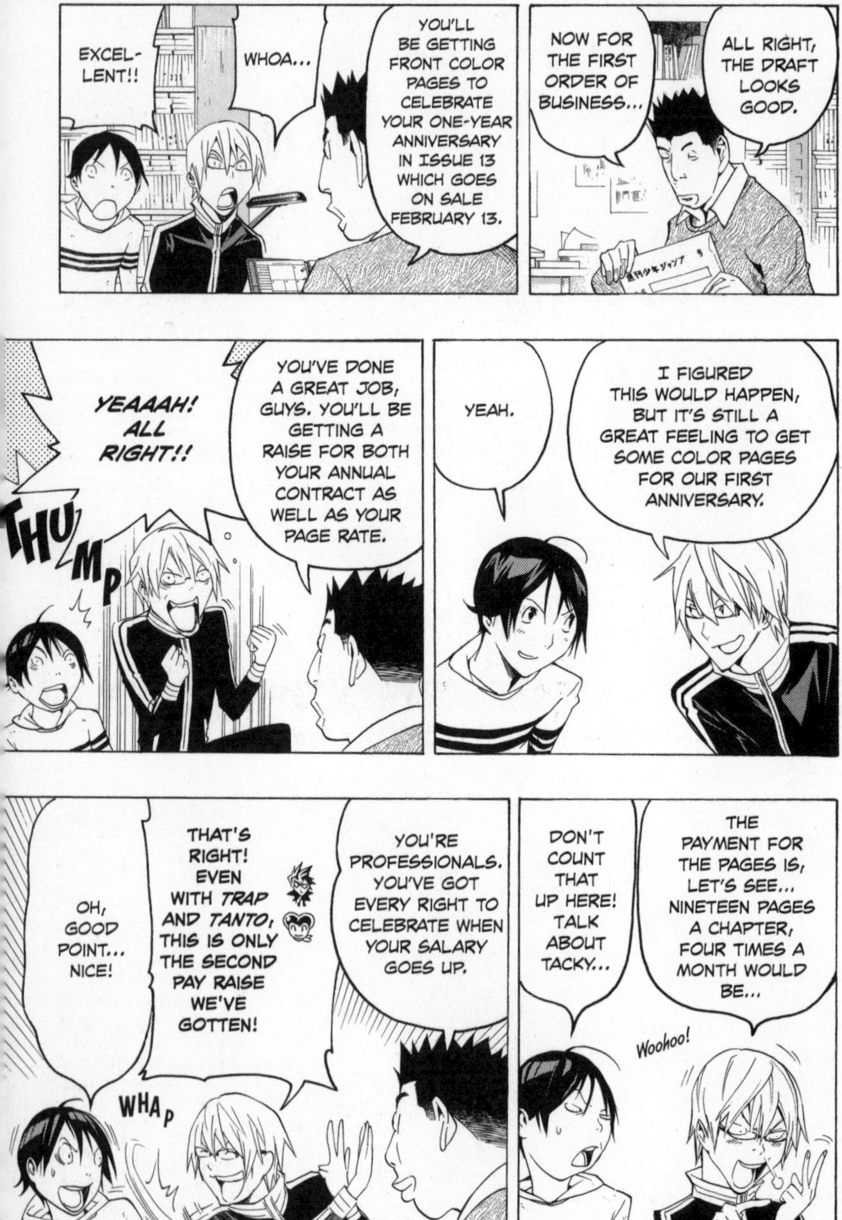
ALL RIGHT, THE DRAFT LOOKS GOOD.
NOW FOR THE FIRST ORDER OF BUSINESS...
YOU'LL BE GETTING FRONT COLOR PAGES TO CELEBRATE YOUR ONE-YEAR ANNIVERSARY IN ISSUE 13 WHICH GOES ON SALE FEBRUARY 13.
WHOA...
EXCEL-LENT!!
I FIGURED THIS WOULD HAPPEN, BUT IT'S STILL A GREAT FEELING TO GET SOME COLOR PAGES FOR OUR FIRST ANNIVERSARY.
YEAH.
YOU'VE DONE A GREAT JOB, GUYS. YOU'LL BE GETTING A RAISE FOR BOTH YOUR ANNUAL CONTRACT AS WELL AS YOUR PAGE RATE.
YEAAAH! ALL RIGHT!!
THUMP
THE PAYMENT FOR THE PAGES IS, LET'S SEE... NINETEEN PAGES A CHAPTER, FOUR TIMES A MONTH WOULD BE...
DON'T COUNT THAT UP HERE! TALK ABOUT TACKY...
Woohoo!
YOU'RE PROFESSIONALS. YOU'VE GOT EVERY RIGHT TO CELEBRATE WHEN YOUR SALARY GOES UP.
THAT'S RIGHT! EVEN WITH *TRAP* AND *TANTO*, THIS IS ONLY THE SECOND PAY RAISE WE'VE GOTTEN!
OH, GOOD POINT... NICE!
WHAP

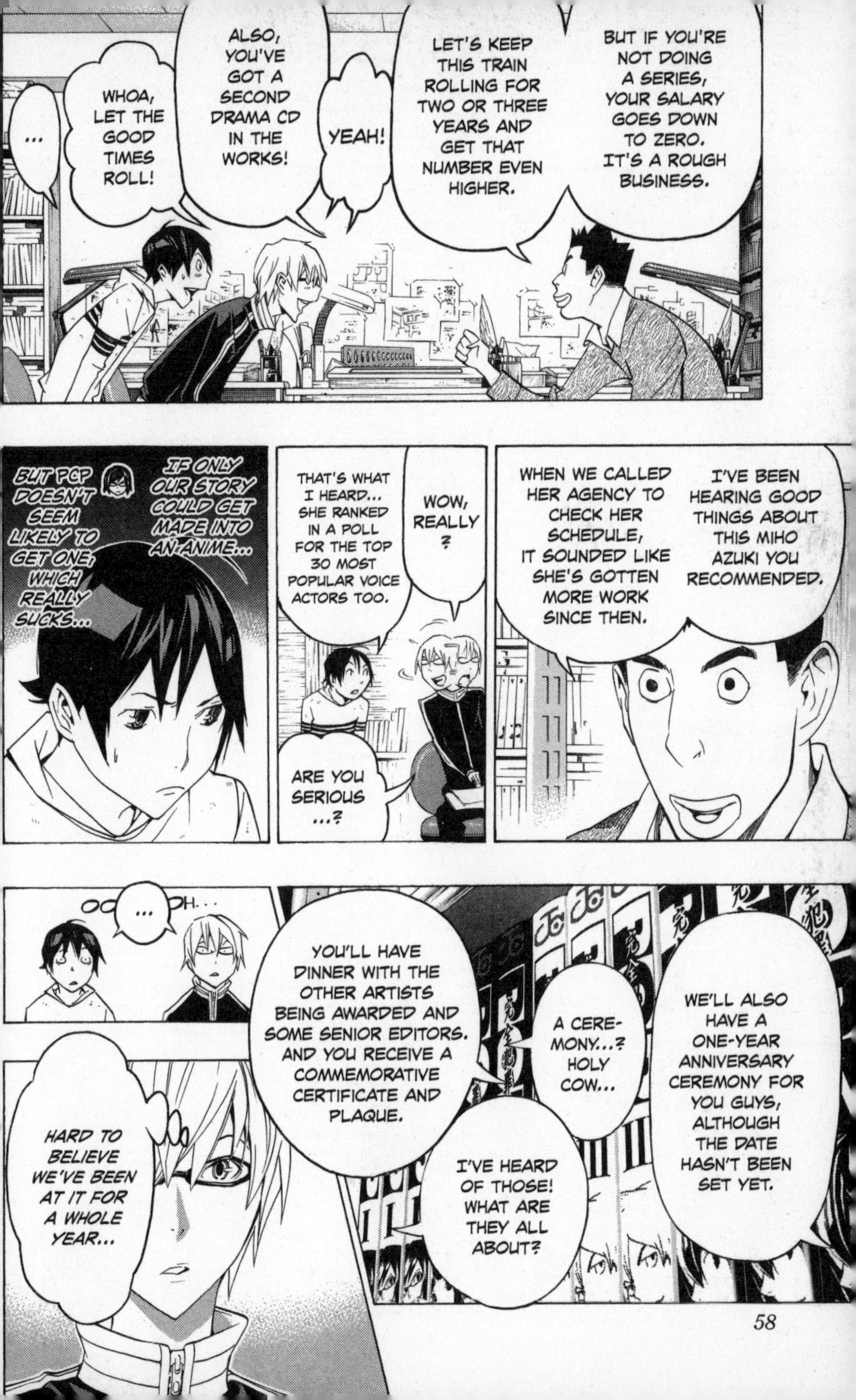
BUT IF YOU'RE NOT DOING A SERIES, YOUR SALARY GOES DOWN TO ZERO. IT'S A ROUGH BUSINESS.
LET'S KEEP THIS TRAIN ROLLING FOR TWO OR THREE YEARS AND GET THAT NUMBER EVEN HIGHER.
YEAH!
ALSO, YOU'VE GOT A SECOND DRAMA CD IN THE WORKS!
WHOA, LET THE GOOD TIMES ROLL!
...
I'VE BEEN HEARING GOOD THINGS ABOUT THIS MIHO AZUKI YOU RECOMMENDED.
WHEN WE CALLED HER AGENCY TO CHECK HER SCHEDULE, IT SOUNDED LIKE SHE'S GOTTEN MORE WORK SINCE THEN.
WOW, REALLY?
THAT'S WHAT I HEARD... SHE RANKED IN A POLL FOR THE TOP 30 MOST POPULAR VOICE ACTORS TOO.
ARE YOU SERIOUS...?
IF ONLY OUR STORY COULD GET MADE INTO AN ANIME...
BUT PCP DOESN'T SEEM LIKELY TO GET ONE, WHICH REALLY SUCKS...
WE'LL ALSO HAVE A ONE-YEAR ANNIVERSARY CEREMONY FOR YOU GUYS, ALTHOUGH THE DATE HASN'T BEEN SET YET.
A CERE-MONY...? HOLY COW...
I'VE HEARD OF THOSE! WHAT ARE THEY ALL ABOUT?
YOU'LL HAVE DINNER WITH THE OTHER ARTISTS BEING AWARDED AND SOME SENIOR EDITORS. AND YOU RECEIVE A COMMEMORATIVE CERTIFICATE AND PLAQUE.
OOOH...
...
HARD TO BELIEVE WE'VE BEEN AT IT FOR A WHOLE YEAR...

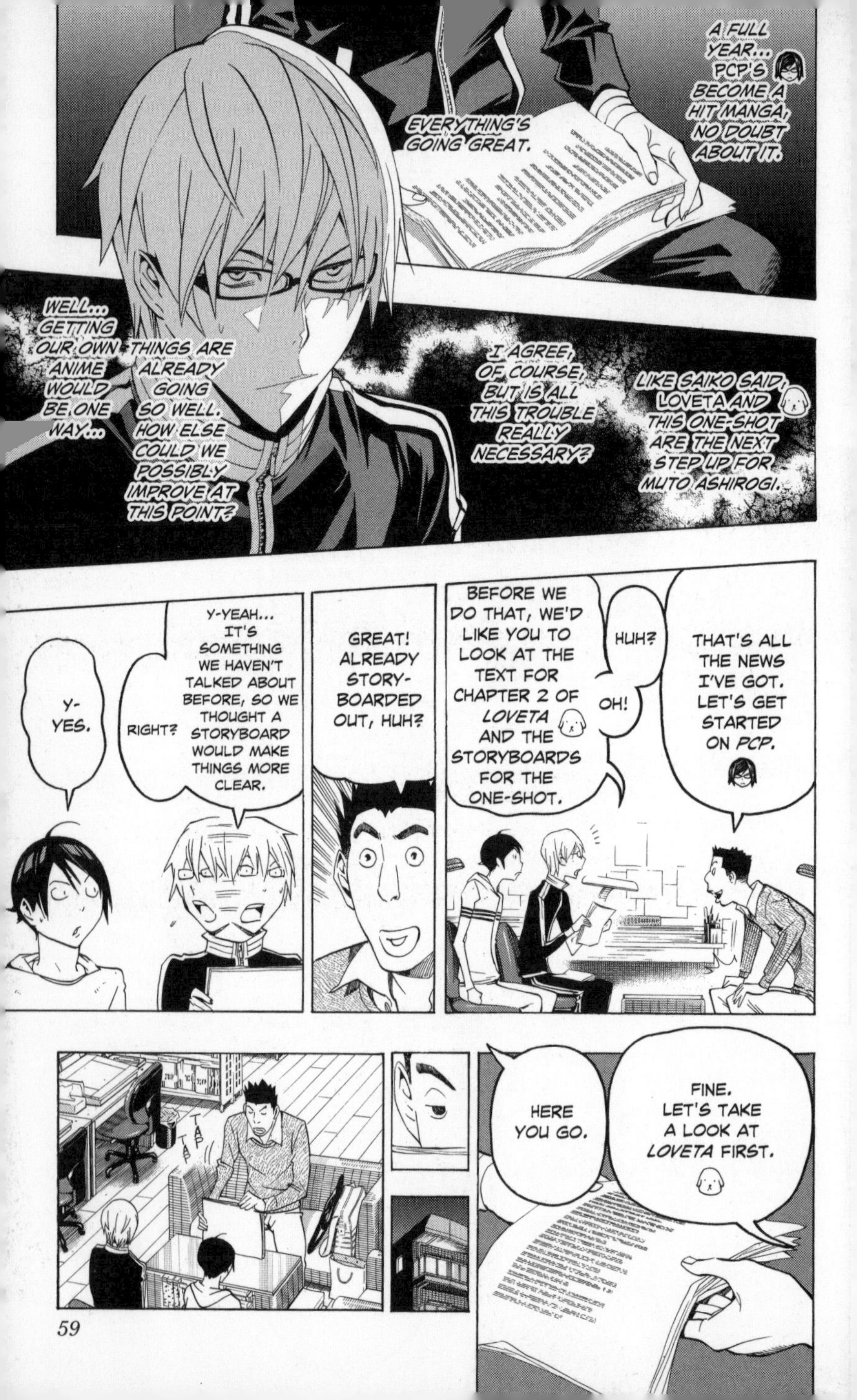
A FULL YEAR... PCP'S BECOME A HIT MANGA, NO DOUBT ABOUT IT.
EVERYTHING'S GOING GREAT.
LIKE SAIKO SAID, LOVETA AND THIS ONE-SHOT ARE THE NEXT STEP UP FOR MUTO ASHIROGI.
I AGREE, OF COURSE, BUT IS ALL THIS TROUBLE REALLY NECESSARY?
THINGS ARE ALREADY GOING SO WELL. HOW ELSE COULD WE POSSIBLY IMPROVE AT THIS POINT?
WELL... GETTING OUR OWN ANIME WOULD BE ONE WAY...
THAT'S ALL THE NEWS I'VE GOT. LET'S GET STARTED ON PCP.
HUH?
OH!
BEFORE WE DO THAT, WE'D LIKE YOU TO LOOK AT THE TEXT FOR CHAPTER 2 OF LOVETA AND THE STORYBOARDS FOR THE ONE-SHOT.
GREAT! ALREADY STORY-BOARDED OUT, HUH?
Y-YEAH... IT'S SOMETHING WE HAVEN'T TALKED ABOUT BEFORE, SO WE THOUGHT A STORYBOARD WOULD MAKE THINGS MORE CLEAR.
RIGHT?
Y- YES.
FINE. LET'S TAKE A LOOK AT LOVETA FIRST.
HERE YOU GO.
TAP TAP

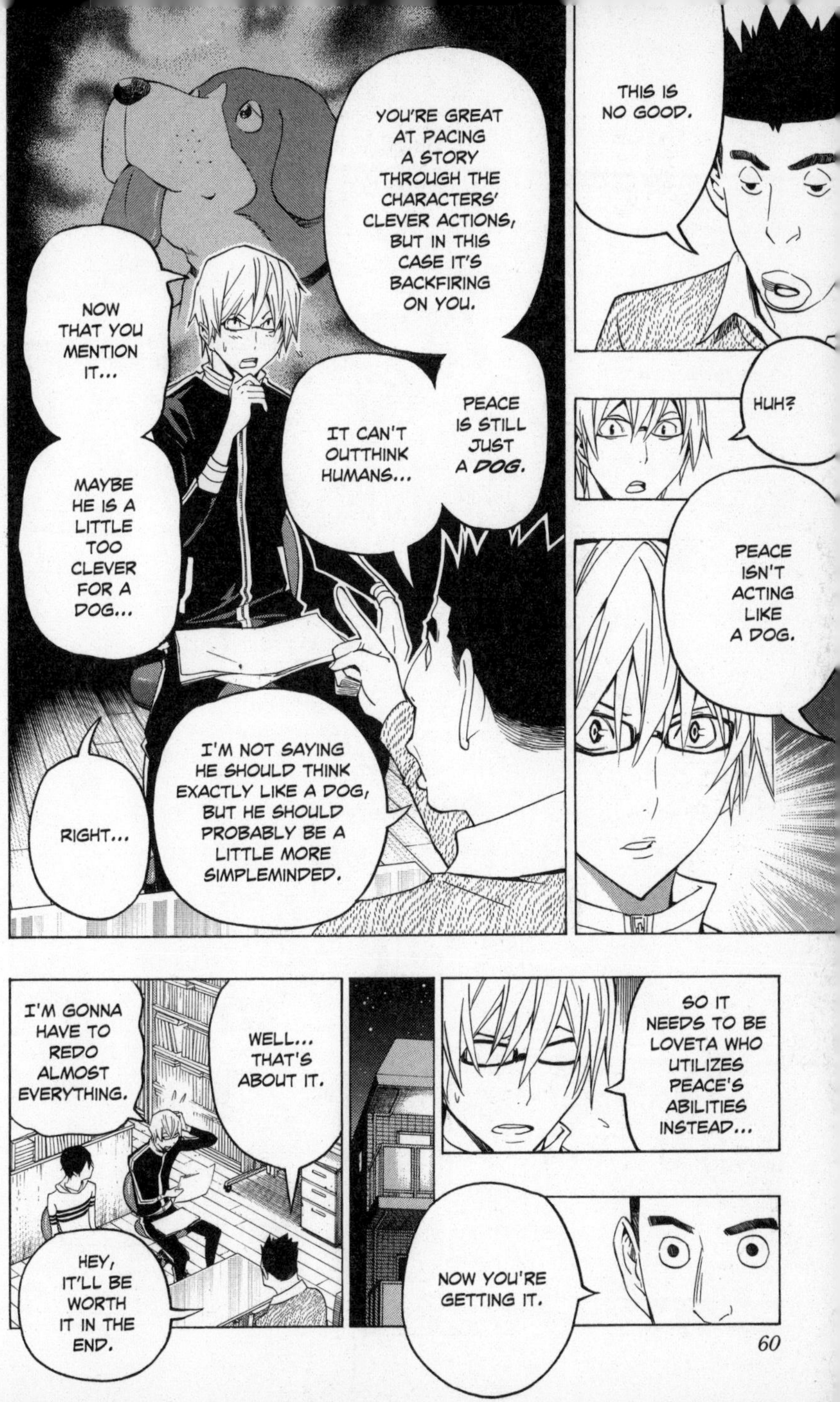
THIS IS NO GOOD.
HUH?
PEACE ISN'T ACTING LIKE A DOG.
YOU'RE GREAT AT PACING A STORY THROUGH THE CHARACTERS' CLEVER ACTIONS, BUT IN THIS CASE IT'S BACKFIRING ON YOU.
NOW THAT YOU MENTION IT...
PEACE IS STILL JUST A *DOG*.
IT CAN'T OUTTHINK HUMANS...
MAYBE HE IS A LITTLE TOO CLEVER FOR A DOG...
I'M NOT SAYING HE SHOULD THINK EXACTLY LIKE A DOG, BUT HE SHOULD PROBABLY BE A LITTLE MORE SIMPLEMINDED.
RIGHT...
SO IT NEEDS TO BE LOVETA WHO UTILIZES PEACE'S ABILITIES INSTEAD...
NOW YOU'RE GETTING IT.
WELL... THAT'S ABOUT IT.
I'M GONNA HAVE TO REDO ALMOST EVERYTHING.
HEY, IT'LL BE WORTH IT IN THE END.

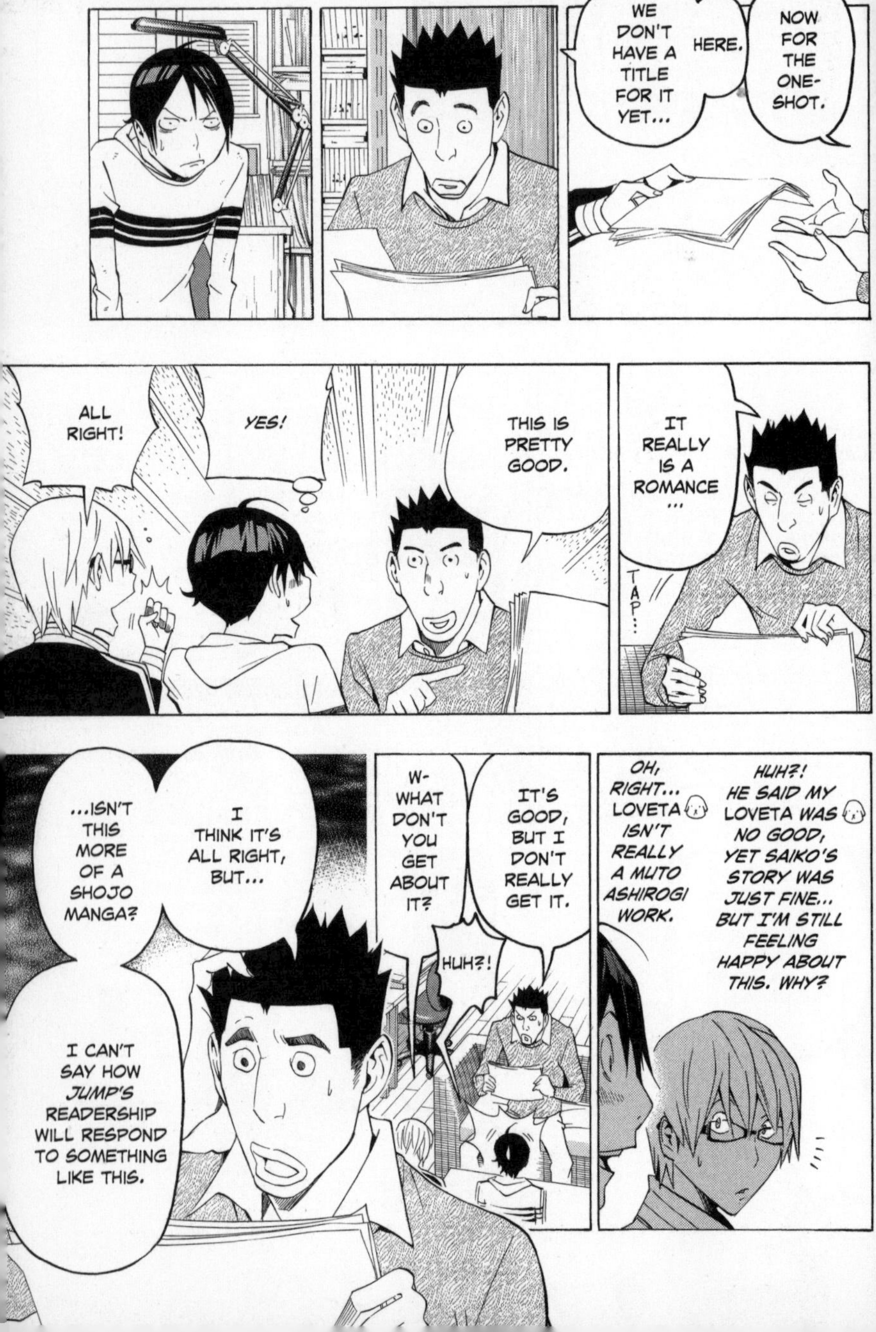
NOW FOR THE ONE-SHOT.
WE DON'T HAVE A TITLE FOR IT YET...
HERE.
IT REALLY IS A ROMANCE ...
TAP...
THIS IS PRETTY GOOD.
YES!
ALL RIGHT!
HUH?! HE SAID MY LOVETA WAS NO GOOD, YET SAIKO'S STORY WAS JUST FINE... BUT I'M STILL FEELING HAPPY ABOUT THIS. WHY?
OH, RIGHT... LOVETA ISN'T REALLY A MUTO ASHIROGI WORK.
IT'S GOOD, BUT I DON'T REALLY GET IT.
W-WHAT DON'T YOU GET ABOUT IT?
HUH?!
I THINK IT'S ALL RIGHT, BUT...
...ISN'T THIS MORE OF A SHOJO MANGA?
I CAN'T SAY HOW *JUMP'S* READERSHIP WILL RESPOND TO SOMETHING LIKE THIS.

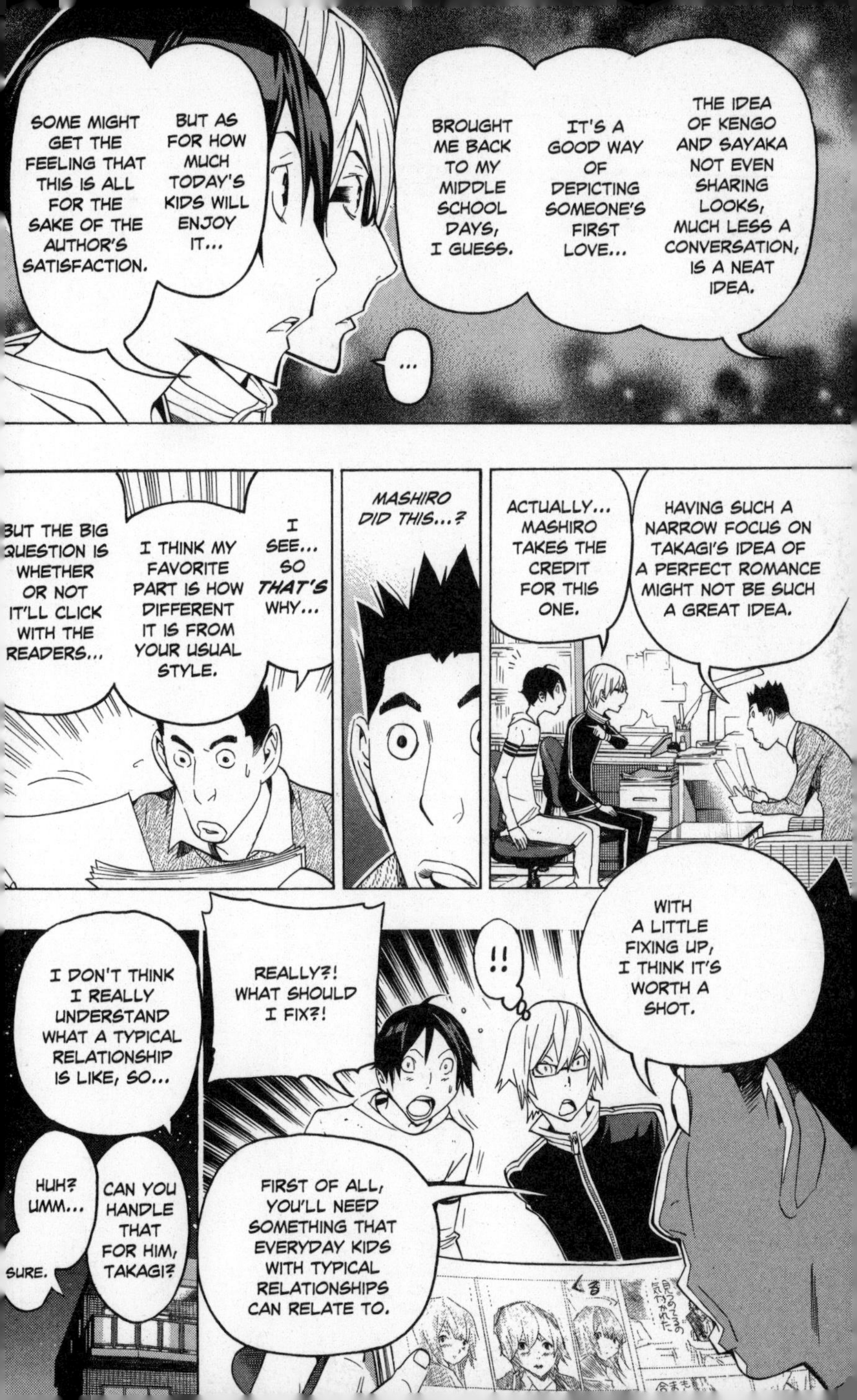
THE IDEA OF KENGO AND SAYAKA NOT EVEN SHARING LOOKS, MUCH LESS A CONVERSATION, IS A NEAT IDEA.
IT'S A GOOD WAY OF DEPICTING SOMEONE'S FIRST LOVE...
BROUGHT ME BACK TO MY MIDDLE SCHOOL DAYS, I GUESS.
...
BUT AS FOR HOW MUCH TODAY'S KIDS WILL ENJOY IT...
SOME MIGHT GET THE FEELING THAT THIS IS ALL FOR THE SAKE OF THE AUTHOR'S SATISFACTION.
HAVING SUCH A NARROW FOCUS ON TAKAGI'S IDEA OF A PERFECT ROMANCE MIGHT NOT BE SUCH A GREAT IDEA.
ACTUALLY... MASHIRO TAKES THE CREDIT FOR THIS ONE.
MASHIRO DID THIS...?
I SEE... SO *THAT'S* WHY...
I THINK MY FAVORITE PART IS HOW DIFFERENT IT IS FROM YOUR USUAL STYLE.
BUT THE BIG QUESTION IS WHETHER OR NOT IT'LL CLICK WITH THE READERS...
WITH A LITTLE FIXING UP, I THINK IT'S WORTH A SHOT.
!!
REALLY?! WHAT SHOULD I FIX?!
I DON'T THINK I REALLY UNDERSTAND WHAT A TYPICAL RELATIONSHIP IS LIKE, SO...
FIRST OF ALL, YOU'LL NEED SOMETHING THAT EVERYDAY KIDS WITH TYPICAL RELATIONSHIPS CAN RELATE TO.
CAN YOU HANDLE THAT FOR HIM, TAKAGI?
HUH? UMM...
SURE.

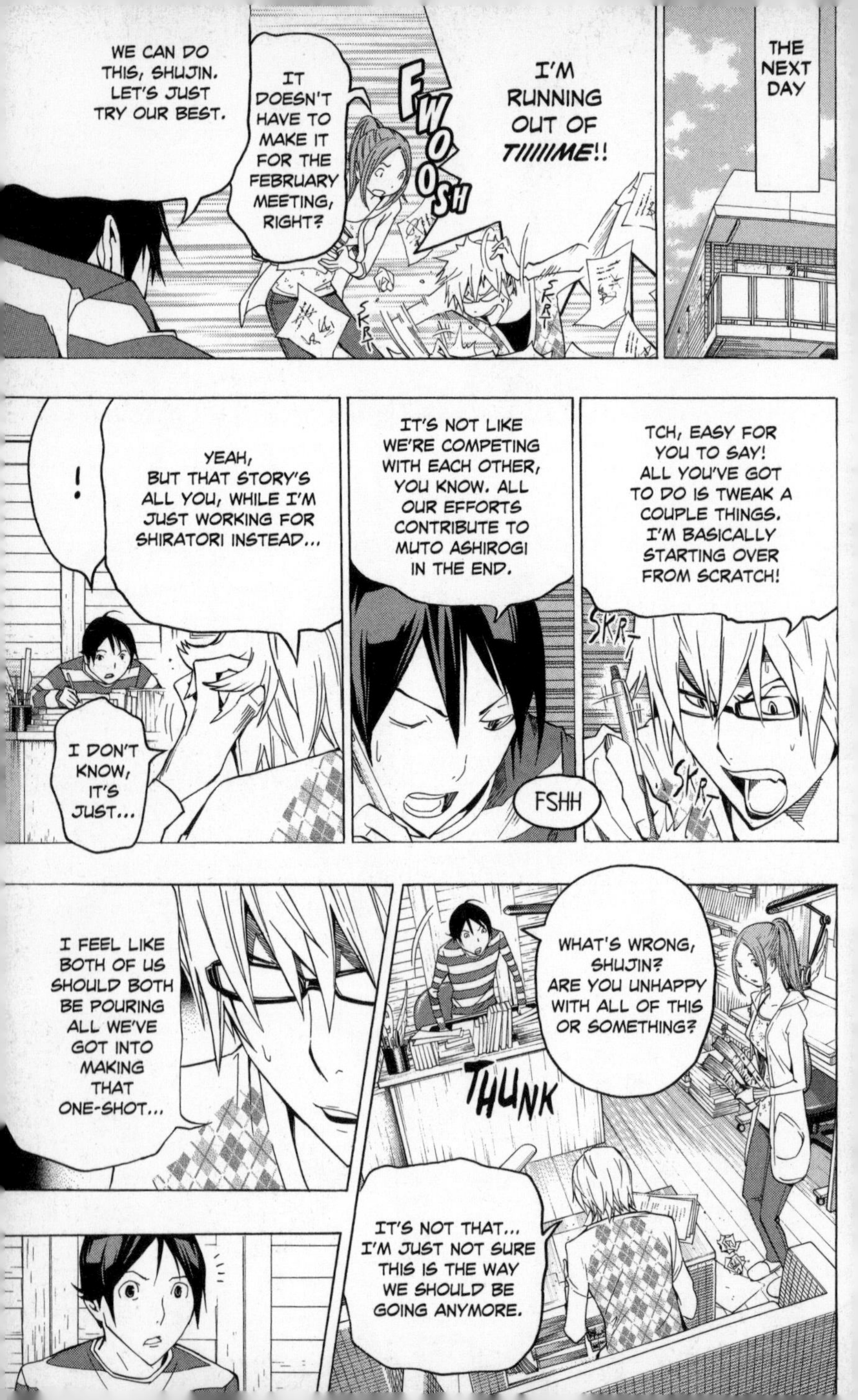
THE NEXT DAY
I'M RUNNING OUT OF TIIIIIME!!
FWOOSH
SKRT
SKRT
IT DOESN'T HAVE TO MAKE IT FOR THE FEBRUARY MEETING, RIGHT?
WE CAN DO THIS, SHUJIN. LET'S JUST TRY OUR BEST.
TCH, EASY FOR YOU TO SAY! ALL YOU'VE GOT TO DO IS TWEAK A COUPLE THINGS. I'M BASICALLY STARTING OVER FROM SCRATCH!
SKRT
SKRT
FSHH
IT'S NOT LIKE WE'RE COMPETING WITH EACH OTHER, YOU KNOW. ALL OUR EFFORTS CONTRIBUTE TO MUTO ASHIROGI IN THE END.
YEAH, BUT THAT STORY'S ALL YOU, WHILE I'M JUST WORKING FOR SHIRATORI INSTEAD...
!
I DON'T KNOW, IT'S JUST...
WHAT'S WRONG, SHUJIN? ARE YOU UNHAPPY WITH ALL OF THIS OR SOMETHING?
THUNK
IT'S NOT THAT... I'M JUST NOT SURE THIS IS THE WAY WE SHOULD BE GOING ANYMORE.
I FEEL LIKE BOTH OF US SHOULD BOTH BE POURING ALL WE'VE GOT INTO MAKING THAT ONE-SHOT...

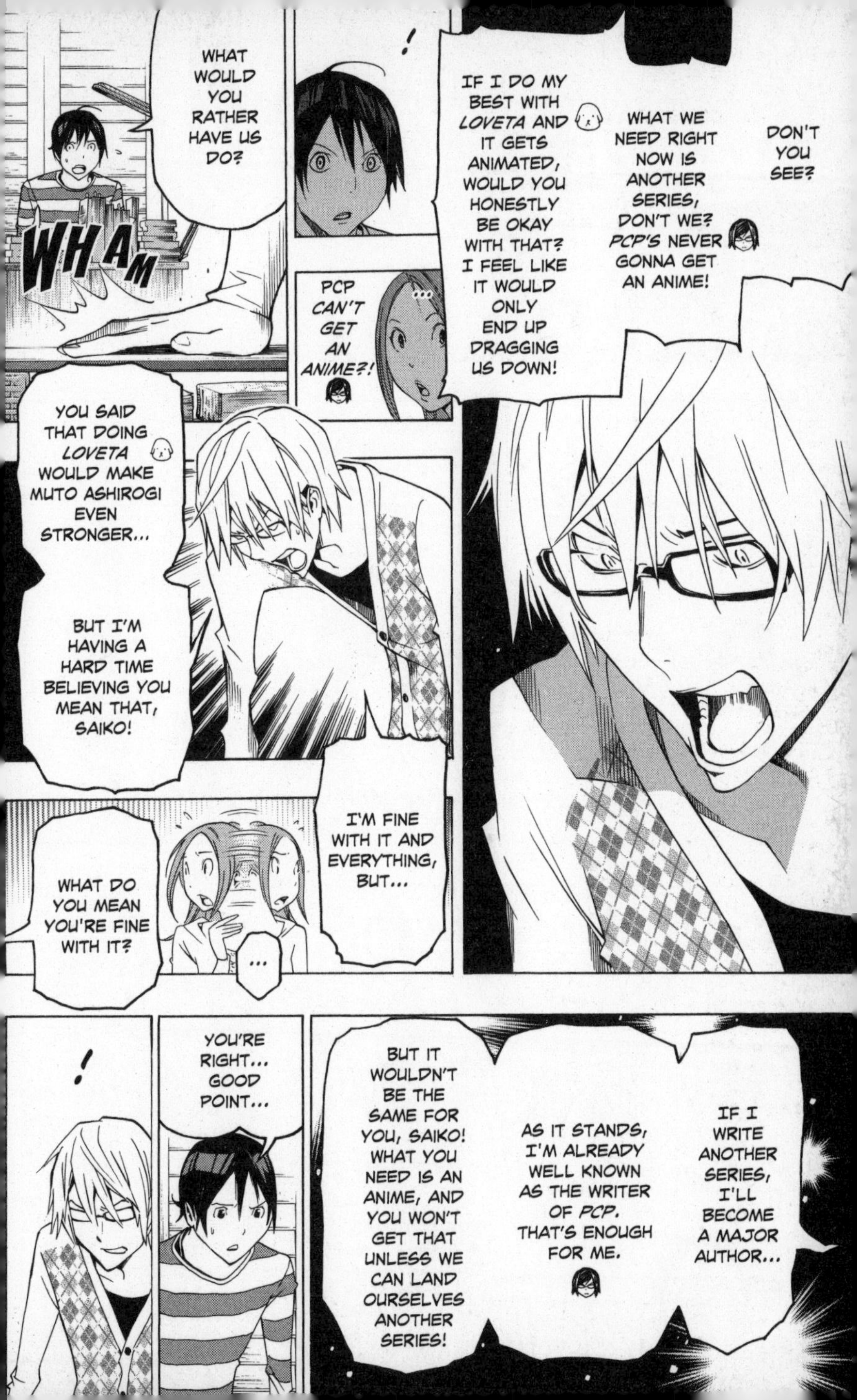
IF I DO MY BEST WITH LOVETA AND IT GETS ANIMATED, WOULD YOU HONESTLY BE OKAY WITH THAT? I FEEL LIKE IT WOULD ONLY END UP DRAGGING US DOWN!
WHAT WE NEED RIGHT NOW IS ANOTHER SERIES, DON'T WE? PCP'S NEVER GONNA GET AN ANIME!
DON'T YOU SEE?
!
PCP CAN'T GET AN ANIME?!
...
WHAT WOULD YOU RATHER HAVE US DO?
WHAM
YOU SAID THAT DOING LOVETA WOULD MAKE MUTO ASHIROGI EVEN STRONGER...
BUT I'M HAVING A HARD TIME BELIEVING YOU MEAN THAT, SAIKO!
I'M FINE WITH IT AND EVERYTHING, BUT...
WHAT DO YOU MEAN YOU'RE FINE WITH IT?
...
IF I WRITE ANOTHER SERIES, I'LL BECOME A MAJOR AUTHOR...
AS IT STANDS, I'M ALREADY WELL KNOWN AS THE WRITER OF PCP. THAT'S ENOUGH FOR ME.
BUT IT WOULDN'T BE THE SAME FOR YOU, SAIKO! WHAT YOU NEED IS AN ANIME, AND YOU WON'T GET THAT UNLESS WE CAN LAND OURSELVES ANOTHER SERIES!
YOU'RE RIGHT... GOOD POINT...
!

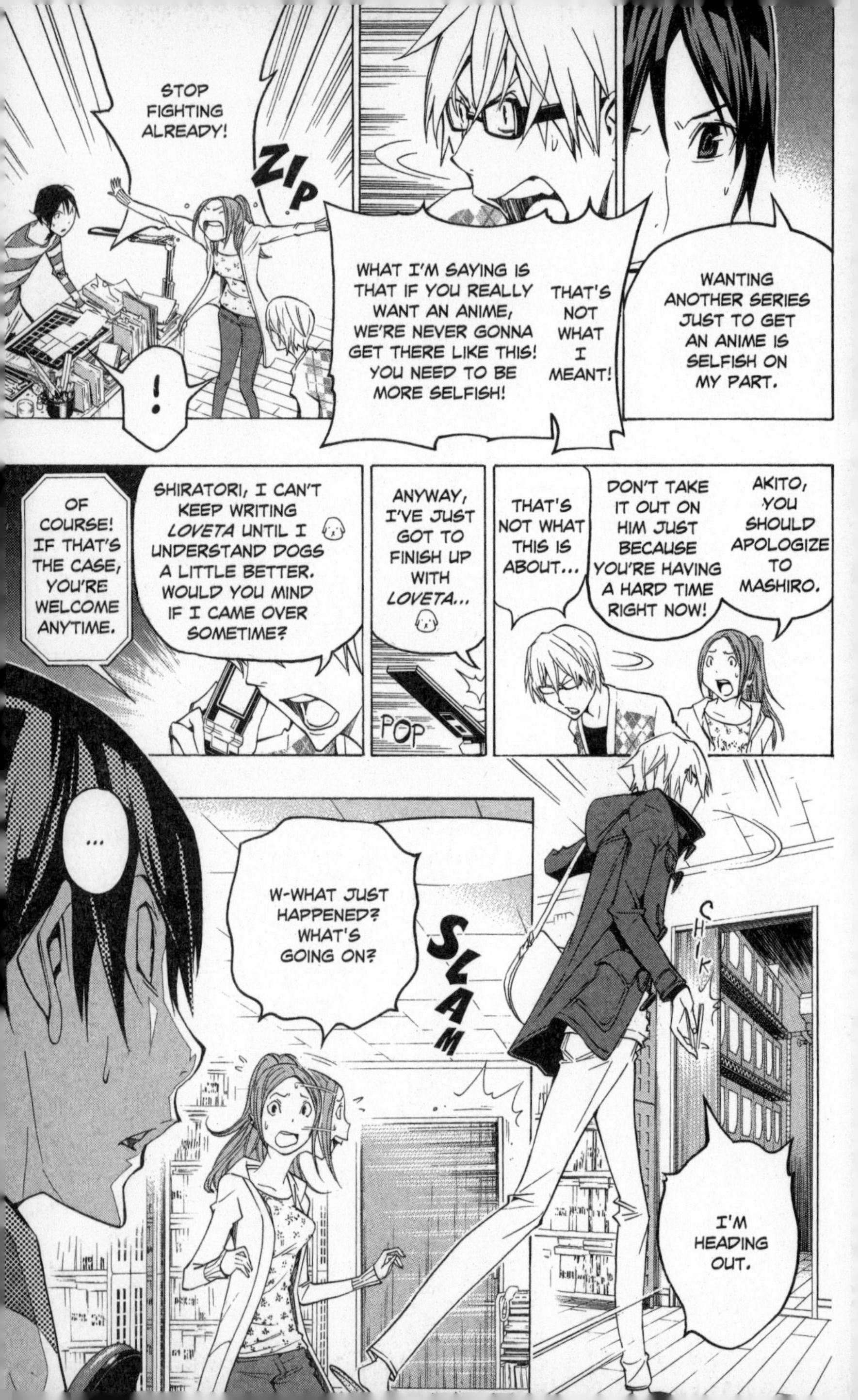
WANTING ANOTHER SERIES JUST TO GET AN ANIME IS SELFISH ON MY PART.
THAT'S NOT WHAT I MEANT!
WHAT I'M SAYING IS THAT IF YOU REALLY WANT AN ANIME, WE'RE NEVER GONNA GET THERE LIKE THIS! YOU NEED TO BE MORE SELFISH!
STOP FIGHTING ALREADY!
ZIP
!
AKITO, YOU SHOULD APOLOGIZE TO MASHIRO.
DON'T TAKE IT OUT ON HIM JUST BECAUSE YOU'RE HAVING A HARD TIME RIGHT NOW!
THAT'S NOT WHAT THIS IS ABOUT...
ANYWAY, I'VE JUST GOT TO FINISH UP WITH *LOVETA*...
POP
SHIRATORI, I CAN'T KEEP WRITING *LOVETA* UNTIL I UNDERSTAND DOGS A LITTLE BETTER. WOULD YOU MIND IF I CAME OVER SOMETIME?
OF COURSE! IF THAT'S THE CASE, YOU'RE WELCOME ANYTIME.
I'M HEADING OUT.
SLAM
W-WHAT JUST HAPPENED? WHAT'S GOING ON?
...

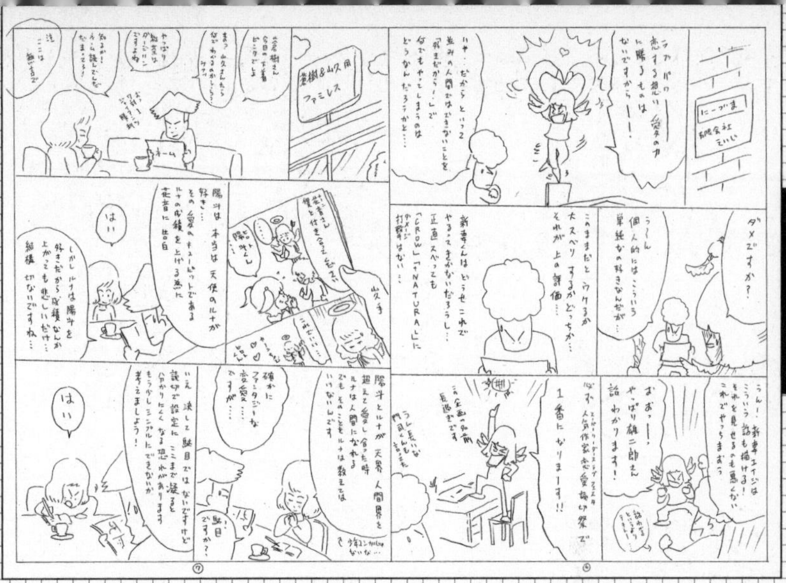
ラブパワ 恋する想い 愛の力に勝るものはないですから〜!
いや…だからといって並みの人間ができないことを「好きだから!」で何でもやってしまうのはどうなんだろうかと…
ダメですか?
う〜ん 個人的にはこういう単純なの好きなんだが…
このままだとウケるか大スベリするかどっちか… それが上の評価…
「CROW」「+NATURAL」に打撃はない…
うん! 新妻エイジはこういう話も描ける これを見せるのも悪くない これでやっちまおう
おおっ! やっぱり雄二郎さん話わかります!
1番になりまーす!!
ファミレス
はい
しかしルナは陽斗を好きだから成績なんか上がっても悲しいだけ… 結構切ないですね…
陽斗とルナが天界人間界を超えて愛し合った時 ルナは人間になれる でもそのことをルナは教えてはいけないんです
確かにファンタジーな恋愛…ですが…
駄目ですか?
いえ 決して駄目ではないですけど 読切で設定にここまで凝ると分かりにくくなる恐れがあります もう少しシンプルにできないか考えましょう!
はい

OHBA'S STORYBOARD

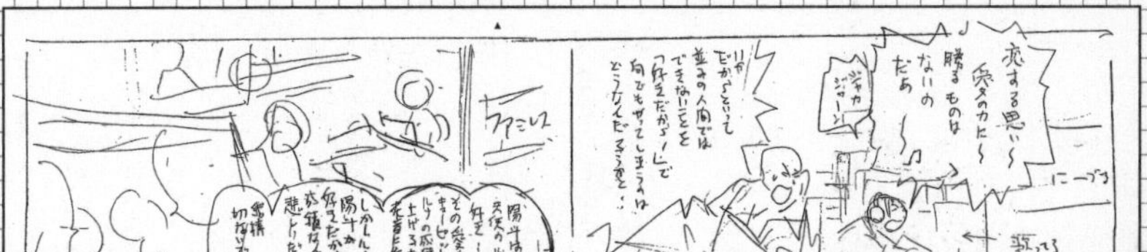

OBATA'S STORYBOARD

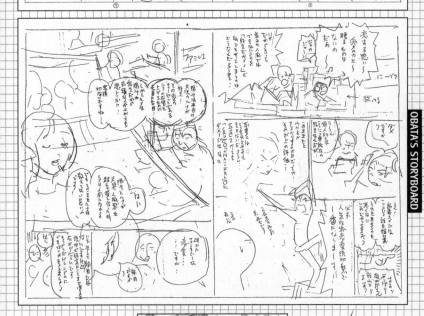

COMPLETE!

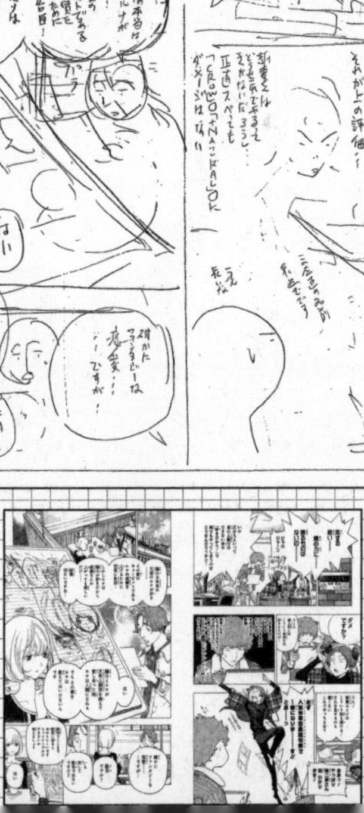

*CREATOR STORYBOARDS AND FINISHED PAGES IN JAPANESE

BAKUMAN。 vol.13

"Until the Final Draft Is Complete"

Chapter 109, pp. 52-53

The Bakuman。 Character Popularity Poll Results!!

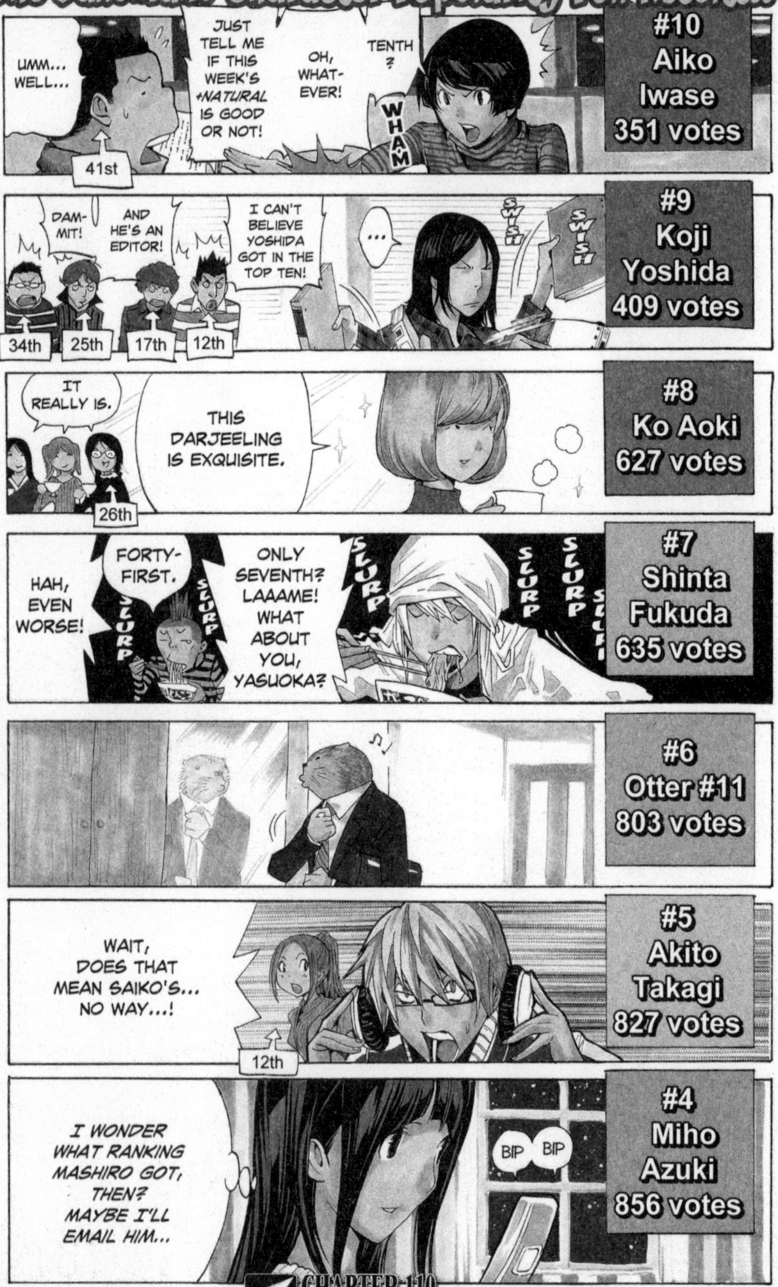

#10 Aiko Iwase 351 votes
TENTH?
WHAM
OH, WHATEVER!
JUST TELL ME IF THIS WEEK'S +NATURAL IS GOOD OR NOT!
UMM... WELL...
41st
#9 Koji Yoshida 409 votes
SWISH
SWISH
...
I CAN'T BELIEVE YOSHIDA GOT IN THE TOP TEN!
AND HE'S AN EDITOR!
DAMMIT!
12th
17th
25th
34th
#8 Ko Aoki 627 votes
THIS DARJEELING IS EXQUISITE.
IT REALLY IS.
26th
#7 Shinta Fukuda 635 votes
SLURP
SLURP
SLURP
ONLY SEVENTH? LAAAME! WHAT ABOUT YOU, YASUOKA?
SLURP
SLURP
FORTY-FIRST.
HAH, EVEN WORSE!
#6 Otter #11 803 votes
#5 Akito Takagi 827 votes
WAIT, DOES THAT MEAN SAIKO'S... NO WAY...!
12th
#4 Miho Azuki 856 votes
BIP
BIP
I WONDER WHAT RANKING MASHIRO GOT, THEN? MAYBE I'LL EMAIL HIM...

CHAPTER 110
TOGETHER AND SEPARATE

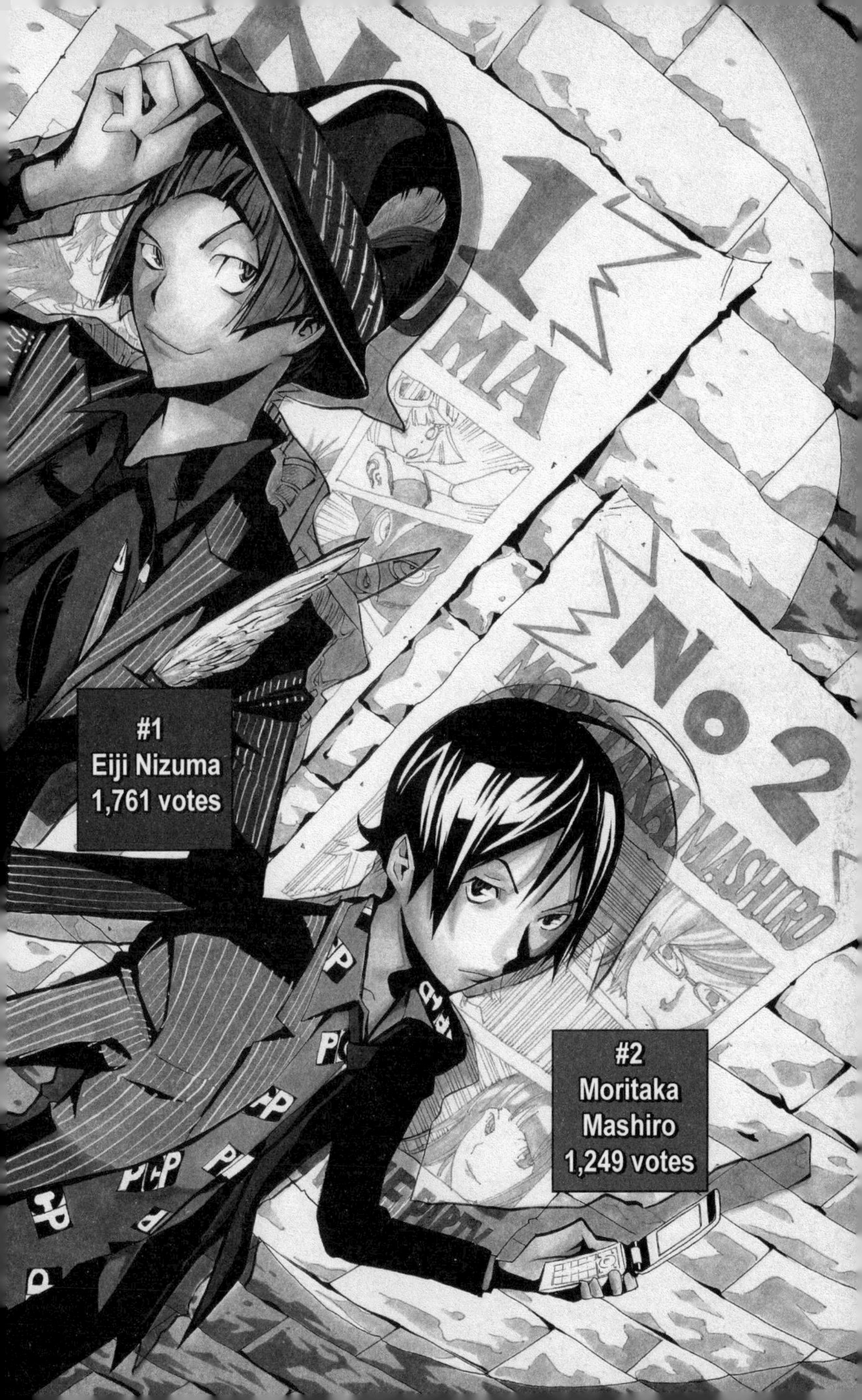
No 2
M.MASHIRO
#1
Eiji Nizuma
1,761 votes
#2
Moritaka
Mashiro
1,249 votes

CHAPTER 110
TOGETHER AND SEPARATE

*11TH PLACE AND BELOW ARE ON THE NEXT PAGE!

THE BAKUMAN。CHARACTER POPULARITY POLL RESULTS!!

HERE'S THE LIST FOR 11TH PLACE AND BELOW, WHICH WASN'T REVEALED WHEN THESE RESULTS WERE FIRST PUBLISHED IN *WEEKLY SHONEN JUMP*!!

11TH:	CROW	287 VOTES	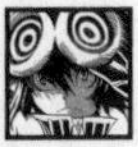
12TH:	KAYA MIYOSHI	246 VOTES	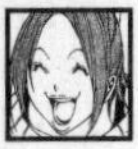
	AKIRA HATTORI	246 VOTES	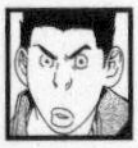
14TH:	TAKURO NAKAI	183 VOTES	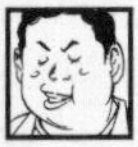
15TH:	MAKOTO DOMOTO	154 VOTES	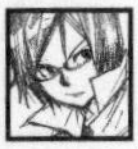
16TH:	EDITOR IN CHIEF SASAKI	132 VOTES	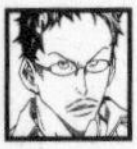
17TH:	YUJIRO HATTORI	104 VOTES	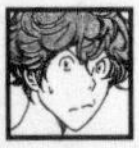
18TH:	SHUN SHIRATORI	94 VOTES	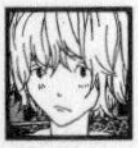
	RYU SHIZUKA	94 VOTES	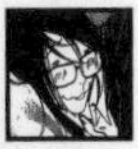
20TH:	TARO KAWAGUCHI	85 VOTES	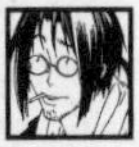
21ST:	DETECTIVE TRAP	82 VOTES	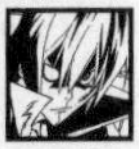
22ND:	MIYUKI AZUKI	79 VOTES	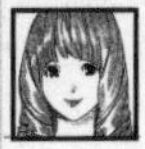
23TH:	ICHIRIKI ORIHARA	68 VOTES	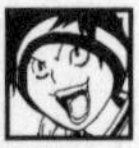
24TH:	DEPUTY EDITOR IN CHIEF HEISHI	62 VOTES	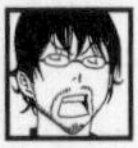
25TH:	MASAKAZU YAMAHISA	60 VOTES	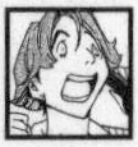
26TH:	NATSUMI KATO	38 VOTES	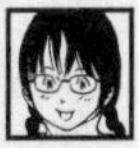
27TH:	MINA AZUKI	30 VOTES	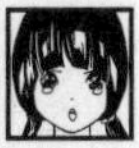
28TH:	ONODERA	23 VOTES	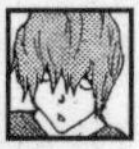
29TH:	SHOYO TAKAHAMA	19 VOTES	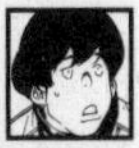
30TH:	KOOGY	14 VOTES	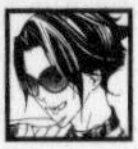
	EXECUTIVE DIRECTOR TORISHIMA	14 VOTES	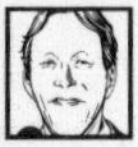
	JUMP SQ EDITOR IN CHIEF IBARAKI	14 VOTES	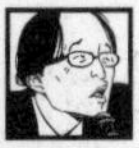
	PRINCE EIGHT PRESIDENT	14 VOTES	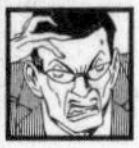

*THIS SURVEY WAS ORIGINALLY ANNOUNCED IN THE #39 ISSUE OF 2010 AND THE RESULTS WERE PUBLISHED IN THE #51 ISSUE OF THAT YEAR.

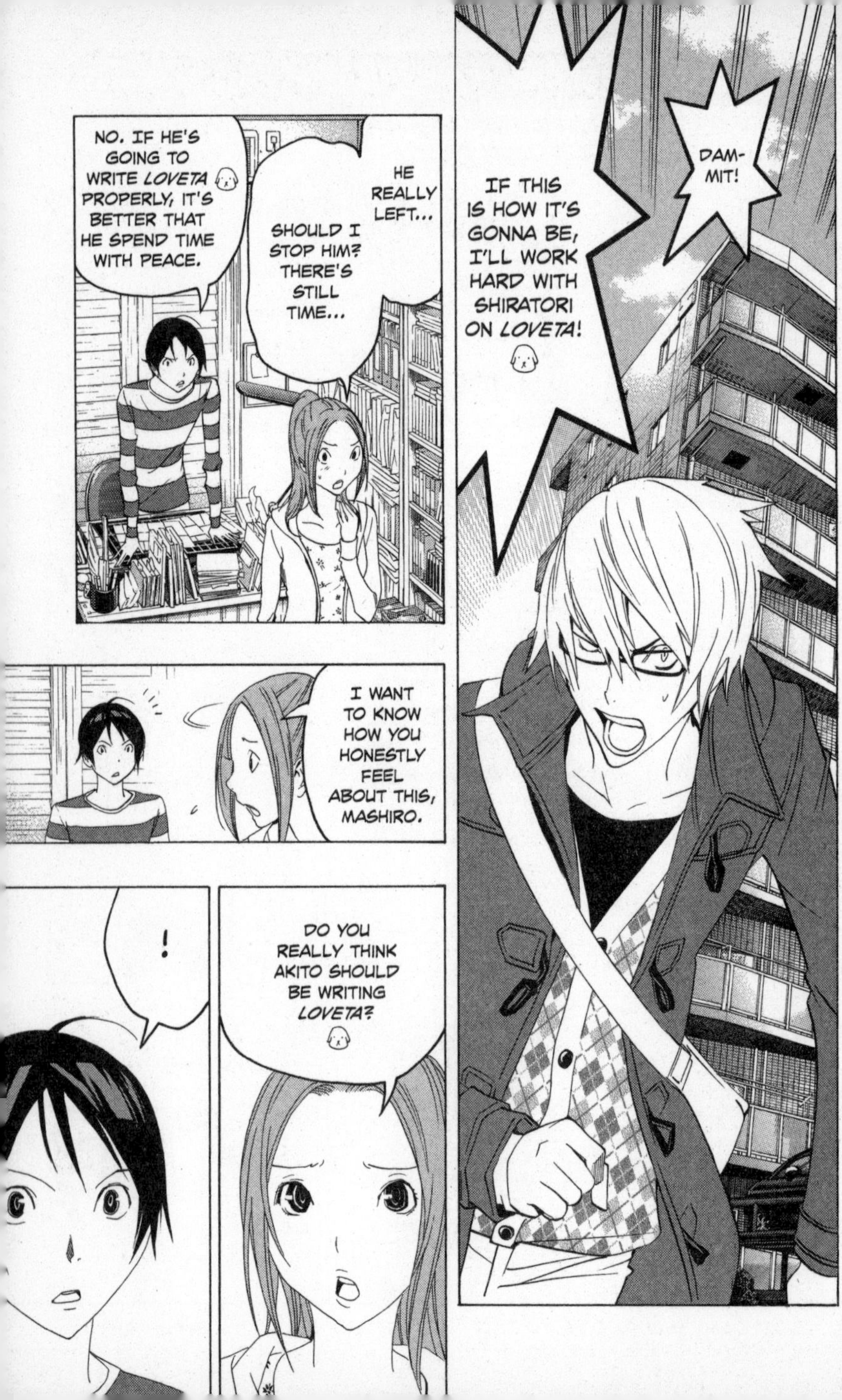
DAM-MIT!
IF THIS IS HOW IT'S GONNA BE, I'LL WORK HARD WITH SHIRATORI ON *LOVETA*!
HE REALLY LEFT...
SHOULD I STOP HIM? THERE'S STILL TIME...
NO. IF HE'S GOING TO WRITE *LOVETA* PROPERLY, IT'S BETTER THAT HE SPEND TIME WITH PEACE.
I WANT TO KNOW HOW YOU HONESTLY FEEL ABOUT THIS, MASHIRO.
DO YOU REALLY THINK AKITO SHOULD BE WRITING *LOVETA*?
!

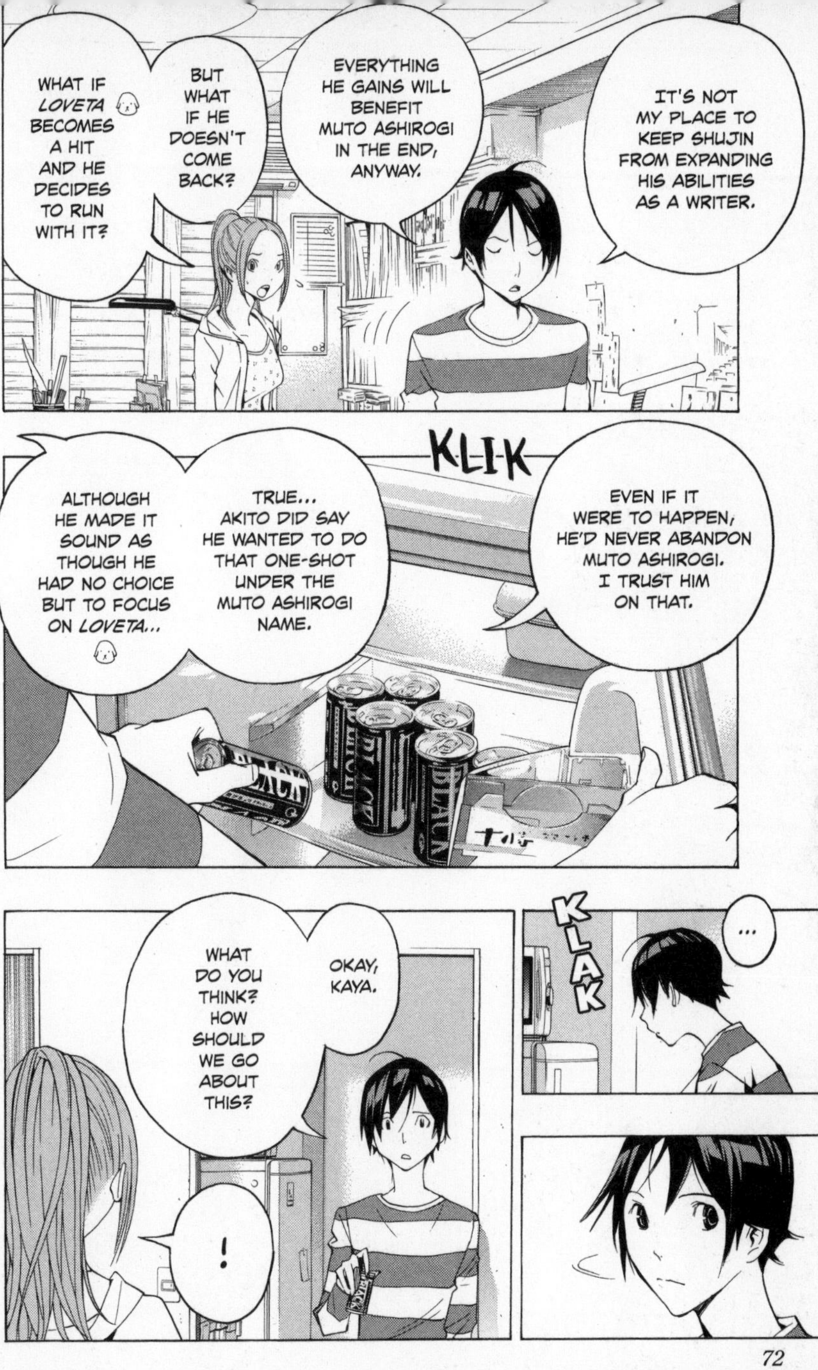
IT'S NOT MY PLACE TO KEEP SHUJIN FROM EXPANDING HIS ABILITIES AS A WRITER.
EVERYTHING HE GAINS WILL BENEFIT MUTO ASHIROGI IN THE END, ANYWAY.
BUT WHAT IF HE DOESN'T COME BACK?
WHAT IF *LOVETA* BECOMES A HIT AND HE DECIDES TO RUN WITH IT?
EVEN IF IT WERE TO HAPPEN, HE'D NEVER ABANDON MUTO ASHIROGI. I TRUST HIM ON THAT.
KLIK
TRUE... AKITO DID SAY HE WANTED TO DO THAT ONE-SHOT UNDER THE MUTO ASHIROGI NAME.
ALTHOUGH HE MADE IT SOUND AS THOUGH HE HAD NO CHOICE BUT TO FOCUS ON *LOVETA*...
...
KLAK
OKAY, KAYA.
WHAT DO YOU THINK? HOW SHOULD WE GO ABOUT THIS?
!

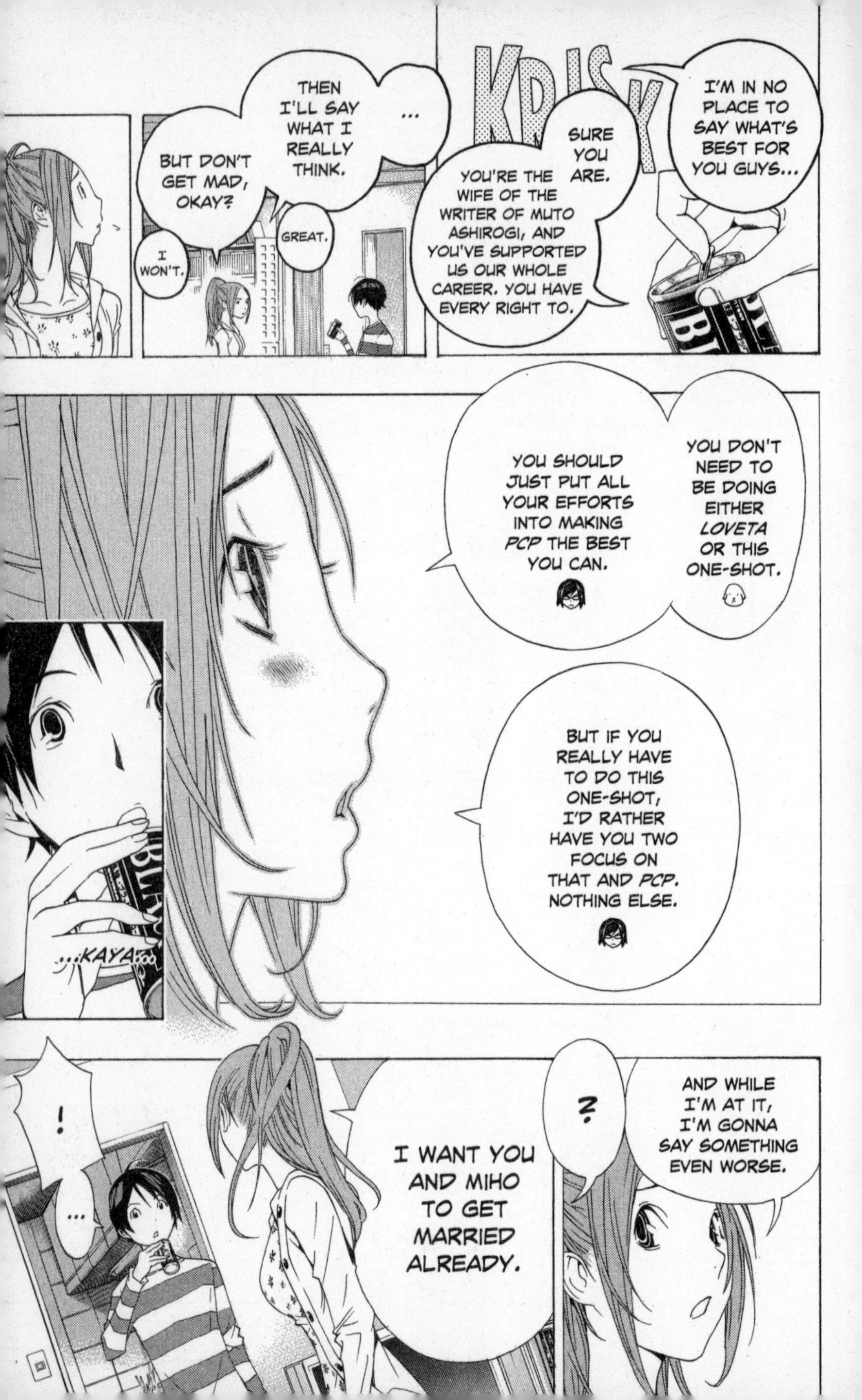

I'M IN NO PLACE TO SAY WHAT'S BEST FOR YOU GUYS...
SURE YOU ARE.
YOU'RE THE WIFE OF THE WRITER OF MUTO ASHIROGI, AND YOU'VE SUPPORTED US OUR WHOLE CAREER. YOU HAVE EVERY RIGHT TO.
...
THEN I'LL SAY WHAT I REALLY THINK.
BUT DON'T GET MAD, OKAY?
GREAT.
I WON'T.
YOU DON'T NEED TO BE DOING EITHER *LOVETA* OR THIS ONE-SHOT.
YOU SHOULD JUST PUT ALL YOUR EFFORTS INTO MAKING *PCP* THE BEST YOU CAN.
BUT IF YOU REALLY HAVE TO DO THIS ONE-SHOT, I'D RATHER HAVE YOU TWO FOCUS ON THAT AND *PCP*. NOTHING ELSE.
...KAYA...
AND WHILE I'M AT IT, I'M GONNA SAY SOMETHING EVEN WORSE.
?
I WANT YOU AND MIHO TO GET MARRIED ALREADY.
!
...

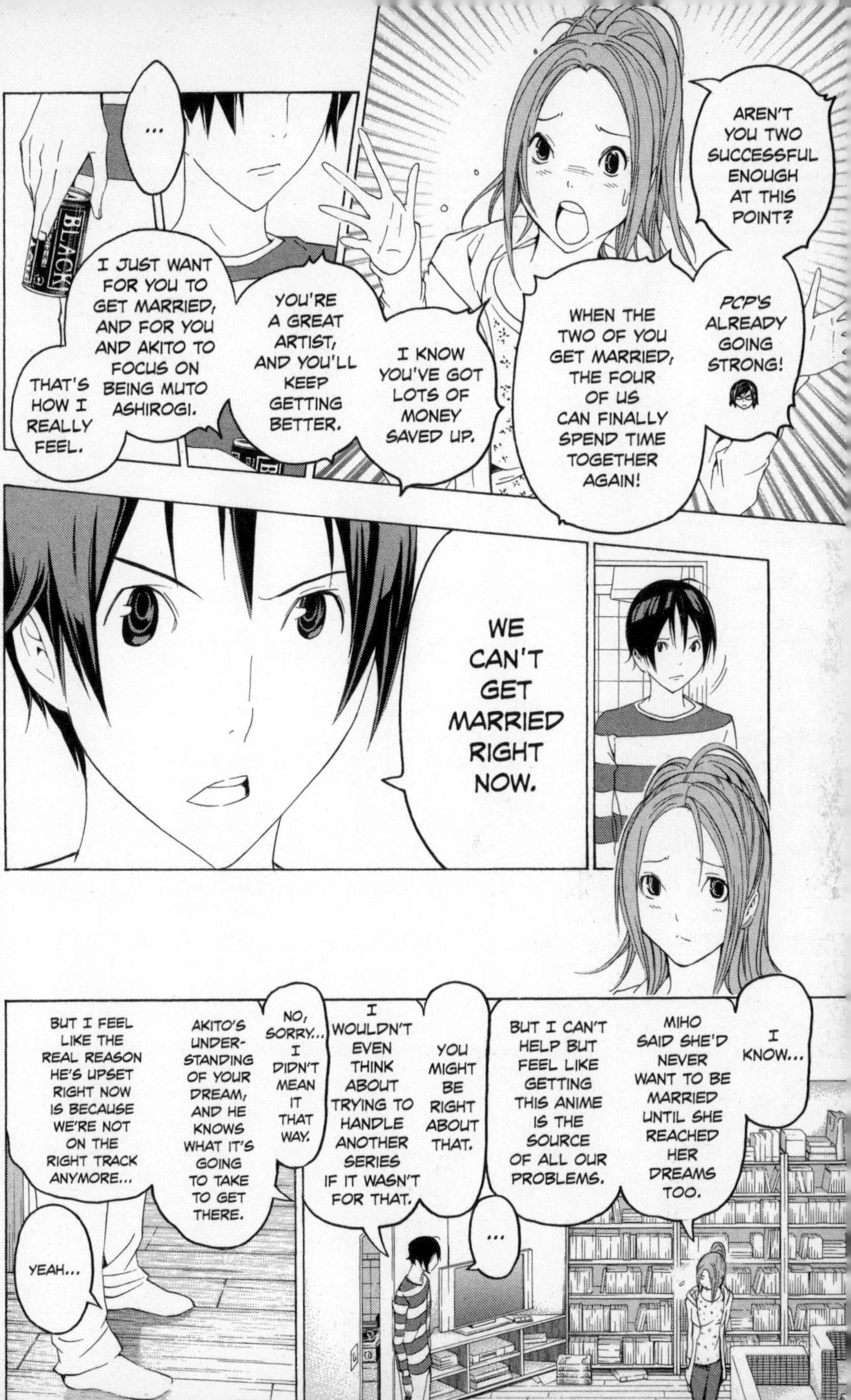

AREN'T YOU TWO SUCCESSFUL ENOUGH AT THIS POINT?
PCP'S ALREADY GOING STRONG!
WHEN THE TWO OF YOU GET MARRIED, THE FOUR OF US CAN FINALLY SPEND TIME TOGETHER AGAIN!
I KNOW YOU'VE GOT LOTS OF MONEY SAVED UP.
YOU'RE A GREAT ARTIST, AND YOU'LL KEEP GETTING BETTER.
...
I JUST WANT FOR YOU TO GET MARRIED, AND FOR YOU AND AKITO TO FOCUS ON BEING MUTO ASHIROGI.
THAT'S HOW I REALLY FEEL.
WE CAN'T GET MARRIED RIGHT NOW.
I KNOW...
MIHO SAID SHE'D NEVER WANT TO BE MARRIED UNTIL SHE REACHED HER DREAMS TOO.
BUT I CAN'T HELP BUT FEEL LIKE GETTING THIS ANIME IS THE SOURCE OF ALL OUR PROBLEMS.
YOU MIGHT BE RIGHT ABOUT THAT.
I WOULDN'T EVEN THINK ABOUT TRYING TO HANDLE ANOTHER SERIES IF IT WASN'T FOR THAT.
...
NO, SORRY... I DIDN'T MEAN IT THAT WAY.
AKITO'S UNDER-STANDING OF YOUR DREAM, AND HE KNOWS WHAT IT'S GOING TO TAKE TO GET THERE.
BUT I FEEL LIKE THE REAL REASON HE'S UPSET RIGHT NOW IS BECAUSE WE'RE NOT ON THE RIGHT TRACK ANYMORE...
YEAH...

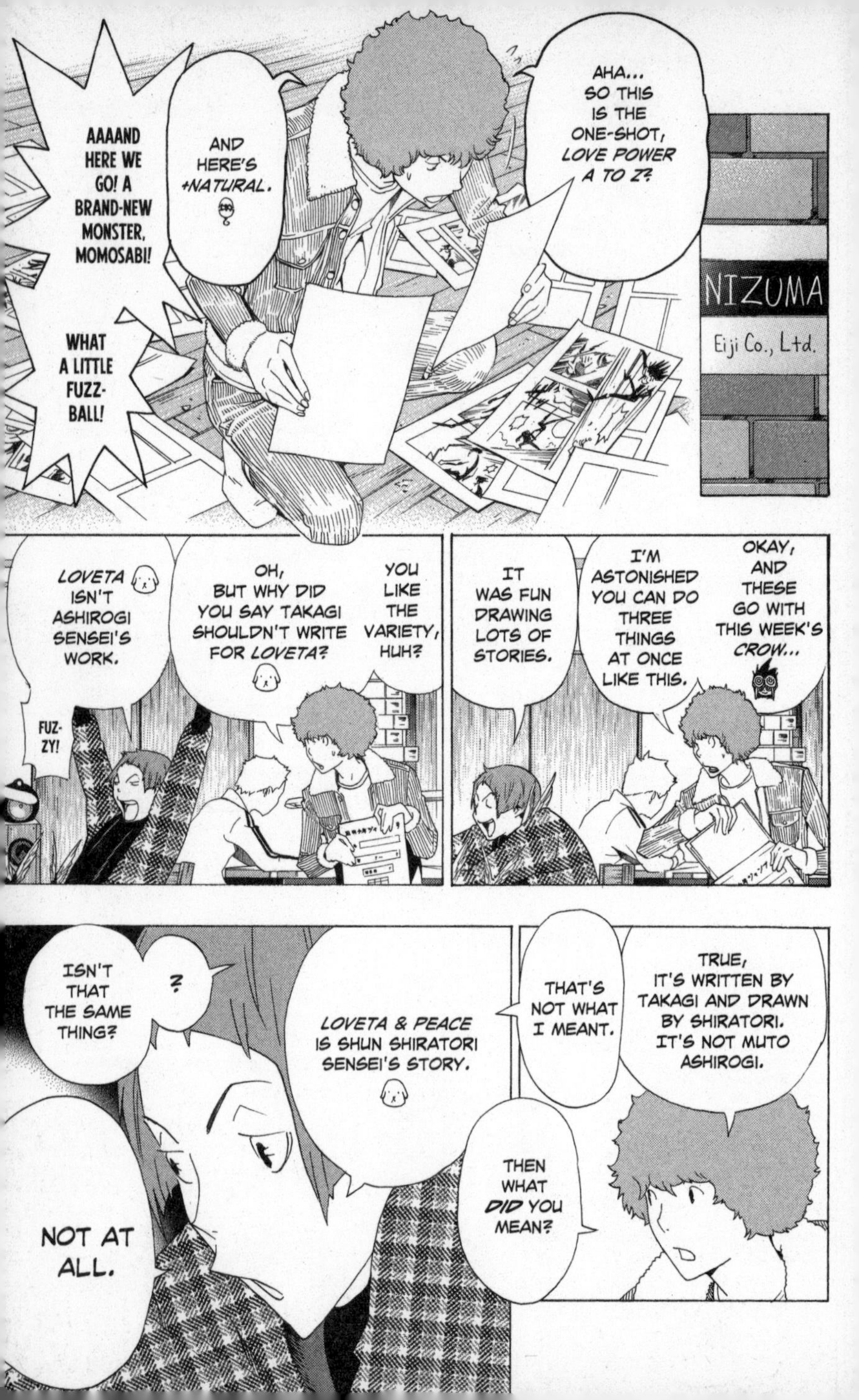
NIZUMA
Eiji Co., Ltd.
AHA... SO THIS IS THE ONE-SHOT, *LOVE POWER A TO Z*?
AND HERE'S *+NATURAL*.
AAAAND HERE WE GO! A BRAND-NEW MONSTER, MOMOSABI!
WHAT A LITTLE FUZZ-BALL!
OKAY, AND THESE GO WITH THIS WEEK'S *CROW*...
I'M ASTONISHED YOU CAN DO THREE THINGS AT ONCE LIKE THIS.
IT WAS FUN DRAWING LOTS OF STORIES.
YOU LIKE THE VARIETY, HUH?
OH, BUT WHY DID YOU SAY TAKAGI SHOULDN'T WRITE FOR *LOVETA*?
LOVETA ISN'T ASHIROGI SENSEI'S WORK.
FUZ-ZY!
TRUE, IT'S WRITTEN BY TAKAGI AND DRAWN BY SHIRATORI. IT'S NOT MUTO ASHIROGI.
THAT'S NOT WHAT I MEANT.
THEN WHAT *DID* YOU MEAN?
LOVETA & PEACE IS SHUN SHIRATORI SENSEI'S STORY.
?
ISN'T THAT THE SAME THING?
NOT AT ALL.

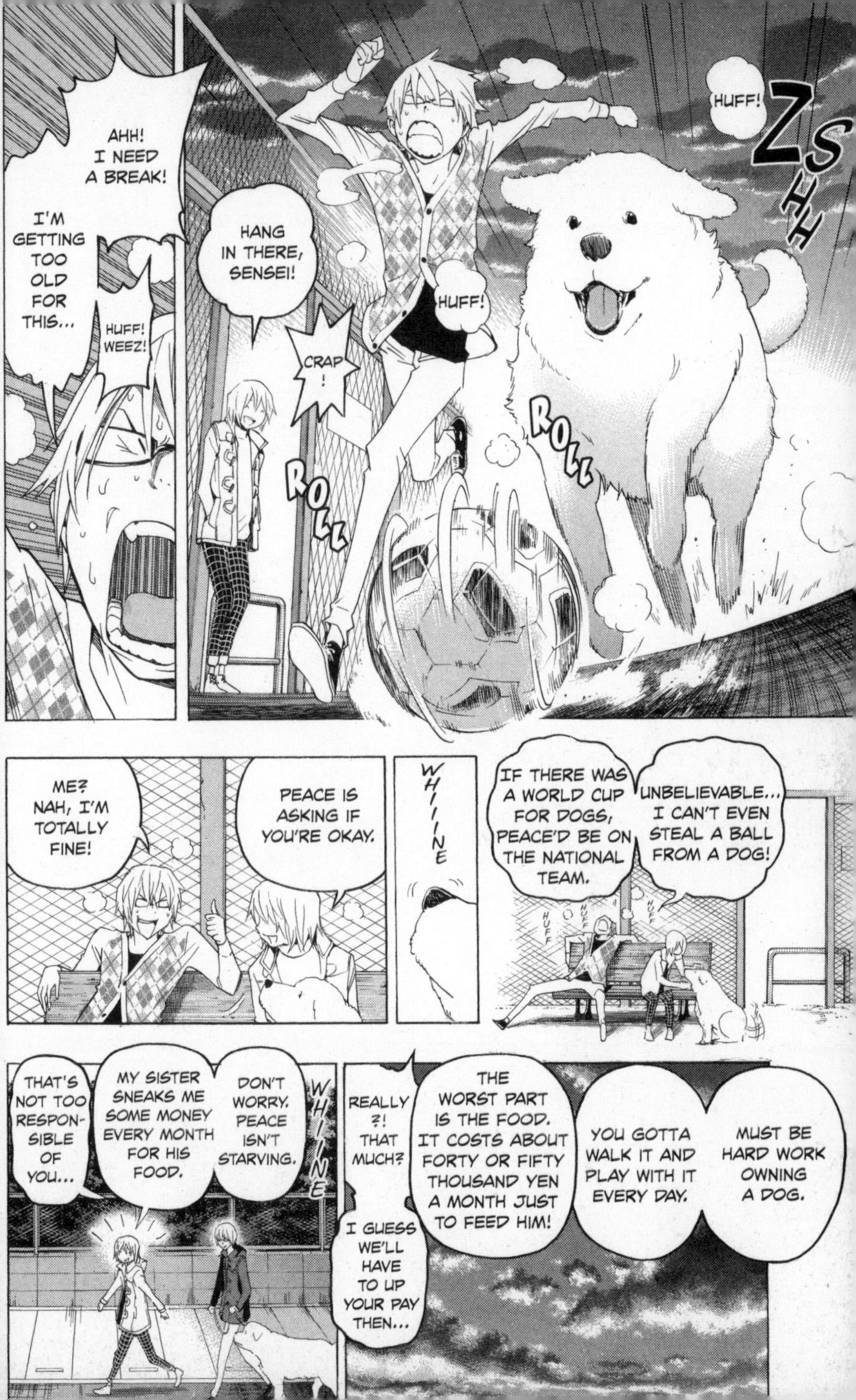
HUFF!
ZSHH
HUFF!
HANG IN THERE, SENSEI!
CRAP!
ROLL
ROLL
AHH! I NEED A BREAK!
I'M GETTING TOO OLD FOR THIS...
HUFF! WEEZ!
UNBELIEVABLE... I CAN'T EVEN STEAL A BALL FROM A DOG!
IF THERE WAS A WORLD CUP FOR DOGS, PEACE'D BE ON THE NATIONAL TEAM.
HUFF
HUFF
HUFF
WHIIIINE
PEACE IS ASKING IF YOU'RE OKAY.
ME? NAH, I'M TOTALLY FINE!
MUST BE HARD WORK OWNING A DOG.
YOU GOTTA WALK IT AND PLAY WITH IT EVERY DAY.
THE WORST PART IS THE FOOD. IT COSTS ABOUT FORTY OR FIFTY THOUSAND YEN A MONTH JUST TO FEED HIM!
REALLY?! THAT MUCH?
I GUESS WE'LL HAVE TO UP YOUR PAY THEN...
WHIIINE
DON'T WORRY. PEACE ISN'T STARVING.
MY SISTER SNEAKS ME SOME MONEY EVERY MONTH FOR HIS FOOD.
THAT'S NOT TOO RESPONSIBLE OF YOU...

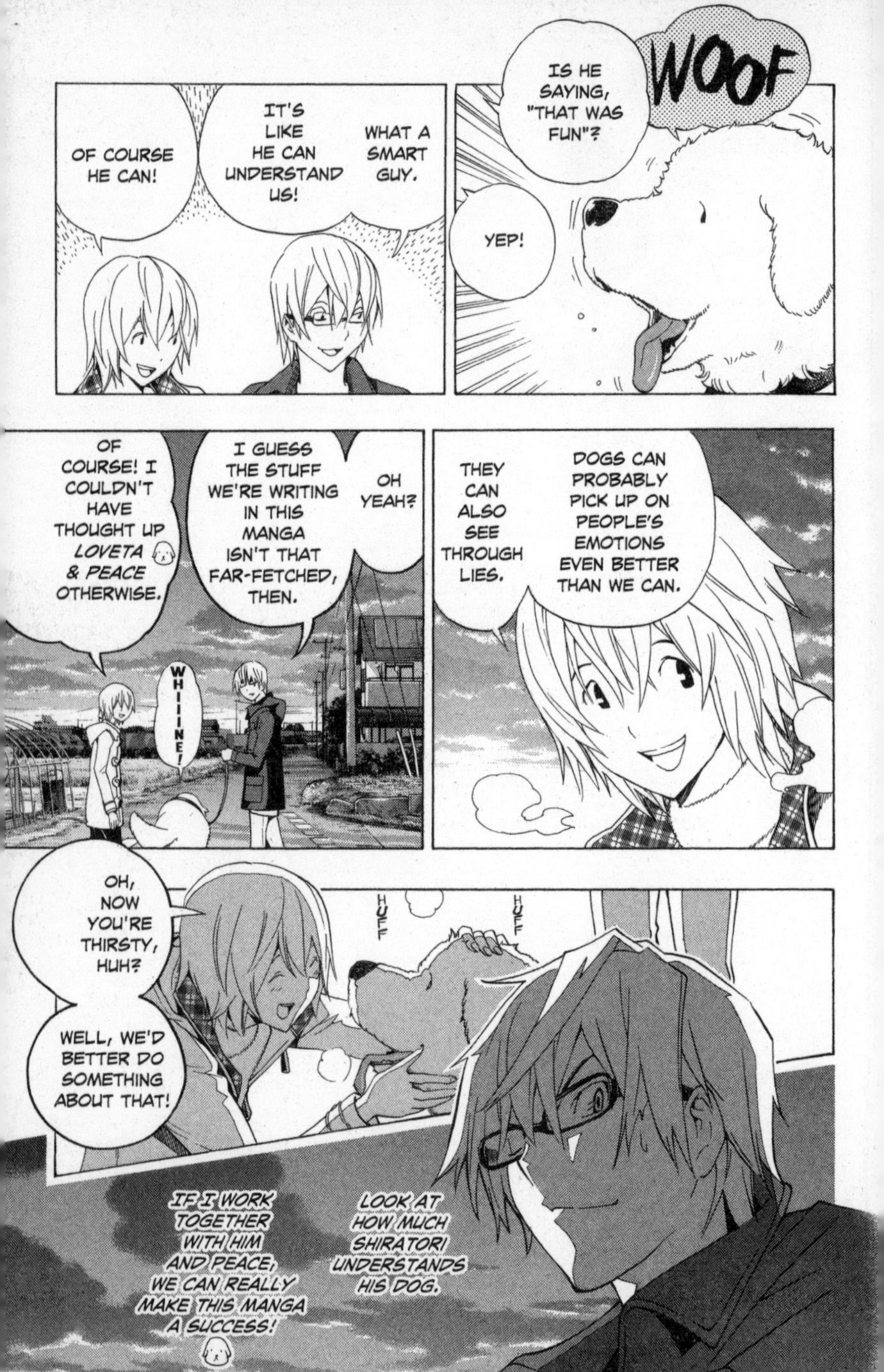
WOOF
IS HE SAYING, "THAT WAS FUN"?
YEP!
WHAT A SMART GUY.
IT'S LIKE HE CAN UNDERSTAND US!
OF COURSE HE CAN!
DOGS CAN PROBABLY PICK UP ON PEOPLE'S EMOTIONS EVEN BETTER THAN WE CAN.
THEY CAN ALSO SEE THROUGH LIES.
OH YEAH?
I GUESS THE STUFF WE'RE WRITING IN THIS MANGA ISN'T THAT FAR-FETCHED, THEN.
OF COURSE! I COULDN'T HAVE THOUGHT UP *LOVETA & PEACE* OTHERWISE.
WHIIINE!
HUFF
HUFF
OH, NOW YOU'RE THIRSTY, HUH?
WELL, WE'D BETTER DO SOMETHING ABOUT THAT!
LOOK AT HOW MUCH SHIRATORI UNDERSTANDS HIS DOG.
IF I WORK TOGETHER WITH HIM AND PEACE, WE CAN REALLY MAKE THIS MANGA A SUCCESS!

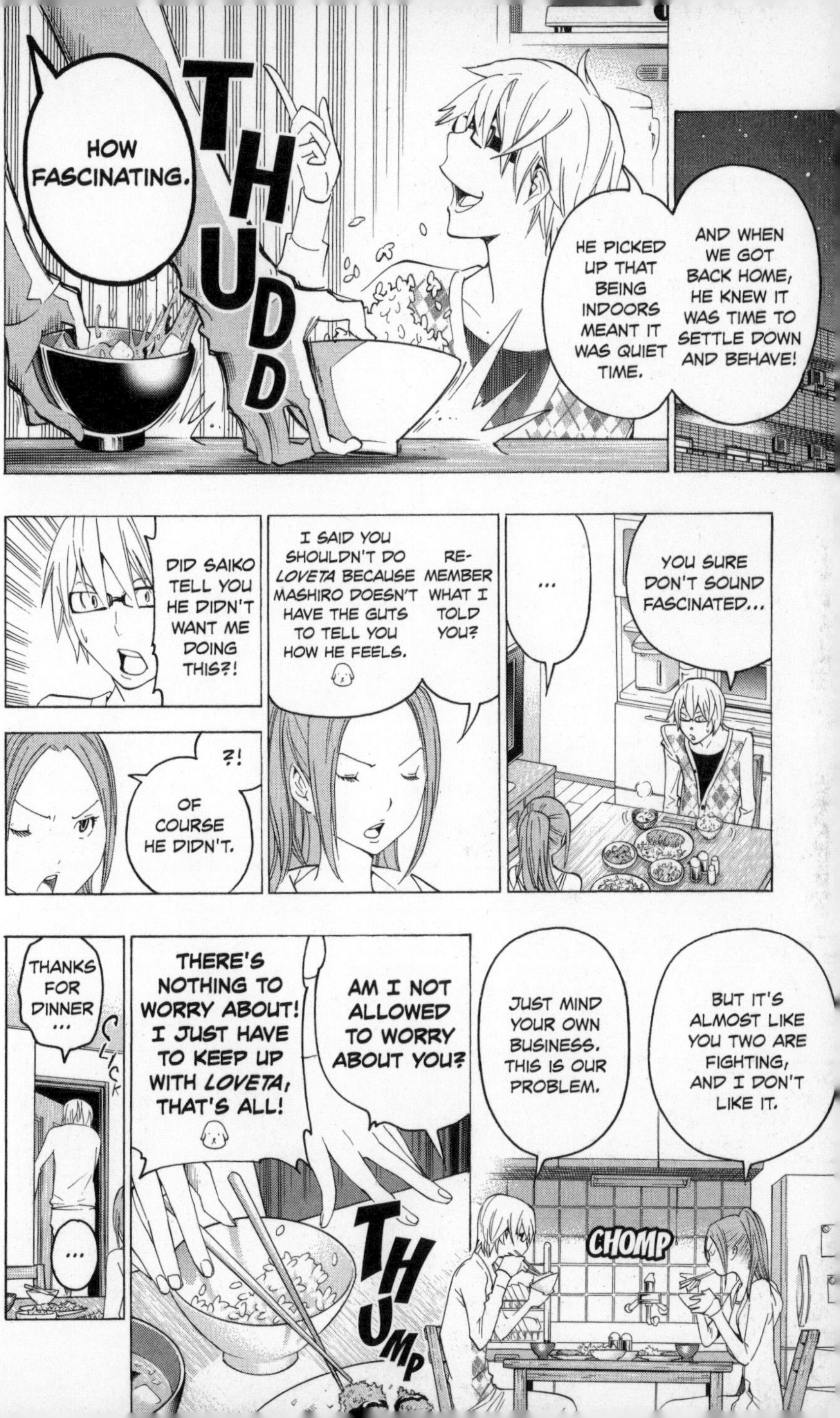
AND WHEN WE GOT BACK HOME, HE KNEW IT WAS TIME TO SETTLE DOWN AND BEHAVE!
HE PICKED UP THAT BEING INDOORS MEANT IT WAS QUIET TIME.
THUDD
HOW FASCINATING.
YOU SURE DON'T SOUND FASCINATED...
...
REMEMBER WHAT I TOLD YOU?
I SAID YOU SHOULDN'T DO *LOVETA* BECAUSE MASHIRO DOESN'T HAVE THE GUTS TO TELL YOU HOW HE FEELS.
DID SAIKO TELL YOU HE DIDN'T WANT ME DOING THIS?!
?!
OF COURSE HE DIDN'T.
BUT IT'S ALMOST LIKE YOU TWO ARE FIGHTING, AND I DON'T LIKE IT.
JUST MIND YOUR OWN BUSINESS. THIS IS OUR PROBLEM.
CHOMP
AM I NOT ALLOWED TO WORRY ABOUT YOU?
THERE'S NOTHING TO WORRY ABOUT! I JUST HAVE TO KEEP UP WITH *LOVETA*, THAT'S ALL!
THUMP
THANKS FOR DINNER...
CLICK
...

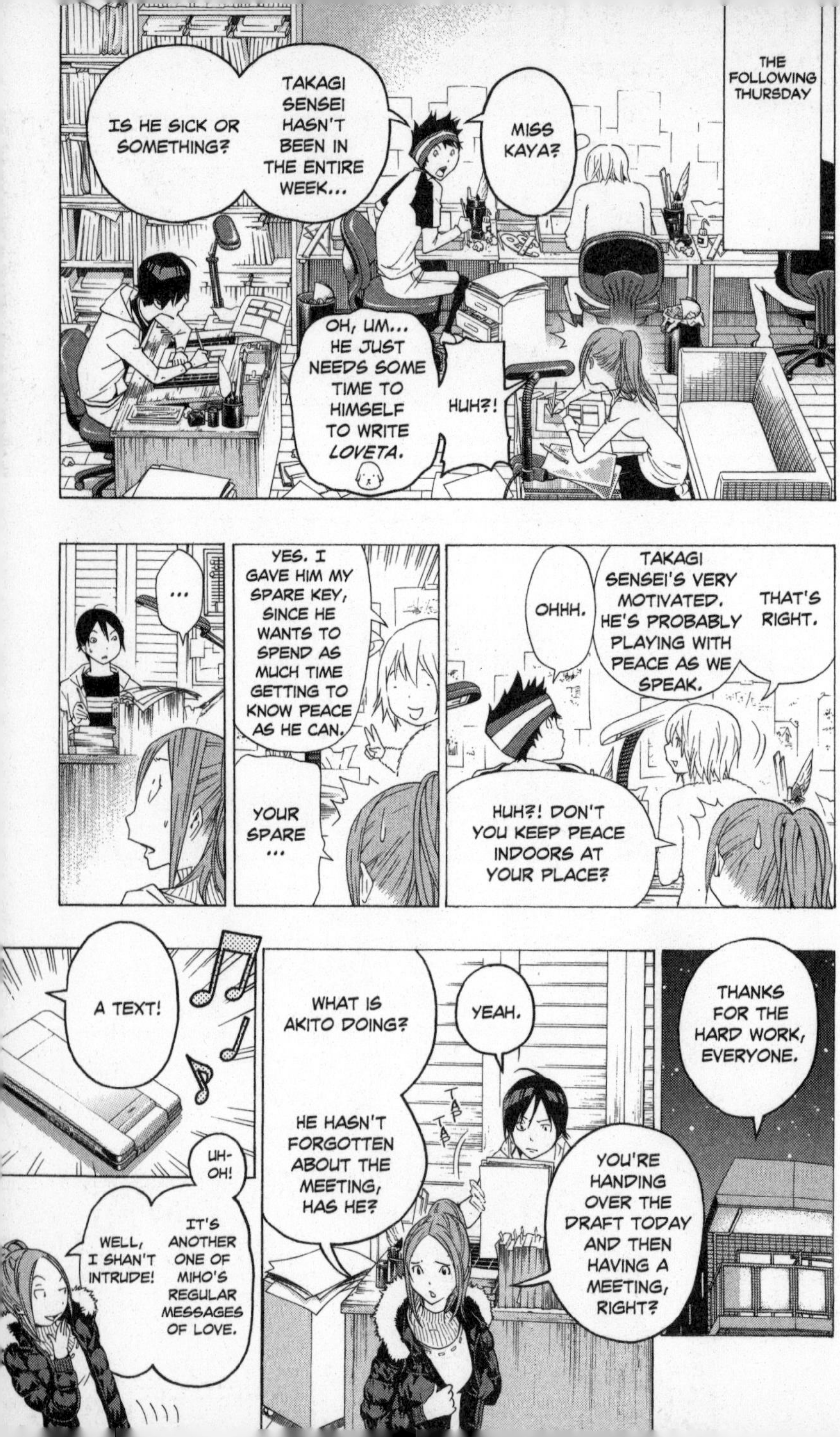
THE FOLLOWING THURSDAY
MISS KAYA?
TAKAGI SENSEI HASN'T BEEN IN THE ENTIRE WEEK...
IS HE SICK OR SOMETHING?
HUH?!
OH, UM... HE JUST NEEDS SOME TIME TO HIMSELF TO WRITE *LOVETA*.
THAT'S RIGHT.
TAKAGI SENSEI'S VERY MOTIVATED. HE'S PROBABLY PLAYING WITH PEACE AS WE SPEAK.
OHHH.
HUH?! DON'T YOU KEEP PEACE INDOORS AT YOUR PLACE?
YES. I GAVE HIM MY SPARE KEY, SINCE HE WANTS TO SPEND AS MUCH TIME GETTING TO KNOW PEACE AS HE CAN.
YOUR SPARE...
...
THANKS FOR THE HARD WORK, EVERYONE.
YOU'RE HANDING OVER THE DRAFT TODAY AND THEN HAVING A MEETING, RIGHT?
YEAH.
TAP TAP
WHAT IS AKITO DOING?
HE HASN'T FORGOTTEN ABOUT THE MEETING, HAS HE?
A TEXT!
UH-OH!
IT'S ANOTHER ONE OF MIHO'S REGULAR MESSAGES OF LOVE.
WELL, I SHAN'T INTRUDE!

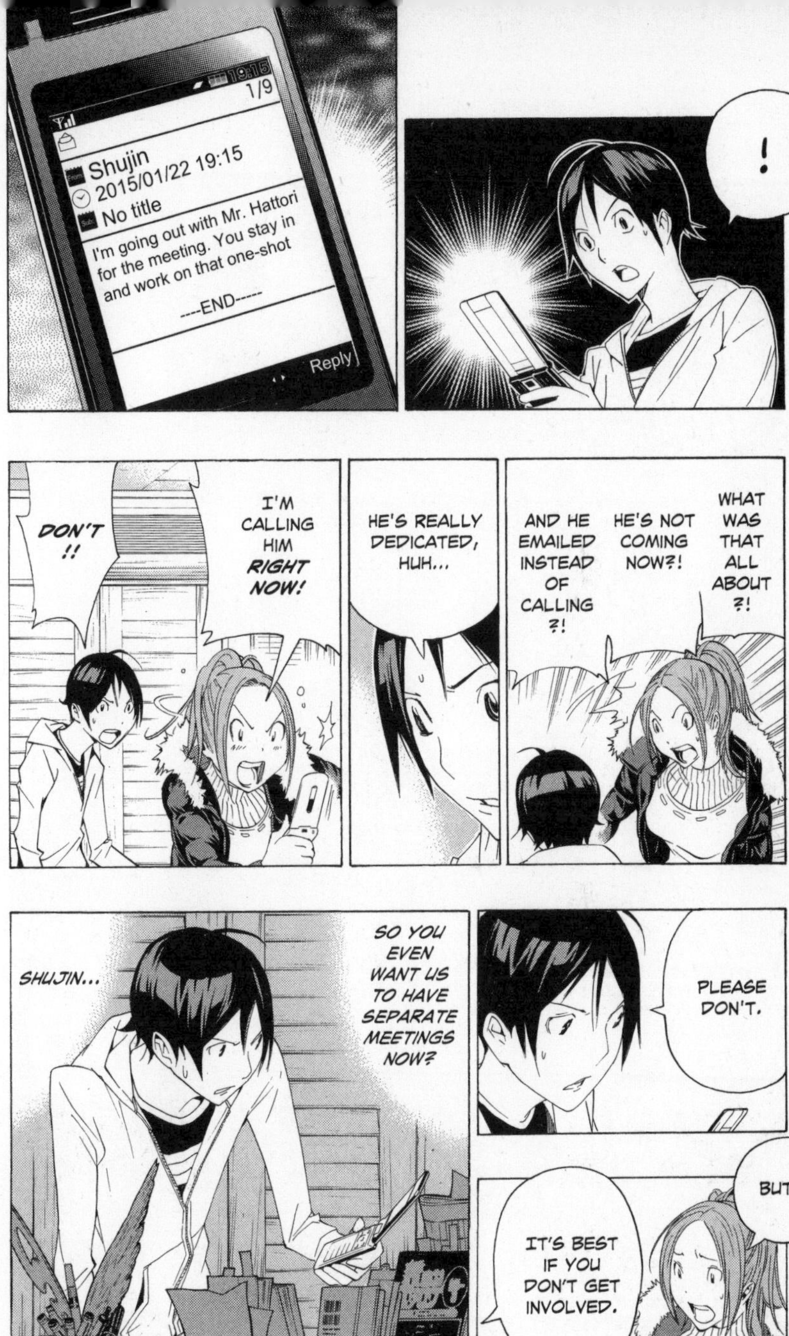
!
19:15
1/9
Shujin
2015/01/22 19:15
No title
I'm going out with Mr. Hattori for the meeting. You stay in and work on that one-shot
---END-----
Reply
WHAT WAS THAT ALL ABOUT?!
HE'S NOT COMING NOW?!
AND HE EMAILED INSTEAD OF CALLING?!
HE'S REALLY DEDICATED, HUH...
I'M CALLING HIM *RIGHT NOW!*
DON'T!!
PLEASE DON'T.
BUT...
IT'S BEST IF YOU DON'T GET INVOLVED.
SO YOU EVEN WANT US TO HAVE SEPARATE MEETINGS NOW?
SHUJIN...

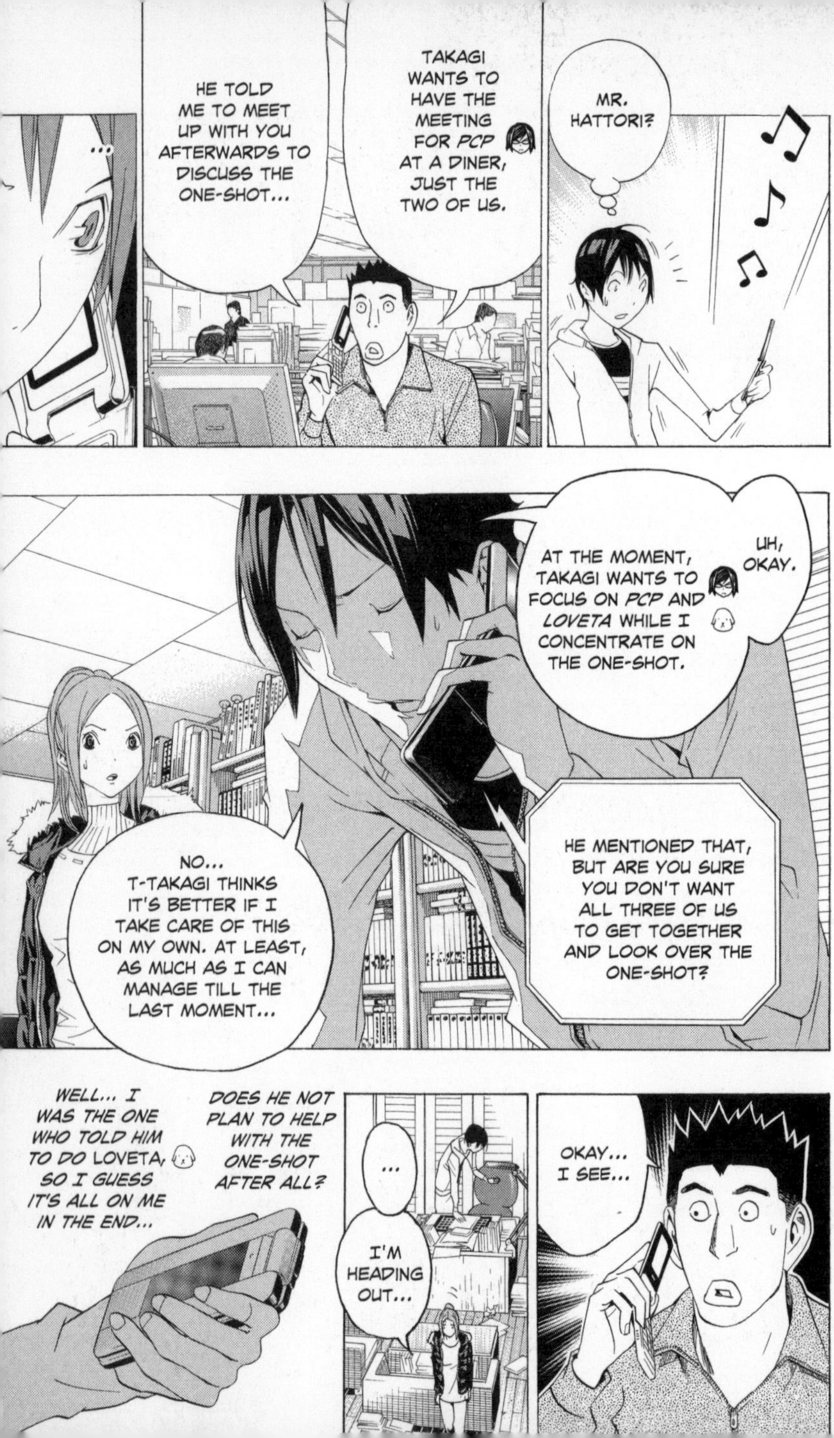
MR. HATTORI?
TAKAGI WANTS TO HAVE THE MEETING FOR *PCP* AT A DINER, JUST THE TWO OF US.
HE TOLD ME TO MEET UP WITH YOU AFTERWARDS TO DISCUSS THE ONE-SHOT...
...
UH, OKAY.
AT THE MOMENT, TAKAGI WANTS TO FOCUS ON *PCP* AND *LOVETA* WHILE I CONCENTRATE ON THE ONE-SHOT.
HE MENTIONED THAT, BUT ARE YOU SURE YOU DON'T WANT ALL THREE OF US TO GET TOGETHER AND LOOK OVER THE ONE-SHOT?
NO... T-TAKAGI THINKS IT'S BETTER IF I TAKE CARE OF THIS ON MY OWN. AT LEAST, AS MUCH AS I CAN MANAGE TILL THE LAST MOMENT...
OKAY... I SEE...
...
I'M HEADING OUT...
DOES HE NOT PLAN TO HELP WITH THE ONE-SHOT AFTER ALL?
WELL... I WAS THE ONE WHO TOLD HIM TO DO LOVETA, SO I GUESS IT'S ALL ON ME IN THE END...

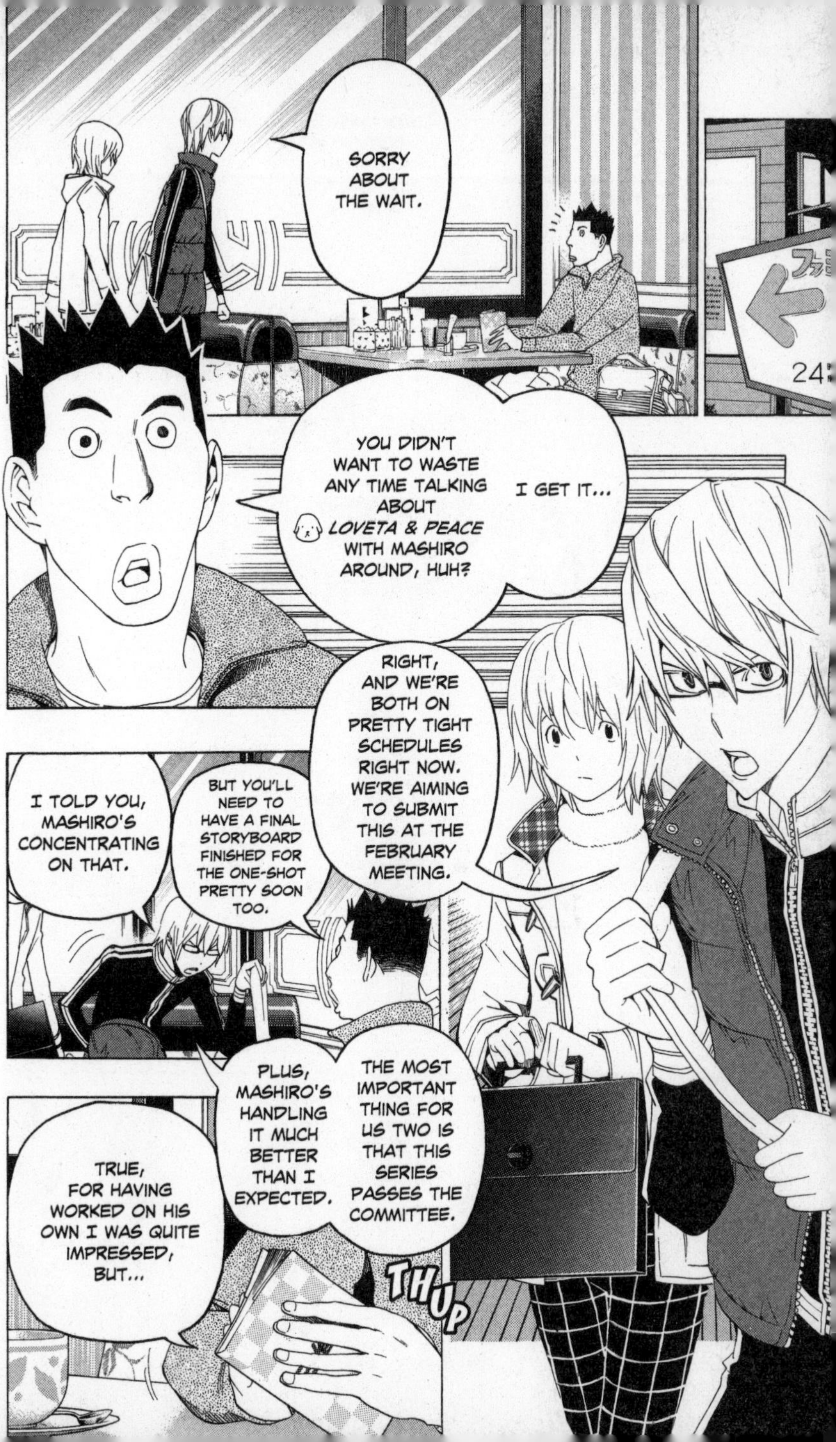
SORRY ABOUT THE WAIT.
I GET IT...
YOU DIDN'T WANT TO WASTE ANY TIME TALKING ABOUT *LOVETA & PEACE* WITH MASHIRO AROUND, HUH?
RIGHT, AND WE'RE BOTH ON PRETTY TIGHT SCHEDULES RIGHT NOW. WE'RE AIMING TO SUBMIT THIS AT THE FEBRUARY MEETING.
BUT YOU'LL NEED TO HAVE A FINAL STORYBOARD FINISHED FOR THE ONE-SHOT PRETTY SOON TOO.
I TOLD YOU, MASHIRO'S CONCENTRATING ON THAT.
THE MOST IMPORTANT THING FOR US TWO IS THAT THIS SERIES PASSES THE COMMITTEE.
PLUS, MASHIRO'S HANDLING IT MUCH BETTER THAN I EXPECTED.
THUP
TRUE, FOR HAVING WORKED ON HIS OWN I WAS QUITE IMPRESSED, BUT...

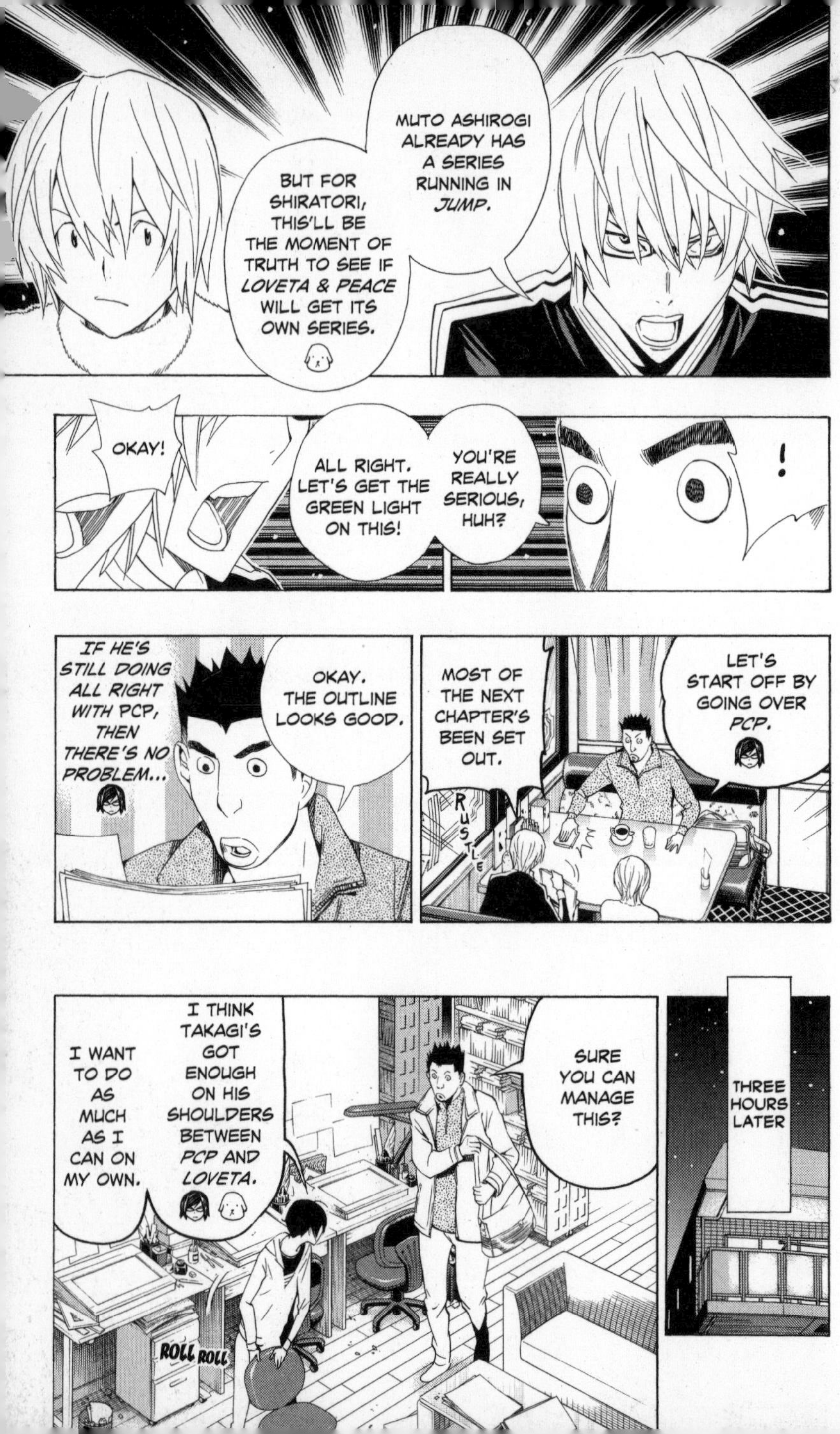
MUTO ASHIROGI ALREADY HAS A SERIES RUNNING IN JUMP.
BUT FOR SHIRATORI, THIS'LL BE THE MOMENT OF TRUTH TO SEE IF LOVETA & PEACE WILL GET ITS OWN SERIES.
!
YOU'RE REALLY SERIOUS, HUH?
ALL RIGHT. LET'S GET THE GREEN LIGHT ON THIS!
OKAY!
LET'S START OFF BY GOING OVER PCP.
MOST OF THE NEXT CHAPTER'S BEEN SET OUT.
RUSTLE
OKAY. THE OUTLINE LOOKS GOOD.
IF HE'S STILL DOING ALL RIGHT WITH PCP, THEN THERE'S NO PROBLEM...
THREE HOURS LATER
SURE YOU CAN MANAGE THIS?
I THINK TAKAGI'S GOT ENOUGH ON HIS SHOULDERS BETWEEN PCP AND LOVETA.
I WANT TO DO AS MUCH AS I CAN ON MY OWN.
ROLL ROLL

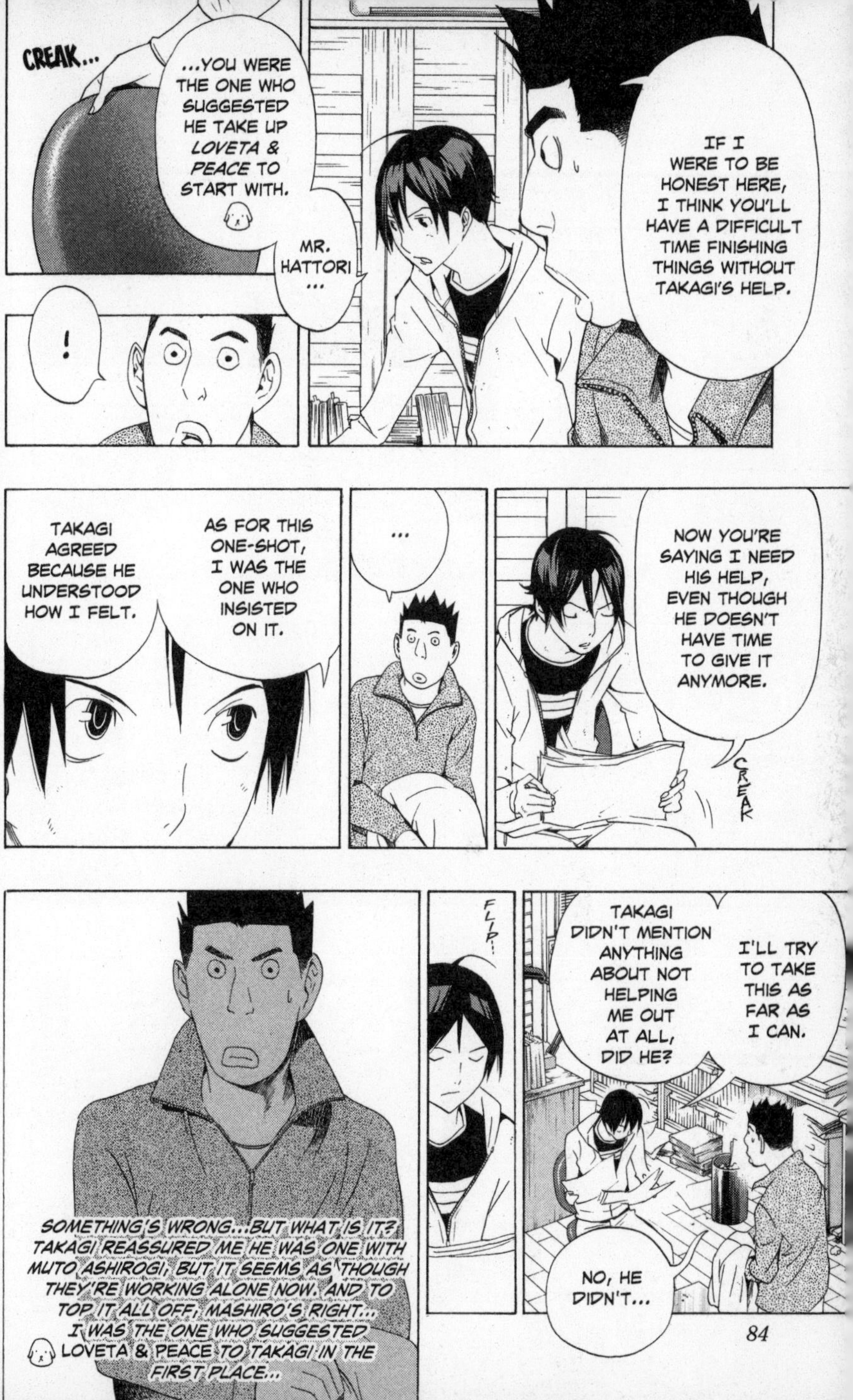
IF I WERE TO BE HONEST HERE, I THINK YOU'LL HAVE A DIFFICULT TIME FINISHING THINGS WITHOUT TAKAGI'S HELP.
MR. HATTORI...
...YOU WERE THE ONE WHO SUGGESTED HE TAKE UP *LOVETA & PEACE* TO START WITH.
CREAK...
!
NOW YOU'RE SAYING I NEED HIS HELP, EVEN THOUGH HE DOESN'T HAVE TIME TO GIVE IT ANYMORE.
CREAK
...
AS FOR THIS ONE-SHOT, I WAS THE ONE WHO INSISTED ON IT.
TAKAGI AGREED BECAUSE HE UNDERSTOOD HOW I FELT.
TAKAGI DIDN'T MENTION ANYTHING ABOUT NOT HELPING ME OUT AT ALL, DID HE?
NO, HE DIDN'T...
I'LL TRY TO TAKE THIS AS FAR AS I CAN.
FLIP!!
SOMETHING'S WRONG...BUT WHAT IS IT? TAKAGI REASSURED ME HE WAS ONE WITH MUTO ASHIROGI, BUT IT SEEMS AS THOUGH THEY'RE WORKING ALONE NOW. AND TO TOP IT ALL OFF, MASHIRO'S RIGHT... I WAS THE ONE WHO SUGGESTED LOVETA & PEACE TO TAKAGI IN THE FIRST PLACE...

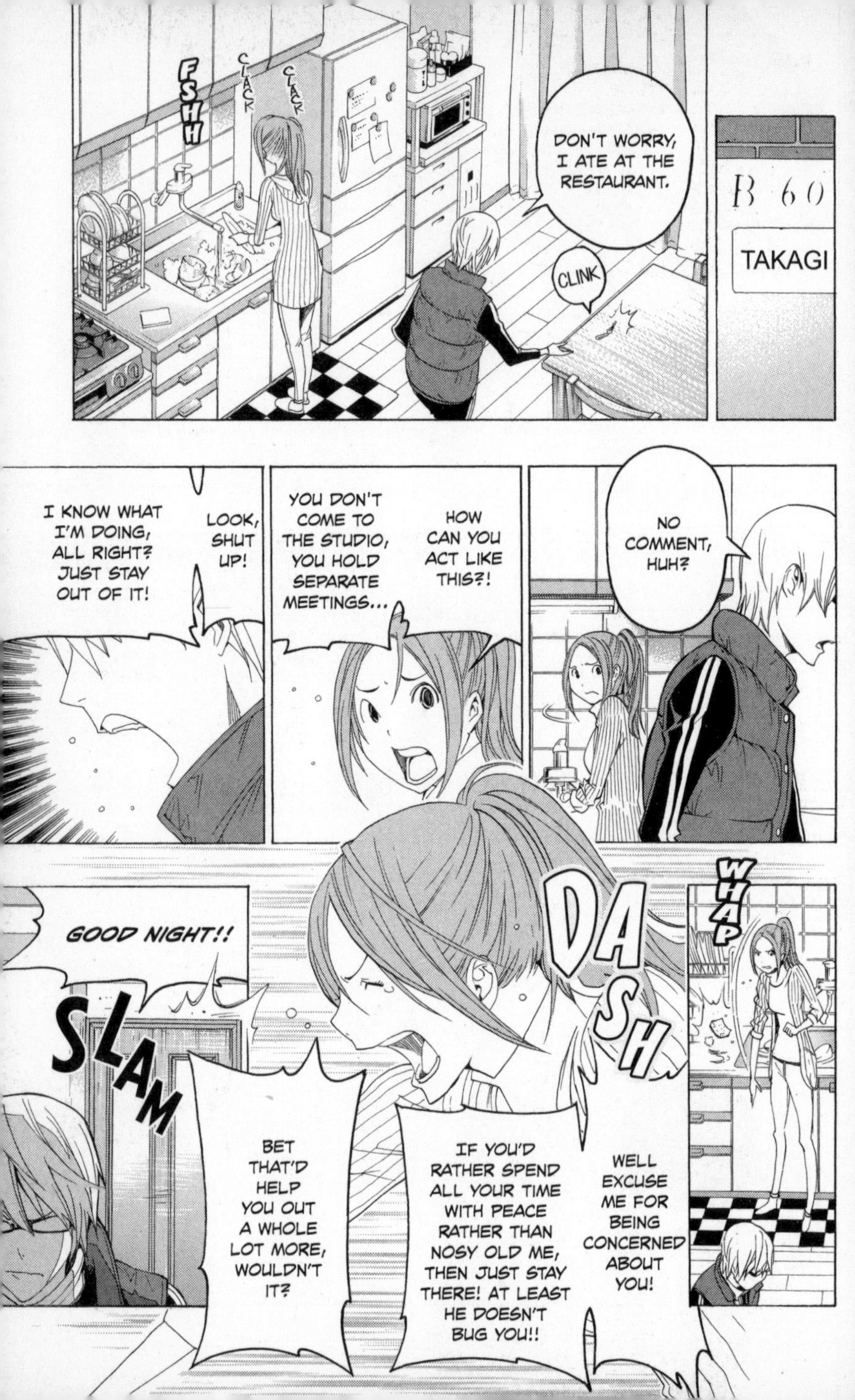
B 60
TAKAGI
DON'T WORRY, I ATE AT THE RESTAURANT.
CLINK
CLACK
CLACK
FSHH
NO COMMENT, HUH?
HOW CAN YOU ACT LIKE THIS?!
YOU DON'T COME TO THE STUDIO, YOU HOLD SEPARATE MEETINGS...
LOOK, SHUT UP!
I KNOW WHAT I'M DOING, ALL RIGHT? JUST STAY OUT OF IT!
WHAP
DASH
WELL EXCUSE ME FOR BEING CONCERNED ABOUT YOU!
IF YOU'D RATHER SPEND ALL YOUR TIME WITH PEACE RATHER THAN NOSY OLD ME, THEN JUST STAY THERE! AT LEAST HE DOESN'T BUG YOU!!
BET THAT'D HELP YOU OUT A WHOLE LOT MORE, WOULDN'T IT?
GOOD NIGHT!!
SLAM

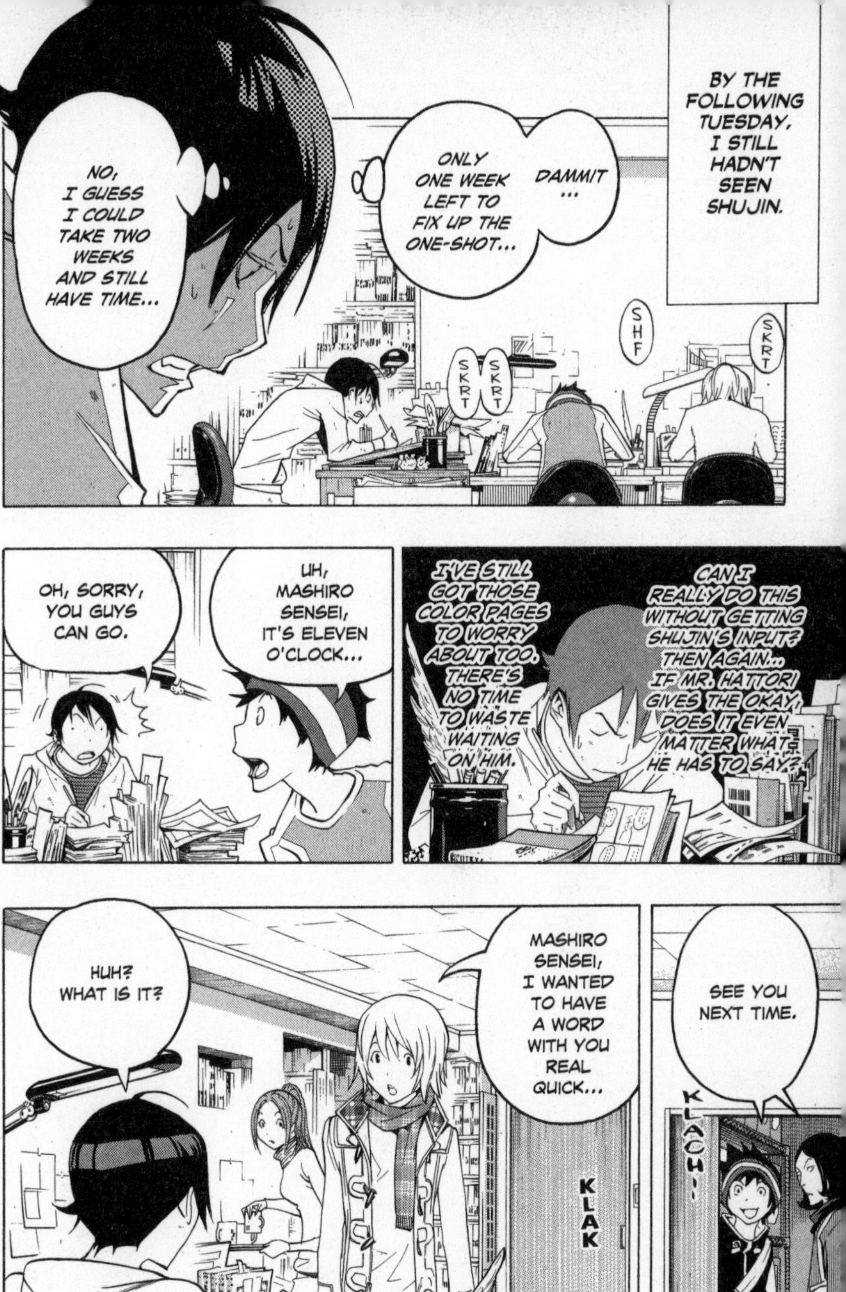
BY THE FOLLOWING TUESDAY, I STILL HADN'T SEEN SHUJIN.
DAMMIT...
ONLY ONE WEEK LEFT TO FIX UP THE ONE-SHOT...
SKRT
SHF
SKRT
SKRT
NO, I GUESS I COULD TAKE TWO WEEKS AND STILL HAVE TIME...
CAN I REALLY DO THIS WITHOUT GETTING SHUJIN'S INPUT? THEN AGAIN... IF MR. HATTORI GIVES THE OKAY, DOES IT EVEN MATTER WHAT HE HAS TO SAY?
I'VE STILL GOT THOSE COLOR PAGES TO WORRY ABOUT TOO. THERE'S NO TIME TO WASTE WAITING ON HIM.
UH, MASHIRO SENSEI, IT'S ELEVEN O'CLOCK...
OH, SORRY, YOU GUYS CAN GO.
SEE YOU NEXT TIME.
KLACHI
MASHIRO SENSEI, I WANTED TO HAVE A WORD WITH YOU REAL QUICK...
KLAK
HUH? WHAT IS IT?

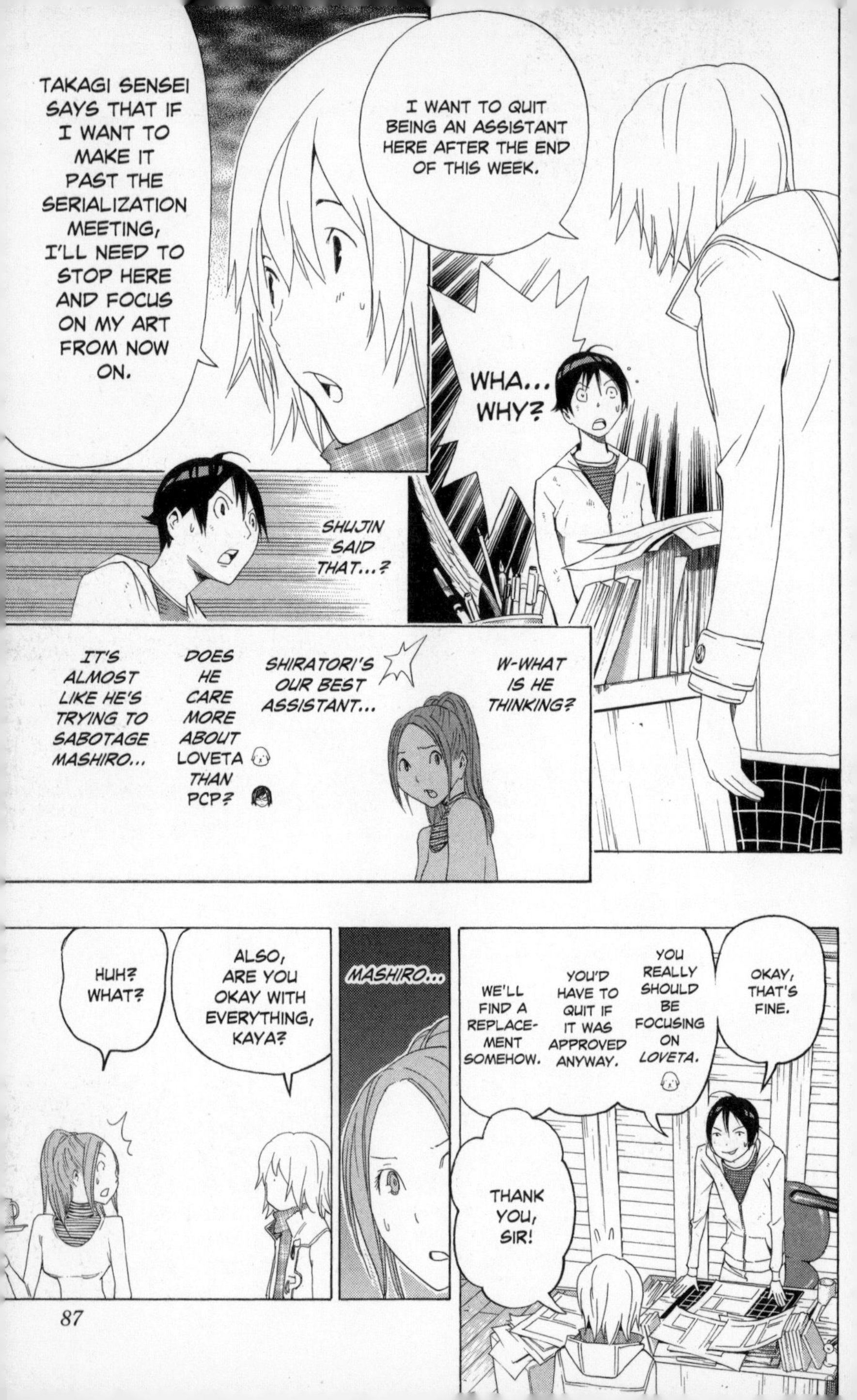
I WANT TO QUIT BEING AN ASSISTANT HERE AFTER THE END OF THIS WEEK.
WHA... WHY?
TAKAGI SENSEI SAYS THAT IF I WANT TO MAKE IT PAST THE SERIALIZATION MEETING, I'LL NEED TO STOP HERE AND FOCUS ON MY ART FROM NOW ON.
SHUJIN SAID THAT...?
W-WHAT IS HE THINKING?
SHIRATORI'S OUR BEST ASSISTANT...
DOES HE CARE MORE ABOUT LOVETA THAN PCP?
IT'S ALMOST LIKE HE'S TRYING TO SABOTAGE MASHIRO...
OKAY, THAT'S FINE.
YOU REALLY SHOULD BE FOCUSING ON LOVETA.
YOU'D HAVE TO QUIT IF IT WAS APPROVED ANYWAY.
WE'LL FIND A REPLACEMENT SOMEHOW.
THANK YOU, SIR!
MASHIRO...
ALSO, ARE YOU OKAY WITH EVERYTHING, KAYA?
HUH? WHAT?

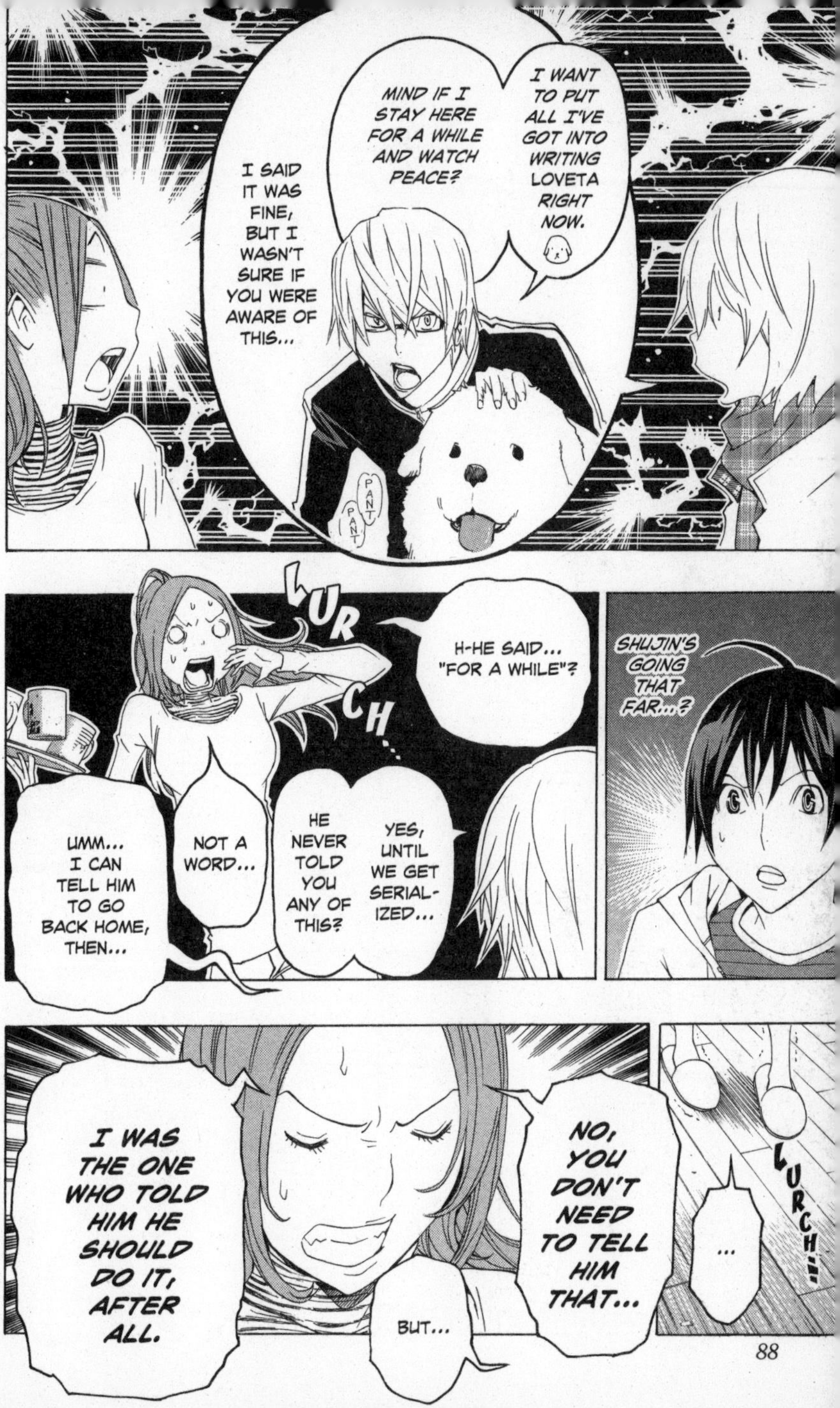
I WANT TO PUT ALL I'VE GOT INTO WRITING LOVETA RIGHT NOW.
MIND IF I STAY HERE FOR A WHILE AND WATCH PEACE?
I SAID IT WAS FINE, BUT I WASN'T SURE IF YOU WERE AWARE OF THIS...
PANT PANT
SHUJIN'S GOING THAT FAR...?
H-HE SAID... "FOR A WHILE"?
LURCH...
YES, UNTIL WE GET SERIAL-IZED...
HE NEVER TOLD YOU ANY OF THIS?
NOT A WORD...
UMM... I CAN TELL HIM TO GO BACK HOME, THEN...
...
LURCH...
NO, YOU DON'T NEED TO TELL HIM THAT...
BUT...
I WAS THE ONE WHO TOLD HIM HE SHOULD DO IT, AFTER ALL.

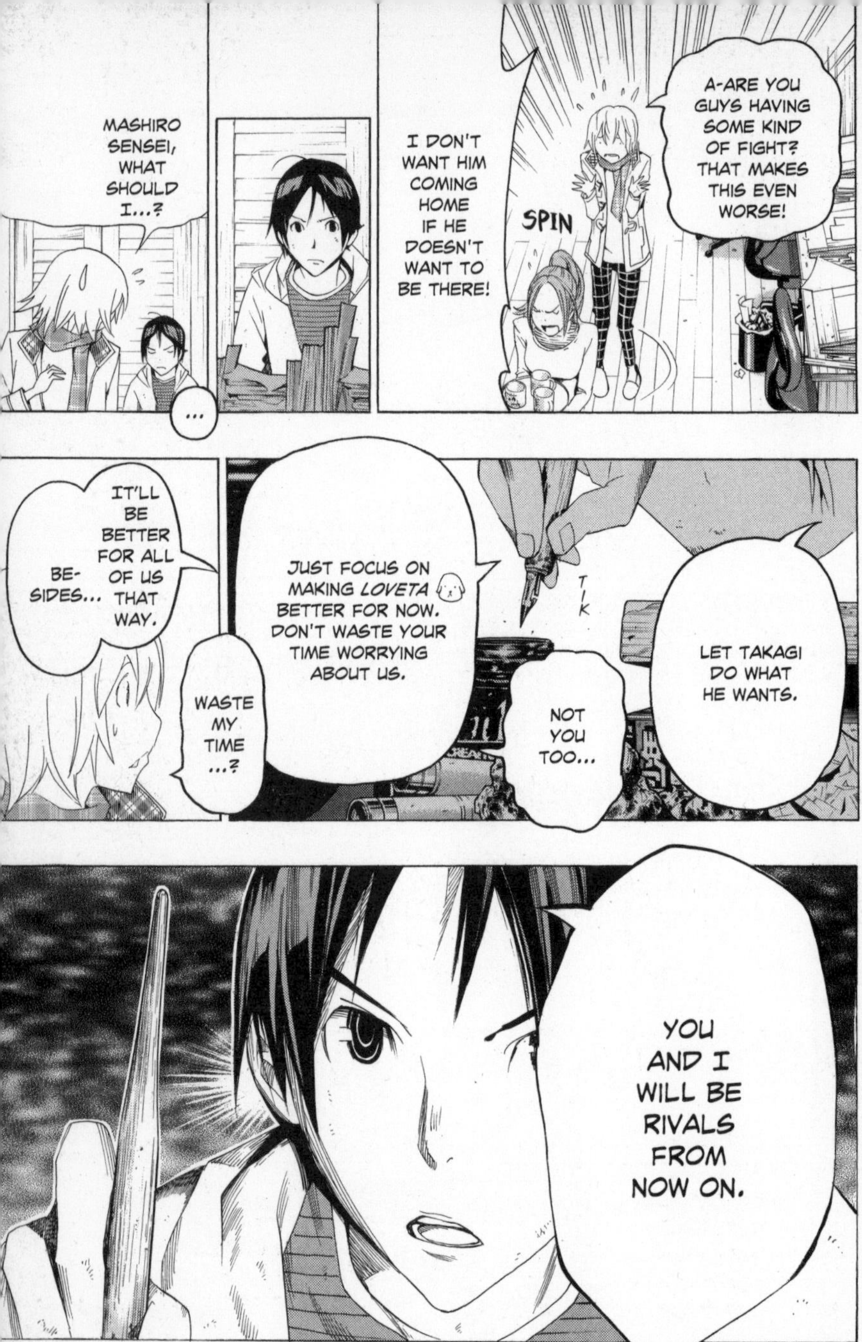
A-ARE YOU GUYS HAVING SOME KIND OF FIGHT? THAT MAKES THIS EVEN WORSE!
SPIN
I DON'T WANT HIM COMING HOME IF HE DOESN'T WANT TO BE THERE!
MASHIRO SENSEI, WHAT SHOULD I...?
...
LET TAKAGI DO WHAT HE WANTS.
TIK
NOT YOU TOO...
JUST FOCUS ON MAKING *LOVETA* BETTER FOR NOW. DON'T WASTE YOUR TIME WORRYING ABOUT US.
WASTE MY TIME ...?
BESIDES... IT'LL BE BETTER FOR ALL OF US THAT WAY.
YOU AND I WILL BE RIVALS FROM NOW ON.

OHBA'S STORYBOARD

広い空地的な
高木さん頑張れ
はーはーくそっ
ちょ 休憩…
はーはー俺も歳だな
はは
犬のピースから球獲れないって情けねーな 犬のW杯あったらピース絶対代表だ
はーはー
クゥ〜ン
ピースが大丈夫か聞いてます
お…大丈夫
犬飼うのって大変なんだな… 毎日散歩させて遊んでやって…
1番大変なのはエサ代ですよ ピースだと月4くらいか
ええ…!? そうなんだ アシスタント代上げてあげないと
クゥ〜ン
ピースは心配しなくて大丈夫だよ 姉さんがこっそりエサ代回してくれてるから
なんだ… ダメじゃん…
ウォ
良かったって言ってんだ?
はい
本当に利口だよなー 人間の言葉ほとんど理解してるよな
もちろんですよ
表情から人の心情読み取るのはもしかしたら人間以上です 嘘も見抜きますしね
へー…
マンガで描いてることあながち嘘じゃないんだ
そうですよ? じゃなきゃ「恋太&ピース」は思い付きませんでした
クゥン
今度は喉が渇いたか… しょうがないな〜
白鳥くんがピース…犬をこれだけ理解してるんだ
白鳥くんとピースと力を合わせれば「恋太」は必ずスゲー作品になる!…

OBATA'S STORYBOARD

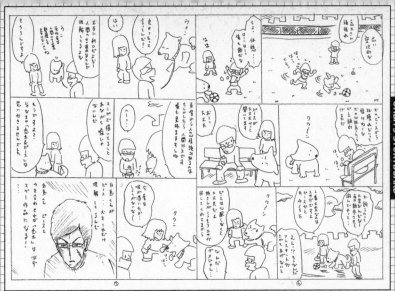

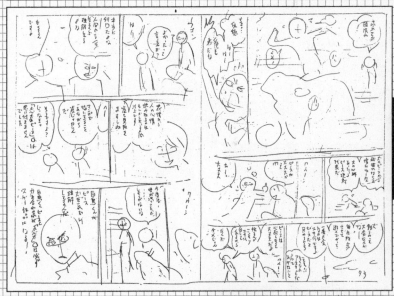

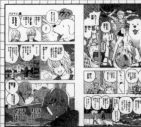

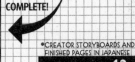

COMPLETE!

*CREATOR STORYBOARDS AND FINISHED PAGES IN JAPANESE

BAKUMAN。 vol.13

"Until the Final Draft Is Complete"

Chapter 110, pp. 76-77

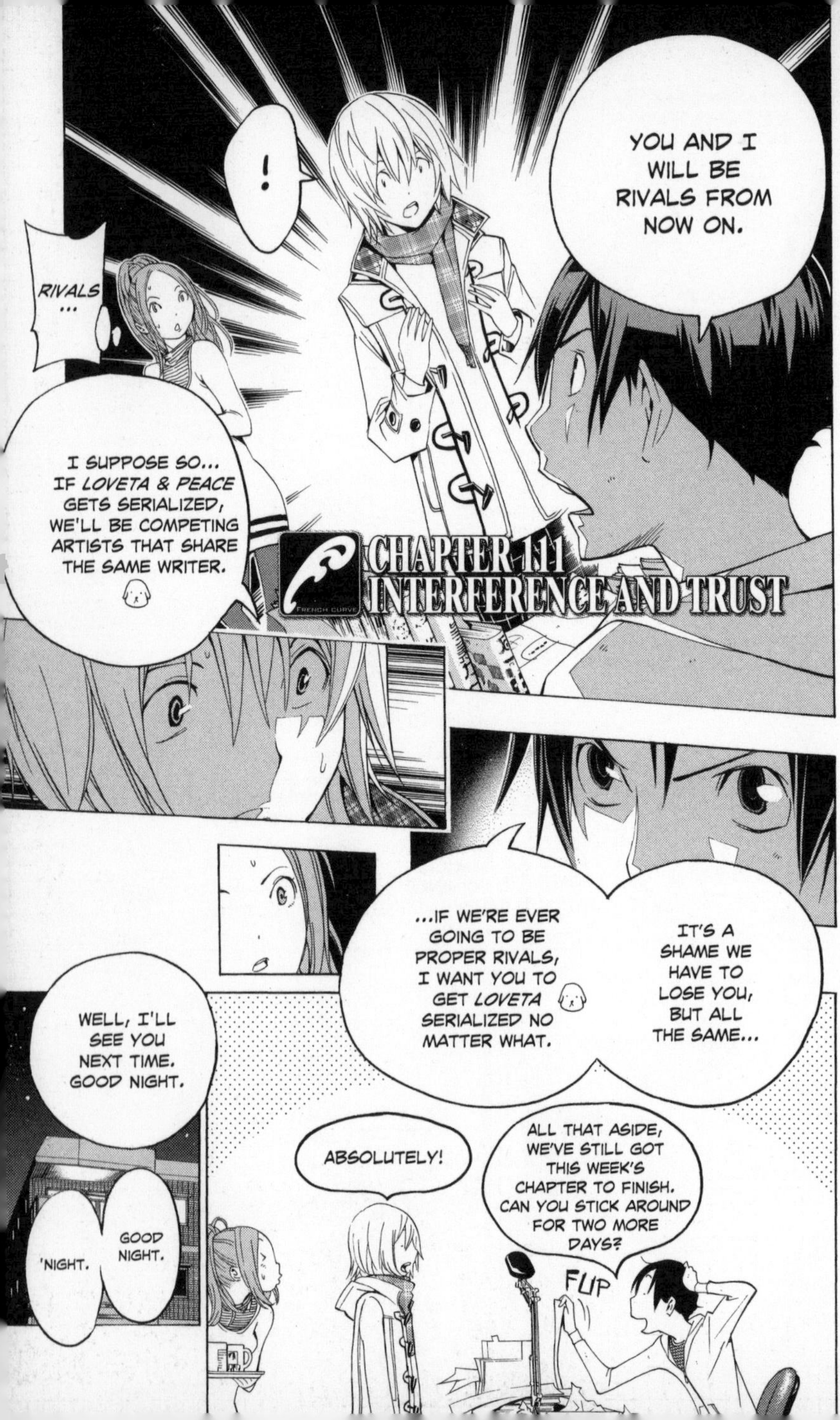
YOU AND I WILL BE RIVALS FROM NOW ON.
!
RIVALS...
I SUPPOSE SO... IF *LOVETA & PEACE* GETS SERIALIZED, WE'LL BE COMPETING ARTISTS THAT SHARE THE SAME WRITER.
CHAPTER 111
INTERFERENCE AND TRUST
IT'S A SHAME WE HAVE TO LOSE YOU, BUT ALL THE SAME...
...IF WE'RE EVER GOING TO BE PROPER RIVALS, I WANT YOU TO GET *LOVETA* SERIALIZED NO MATTER WHAT.
ALL THAT ASIDE, WE'VE STILL GOT THIS WEEK'S CHAPTER TO FINISH. CAN YOU STICK AROUND FOR TWO MORE DAYS?
FLIP
ABSOLUTELY!
WELL, I'LL SEE YOU NEXT TIME. GOOD NIGHT.
GOOD NIGHT.
'NIGHT.

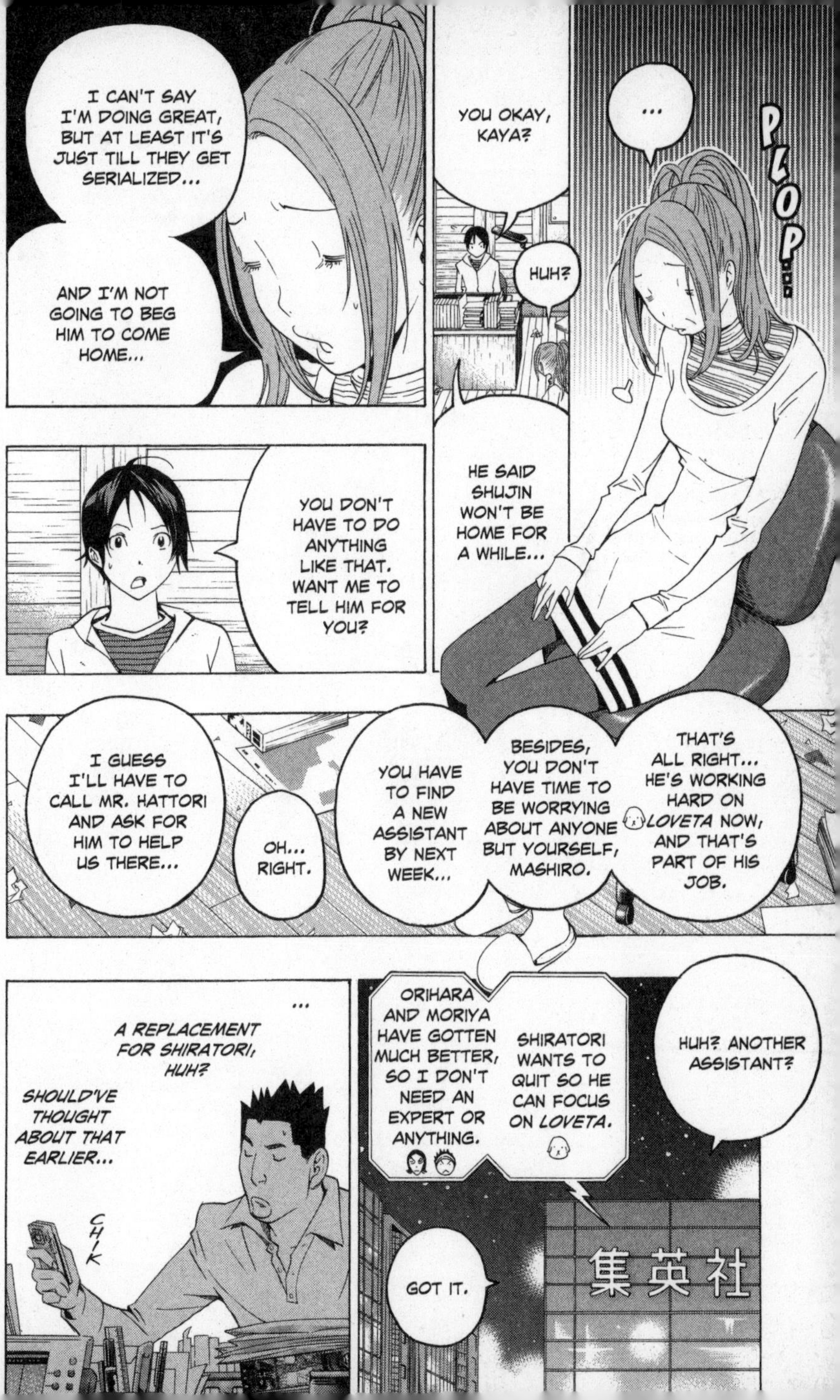
...
PLOP...
YOU OKAY, KAYA?
HUH?
HE SAID SHUJIN WON'T BE HOME FOR A WHILE...
I CAN'T SAY I'M DOING GREAT, BUT AT LEAST IT'S JUST TILL THEY GET SERIALIZED...
AND I'M NOT GOING TO BEG HIM TO COME HOME...
YOU DON'T HAVE TO DO ANYTHING LIKE THAT. WANT ME TO TELL HIM FOR YOU?
THAT'S ALL RIGHT... HE'S WORKING HARD ON *LOVETA* NOW, AND THAT'S PART OF HIS JOB.
BESIDES, YOU DON'T HAVE TIME TO BE WORRYING ABOUT ANYONE BUT YOURSELF, MASHIRO.
YOU HAVE TO FIND A NEW ASSISTANT BY NEXT WEEK...
OH... RIGHT.
I GUESS I'LL HAVE TO CALL MR. HATTORI AND ASK FOR HIM TO HELP US THERE...
HUH? ANOTHER ASSISTANT?
SHIRATORI WANTS TO QUIT SO HE CAN FOCUS ON *LOVETA*.
ORIHARA AND MORIYA HAVE GOTTEN MUCH BETTER, SO I DON'T NEED AN EXPERT OR ANYTHING.
集英社
GOT IT.
...
A REPLACEMENT FOR SHIRATORI, HUH?
SHOULD'VE THOUGHT ABOUT THAT EARLIER...
CHIK

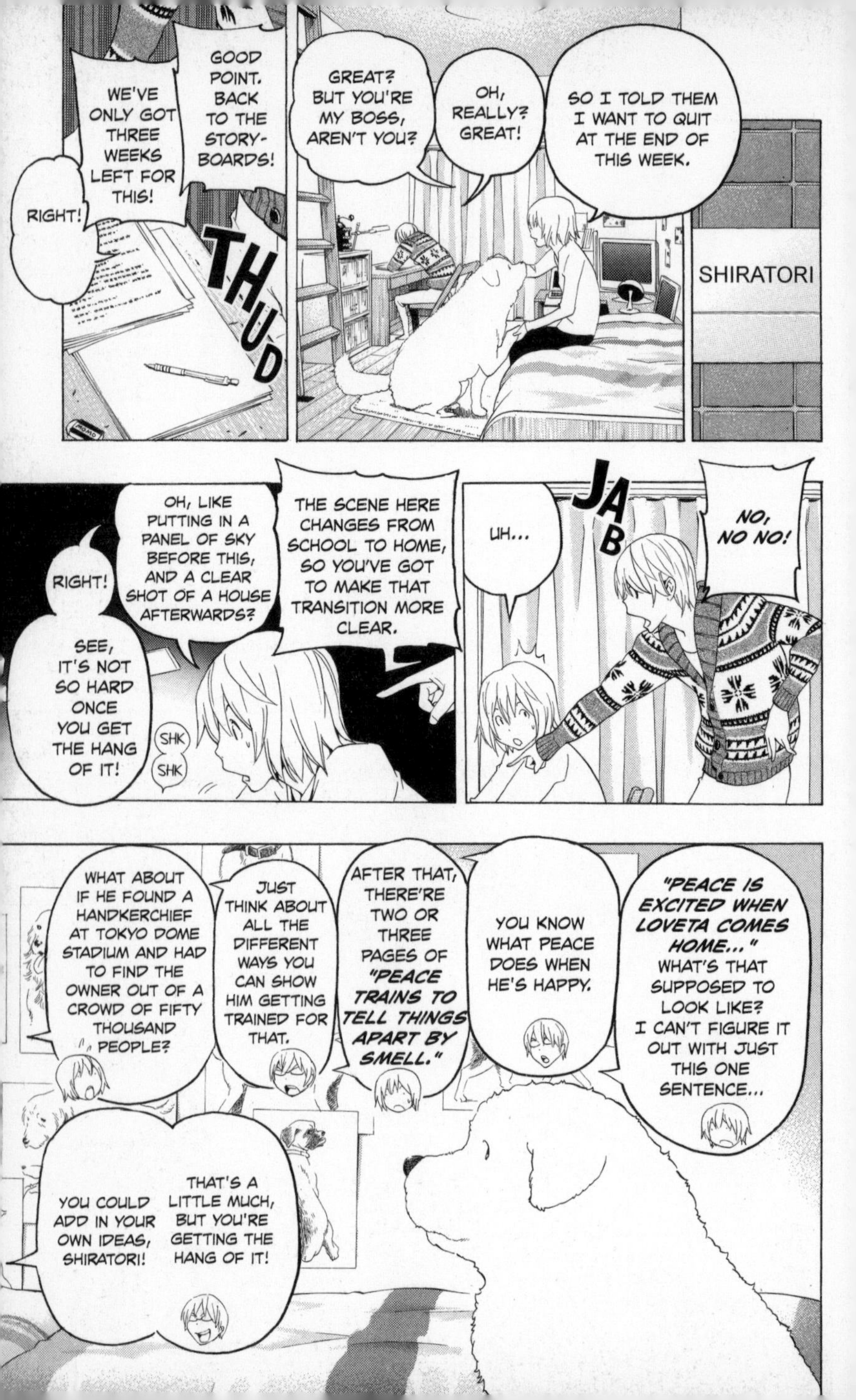
SHIRATORI
SO I TOLD THEM I WANT TO QUIT AT THE END OF THIS WEEK.
OH, REALLY? GREAT!
GREAT? BUT YOU'RE MY BOSS, AREN'T YOU?
GOOD POINT. BACK TO THE STORY-BOARDS!
THUD
WE'VE ONLY GOT THREE WEEKS LEFT FOR THIS!
RIGHT!
NO, NO NO!
JAB
UH...
THE SCENE HERE CHANGES FROM SCHOOL TO HOME, SO YOU'VE GOT TO MAKE THAT TRANSITION MORE CLEAR.
OH, LIKE PUTTING IN A PANEL OF SKY BEFORE THIS, AND A CLEAR SHOT OF A HOUSE AFTERWARDS?
RIGHT!
SEE, IT'S NOT SO HARD ONCE YOU GET THE HANG OF IT!
SHK
SHK
"PEACE IS EXCITED WHEN LOVETA COMES HOME..." WHAT'S THAT SUPPOSED TO LOOK LIKE? I CAN'T FIGURE IT OUT WITH JUST THIS ONE SENTENCE...
YOU KNOW WHAT PEACE DOES WHEN HE'S HAPPY.
AFTER THAT, THERE'RE TWO OR THREE PAGES OF "PEACE TRAINS TO TELL THINGS APART BY SMELL."
JUST THINK ABOUT ALL THE DIFFERENT WAYS YOU CAN SHOW HIM GETTING TRAINED FOR THAT.
WHAT ABOUT IF HE FOUND A HANDKERCHIEF AT TOKYO DOME STADIUM AND HAD TO FIND THE OWNER OUT OF A CROWD OF FIFTY THOUSAND PEOPLE?
THAT'S A LITTLE MUCH, BUT YOU'RE GETTING THE HANG OF IT!
YOU COULD ADD IN YOUR OWN IDEAS, SHIRATORI!

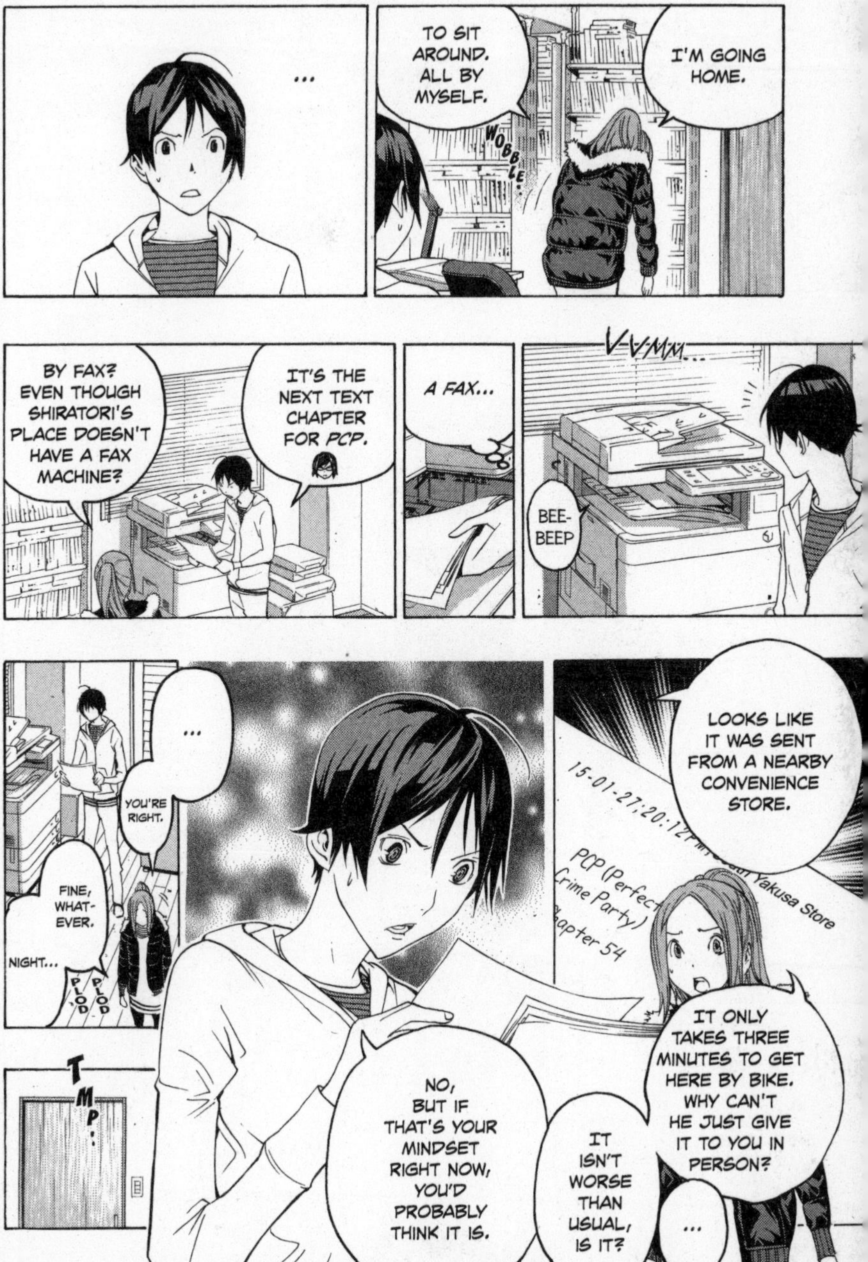
I'M GOING HOME.
TO SIT AROUND. ALL BY MYSELF.
WOBBLE
...
V-V-MM...
BEE-BEEP
A FAX...
IT'S THE NEXT TEXT CHAPTER FOR *PCP*.
BY FAX? EVEN THOUGH SHIRATORI'S PLACE DOESN'T HAVE A FAX MACHINE?
LOOKS LIKE IT WAS SENT FROM A NEARBY CONVENIENCE STORE.
15-01-27;20:12
Yakusa Store
PCP (Perfec
rime Party)
apter 54
IT ONLY TAKES THREE MINUTES TO GET HERE BY BIKE. WHY CAN'T HE JUST GIVE IT TO YOU IN PERSON?
...
IT ISN'T WORSE THAN USUAL, IS IT?
NO, BUT IF THAT'S YOUR MINDSET RIGHT NOW, YOU'D PROBABLY THINK IT IS.
...
YOU'RE RIGHT.
FINE, WHATEVER.
NIGHT...
PLOD PLOD
TMP

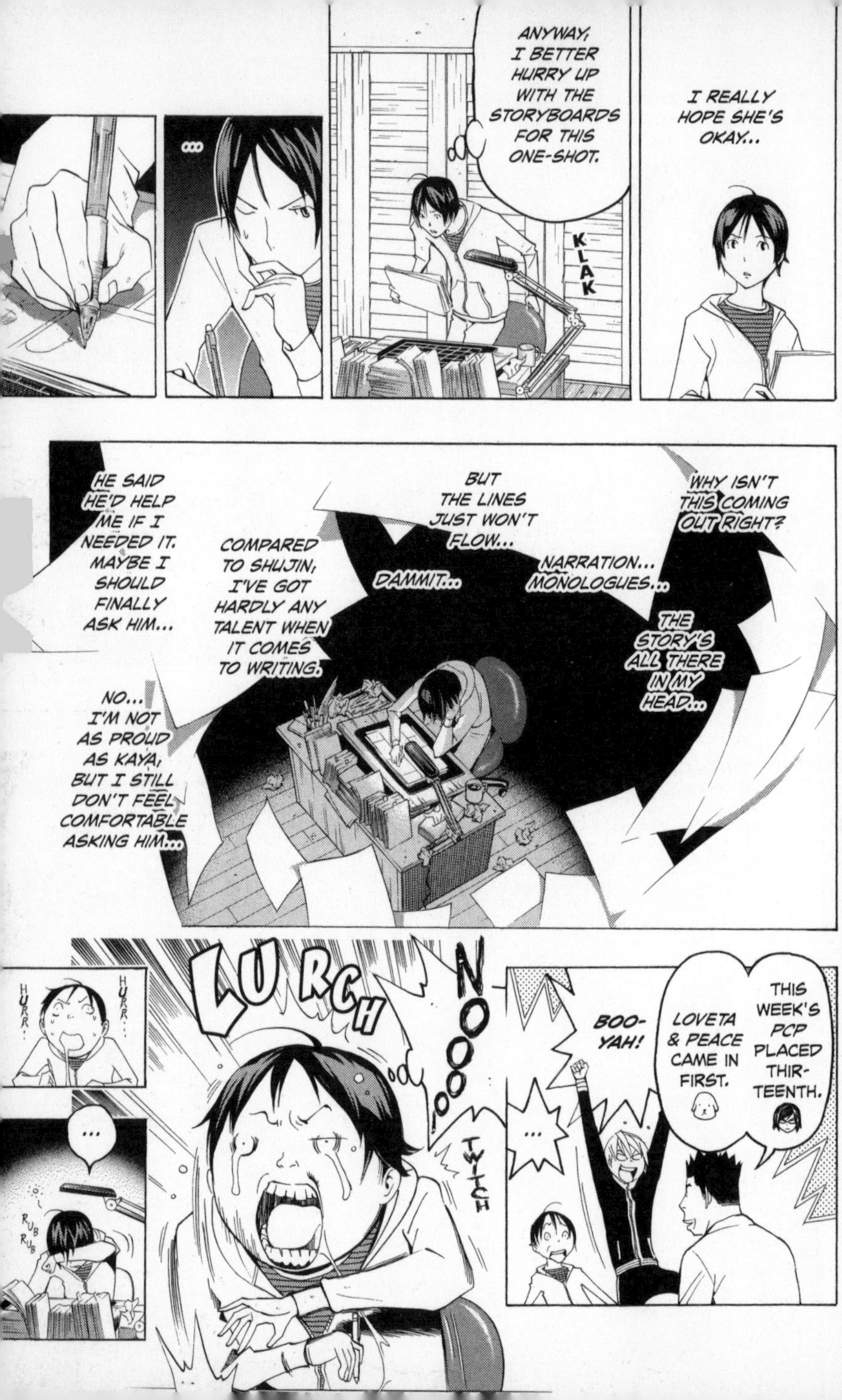
I REALLY HOPE SHE'S OKAY...
ANYWAY, I BETTER HURRY UP WITH THE STORYBOARDS FOR THIS ONE-SHOT.
KLAK
...
WHY ISN'T THIS COMING OUT RIGHT?
BUT THE LINES JUST WON'T FLOW...
NARRATION... MONOLOGUES...
THE STORY'S ALL THERE IN MY HEAD...
DAMMIT...
COMPARED TO SHUJIN, I'VE GOT HARDLY ANY TALENT WHEN IT COMES TO WRITING.
HE SAID HE'D HELP ME IF I NEEDED IT. MAYBE I SHOULD FINALLY ASK HIM...
NO... I'M NOT AS PROUD AS KAYA, BUT I STILL DON'T FEEL COMFORTABLE ASKING HIM...
THIS WEEK'S PCP PLACED THIR-TEENTH.
LOVETA & PEACE CAME IN FIRST.
BOO-YAH!
...
LURCH
NOOOO
TWITCH
HURR... HURR...
...
RUB RUB

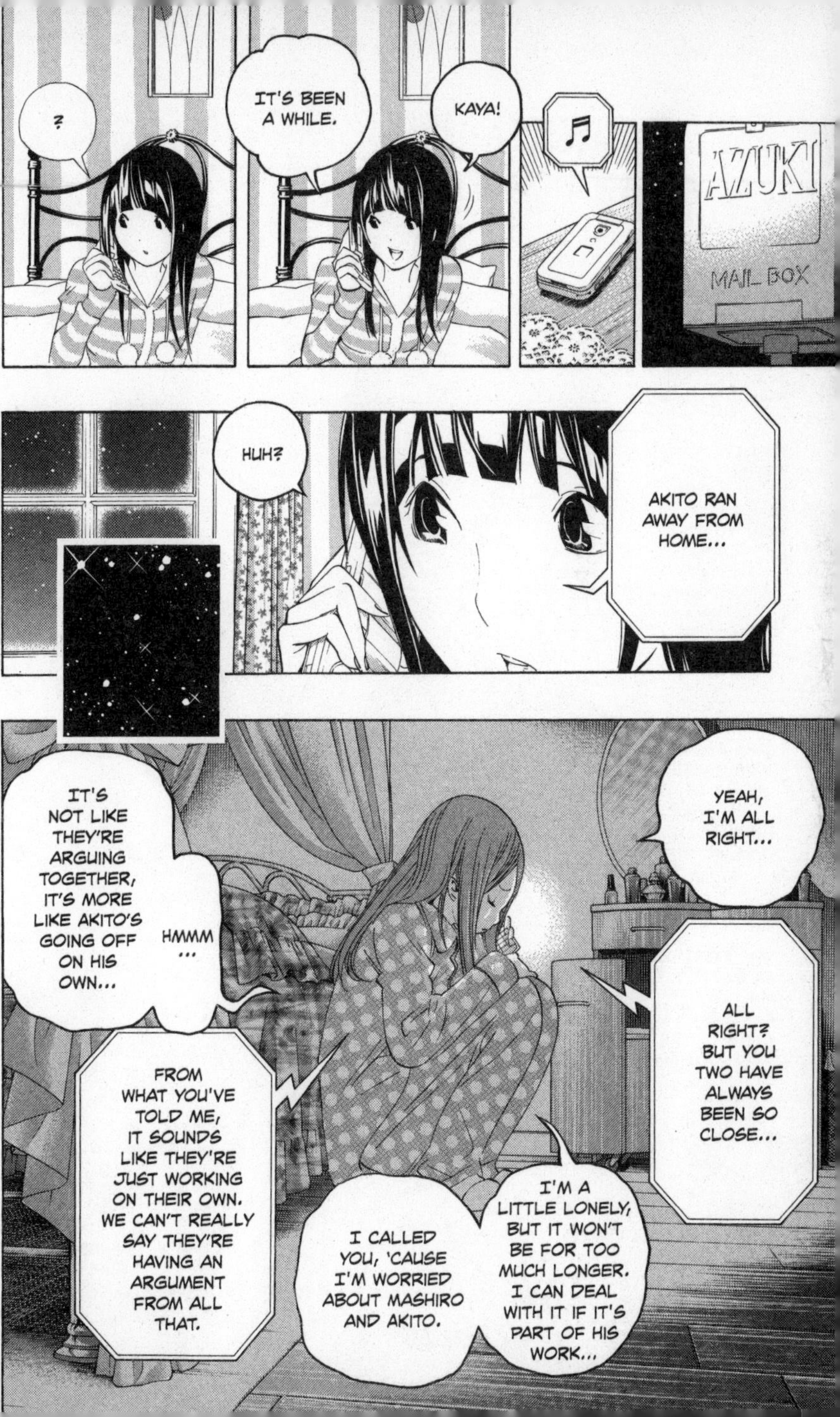
AZUKI
MAIL BOX
♫
KAYA!
IT'S BEEN A WHILE.
?
AKITO RAN AWAY FROM HOME...
HUH?
YEAH, I'M ALL RIGHT...
ALL RIGHT? BUT YOU TWO HAVE ALWAYS BEEN SO CLOSE...
I'M A LITTLE LONELY, BUT IT WON'T BE FOR TOO MUCH LONGER. I CAN DEAL WITH IT IF IT'S PART OF HIS WORK...
I CALLED YOU, 'CAUSE I'M WORRIED ABOUT MASHIRO AND AKITO.
FROM WHAT YOU'VE TOLD ME, IT SOUNDS LIKE THEY'RE JUST WORKING ON THEIR OWN. WE CAN'T REALLY SAY THEY'RE HAVING AN ARGUMENT FROM ALL THAT.
IT'S NOT LIKE THEY'RE ARGUING TOGETHER, IT'S MORE LIKE AKITO'S GOING OFF ON HIS OWN...
HMMM...

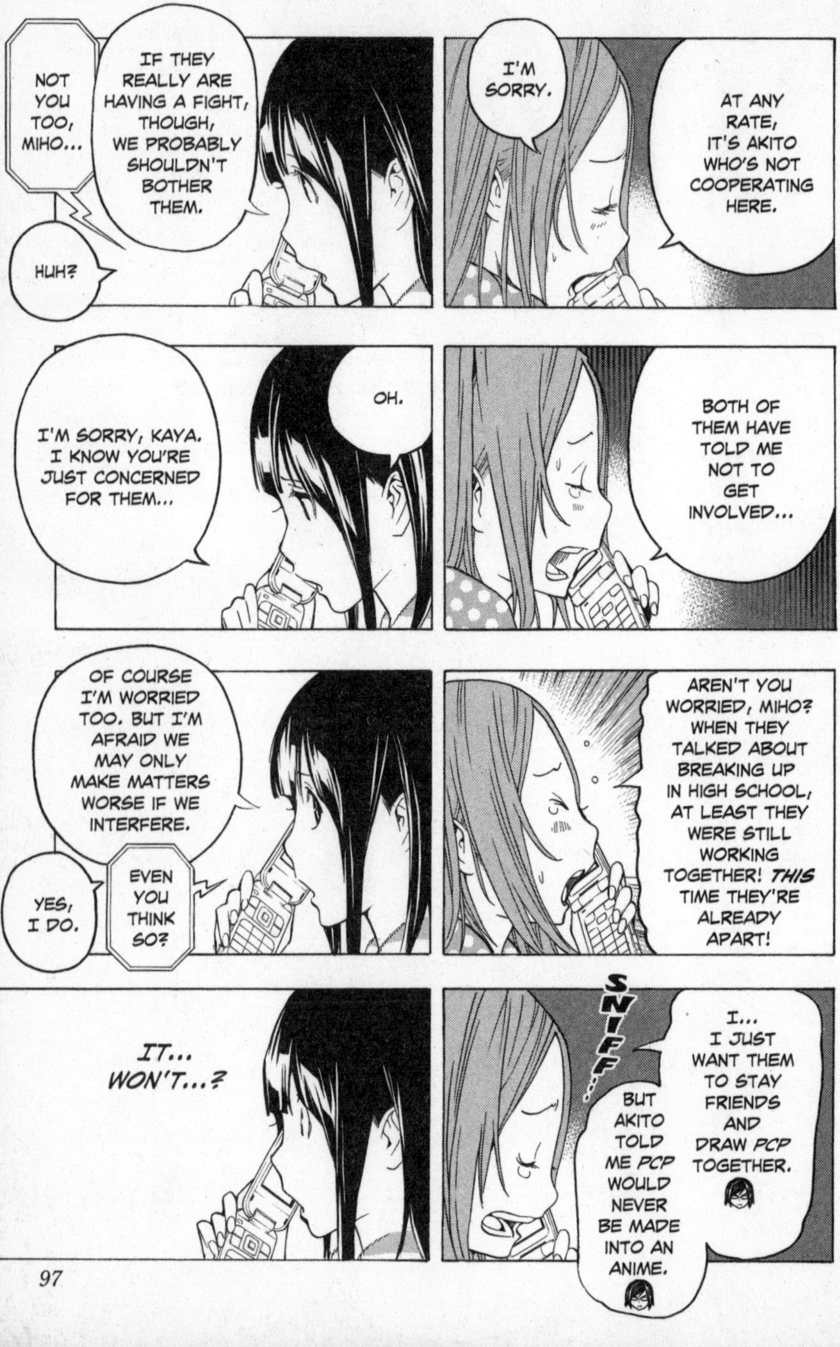
AT ANY RATE, IT'S AKITO WHO'S NOT COOPERATING HERE.
I'M SORRY.
IF THEY REALLY ARE HAVING A FIGHT, THOUGH, WE PROBABLY SHOULDN'T BOTHER THEM.
NOT YOU TOO, MIHO...
HUH?
BOTH OF THEM HAVE TOLD ME NOT TO GET INVOLVED...
OH.
I'M SORRY, KAYA. I KNOW YOU'RE JUST CONCERNED FOR THEM...
AREN'T YOU WORRIED, MIHO? WHEN THEY TALKED ABOUT BREAKING UP IN HIGH SCHOOL, AT LEAST THEY WERE STILL WORKING TOGETHER! *THIS* TIME THEY'RE ALREADY APART!
OF COURSE I'M WORRIED TOO. BUT I'M AFRAID WE MAY ONLY MAKE MATTERS WORSE IF WE INTERFERE.
EVEN YOU THINK SO?
YES, I DO.
SNIFF...
I... I JUST WANT THEM TO STAY FRIENDS AND DRAW *PCP* TOGETHER.
BUT AKITO TOLD ME *PCP* WOULD NEVER BE MADE INTO AN ANIME.
IT... WON'T...?

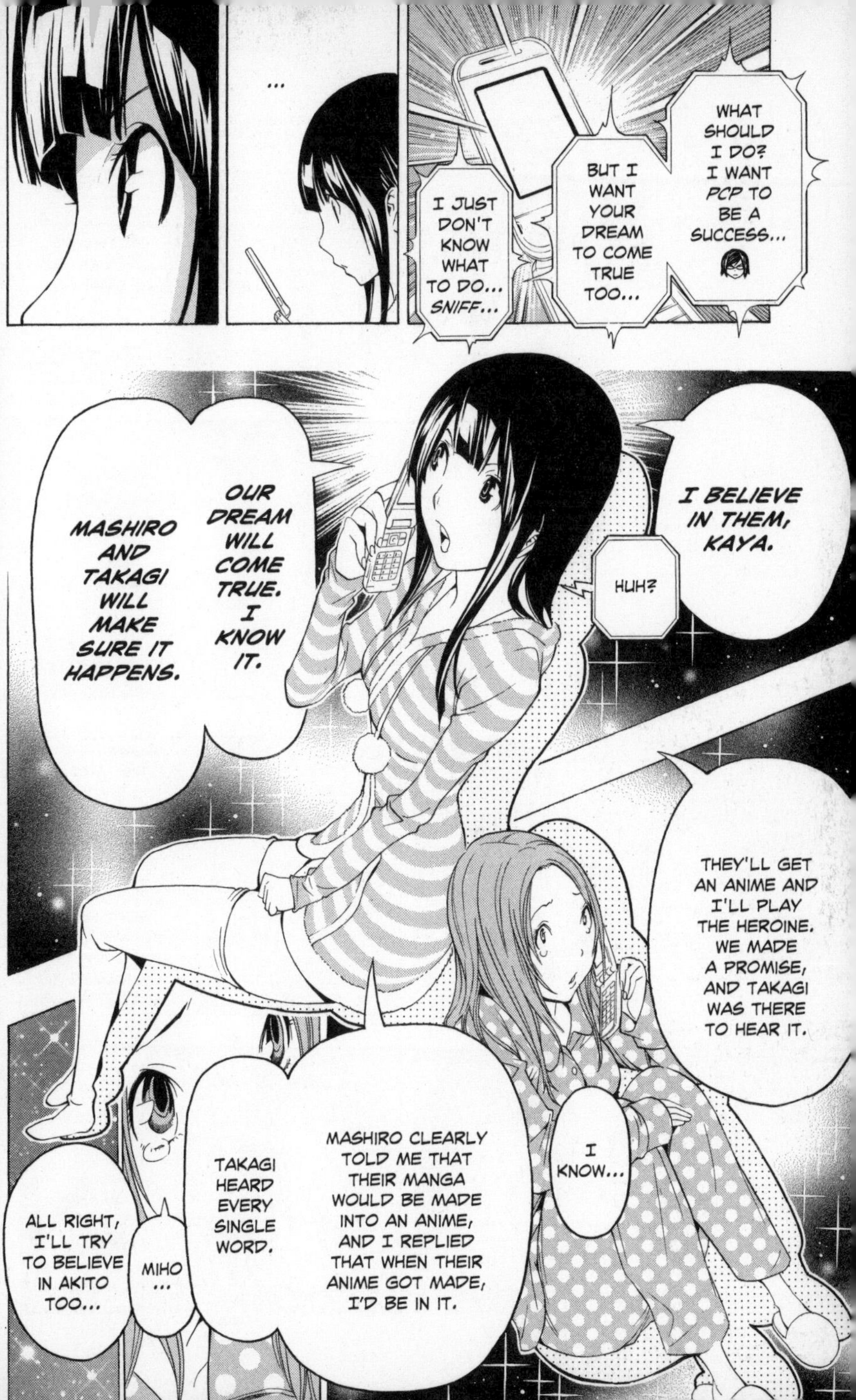
WHAT SHOULD I DO? I WANT PCP TO BE A SUCCESS...
BUT I WANT YOUR DREAM TO COME TRUE TOO...
I JUST DON'T KNOW WHAT TO DO... SNIFF...
...
I BELIEVE IN THEM, KAYA.
HUH?
OUR DREAM WILL COME TRUE. I KNOW IT.
MASHIRO AND TAKAGI WILL MAKE SURE IT HAPPENS.
THEY'LL GET AN ANIME AND I'LL PLAY THE HEROINE. WE MADE A PROMISE, AND TAKAGI WAS THERE TO HEAR IT.
I KNOW...
MASHIRO CLEARLY TOLD ME THAT THEIR MANGA WOULD BE MADE INTO AN ANIME, AND I REPLIED THAT WHEN THEIR ANIME GOT MADE, I'D BE IN IT.
TAKAGI HEARD EVERY SINGLE WORD.
MIHO...
ALL RIGHT, I'LL TRY TO BELIEVE IN AKITO TOO...

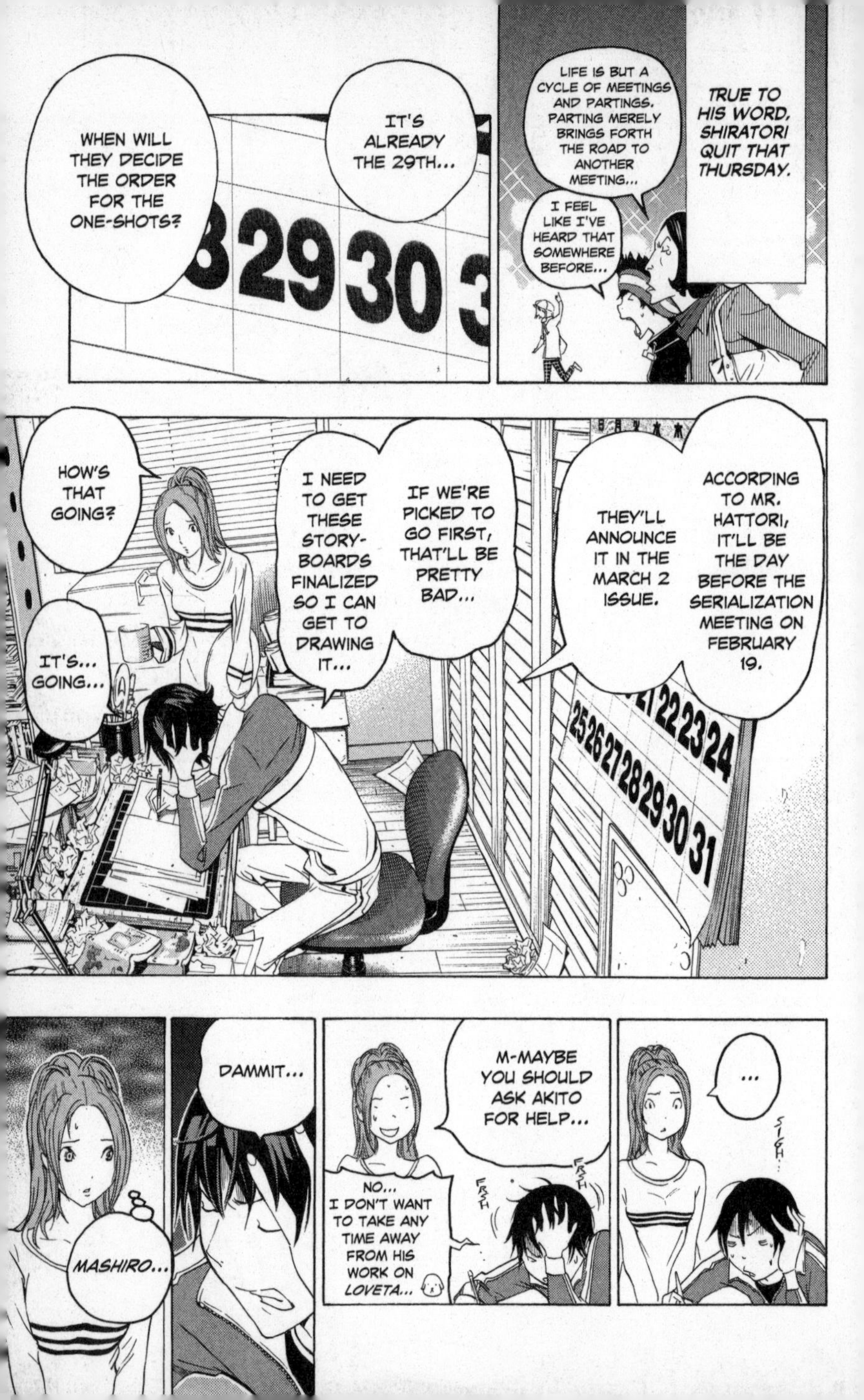
TRUE TO HIS WORD, SHIRATORI QUIT THAT THURSDAY.
LIFE IS BUT A CYCLE OF MEETINGS AND PARTINGS. PARTING MERELY BRINGS FORTH THE ROAD TO ANOTHER MEETING...
I FEEL LIKE I'VE HEARD THAT SOMEWHERE BEFORE...
IT'S ALREADY THE 29TH...
WHEN WILL THEY DECIDE THE ORDER FOR THE ONE-SHOTS?
ACCORDING TO MR. HATTORI, IT'LL BE THE DAY BEFORE THE SERIALIZATION MEETING ON FEBRUARY 19.
THEY'LL ANNOUNCE IT IN THE MARCH 2 ISSUE.
IF WE'RE PICKED TO GO FIRST, THAT'LL BE PRETTY BAD...
I NEED TO GET THESE STORY-BOARDS FINALIZED SO I CAN GET TO DRAWING IT...
HOW'S THAT GOING?
IT'S... GOING...
...
SIGH...
M-MAYBE YOU SHOULD ASK AKITO FOR HELP...
FRSH
FRSH
NO... I DON'T WANT TO TAKE ANY TIME AWAY FROM HIS WORK ON *LOVETA*...
DAMMIT...
MASHIRO...

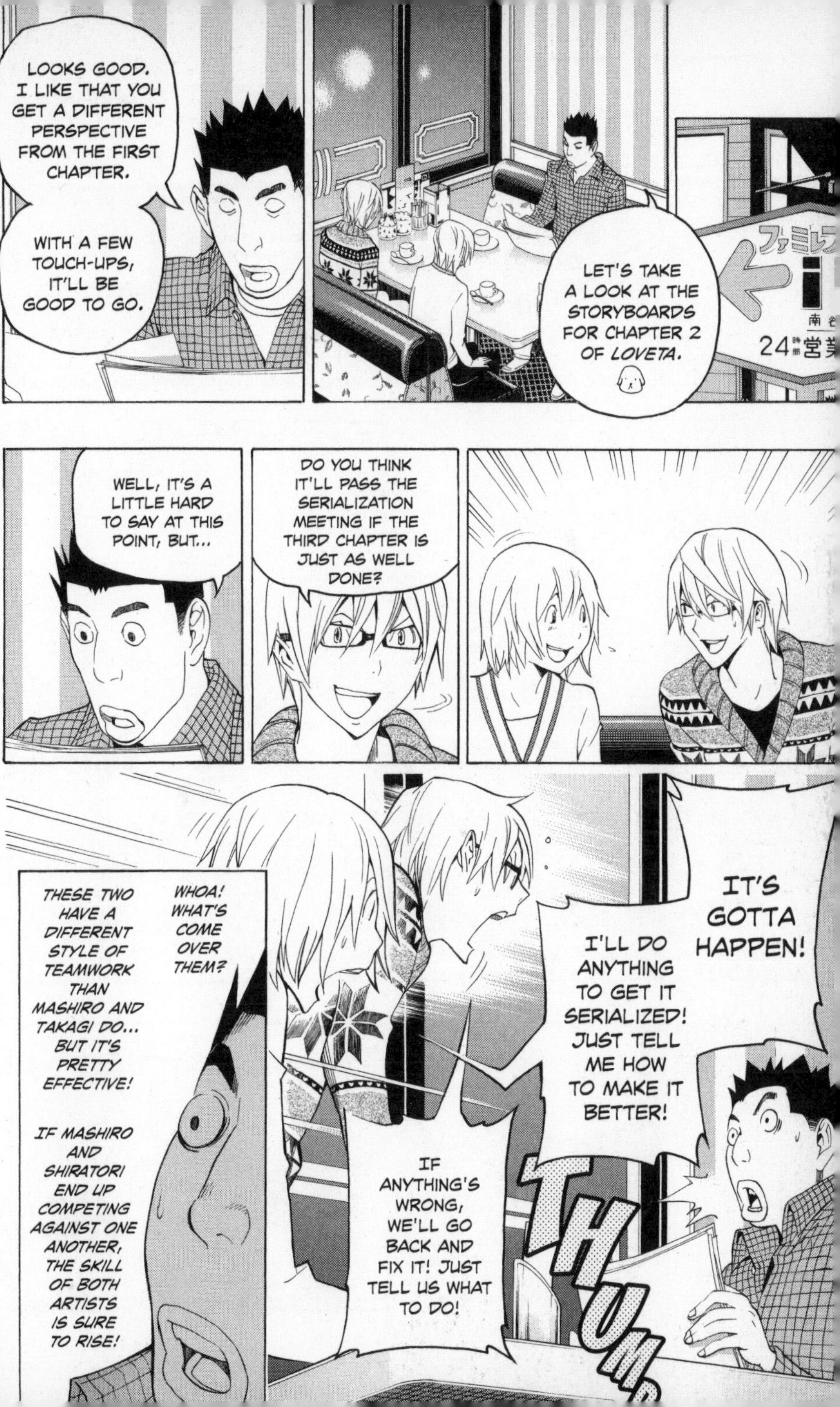
LET'S TAKE A LOOK AT THE STORYBOARDS FOR CHAPTER 2 OF *LOVETA*.
LOOKS GOOD. I LIKE THAT YOU GET A DIFFERENT PERSPECTIVE FROM THE FIRST CHAPTER.
WITH A FEW TOUCH-UPS, IT'LL BE GOOD TO GO.
DO YOU THINK IT'LL PASS THE SERIALIZATION MEETING IF THE THIRD CHAPTER IS JUST AS WELL DONE?
WELL, IT'S A LITTLE HARD TO SAY AT THIS POINT, BUT...
IT'S GOTTA HAPPEN!
I'LL DO ANYTHING TO GET IT SERIALIZED! JUST TELL ME HOW TO MAKE IT BETTER!
IF ANYTHING'S WRONG, WE'LL GO BACK AND FIX IT! JUST TELL US WHAT TO DO!
THUM
WHOA! WHAT'S COME OVER THEM?
THESE TWO HAVE A DIFFERENT STYLE OF TEAMWORK THAN MASHIRO AND TAKAGI DO... BUT IT'S PRETTY EFFECTIVE!
IF MASHIRO AND SHIRATORI END UP COMPETING AGAINST ONE ANOTHER, THE SKILL OF BOTH ARTISTS IS SURE TO RISE!

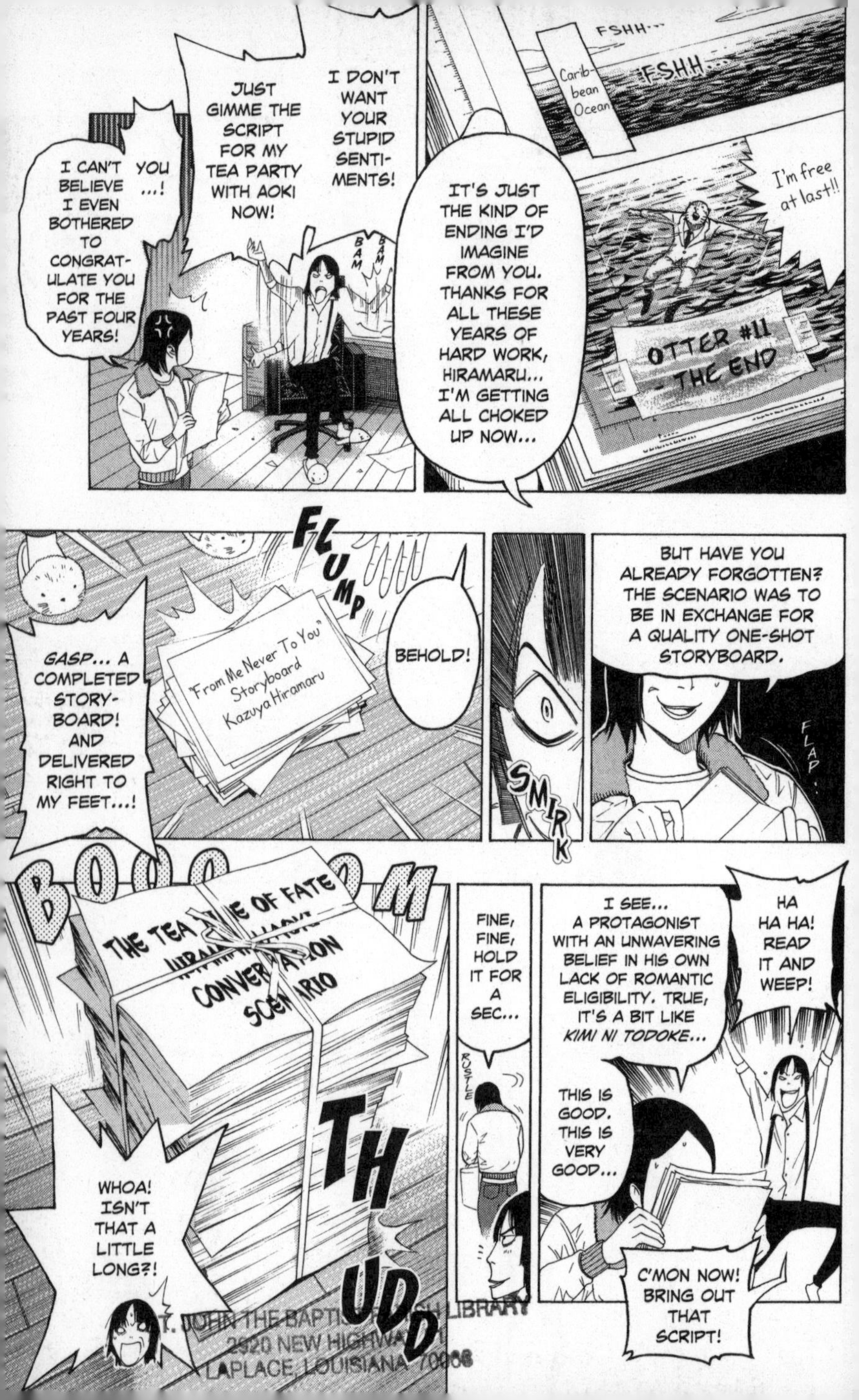
FSHH...
FSHH...
Carib-bean Ocean
I'm free at last!!
OTTER #11 - THE END
IT'S JUST THE KIND OF ENDING I'D IMAGINE FROM YOU. THANKS FOR ALL THESE YEARS OF HARD WORK, HIRAMARU... I'M GETTING ALL CHOKED UP NOW...
I DON'T WANT YOUR STUPID SENTI-MENTS!
JUST GIMME THE SCRIPT FOR MY TEA PARTY WITH AOKI NOW!
BAM BAM
YOU ...!
I CAN'T BELIEVE I EVEN BOTHERED TO CONGRAT-ULATE YOU FOR THE PAST FOUR YEARS!
BUT HAVE YOU ALREADY FORGOTTEN? THE SCENARIO WAS TO BE IN EXCHANGE FOR A QUALITY ONE-SHOT STORYBOARD.
FLAP
SMIRK
BEHOLD!
FLUMP
"From Me Never To You" Storyboard Kazuya Hiramaru
GASP... A COMPLETED STORY-BOARD! AND DELIVERED RIGHT TO MY FEET...!
HA HA HA! READ IT AND WEEP!
I SEE... A PROTAGONIST WITH AN UNWAVERING BELIEF IN HIS OWN LACK OF ROMANTIC ELIGIBILITY. TRUE, IT'S A BIT LIKE *KIMI NI TODOKE*...
THIS IS GOOD. THIS IS VERY GOOD...
C'MON NOW! BRING OUT THAT SCRIPT!
FINE, FINE, HOLD IT FOR A SEC...
RUSTLE
BOOOOOM
CONVERSATION SCENARIO
THUDD
WHOA! ISN'T THAT A LITTLE LONG?!

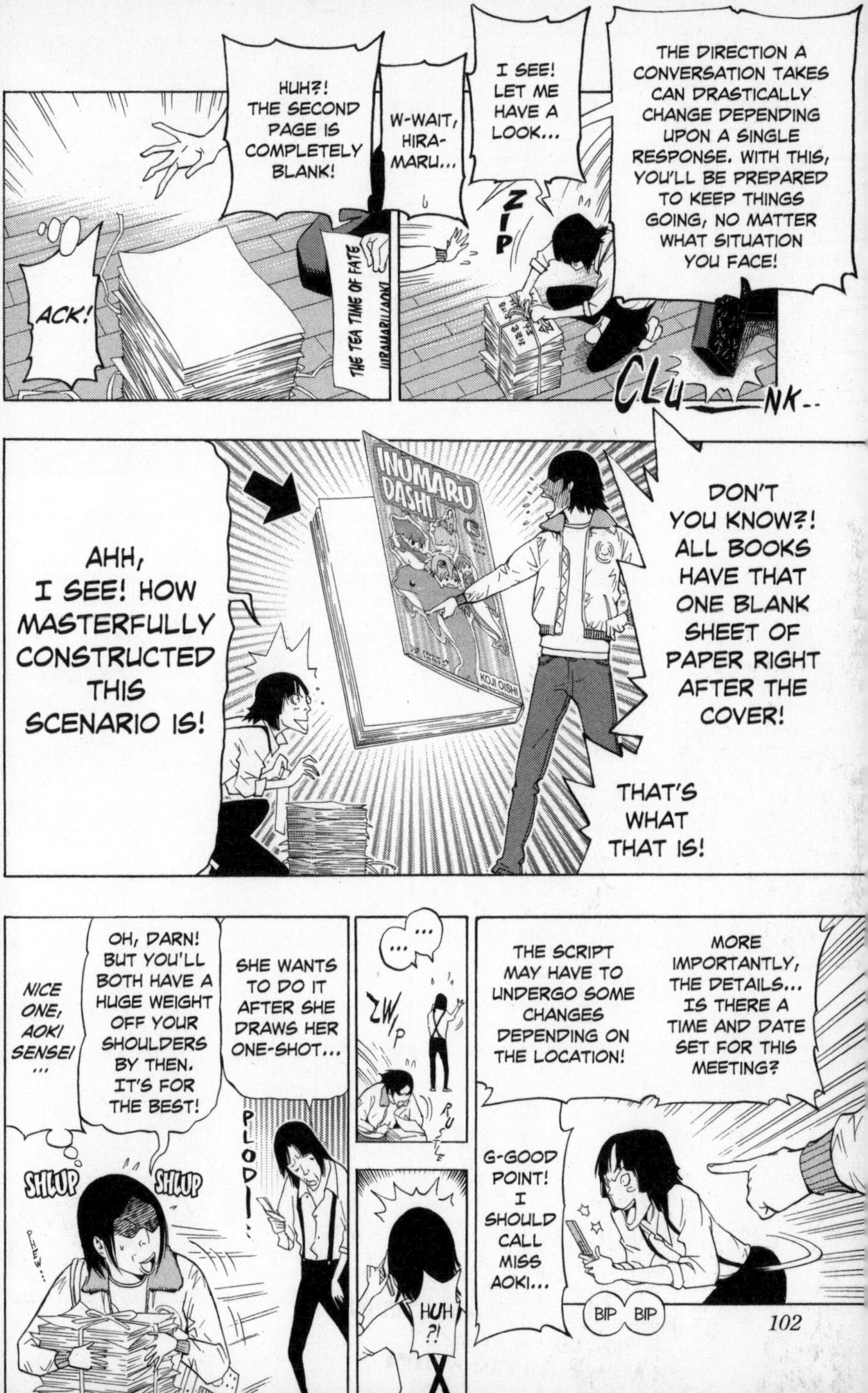
THE DIRECTION A CONVERSATION TAKES CAN DRASTICALLY CHANGE DEPENDING UPON A SINGLE RESPONSE. WITH THIS, YOU'LL BE PREPARED TO KEEP THINGS GOING, NO MATTER WHAT SITUATION YOU FACE!
I SEE! LET ME HAVE A LOOK...
ZIP
CLU---NK..
W-WAIT, HIRA-MARU...
HUH?! THE SECOND PAGE IS COMPLETELY BLANK!
THE TEA TIME OF FATE
HIRAMARU AOKI
ACK!
DON'T YOU KNOW?! ALL BOOKS HAVE THAT ONE BLANK SHEET OF PAPER RIGHT AFTER THE COVER!
THAT'S WHAT THAT IS!
INUMARU DASHI
KOJI OISHI
AHH, I SEE! HOW MASTERFULLY CONSTRUCTED THIS SCENARIO IS!
MORE IMPORTANTLY, THE DETAILS... IS THERE A TIME AND DATE SET FOR THIS MEETING?
THE SCRIPT MAY HAVE TO UNDERGO SOME CHANGES DEPENDING ON THE LOCATION!
G-GOOD POINT! I SHOULD CALL MISS AOKI...
BIP
BIP
... ...
ZWIP
RUSTLE
HUH?!
SHE WANTS TO DO IT AFTER SHE DRAWS HER ONE-SHOT...
PLOD
OH, DARN! BUT YOU'LL BOTH HAVE A HUGE WEIGHT OFF YOUR SHOULDERS BY THEN. IT'S FOR THE BEST!
NICE ONE, AOKI SENSEI...
SHLUP
SHLUP
PHEW...

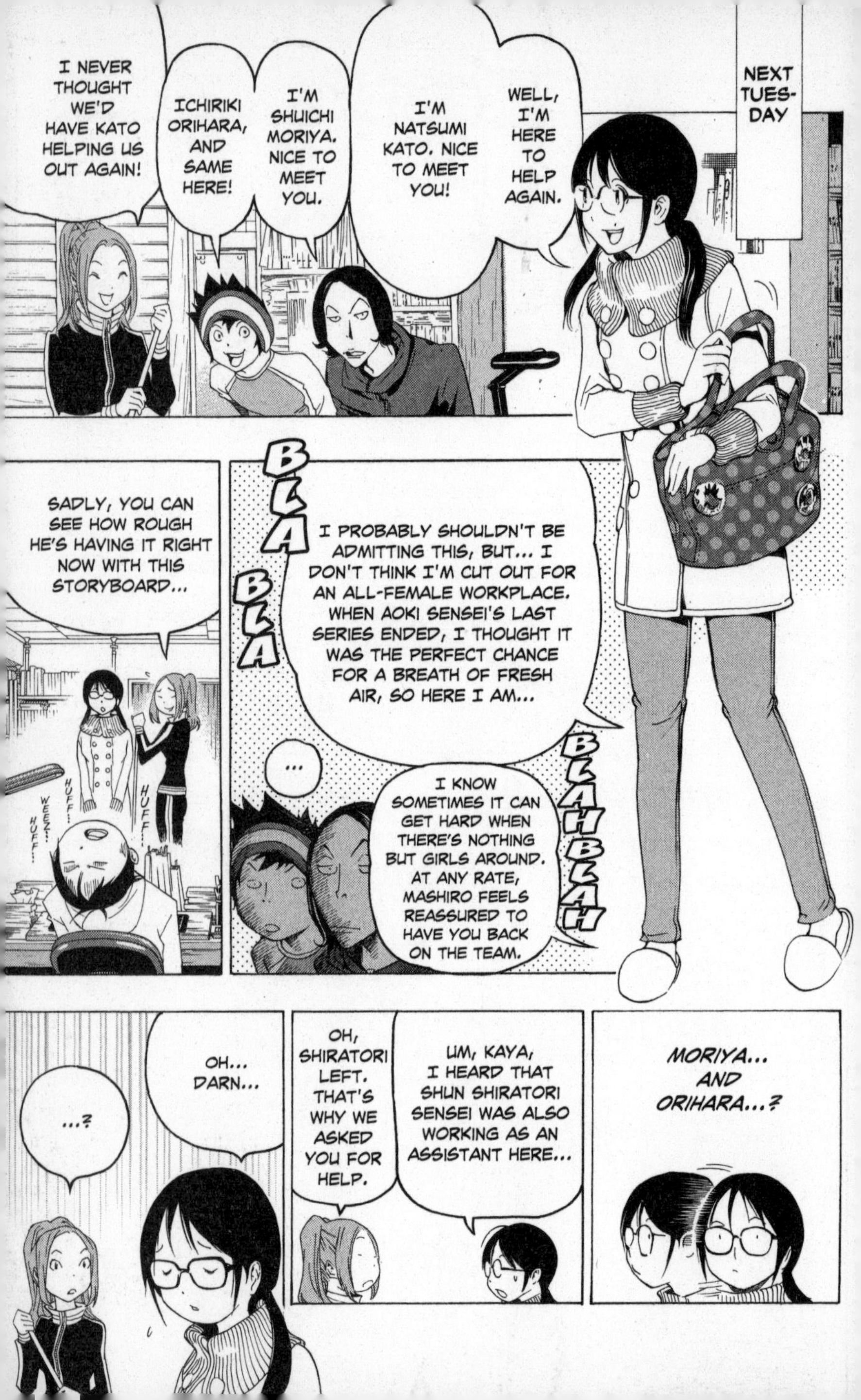
NEXT TUES-DAY
WELL, I'M HERE TO HELP AGAIN.
I'M NATSUMI KATO. NICE TO MEET YOU!
I'M SHUICHI MORIYA. NICE TO MEET YOU.
ICHIRIKI ORIHARA, AND SAME HERE!
I NEVER THOUGHT WE'D HAVE KATO HELPING US OUT AGAIN!
BLA BLA
I PROBABLY SHOULDN'T BE ADMITTING THIS, BUT... I DON'T THINK I'M CUT OUT FOR AN ALL-FEMALE WORKPLACE. WHEN AOKI SENSEI'S LAST SERIES ENDED, I THOUGHT IT WAS THE PERFECT CHANCE FOR A BREATH OF FRESH AIR, SO HERE I AM...
BLAH BLAH
...
I KNOW SOMETIMES IT CAN GET HARD WHEN THERE'S NOTHING BUT GIRLS AROUND. AT ANY RATE, MASHIRO FEELS REASSURED TO HAVE YOU BACK ON THE TEAM.
SADLY, YOU CAN SEE HOW ROUGH HE'S HAVING IT RIGHT NOW WITH THIS STORYBOARD...
HUFF...
HUFF...
WEEZ...
HUFF!...
MORIYA... AND ORIHARA...?
UM, KAYA, I HEARD THAT SHUN SHIRATORI SENSEI WAS ALSO WORKING AS AN ASSISTANT HERE...
OH, SHIRATORI LEFT. THAT'S WHY WE ASKED YOU FOR HELP.
OH... DARN...
...?

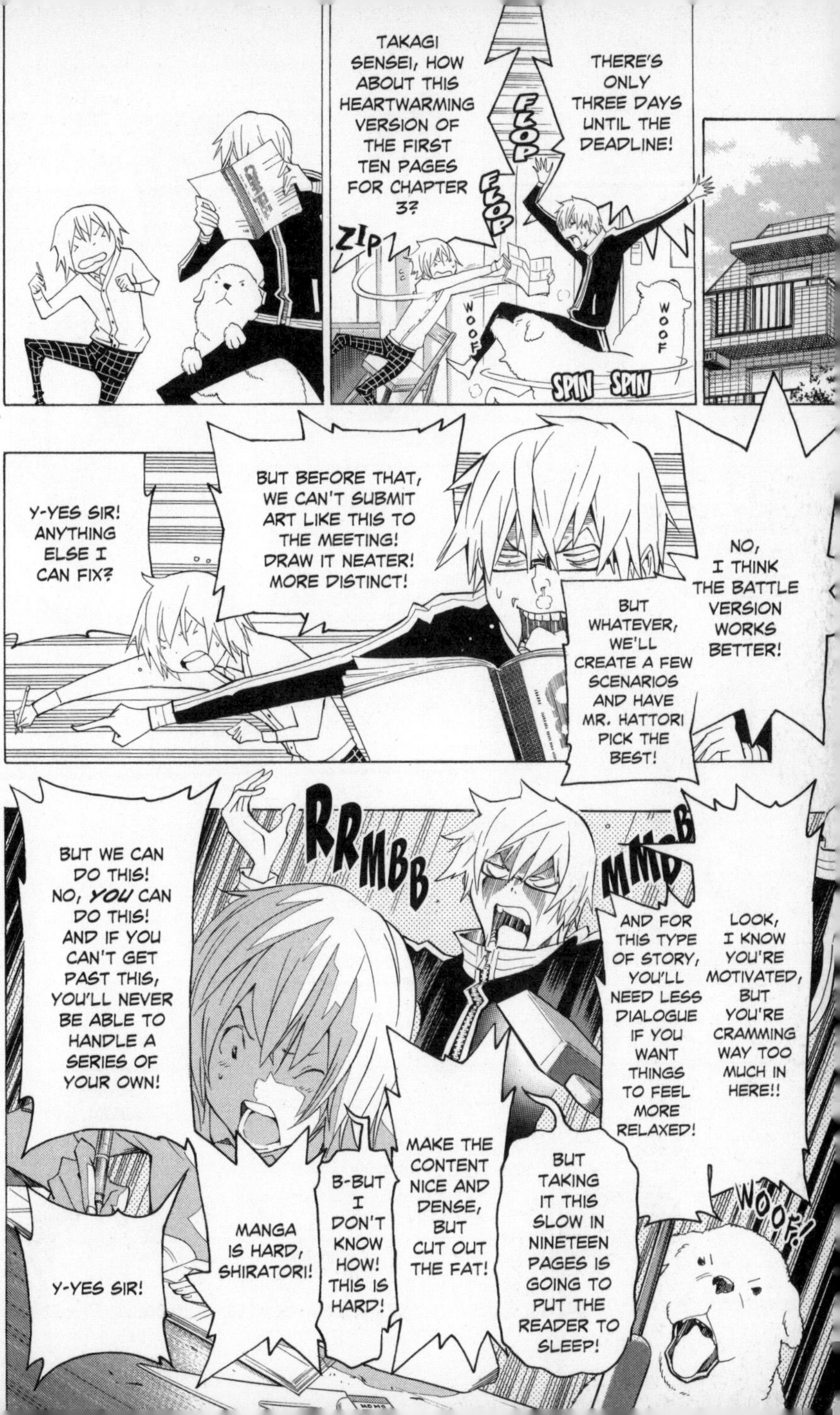
THERE'S ONLY THREE DAYS UNTIL THE DEADLINE!
TAKAGI SENSEI, HOW ABOUT THIS HEARTWARMING VERSION OF THE FIRST TEN PAGES FOR CHAPTER 3?
FLOP
FLOP
ZIP
WOOF
WOOF
SPIN SPIN
NO, I THINK THE BATTLE VERSION WORKS BETTER!
BUT WHATEVER, WE'LL CREATE A FEW SCENARIOS AND HAVE MR. HATTORI PICK THE BEST!
BUT BEFORE THAT, WE CAN'T SUBMIT ART LIKE THIS TO THE MEETING! DRAW IT NEATER! MORE DISTINCT!
Y-YES SIR! ANYTHING ELSE I CAN FIX?
RRMBB
LOOK, I KNOW YOU'RE MOTIVATED, BUT YOU'RE CRAMMING WAY TOO MUCH IN HERE!!
AND FOR THIS TYPE OF STORY, YOU'LL NEED LESS DIALOGUE IF YOU WANT THINGS TO FEEL MORE RELAXED!
BUT WE CAN DO THIS! NO, *YOU* CAN DO THIS! AND IF YOU CAN'T GET PAST THIS, YOU'LL NEVER BE ABLE TO HANDLE A SERIES OF YOUR OWN!
WOOF!
BUT TAKING IT THIS SLOW IN NINETEEN PAGES IS GOING TO PUT THE READER TO SLEEP!
MAKE THE CONTENT NICE AND DENSE, BUT CUT OUT THE FAT!
B-BUT I DON'T KNOW HOW! THIS IS HARD!
MANGA IS HARD, SHIRATORI!
Y-YES SIR!

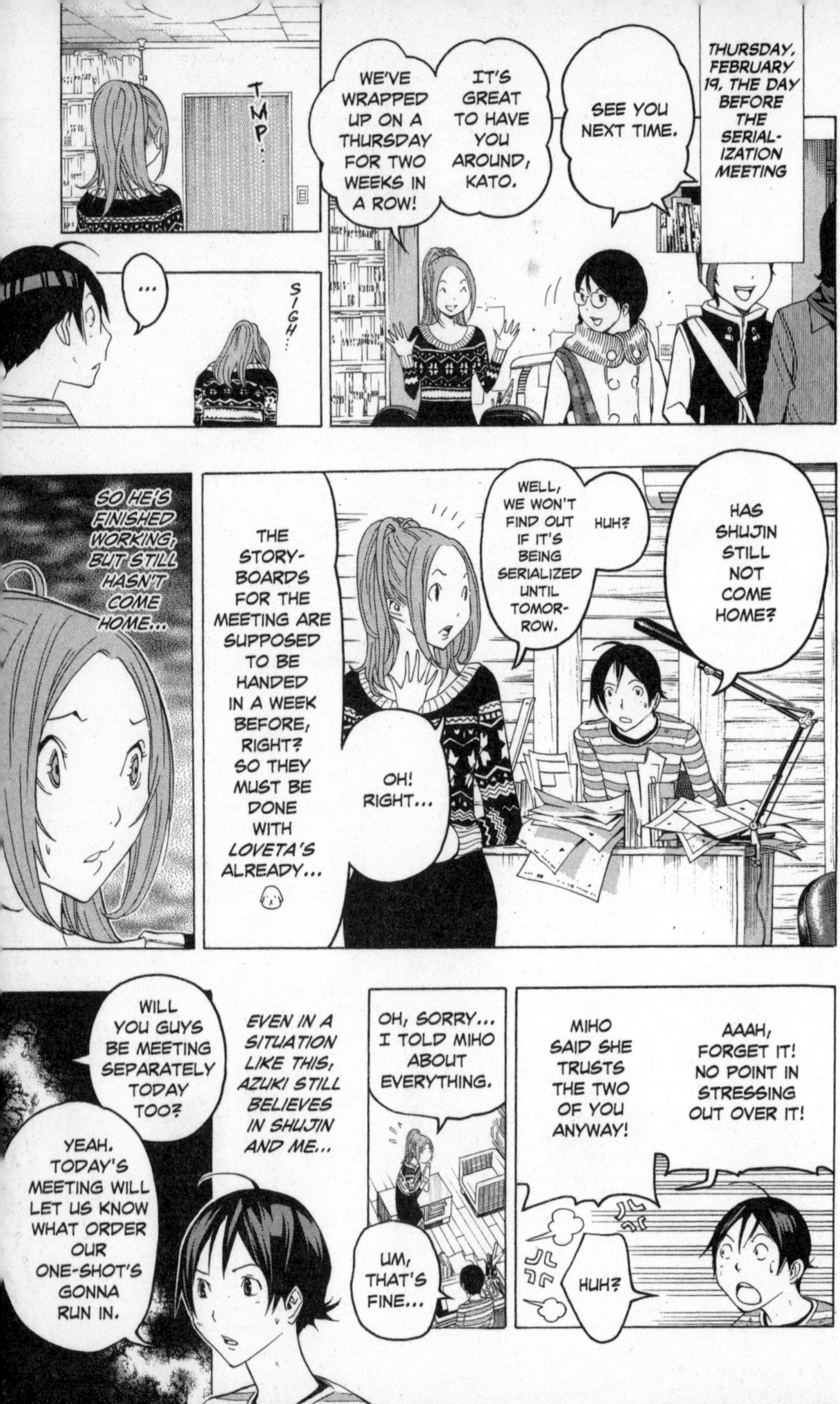
THURSDAY, FEBRUARY 19, THE DAY BEFORE THE SERIALIZATION MEETING
SEE YOU NEXT TIME.
IT'S GREAT TO HAVE YOU AROUND, KATO.
WE'VE WRAPPED UP ON A THURSDAY FOR TWO WEEKS IN A ROW!
TMP...
SIGH...
...
HAS SHUJIN STILL NOT COME HOME?
HUH?
WELL, WE WON'T FIND OUT IF IT'S BEING SERIALIZED UNTIL TOMORROW.
THE STORYBOARDS FOR THE MEETING ARE SUPPOSED TO BE HANDED IN A WEEK BEFORE, RIGHT? SO THEY MUST BE DONE WITH *LOVETA'S* ALREADY...
OH! RIGHT...
SO HE'S FINISHED WORKING, BUT STILL HASN'T COME HOME...
AAAH, FORGET IT! NO POINT IN STRESSING OUT OVER IT!
MIHO SAID SHE TRUSTS THE TWO OF YOU ANYWAY!
HUH?
OH, SORRY... I TOLD MIHO ABOUT EVERYTHING.
UM, THAT'S FINE...
EVEN IN A SITUATION LIKE THIS, AZUKI STILL BELIEVES IN SHUJIN AND ME...
WILL YOU GUYS BE MEETING SEPARATELY TODAY TOO?
YEAH. TODAY'S MEETING WILL LET US KNOW WHAT ORDER OUR ONE-SHOT'S GONNA RUN IN.

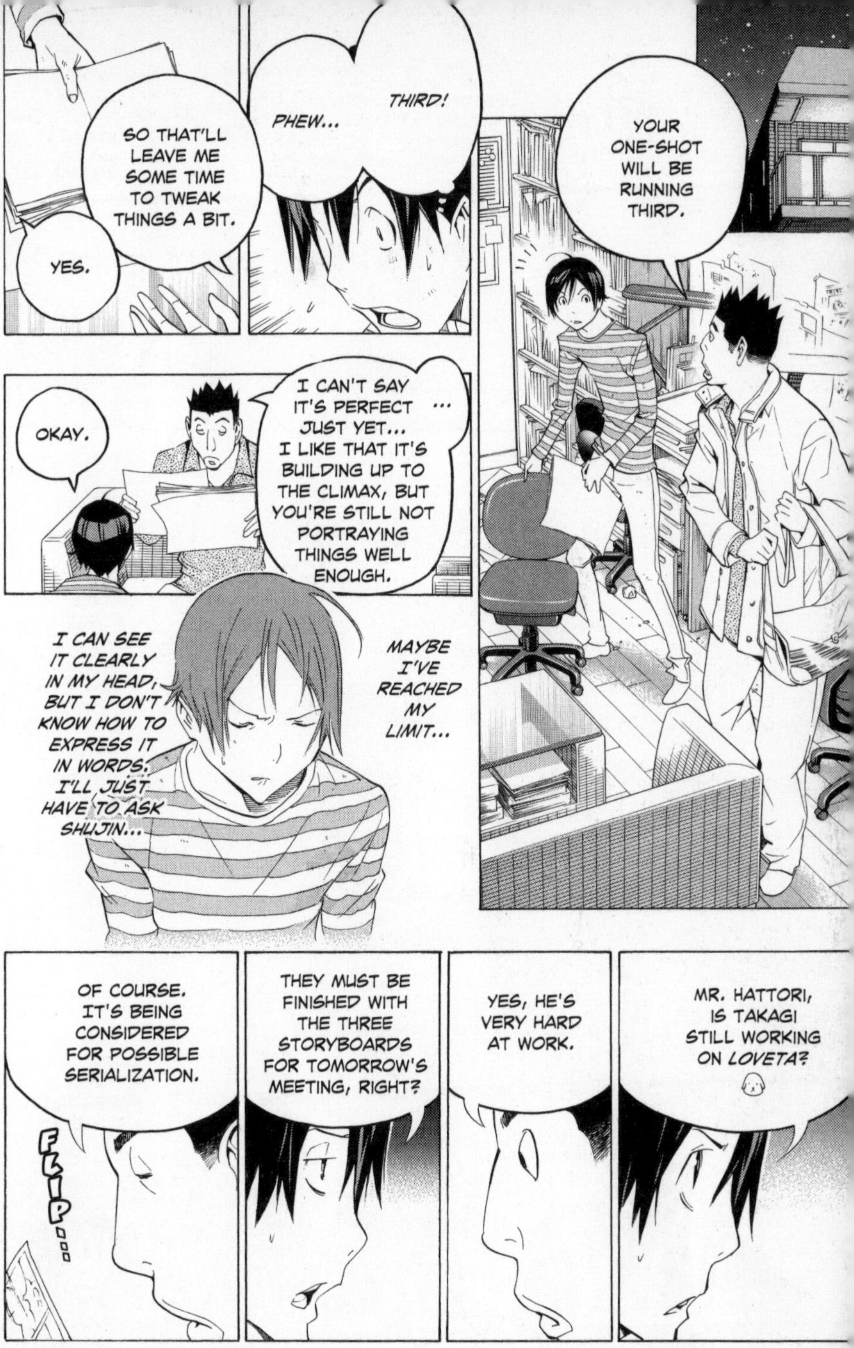
YOUR ONE-SHOT WILL BE RUNNING THIRD.
THIRD!
PHEW...
SO THAT'LL LEAVE ME SOME TIME TO TWEAK THINGS A BIT.
YES.
...
I CAN'T SAY IT'S PERFECT JUST YET... I LIKE THAT IT'S BUILDING UP TO THE CLIMAX, BUT YOU'RE STILL NOT PORTRAYING THINGS WELL ENOUGH.
OKAY.
MAYBE I'VE REACHED MY LIMIT...
I CAN SEE IT CLEARLY IN MY HEAD, BUT I DON'T KNOW HOW TO EXPRESS IT IN WORDS. I'LL JUST HAVE TO ASK SHUJIN...
MR. HATTORI, IS TAKAGI STILL WORKING ON *LOVETA*?
YES, HE'S VERY HARD AT WORK.
THEY MUST BE FINISHED WITH THE THREE STORYBOARDS FOR TOMORROW'S MEETING, RIGHT?
OF COURSE. IT'S BEING CONSIDERED FOR POSSIBLE SERIALIZATION.
FLIP...

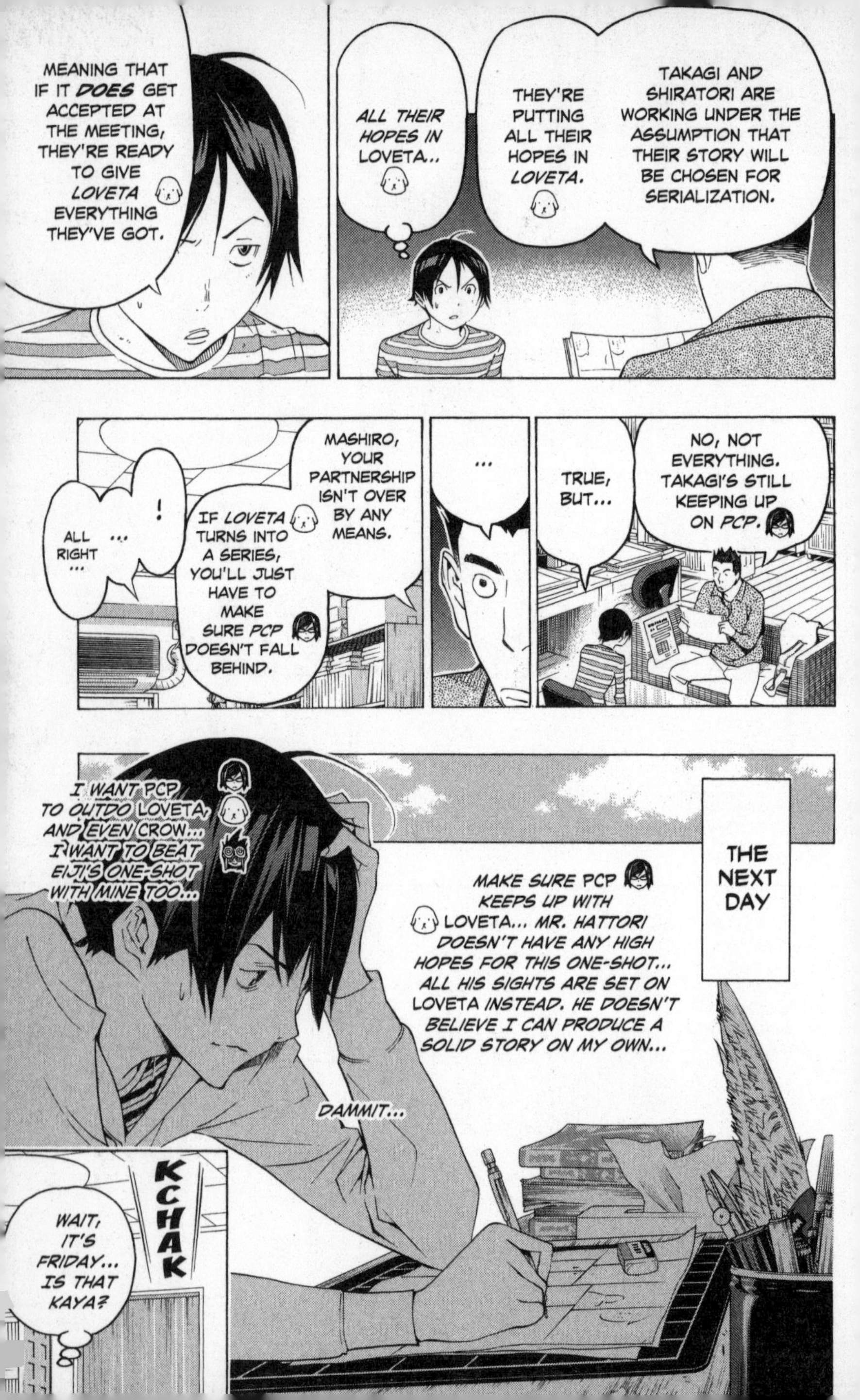
TAKAGI AND SHIRATORI ARE WORKING UNDER THE ASSUMPTION THAT THEIR STORY WILL BE CHOSEN FOR SERIALIZATION.
THEY'RE PUTTING ALL THEIR HOPES IN LOVETA.
ALL THEIR HOPES IN LOVETA...
MEANING THAT IF IT DOES GET ACCEPTED AT THE MEETING, THEY'RE READY TO GIVE LOVETA EVERYTHING THEY'VE GOT.
NO, NOT EVERYTHING. TAKAGI'S STILL KEEPING UP ON PCP.
TRUE, BUT...
...
MASHIRO, YOUR PARTNERSHIP ISN'T OVER BY ANY MEANS.
IF LOVETA TURNS INTO A SERIES, YOU'LL JUST HAVE TO MAKE SURE PCP DOESN'T FALL BEHIND.
!
...
ALL RIGHT ...
THE NEXT DAY
MAKE SURE PCP KEEPS UP WITH LOVETA... MR. HATTORI DOESN'T HAVE ANY HIGH HOPES FOR THIS ONE-SHOT... ALL HIS SIGHTS ARE SET ON LOVETA INSTEAD. HE DOESN'T BELIEVE I CAN PRODUCE A SOLID STORY ON MY OWN...
I WANT PCP TO OUTDO LOVETA, AND EVEN CROW... I WANT TO BEAT EIJI'S ONE-SHOT WITH MINE TOO...
DAMMIT...
KCHAK
WAIT, IT'S FRIDAY... IS THAT KAYA?

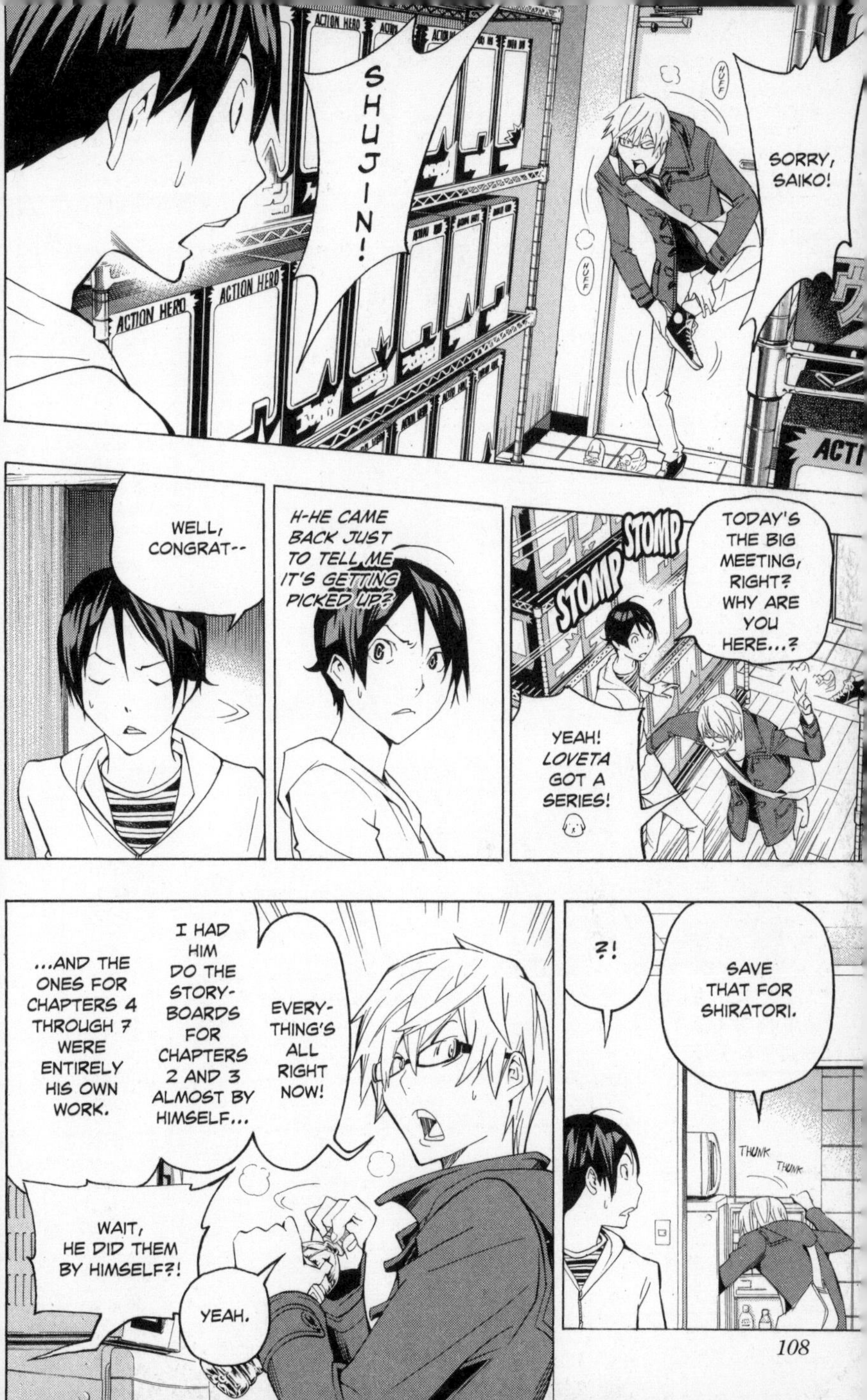
HUFF
HUFF
SORRY, SAIKO!
SHUJIN!
STOMP STOMP
TODAY'S THE BIG MEETING, RIGHT? WHY ARE YOU HERE...?
YEAH! LOVETA GOT A SERIES!
H-HE CAME BACK JUST TO TELL ME IT'S GETTING PICKED UP?
WELL, CONGRAT--
?!
SAVE THAT FOR SHIRATORI.
THUNK THUNK
EVERYTHING'S ALL RIGHT NOW!
I HAD HIM DO THE STORYBOARDS FOR CHAPTERS 2 AND 3 ALMOST BY HIMSELF...
...AND THE ONES FOR CHAPTERS 4 THROUGH 7 WERE ENTIRELY HIS OWN WORK.
WAIT, HE DID THEM BY HIMSELF?!
YEAH.

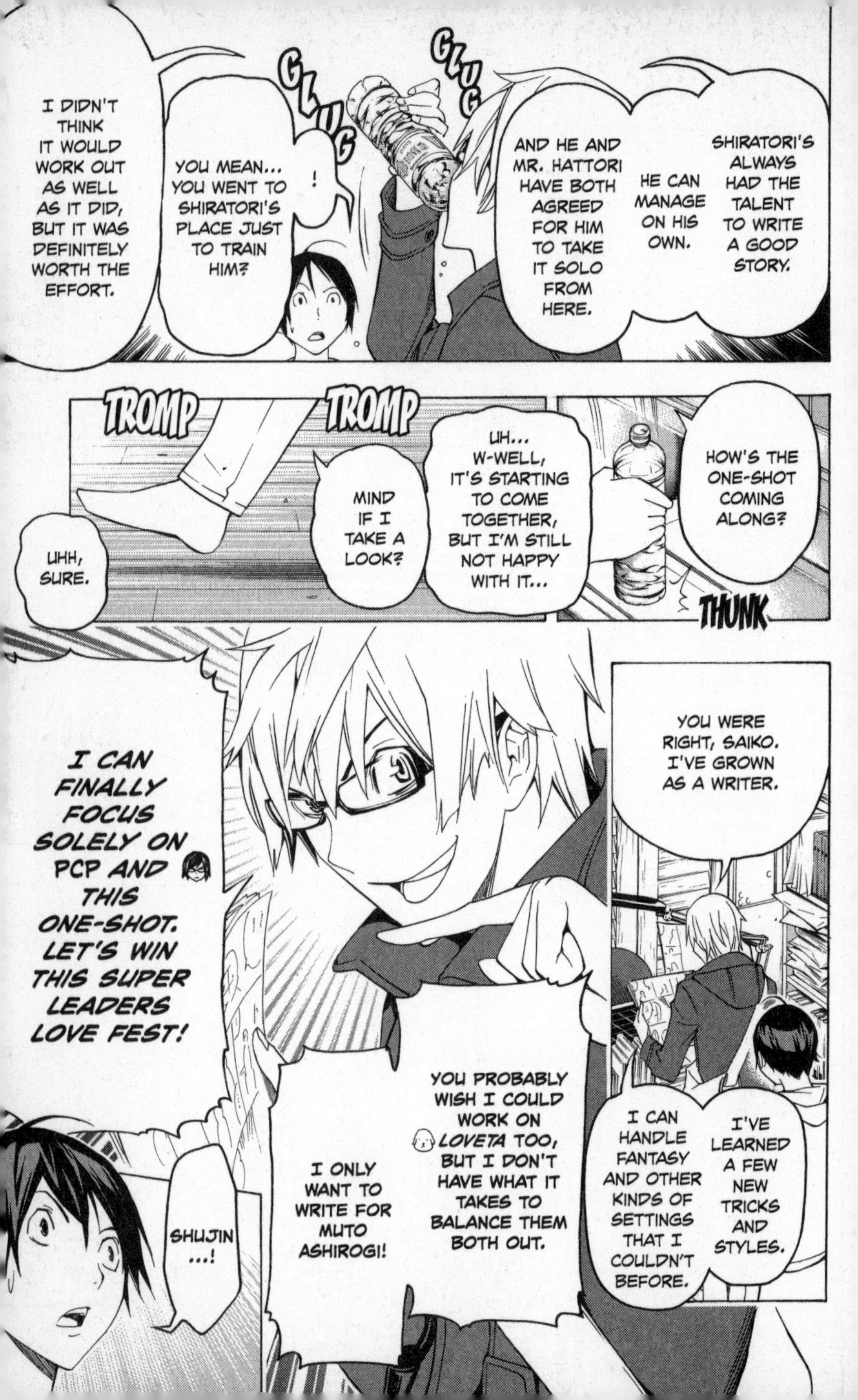
SHIRATORI'S ALWAYS HAD THE TALENT TO WRITE A GOOD STORY.
HE CAN MANAGE ON HIS OWN.
AND HE AND MR. HATTORI HAVE BOTH AGREED FOR HIM TO TAKE IT SOLO FROM HERE.
GLUG
GLUG
!
YOU MEAN... YOU WENT TO SHIRATORI'S PLACE JUST TO TRAIN HIM?
I DIDN'T THINK IT WOULD WORK OUT AS WELL AS IT DID, BUT IT WAS DEFINITELY WORTH THE EFFORT.
HOW'S THE ONE-SHOT COMING ALONG?
THUNK
UH... W-WELL, IT'S STARTING TO COME TOGETHER, BUT I'M STILL NOT HAPPY WITH IT...
TROMP
TROMP
MIND IF I TAKE A LOOK?
UHH, SURE.
YOU WERE RIGHT, SAIKO. I'VE GROWN AS A WRITER.
I'VE LEARNED A FEW NEW TRICKS AND STYLES.
I CAN HANDLE FANTASY AND OTHER KINDS OF SETTINGS THAT I COULDN'T BEFORE.
YOU PROBABLY WISH I COULD WORK ON LOVETA TOO, BUT I DON'T HAVE WHAT IT TAKES TO BALANCE THEM BOTH OUT.
I ONLY WANT TO WRITE FOR MUTO ASHIROGI!
SHUJIN ...!
I CAN FINALLY FOCUS SOLELY ON PCP AND THIS ONE-SHOT. LET'S WIN THIS SUPER LEADERS LOVE FEST!

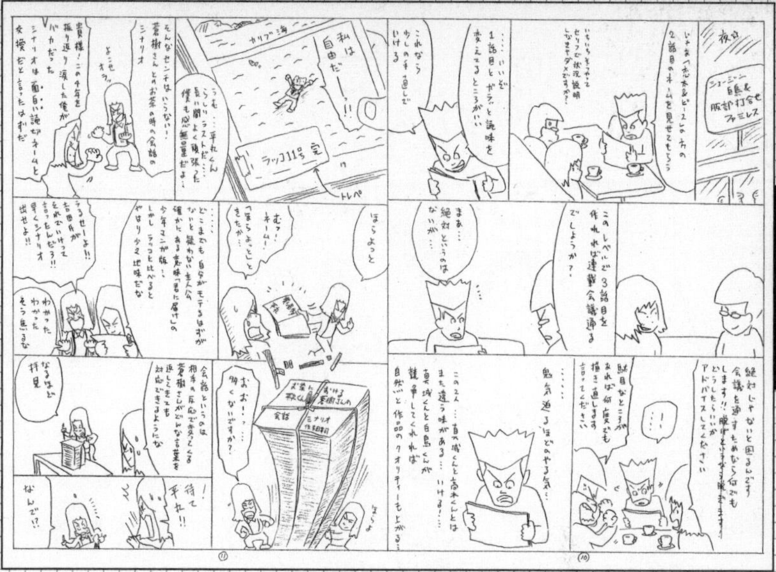
夜のファミレス
シュージン 亜城＆服部打合せ ファミレス
じゃあ「恋太＆ピース」の方の2話目のネームを見せてもらう
……いいぞ 1話目とガラッと読味を変えてるところがいい
これなら少しの手直しでいける
このレベルで3話目を作れれば連載会議通るでしょうか?
まあ… 絶対というのはないが…
絶対じゃないと困るんです 会議を通すためなら何でもします!! どうしたらいいかアドバイスしてください
駄目なところがあれば何度でも描き直しますから言ってください
……
!!
鬼気迫るほどのやる気…
このふん…真城くんと高木くんとはまた違う味がある… いける…!! 競争してくれれば自然と作品のクオリティーも上がる…
カリブ海
私は自由だー!!
ラッコ11号 完
トレペ
うむ…平丸くんらしいラストだ… 良い間よく頑張った 僕も感無量だよ
そんなセンチはいらない! 蒼樹さんとのお茶の時の会話のシナリオ
よこせオラッ
貴様! この半年を振り返り涙した俺がバカだった
シナリオは面白い読切ネームと交換だと言ったはずだ
ほらよっと
むっ ネーム! きたか…
どこまでも自分がモテるはずがないと疑わない主人公 確かにある意味「君に届け」の少年マンガ版… しかしラッコと比べるとやはり少々地味だな
テラセーよ!! 吉田氏がそれないけって言ったんだろ!! 早くシナリオ出せよ!!
わかったわかった そう焦るな
おお…っ 多くないですか?
会話というのは相手の反応で変わってくる どんな言葉を返してきても対応できるようにな
なるほど 拝見
待て 平丸!!
なんで!?

OHBA'S STORYBOARD

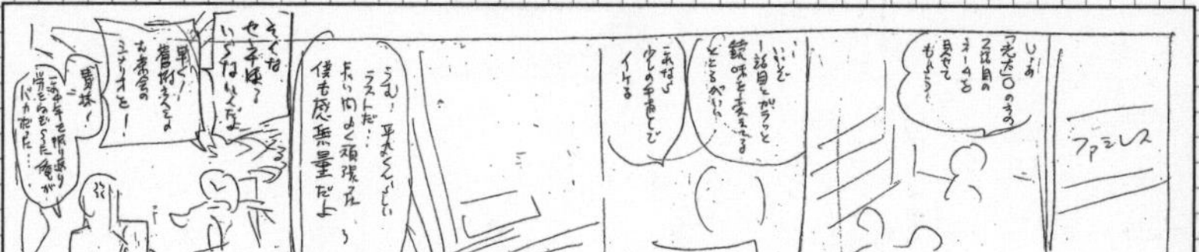
ファミレス

OBATA'S STORYBOARD

COMPLETE!

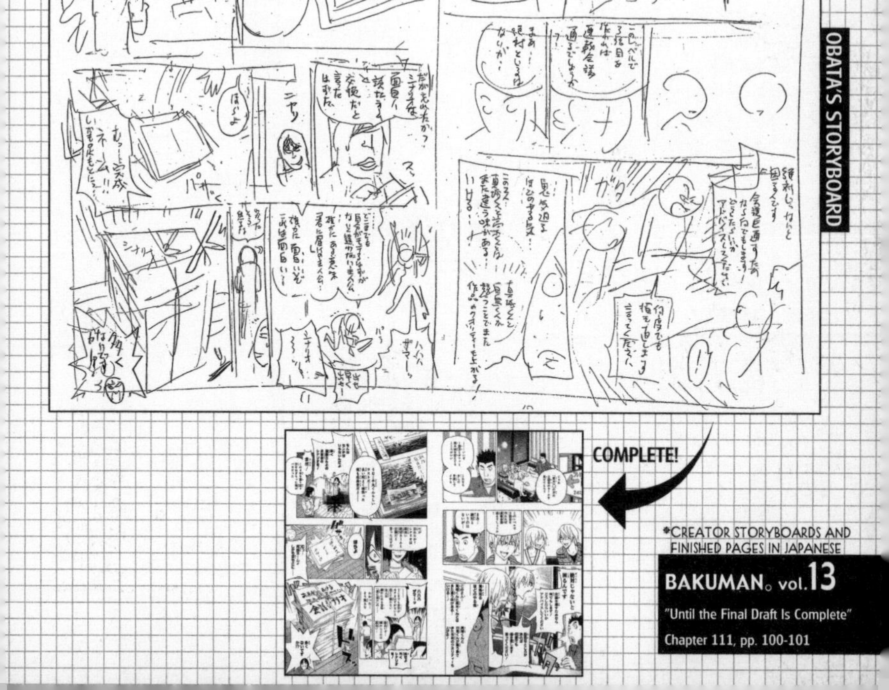

*CREATOR STORYBOARDS AND FINISHED PAGES IN JAPANESE

BAKUMAN。 vol.13

"Until the Final Draft Is Complete"

Chapter 111, pp. 100-101

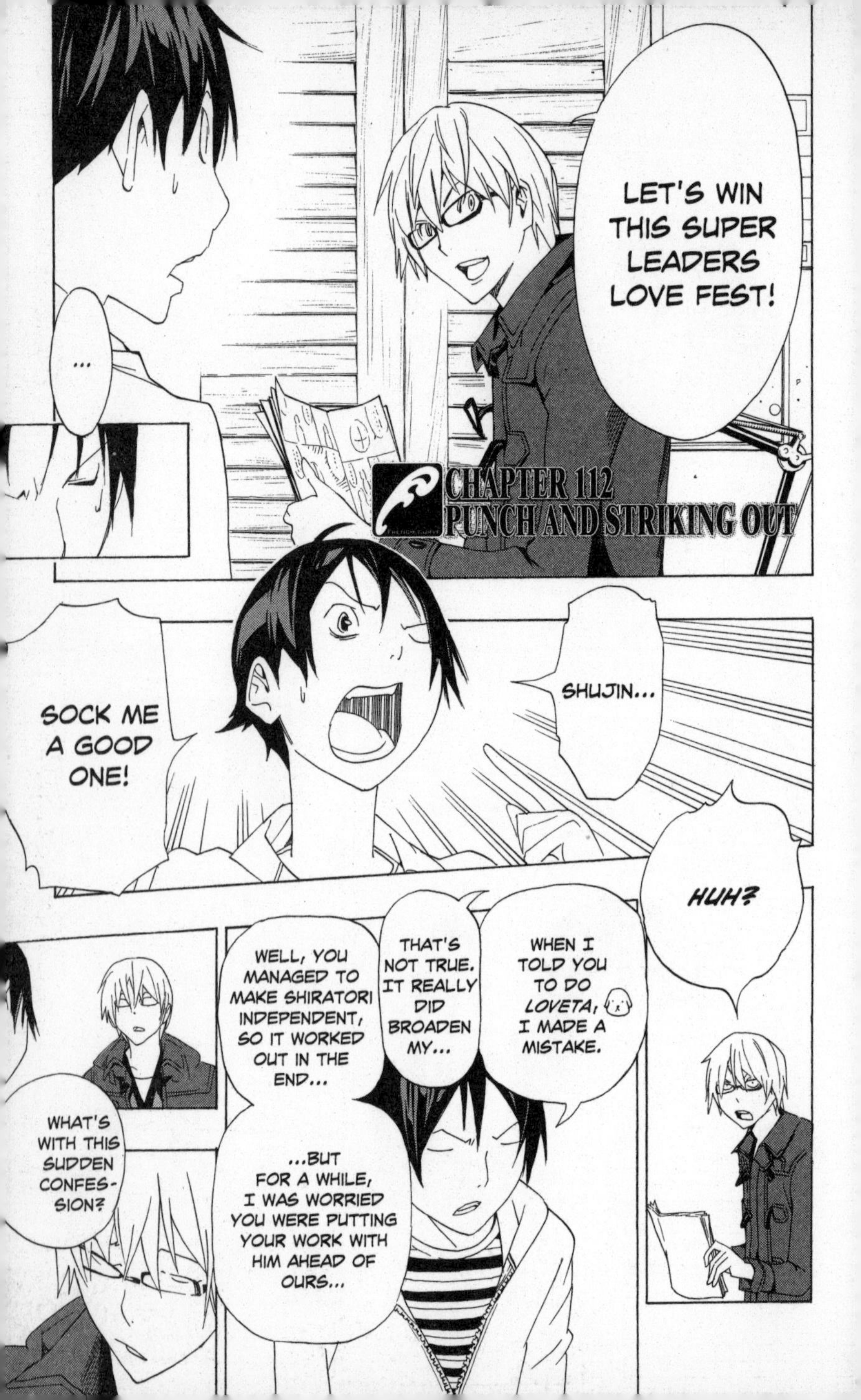
LET'S WIN THIS SUPER LEADERS LOVE FEST!
...
CHAPTER 112 PUNCH AND STRIKING OUT
SHUJIN...
SOCK ME A GOOD ONE!
HUH?
WHEN I TOLD YOU TO DO LOVETA, I MADE A MISTAKE.
THAT'S NOT TRUE. IT REALLY DID BROADEN MY...
WELL, YOU MANAGED TO MAKE SHIRATORI INDEPENDENT, SO IT WORKED OUT IN THE END...
...BUT FOR A WHILE, I WAS WORRIED YOU WERE PUTTING YOUR WORK WITH HIM AHEAD OF OURS...
WHAT'S WITH THIS SUDDEN CONFES-SION?

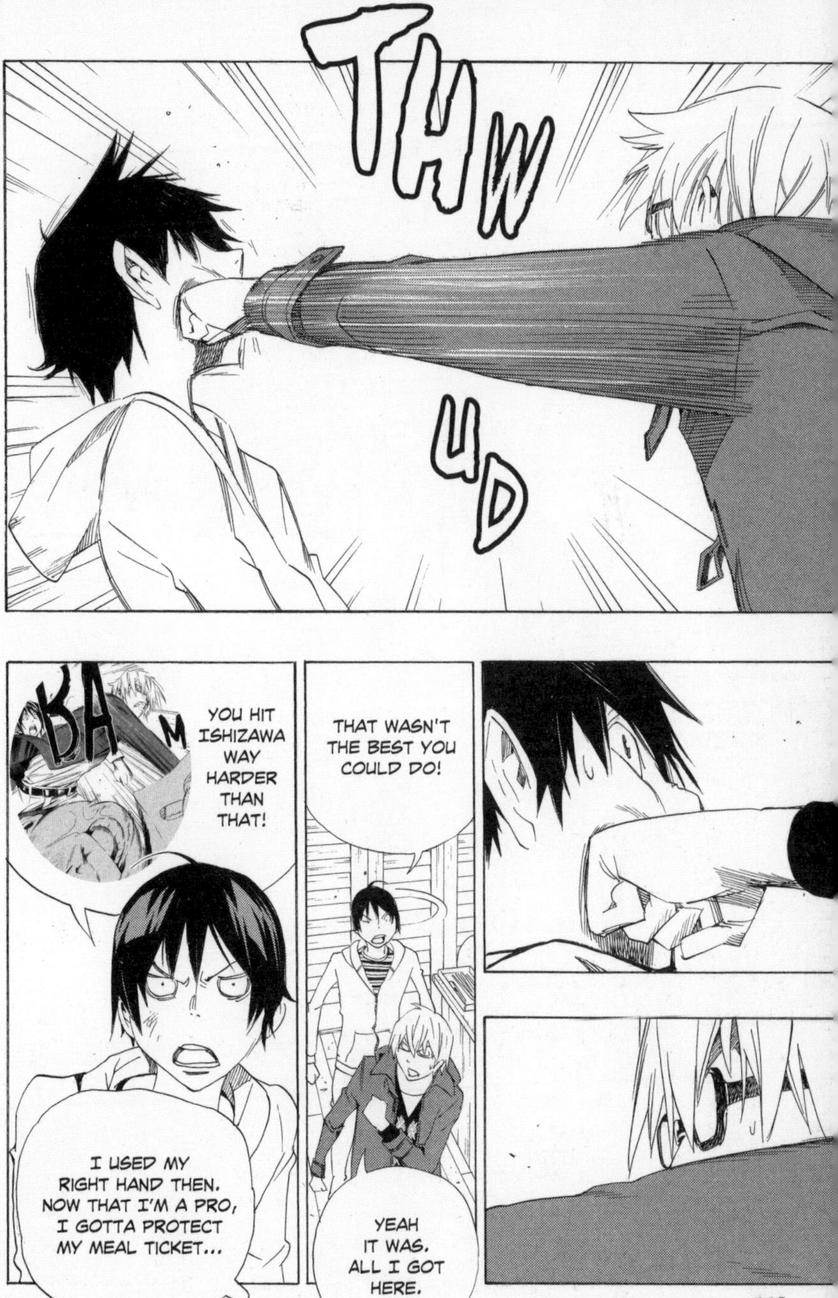
THWUD
THAT WASN'T THE BEST YOU COULD DO!
YEAH IT WAS. ALL I GOT HERE.
YOU HIT ISHIZAWA WAY HARDER THAN THAT!
BAM
I USED MY RIGHT HAND THEN. NOW THAT I'M A PRO, I GOTTA PROTECT MY MEAL TICKET...

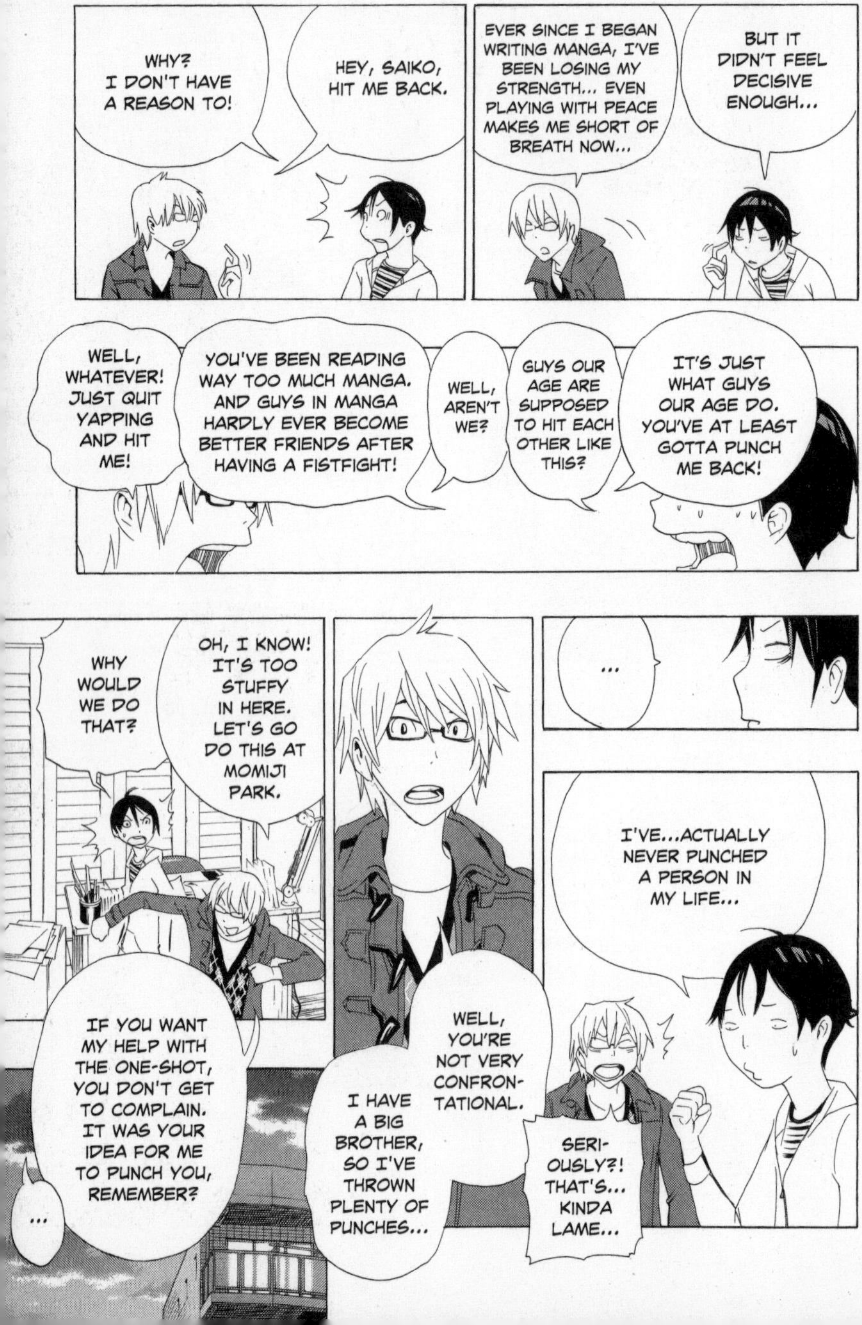

BUT IT DIDN'T FEEL DECISIVE ENOUGH...
EVER SINCE I BEGAN WRITING MANGA, I'VE BEEN LOSING MY STRENGTH... EVEN PLAYING WITH PEACE MAKES ME SHORT OF BREATH NOW...
HEY, SAIKO, HIT ME BACK.
WHY? I DON'T HAVE A REASON TO!
IT'S JUST WHAT GUYS OUR AGE DO. YOU'VE AT LEAST GOTTA PUNCH ME BACK!
GUYS OUR AGE ARE SUPPOSED TO HIT EACH OTHER LIKE THIS?
WELL, AREN'T WE?
YOU'VE BEEN READING WAY TOO MUCH MANGA. AND GUYS IN MANGA HARDLY EVER BECOME BETTER FRIENDS AFTER HAVING A FISTFIGHT!
WELL, WHATEVER! JUST QUIT YAPPING AND HIT ME!
...
I'VE...ACTUALLY NEVER PUNCHED A PERSON IN MY LIFE...
SERI-OUSLY?! THAT'S... KINDA LAME...
WELL, YOU'RE NOT VERY CONFRON-TATIONAL.
I HAVE A BIG BROTHER, SO I'VE THROWN PLENTY OF PUNCHES...
OH, I KNOW! IT'S TOO STUFFY IN HERE. LET'S GO DO THIS AT MOMIJI PARK.
WHY WOULD WE DO THAT?
IF YOU WANT MY HELP WITH THE ONE-SHOT, YOU DON'T GET TO COMPLAIN. IT WAS YOUR IDEA FOR ME TO PUNCH YOU, REMEMBER?
...

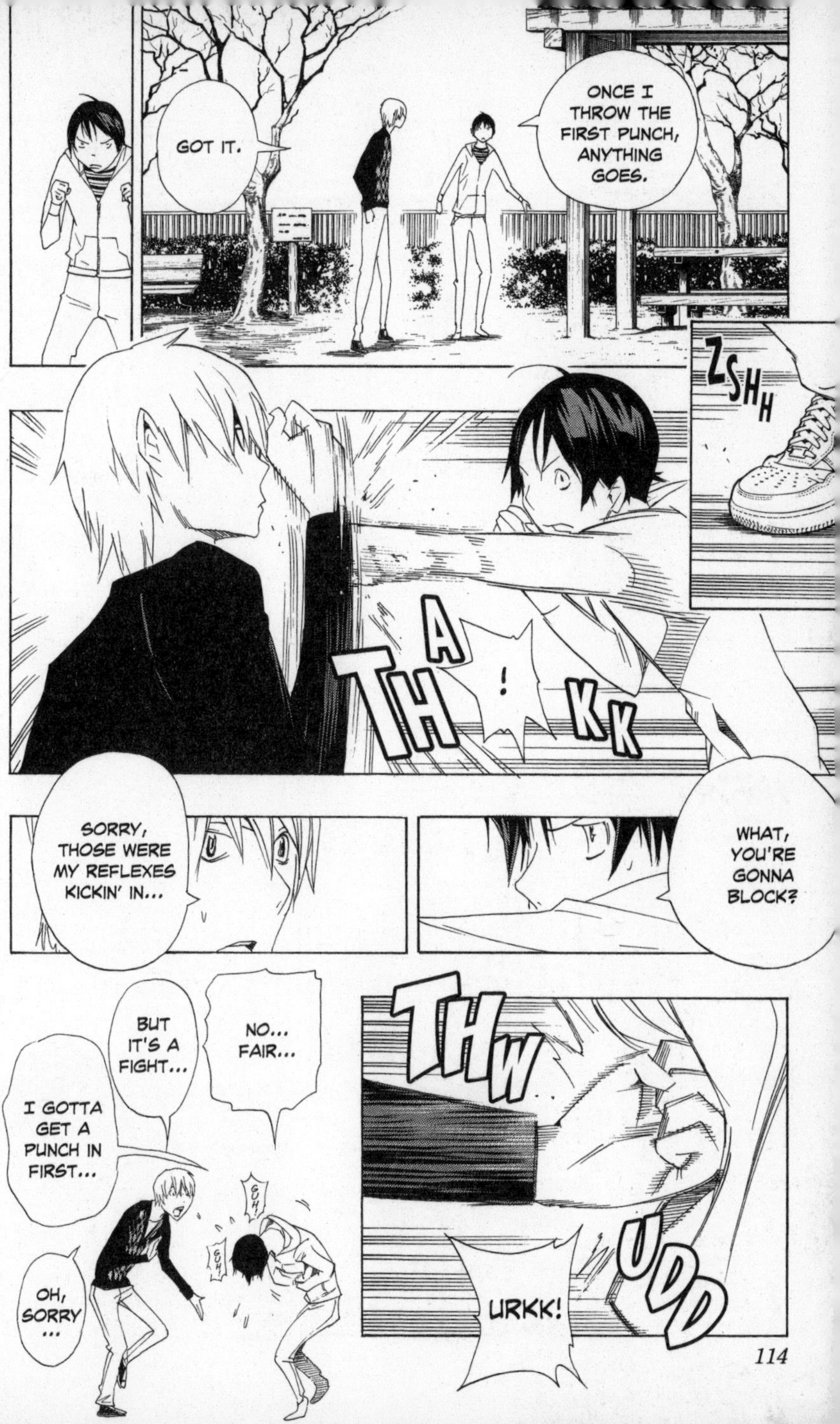
ONCE I THROW THE FIRST PUNCH, ANYTHING GOES.
GOT IT.
ZSHH
THACKK
!
WHAT, YOU'RE GONNA BLOCK?
SORRY, THOSE WERE MY REFLEXES KICKIN' IN...
THWUDD
URKK!
NO... FAIR...
BUT IT'S A FIGHT...
I GOTTA GET A PUNCH IN FIRST...
GUH!
GUH!
OH, SORRY...

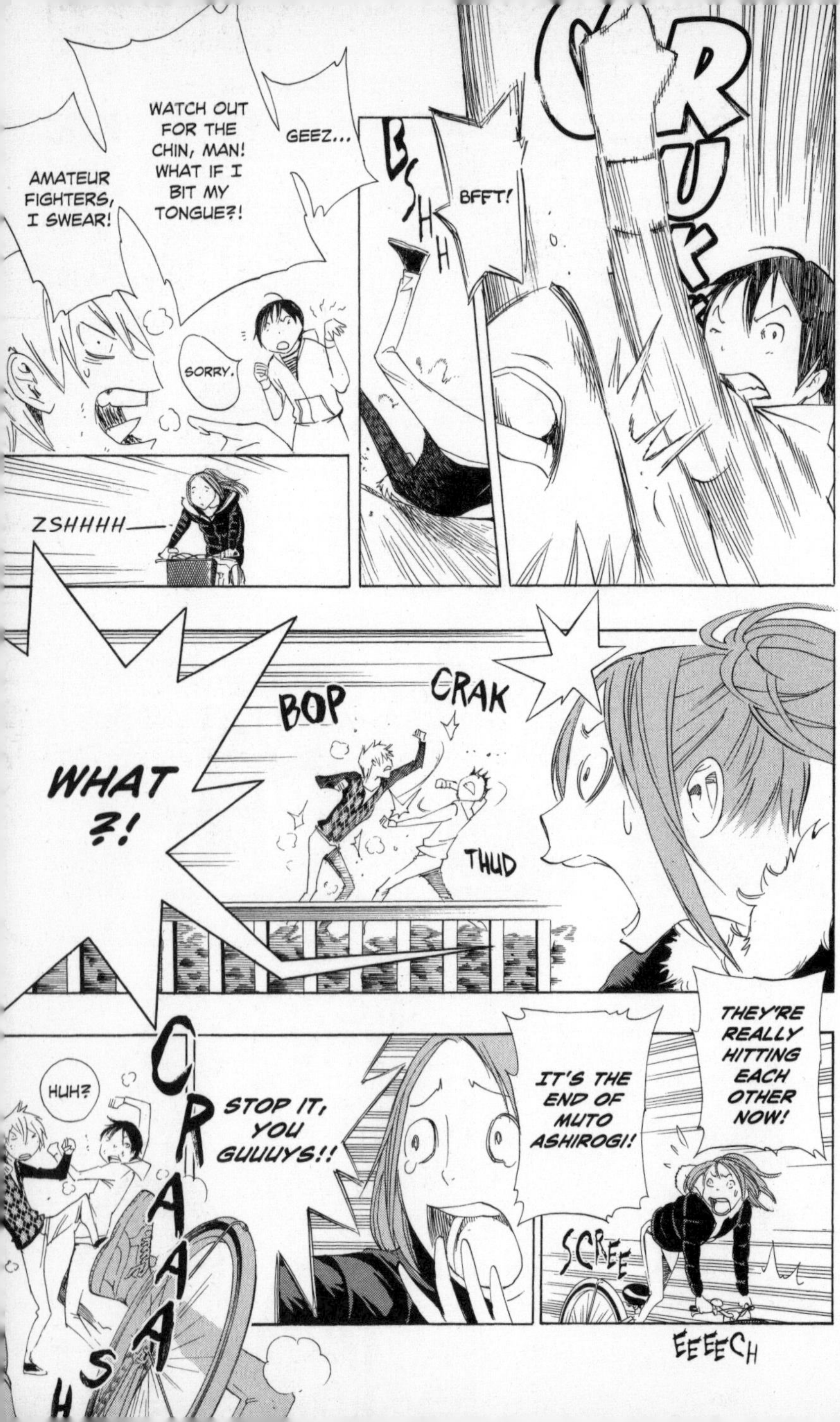
CRUN
BFFT!
BSHH
GEEZ...
WATCH OUT FOR THE CHIN, MAN! WHAT IF I BIT MY TONGUE?!
AMATEUR FIGHTERS, I SWEAR!
SORRY.
ZSHHHH
WHAT?!
CRAK
BOP
THUD
THEY'RE REALLY HITTING EACH OTHER NOW!
SCREE
EEEECH
IT'S THE END OF MUTO ASHIROGI!
STOP IT, YOU GUUUYS!!
CRAAAASH
HUH?

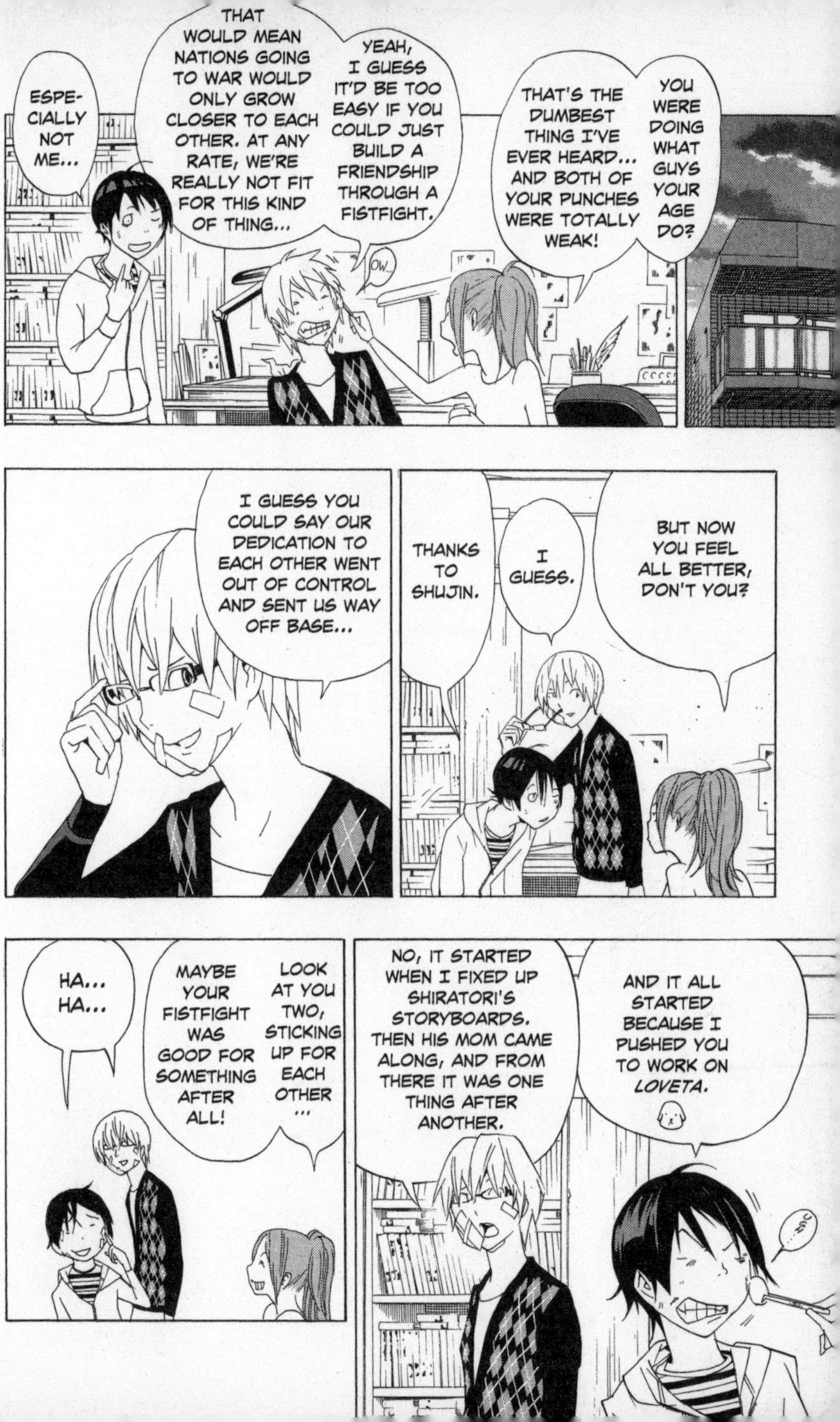
YOU WERE DOING WHAT GUYS YOUR AGE DO?
THAT'S THE DUMBEST THING I'VE EVER HEARD... AND BOTH OF YOUR PUNCHES WERE TOTALLY WEAK!
OW...
YEAH, I GUESS IT'D BE TOO EASY IF YOU COULD JUST BUILD A FRIENDSHIP THROUGH A FISTFIGHT.
THAT WOULD MEAN NATIONS GOING TO WAR WOULD ONLY GROW CLOSER TO EACH OTHER. AT ANY RATE, WE'RE REALLY NOT FIT FOR THIS KIND OF THING...
ESPE-CIALLY NOT ME...
BUT NOW YOU FEEL ALL BETTER, DON'T YOU?
I GUESS.
THANKS TO SHUJIN.
I GUESS YOU COULD SAY OUR DEDICATION TO EACH OTHER WENT OUT OF CONTROL AND SENT US WAY OFF BASE...
AND IT ALL STARTED BECAUSE I PUSHED YOU TO WORK ON *LOVETA*.
NO, IT STARTED WHEN I FIXED UP SHIRATORI'S STORYBOARDS. THEN HIS MOM CAME ALONG, AND FROM THERE IT WAS ONE THING AFTER ANOTHER.
LOOK AT YOU TWO, STICKING UP FOR EACH OTHER...
MAYBE YOUR FISTFIGHT WAS GOOD FOR SOMETHING AFTER ALL!
HA... HA...

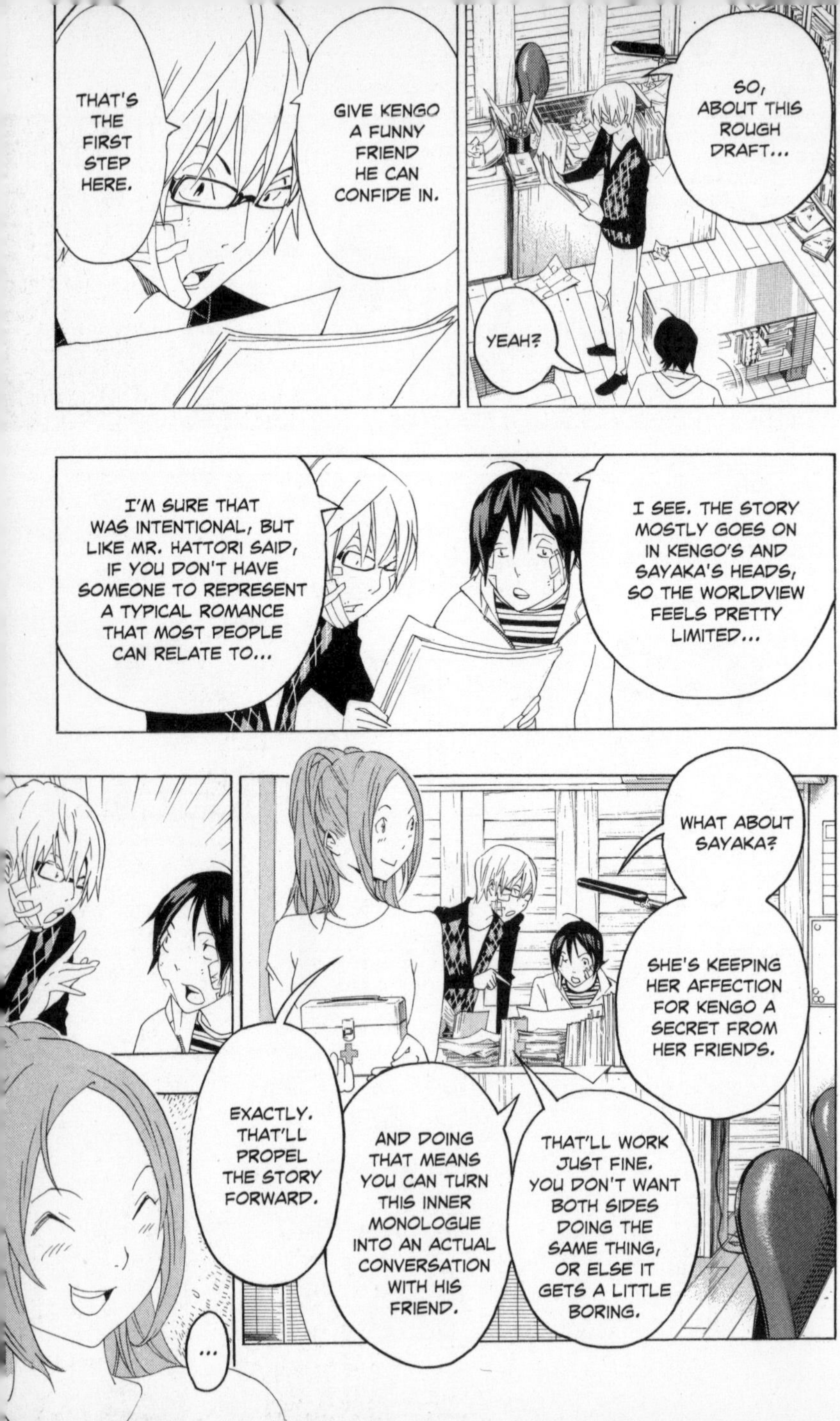

SO, ABOUT THIS ROUGH DRAFT...
YEAH?
GIVE KENGO A FUNNY FRIEND HE CAN CONFIDE IN.
THAT'S THE FIRST STEP HERE.
I SEE. THE STORY MOSTLY GOES ON IN KENGO'S AND SAYAKA'S HEADS, SO THE WORLDVIEW FEELS PRETTY LIMITED...
I'M SURE THAT WAS INTENTIONAL, BUT LIKE MR. HATTORI SAID, IF YOU DON'T HAVE SOMEONE TO REPRESENT A TYPICAL ROMANCE THAT MOST PEOPLE CAN RELATE TO...
WHAT ABOUT SAYAKA?
SHE'S KEEPING HER AFFECTION FOR KENGO A SECRET FROM HER FRIENDS.
THAT'LL WORK JUST FINE. YOU DON'T WANT BOTH SIDES DOING THE SAME THING, OR ELSE IT GETS A LITTLE BORING.
AND DOING THAT MEANS YOU CAN TURN THIS INNER MONOLOGUE INTO AN ACTUAL CONVERSATION WITH HIS FRIEND.
EXACTLY. THAT'LL PROPEL THE STORY FORWARD.
...

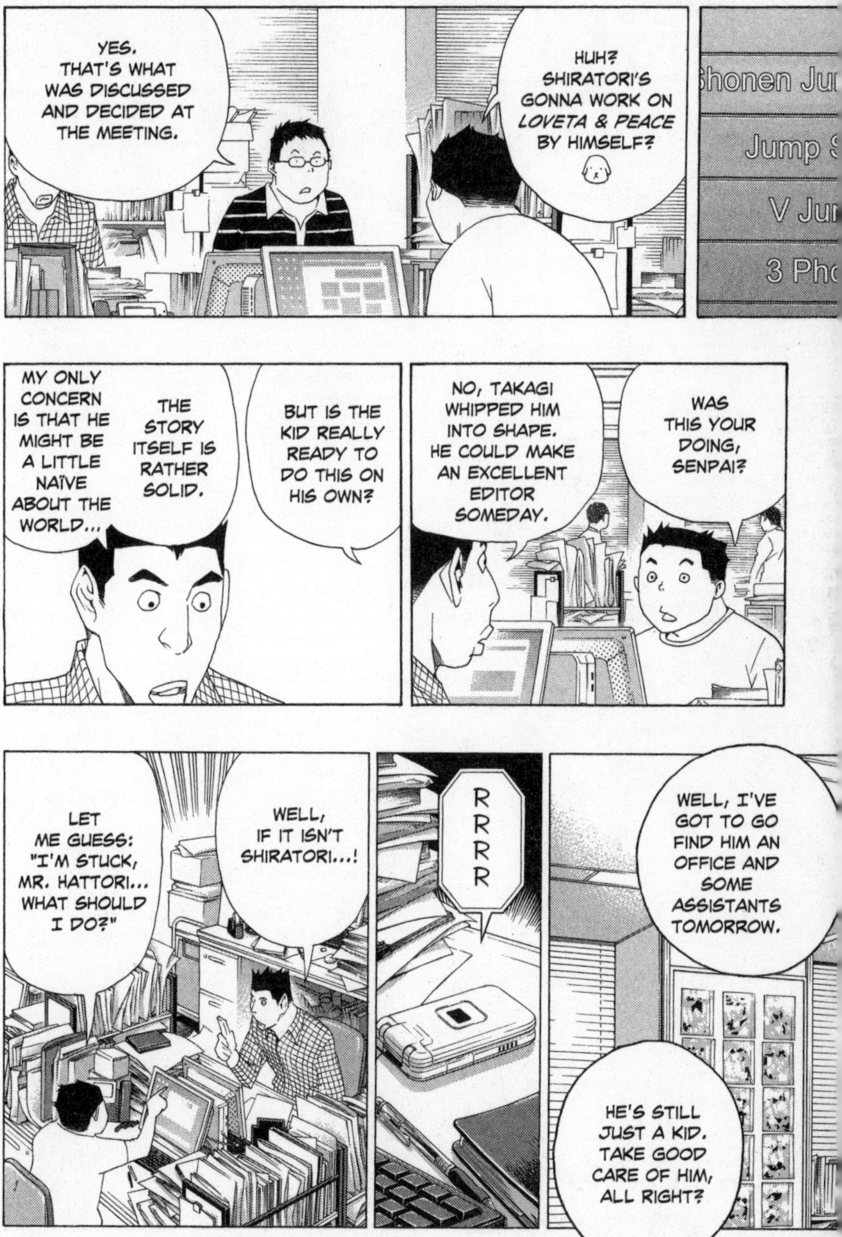
HUH? SHIRATORI'S GONNA WORK ON *LOVETA & PEACE* BY HIMSELF?
YES. THAT'S WHAT WAS DISCUSSED AND DECIDED AT THE MEETING.
WAS THIS YOUR DOING, SENPAI?
NO, TAKAGI WHIPPED HIM INTO SHAPE. HE COULD MAKE AN EXCELLENT EDITOR SOMEDAY.
BUT IS THE KID REALLY READY TO DO THIS ON HIS OWN?
THE STORY ITSELF IS RATHER SOLID.
MY ONLY CONCERN IS THAT HE MIGHT BE A LITTLE NAÏVE ABOUT THE WORLD...
WELL, I'VE GOT TO GO FIND HIM AN OFFICE AND SOME ASSISTANTS TOMORROW.
HE'S STILL JUST A KID. TAKE GOOD CARE OF HIM, ALL RIGHT?
RRRR
WELL, IF IT ISN'T SHIRATORI...!
LET ME GUESS: "I'M STUCK, MR. HATTORI... WHAT SHOULD I DO?"

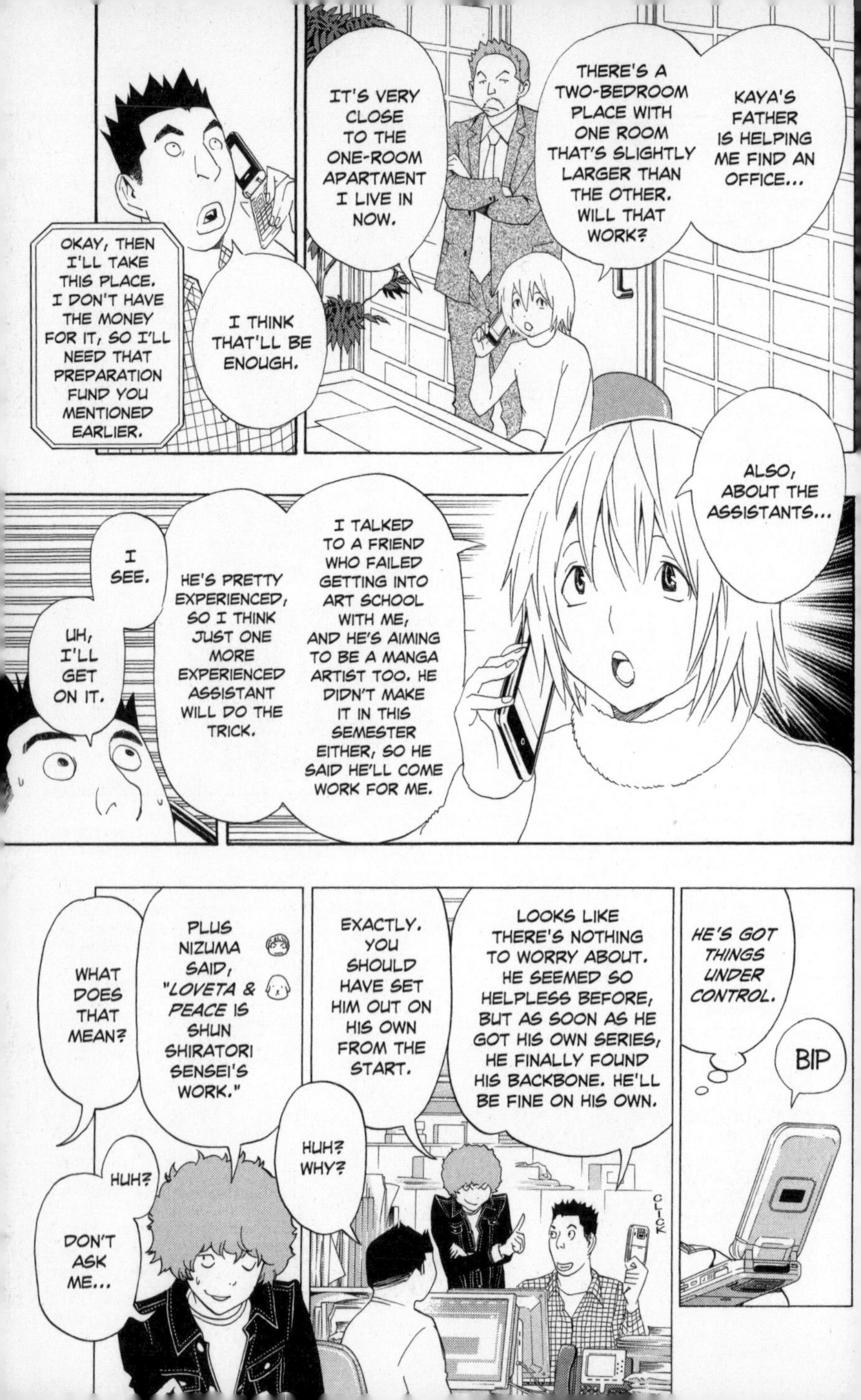

KAYA'S FATHER IS HELPING ME FIND AN OFFICE...
THERE'S A TWO-BEDROOM PLACE WITH ONE ROOM THAT'S SLIGHTLY LARGER THAN THE OTHER. WILL THAT WORK?
IT'S VERY CLOSE TO THE ONE-ROOM APARTMENT I LIVE IN NOW.
I THINK THAT'LL BE ENOUGH.
OKAY, THEN I'LL TAKE THIS PLACE. I DON'T HAVE THE MONEY FOR IT, SO I'LL NEED THAT PREPARATION FUND YOU MENTIONED EARLIER.
ALSO, ABOUT THE ASSISTANTS...
I TALKED TO A FRIEND WHO FAILED GETTING INTO ART SCHOOL WITH ME, AND HE'S AIMING TO BE A MANGA ARTIST TOO. HE DIDN'T MAKE IT IN THIS SEMESTER EITHER, SO HE SAID HE'LL COME WORK FOR ME.
HE'S PRETTY EXPERIENCED, SO I THINK JUST ONE MORE EXPERIENCED ASSISTANT WILL DO THE TRICK.
I SEE.
UH, I'LL GET ON IT.
HE'S GOT THINGS UNDER CONTROL.
BIP
LOOKS LIKE THERE'S NOTHING TO WORRY ABOUT. HE SEEMED SO HELPLESS BEFORE, BUT AS SOON AS HE GOT HIS OWN SERIES, HE FINALLY FOUND HIS BACKBONE. HE'LL BE FINE ON HIS OWN.
CLICK
EXACTLY. YOU SHOULD HAVE SET HIM OUT ON HIS OWN FROM THE START.
HUH? WHY?
PLUS NIZUMA SAID, "LOVETA & PEACE IS SHUN SHIRATORI SENSEI'S WORK."
WHAT DOES THAT MEAN?
HUH?
DON'T ASK ME...

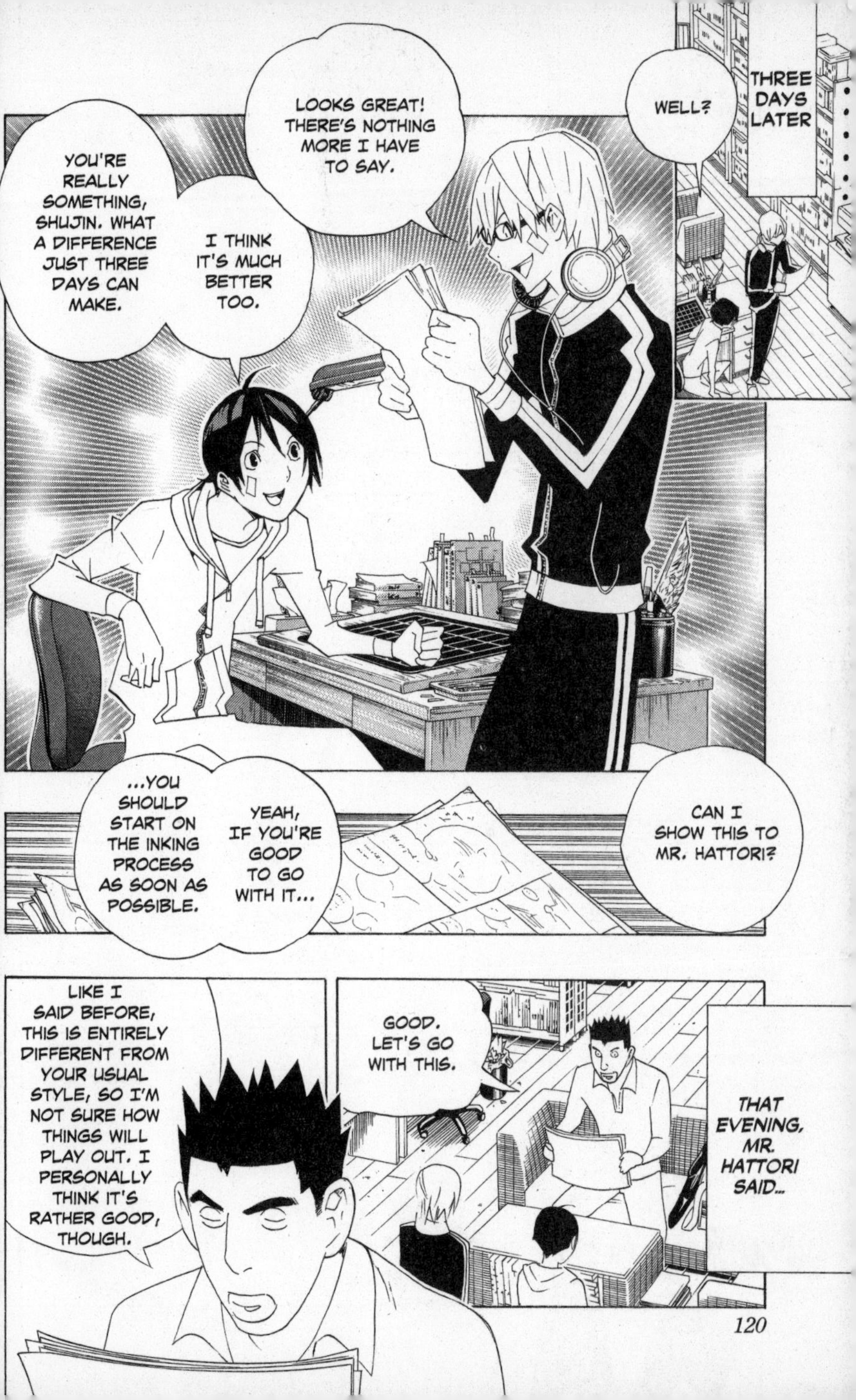
THREE DAYS LATER
WELL?
LOOKS GREAT! THERE'S NOTHING MORE I HAVE TO SAY.
I THINK IT'S MUCH BETTER TOO.
YOU'RE REALLY SOMETHING, SHUJIN. WHAT A DIFFERENCE JUST THREE DAYS CAN MAKE.
CAN I SHOW THIS TO MR. HATTORI?
YEAH, IF YOU'RE GOOD TO GO WITH IT...
...YOU SHOULD START ON THE INKING PROCESS AS SOON AS POSSIBLE.
THAT EVENING, MR. HATTORI SAID...
GOOD. LET'S GO WITH THIS.
LIKE I SAID BEFORE, THIS IS ENTIRELY DIFFERENT FROM YOUR USUAL STYLE, SO I'M NOT SURE HOW THINGS WILL PLAY OUT. I PERSONALLY THINK IT'S RATHER GOOD, THOUGH.

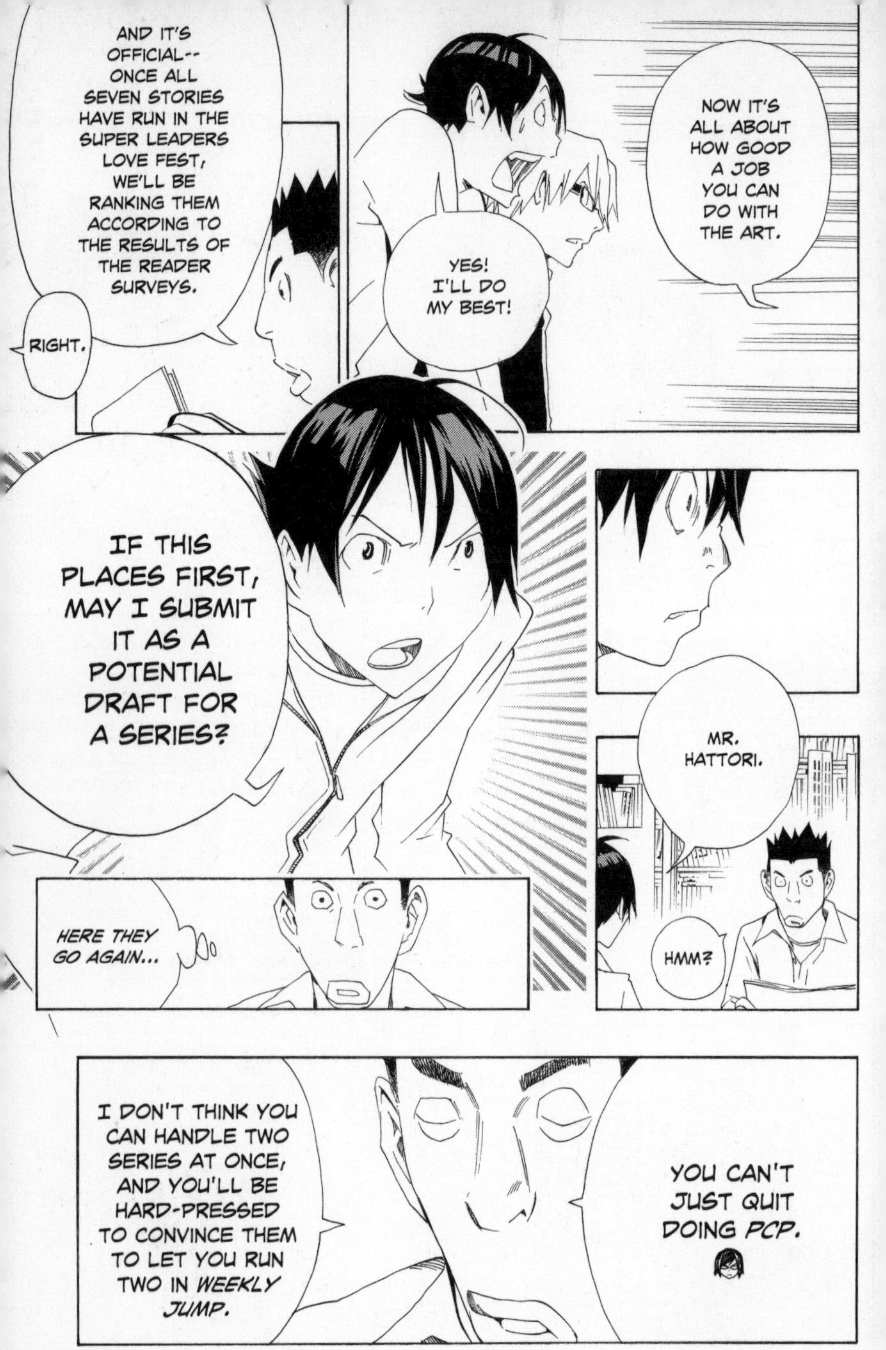
NOW IT'S ALL ABOUT HOW GOOD A JOB YOU CAN DO WITH THE ART.
YES! I'LL DO MY BEST!
AND IT'S OFFICIAL-- ONCE ALL SEVEN STORIES HAVE RUN IN THE SUPER LEADERS LOVE FEST, WE'LL BE RANKING THEM ACCORDING TO THE RESULTS OF THE READER SURVEYS.
RIGHT.
MR. HATTORI.
HMM?
IF THIS PLACES FIRST, MAY I SUBMIT IT AS A POTENTIAL DRAFT FOR A SERIES?
HERE THEY GO AGAIN...
YOU CAN'T JUST QUIT DOING PCP.
I DON'T THINK YOU CAN HANDLE TWO SERIES AT ONCE, AND YOU'LL BE HARD-PRESSED TO CONVINCE THEM TO LET YOU RUN TWO IN WEEKLY JUMP.

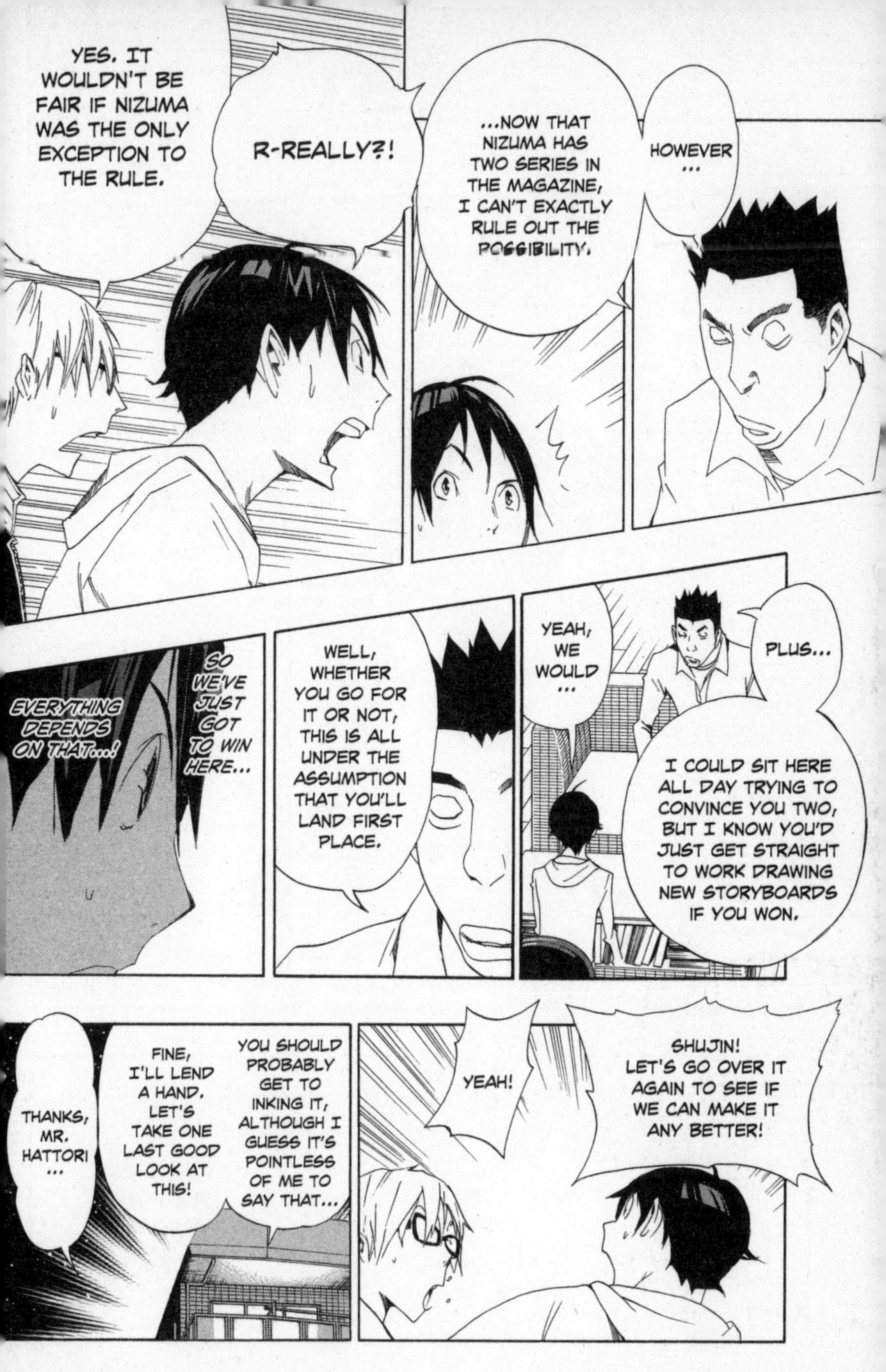
HOWEVER ...
...NOW THAT NIZUMA HAS TWO SERIES IN THE MAGAZINE, I CAN'T EXACTLY RULE OUT THE POSSIBILITY.
R-REALLY?!
YES. IT WOULDN'T BE FAIR IF NIZUMA WAS THE ONLY EXCEPTION TO THE RULE.
PLUS...
I COULD SIT HERE ALL DAY TRYING TO CONVINCE YOU TWO, BUT I KNOW YOU'D JUST GET STRAIGHT TO WORK DRAWING NEW STORYBOARDS IF YOU WON.
YEAH, WE WOULD ...
WELL, WHETHER YOU GO FOR IT OR NOT, THIS IS ALL UNDER THE ASSUMPTION THAT YOU'LL LAND FIRST PLACE.
SO WE'VE JUST GOT TO WIN HERE...
EVERYTHING DEPENDS ON THAT...!
SHUJIN! LET'S GO OVER IT AGAIN TO SEE IF WE CAN MAKE IT ANY BETTER!
YEAH!
YOU SHOULD PROBABLY GET TO INKING IT, ALTHOUGH I GUESS IT'S POINTLESS OF ME TO SAY THAT...
FINE, I'LL LEND A HAND. LET'S TAKE ONE LAST GOOD LOOK AT THIS!
THANKS, MR. HATTORI ...

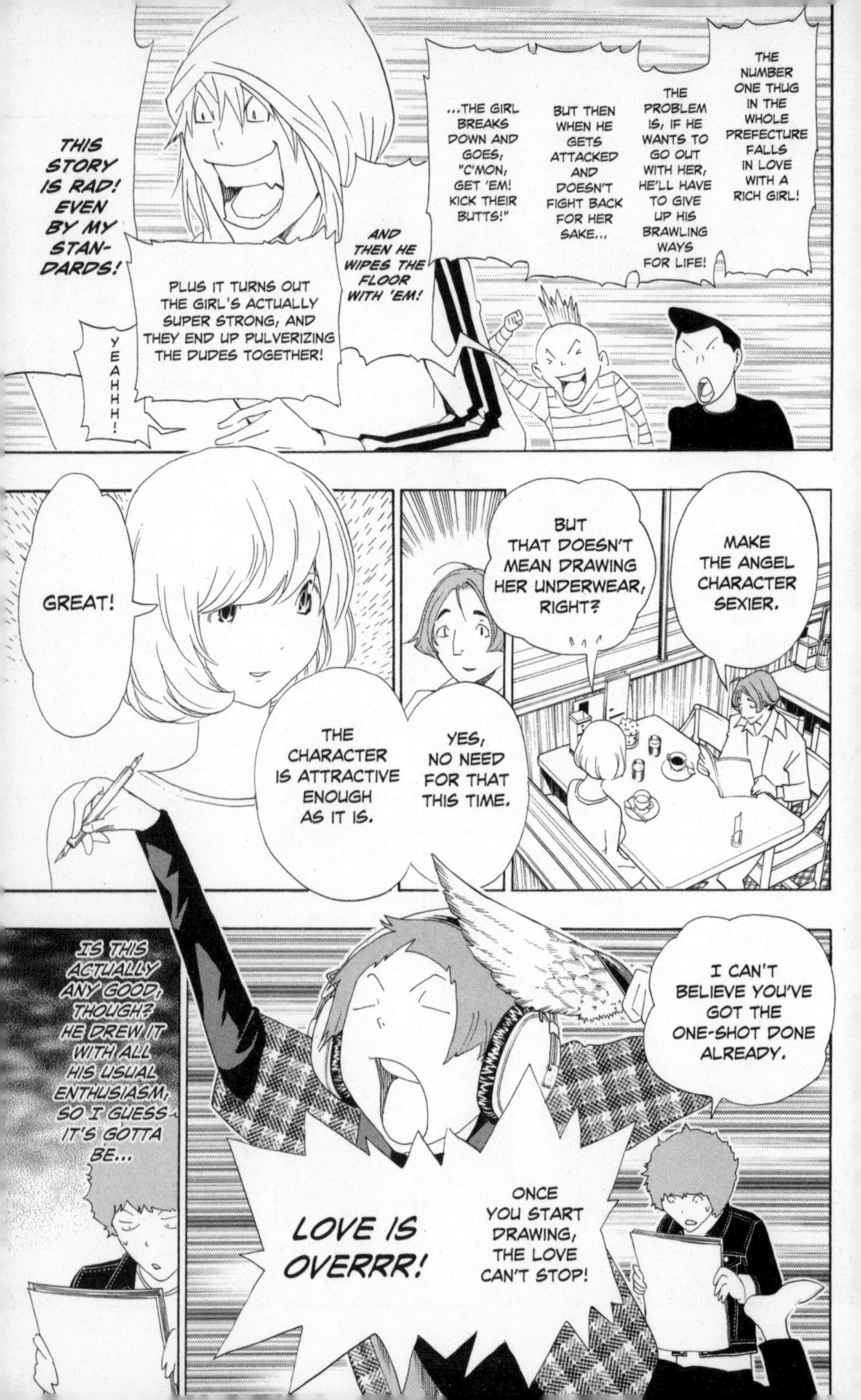
THE NUMBER ONE THUG IN THE WHOLE PREFECTURE FALLS IN LOVE WITH A RICH GIRL!
THE PROBLEM IS, IF HE WANTS TO GO OUT WITH HER, HE'LL HAVE TO GIVE UP HIS BRAWLING WAYS FOR LIFE!
BUT THEN WHEN HE GETS ATTACKED AND DOESN'T FIGHT BACK FOR HER SAKE...
...THE GIRL BREAKS DOWN AND GOES, "C'MON, GET 'EM! KICK THEIR BUTTS!"
AND THEN HE WIPES THE FLOOR WITH 'EM!
PLUS IT TURNS OUT THE GIRL'S ACTUALLY SUPER STRONG, AND THEY END UP PULVERIZING THE DUDES TOGETHER!
THIS STORY IS RAD! EVEN BY MY STAN-DARDS!
YEAHHH!
MAKE THE ANGEL CHARACTER SEXIER.
BUT THAT DOESN'T MEAN DRAWING HER UNDERWEAR, RIGHT?
YES, NO NEED FOR THAT THIS TIME.
THE CHARACTER IS ATTRACTIVE ENOUGH AS IT IS.
GREAT!
I CAN'T BELIEVE YOU'VE GOT THE ONE-SHOT DONE ALREADY.
ONCE YOU START DRAWING, THE LOVE CAN'T STOP!
LOVE IS OVERRR!
IS THIS ACTUALLY ANY GOOD, THOUGH? HE DREW IT WITH ALL HIS USUAL ENTHUSIASM, SO I GUESS IT'S GOTTA BE...

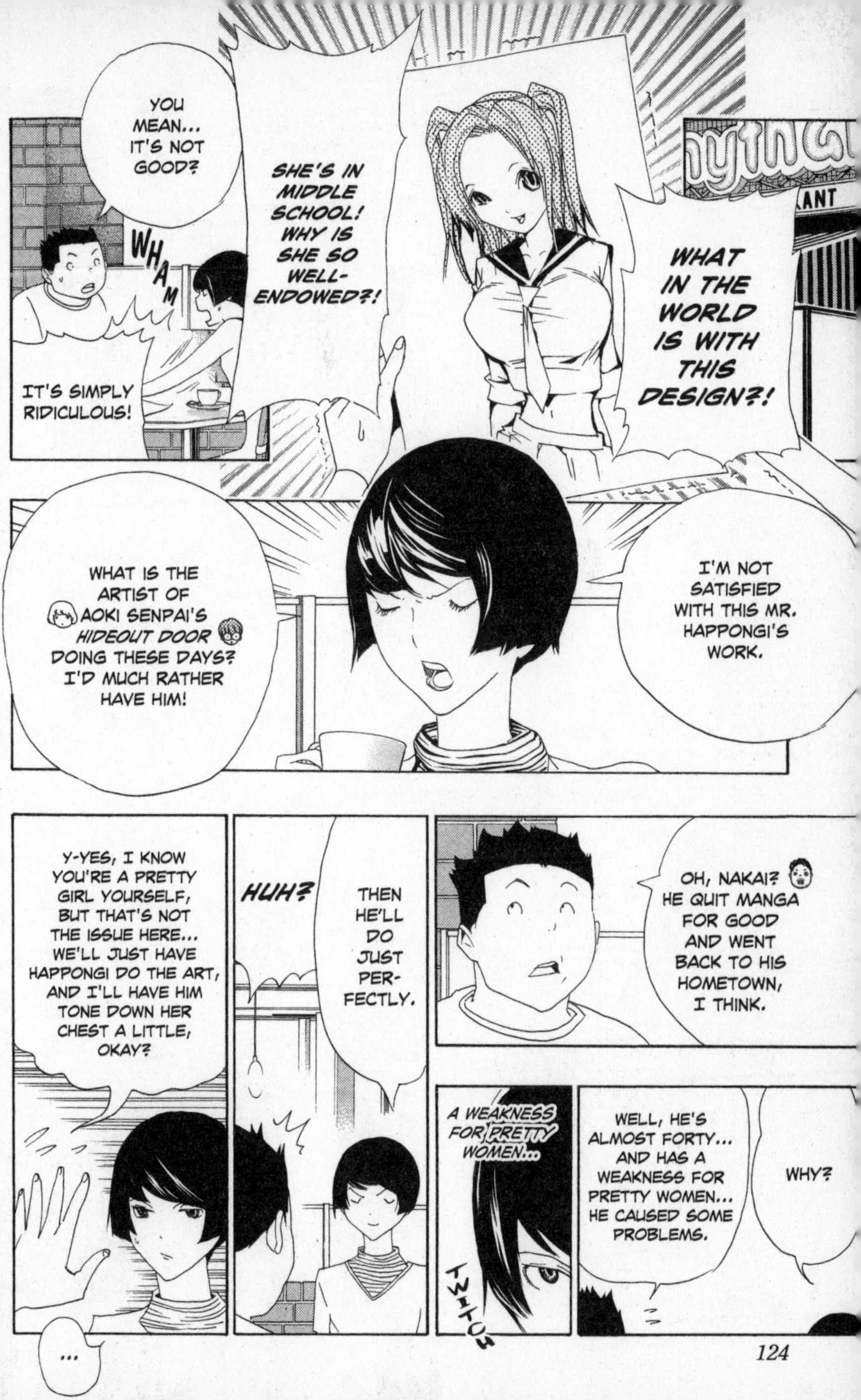
WHAT IN THE WORLD IS WITH THIS DESIGN?!
SHE'S IN MIDDLE SCHOOL! WHY IS SHE SO WELL-ENDOWED?!
YOU MEAN... IT'S NOT GOOD?
WHAM
IT'S SIMPLY RIDICULOUS!
I'M NOT SATISFIED WITH THIS MR. HAPPONGI'S WORK.
WHAT IS THE ARTIST OF AOKI SENPAI'S *HIDEOUT DOOR* DOING THESE DAYS? I'D MUCH RATHER HAVE HIM!
OH, NAKAI? HE QUIT MANGA FOR GOOD AND WENT BACK TO HIS HOMETOWN, I THINK.
WHY?
WELL, HE'S ALMOST FORTY... AND HAS A WEAKNESS FOR PRETTY WOMEN... HE CAUSED SOME PROBLEMS.
A WEAKNESS FOR PRETTY WOMEN...
TWITCH
THEN HE'LL DO JUST PER-FECTLY.
HUH?
Y-YES, I KNOW YOU'RE A PRETTY GIRL YOURSELF, BUT THAT'S NOT THE ISSUE HERE... WE'LL JUST HAVE HAPPONGI DO THE ART, AND I'LL HAVE HIM TONE DOWN HER CHEST A LITTLE, OKAY?
...

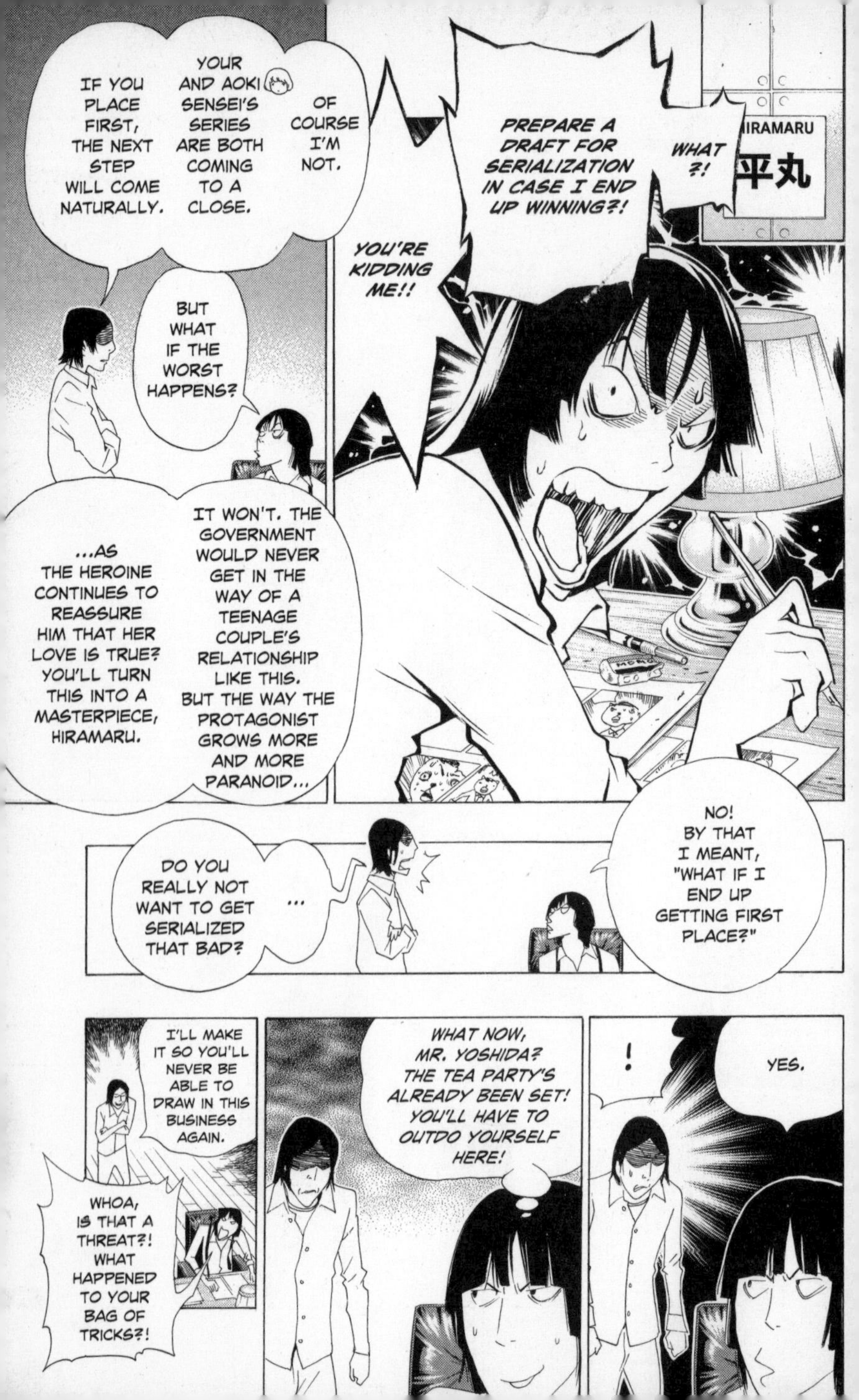
平丸
WHAT?!
PREPARE A DRAFT FOR SERIALIZATION IN CASE I END UP WINNING?!
YOU'RE KIDDING ME!!
OF COURSE I'M NOT.
YOUR AND AOKI SENSEI'S SERIES ARE BOTH COMING TO A CLOSE.
IF YOU PLACE FIRST, THE NEXT STEP WILL COME NATURALLY.
BUT WHAT IF THE WORST HAPPENS?
IT WON'T. THE GOVERNMENT WOULD NEVER GET IN THE WAY OF A TEENAGE COUPLE'S RELATIONSHIP LIKE THIS. BUT THE WAY THE PROTAGONIST GROWS MORE AND MORE PARANOID...
...AS THE HEROINE CONTINUES TO REASSURE HIM THAT HER LOVE IS TRUE? YOU'LL TURN THIS INTO A MASTERPIECE, HIRAMARU.
NO! BY THAT I MEANT, "WHAT IF I END UP GETTING FIRST PLACE?"
...
DO YOU REALLY NOT WANT TO GET SERIALIZED THAT BAD?
YES.
!
WHAT NOW, MR. YOSHIDA? THE TEA PARTY'S ALREADY BEEN SET! YOU'LL HAVE TO OUTDO YOURSELF HERE!
I'LL MAKE IT SO YOU'LL NEVER BE ABLE TO DRAW IN THIS BUSINESS AGAIN.
WHOA, IS THAT A THREAT?! WHAT HAPPENED TO YOUR BAG OF TRICKS?!

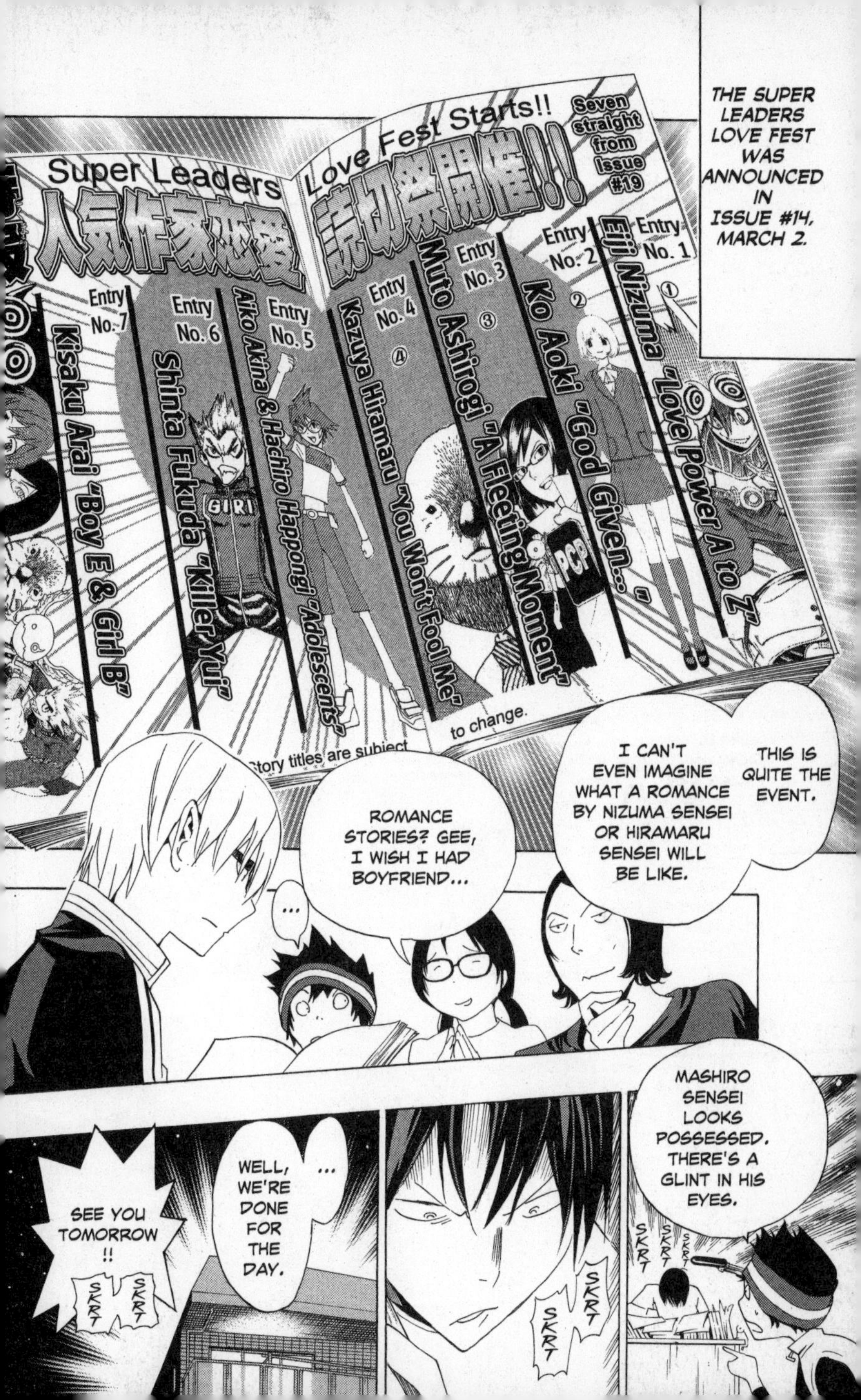
THE SUPER LEADERS LOVE FEST WAS ANNOUNCED IN ISSUE #14, MARCH 2.
Seven straight from Issue #19
Super Leaders Love Fest Starts!!
人気作家恋愛読切祭開催!!
Entry No. 1 ① Eiji Nizuma "Love Power A to Z"
Entry No. 2 ② Ko Aoki "God Given…"
Entry No. 3 ③ Muto Ashirogi "A Fleeting Moment"
Entry No. 4 ④ Kazuya Hiramaru "You Won't Fool Me"
Entry No. 5 Aiko Akina & Hachiro Happongi "Adolescents"
Entry No. 6 Shinta Fukuda "Killer Yui"
Entry No. 7 Kisaku Arai "Boy E & Girl B"
GIRI
PCP
Story titles are subject to change.
THIS IS QUITE THE EVENT.
I CAN'T EVEN IMAGINE WHAT A ROMANCE BY NIZUMA SENSEI OR HIRAMARU SENSEI WILL BE LIKE.
ROMANCE STORIES? GEE, I WISH I HAD BOYFRIEND…
…
MASHIRO SENSEI LOOKS POSSESSED. THERE'S A GLINT IN HIS EYES.
SKRT SKRT SKRT
SKRT SKRT
…
WELL, WE'RE DONE FOR THE DAY.
SEE YOU TOMORROW!!
SKRT SKRT

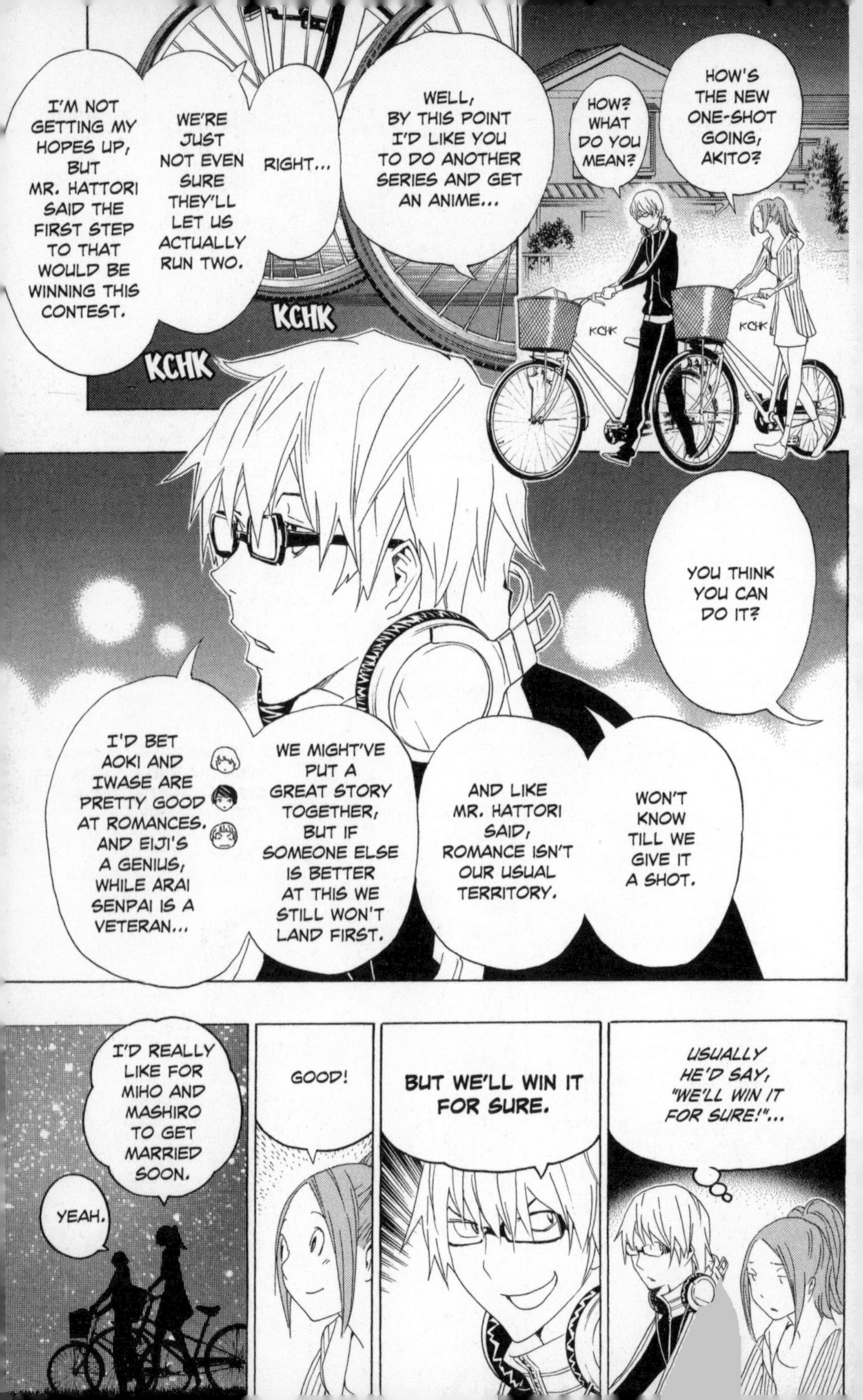
HOW'S THE NEW ONE-SHOT GOING, AKITO?
HOW? WHAT DO YOU MEAN?
KCHK
KCHK
WELL, BY THIS POINT I'D LIKE YOU TO DO ANOTHER SERIES AND GET AN ANIME...
RIGHT...
WE'RE JUST NOT EVEN SURE THEY'LL LET US ACTUALLY RUN TWO.
I'M NOT GETTING MY HOPES UP, BUT MR. HATTORI SAID THE FIRST STEP TO THAT WOULD BE WINNING THIS CONTEST.
KCHK
KCHK
YOU THINK YOU CAN DO IT?
WON'T KNOW TILL WE GIVE IT A SHOT.
AND LIKE MR. HATTORI SAID, ROMANCE ISN'T OUR USUAL TERRITORY.
WE MIGHT'VE PUT A GREAT STORY TOGETHER, BUT IF SOMEONE ELSE IS BETTER AT THIS WE STILL WON'T LAND FIRST.
I'D BET AOKI AND IWASE ARE PRETTY GOOD AT ROMANCES. AND EIJI'S A GENIUS, WHILE ARAI SENPAI IS A VETERAN...
USUALLY HE'D SAY, "WE'LL WIN IT FOR SURE!"...
BUT WE'LL WIN IT FOR SURE.
GOOD!
I'D REALLY LIKE FOR MIHO AND MASHIRO TO GET MARRIED SOON.
YEAH.

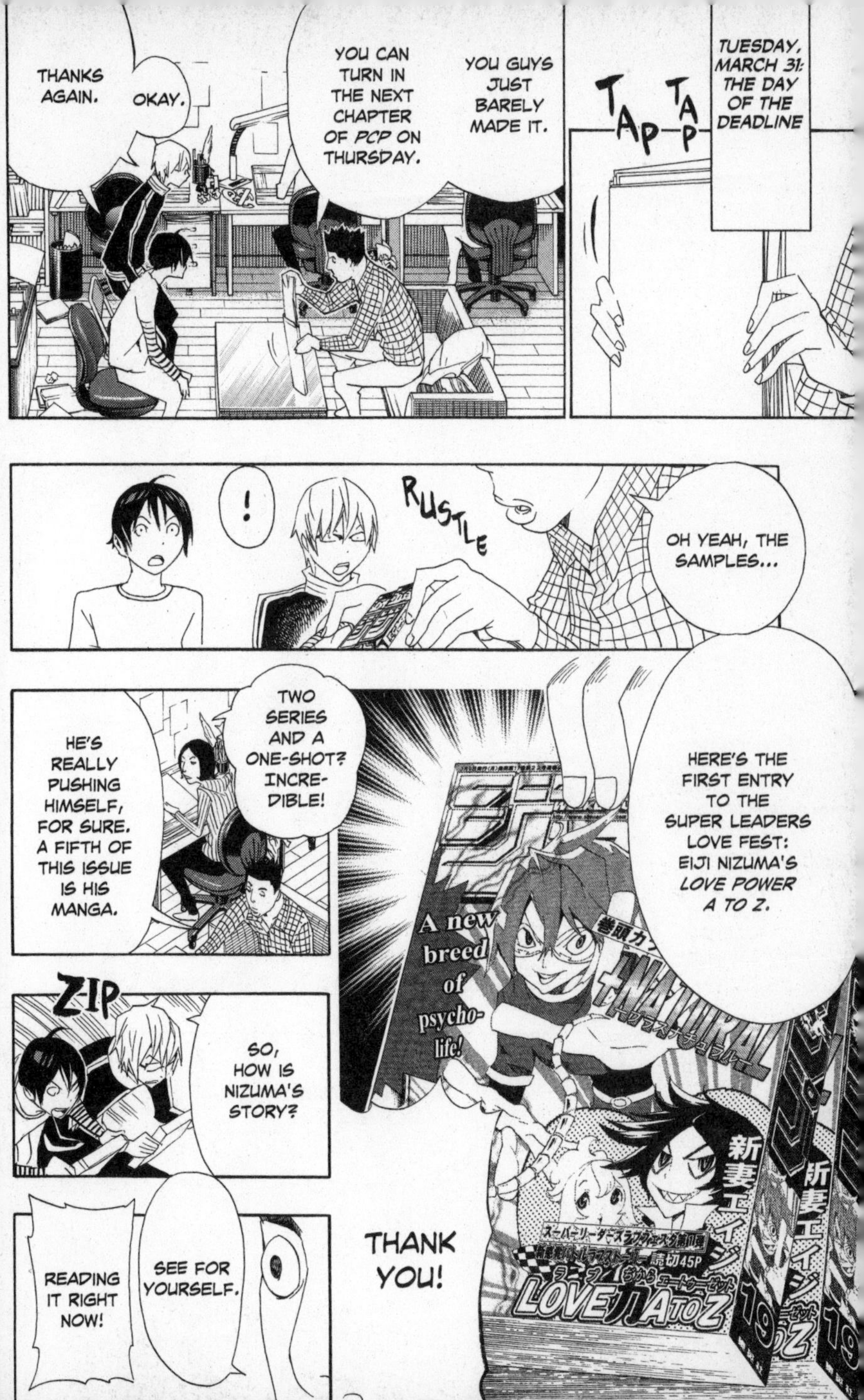
TUESDAY, MARCH 31: THE DAY OF THE DEADLINE
TAP TAP
YOU GUYS JUST BARELY MADE IT.
YOU CAN TURN IN THE NEXT CHAPTER OF *PCP* ON THURSDAY.
OKAY.
THANKS AGAIN.
OH YEAH, THE SAMPLES...
RUSTLE
!
HERE'S THE FIRST ENTRY TO THE SUPER LEADERS LOVE FEST: EIJI NIZUMA'S *LOVE POWER A TO Z*.
A new breed of psycho-life!
新妻エイジ
LOVE A TO Z
TWO SERIES AND A ONE-SHOT? INCREDIBLE!
HE'S REALLY PUSHING HIMSELF, FOR SURE. A FIFTH OF THIS ISSUE IS HIS MANGA.
ZIP
SO, HOW IS NIZUMA'S STORY?
THANK YOU!
SEE FOR YOURSELF.
READING IT RIGHT NOW!

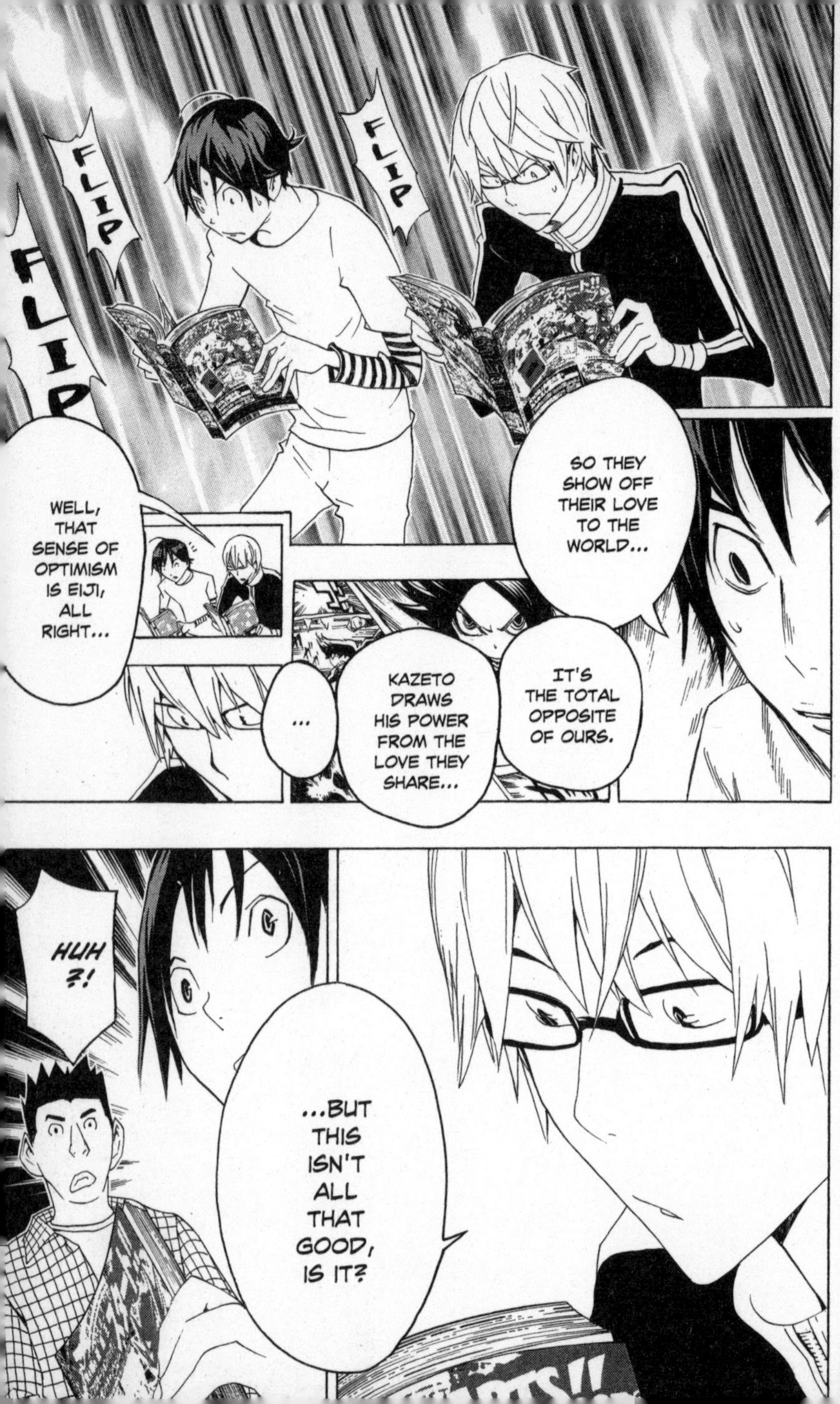
FLIP
FLIP
FLIP
SO THEY SHOW OFF THEIR LOVE TO THE WORLD...
IT'S THE TOTAL OPPOSITE OF OURS.
KAZETO DRAWS HIS POWER FROM THE LOVE THEY SHARE...
...
WELL, THAT SENSE OF OPTIMISM IS EIJI, ALL RIGHT...
...BUT THIS ISN'T ALL THAT GOOD, IS IT?
HUH?!

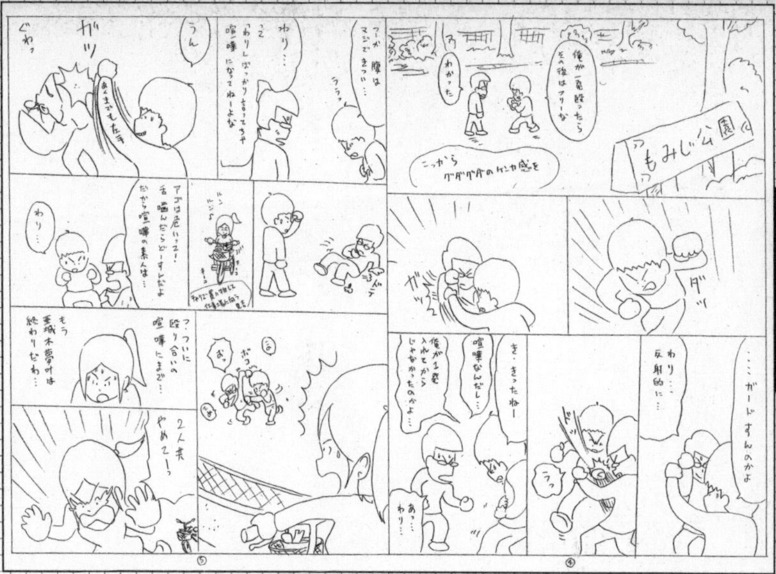
もみじ公園
俺が一発殴ったら その後はフリーな
わかった
ここから グダグダのケンカ感を
ダッ
ガッ
・・・ガードすんのかよ
わり・・・ 反射的に・・・
ドッ
うっ
き・・きったねー
喧嘩なんだし・・・
俺が1発入れたからじゃなかったのかよ・・・
あ・・・ わり・・・
つーか 腹はマジできつい・・・
わり・・・ って「わり」ばっかり言ってちゃ喧嘩になってねーよな
うん
ガツ
あくまでも左手
ぐわっ
わり・・・
アゴは危ないって! 舌噛んだらどーすんだよ だから喧嘩の素人は・・・
ルンルン♪
おっ
ボコッ
つ・・ついに殴り合いの喧嘩にまで・・・ もう亜城木夢叶は終わりだわ・・・
2人共やめて−!

OHBA'S STORYBOARD

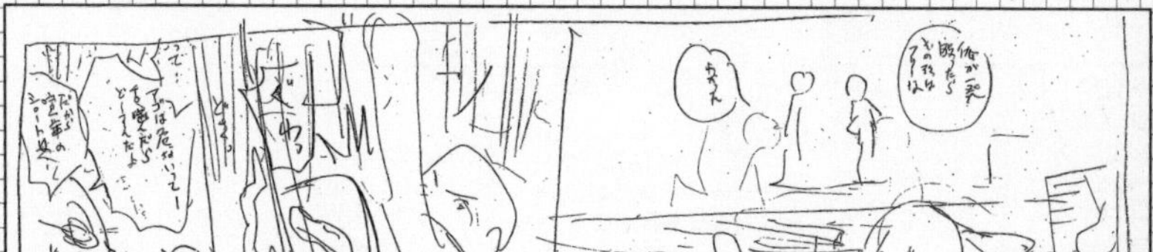

OBATA'S STORYBOARD

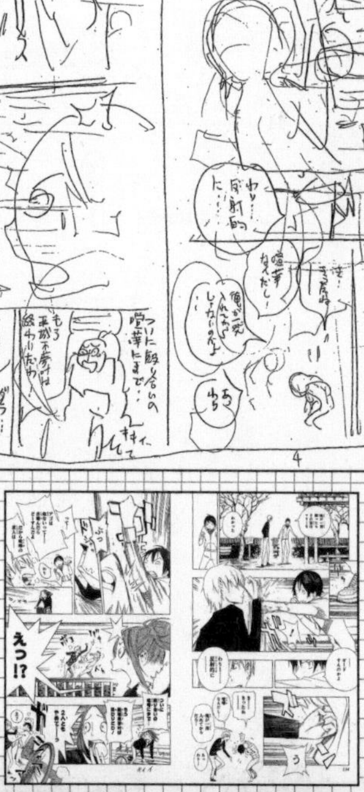
えっ!?

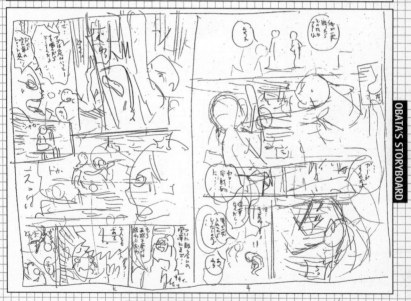

COMPLETE!

*CREATOR STORYBOARDS AND FINISHED PAGES IN JAPANESE

BAKUMAN。 vol.13

"Until the Final Draft Is Complete"

Chapter 112, pp. 114-115

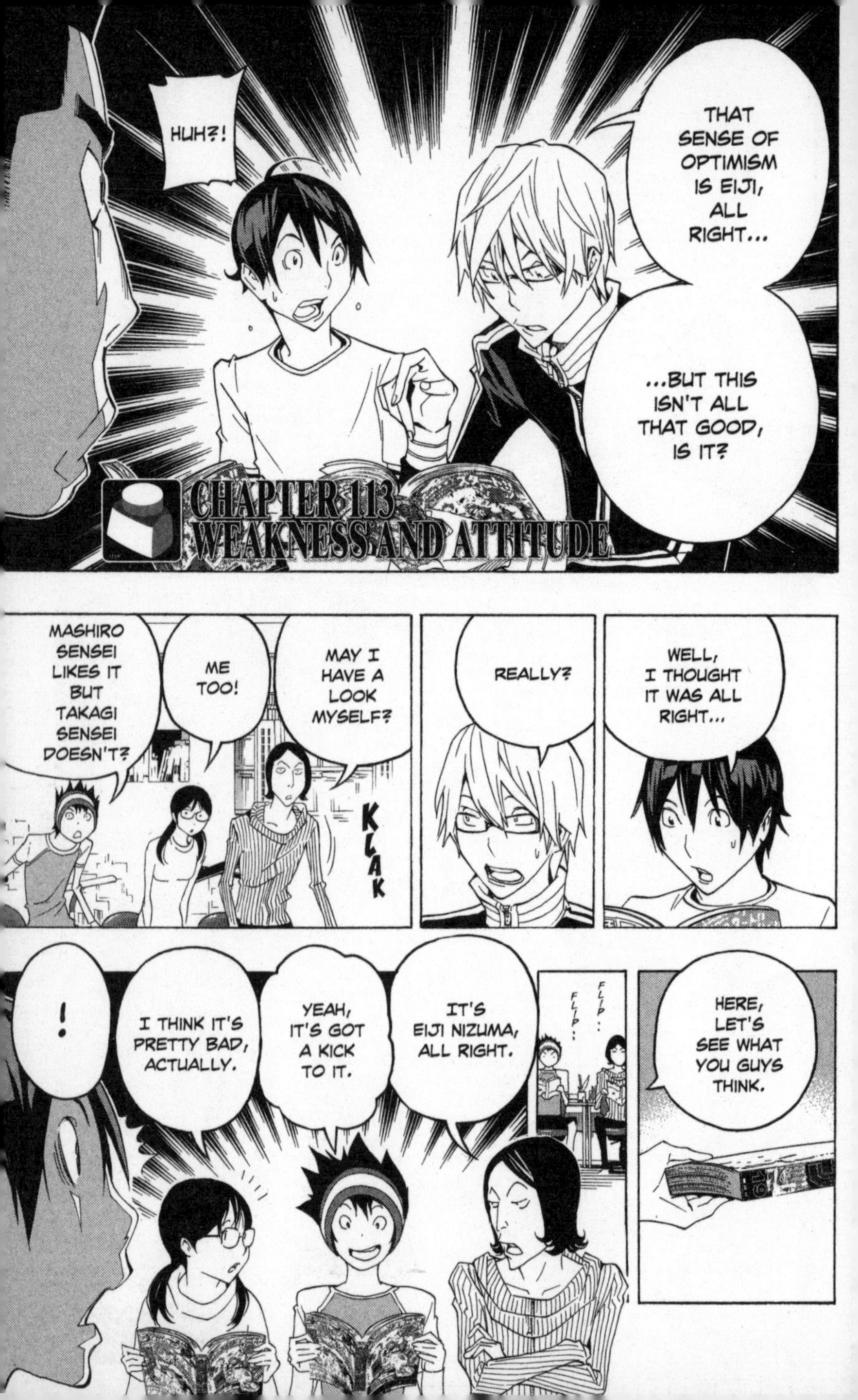
THAT SENSE OF OPTIMISM IS EIJI, ALL RIGHT...
...BUT THIS ISN'T ALL THAT GOOD, IS IT?
HUH?!
CHAPTER 113 WEAKNESS AND ATTITUDE
WELL, I THOUGHT IT WAS ALL RIGHT...
REALLY?
MAY I HAVE A LOOK MYSELF?
KLAK
ME TOO!
MASHIRO SENSEI LIKES IT BUT TAKAGI SENSEI DOESN'T?
HERE, LET'S SEE WHAT YOU GUYS THINK.
FLIP FLIP
IT'S EIJI NIZUMA, ALL RIGHT.
YEAH, IT'S GOT A KICK TO IT.
I THINK IT'S PRETTY BAD, ACTUALLY.
!

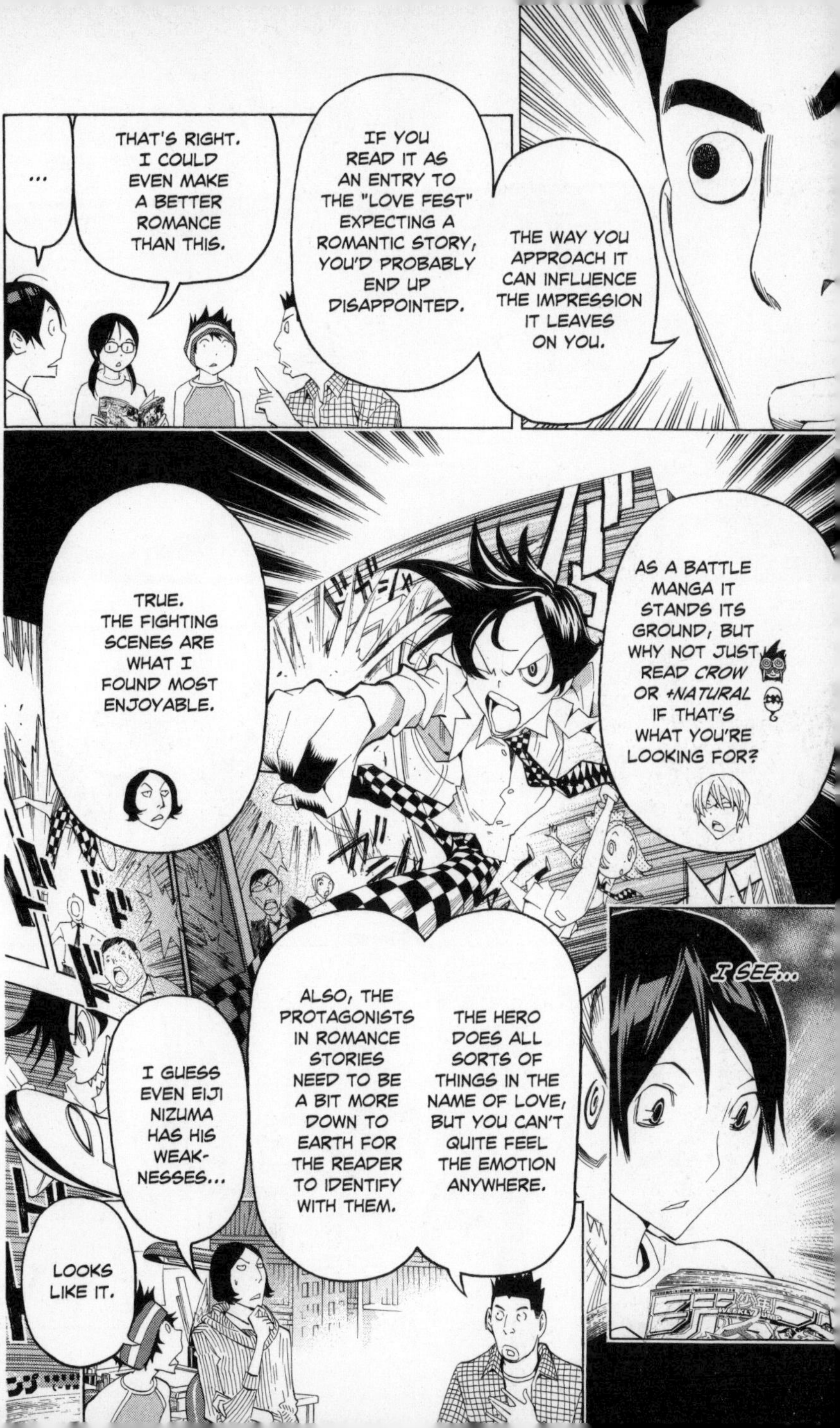
IF YOU READ IT AS AN ENTRY TO THE "LOVE FEST" EXPECTING A ROMANTIC STORY, YOU'D PROBABLY END UP DISAPPOINTED.
THE WAY YOU APPROACH IT CAN INFLUENCE THE IMPRESSION IT LEAVES ON YOU.
THAT'S RIGHT. I COULD EVEN MAKE A BETTER ROMANCE THAN THIS.
...
AS A BATTLE MANGA IT STANDS ITS GROUND, BUT WHY NOT JUST READ *CROW* OR *+NATURAL* IF THAT'S WHAT YOU'RE LOOKING FOR?
TRUE. THE FIGHTING SCENES ARE WHAT I FOUND MOST ENJOYABLE.
I SEE...
THE HERO DOES ALL SORTS OF THINGS IN THE NAME OF LOVE, BUT YOU CAN'T QUITE FEEL THE EMOTION ANYWHERE.
ALSO, THE PROTAGONISTS IN ROMANCE STORIES NEED TO BE A BIT MORE DOWN TO EARTH FOR THE READER TO IDENTIFY WITH THEM.
I GUESS EVEN EIJI NIZUMA HAS HIS WEAK-NESSES...
LOOKS LIKE IT.

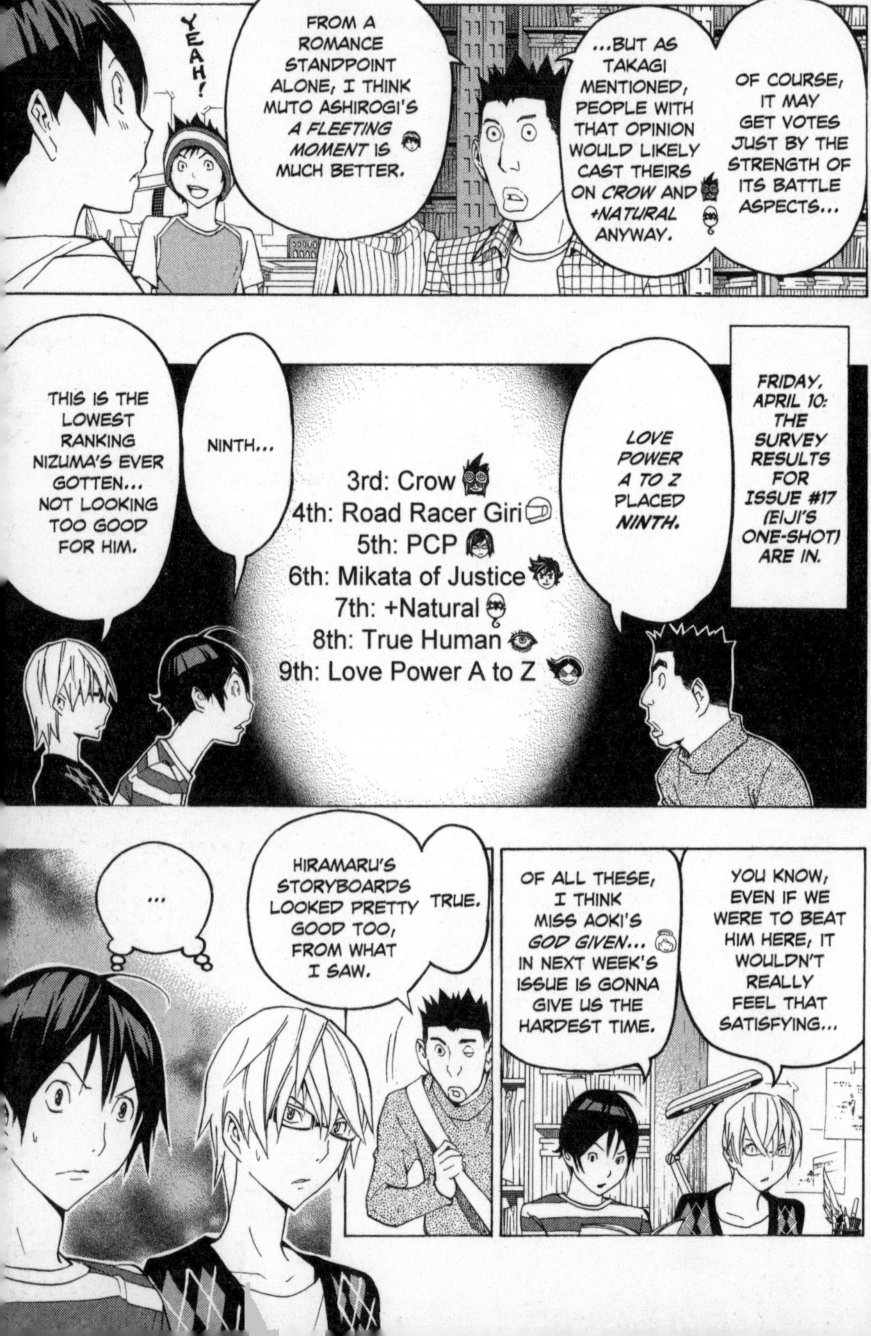
OF COURSE, IT MAY GET VOTES JUST BY THE STRENGTH OF ITS BATTLE ASPECTS...
...BUT AS TAKAGI MENTIONED, PEOPLE WITH THAT OPINION WOULD LIKELY CAST THEIRS ON *CROW* AND *+NATURAL* ANYWAY.
FROM A ROMANCE STANDPOINT ALONE, I THINK MUTO ASHIROGI'S *A FLEETING MOMENT* IS MUCH BETTER.
YEAH!
FRIDAY, APRIL 10: THE SURVEY RESULTS FOR ISSUE #17 (EIJI'S ONE-SHOT) ARE IN.
LOVE POWER A TO Z PLACED *NINTH.*
3rd: Crow
4th: Road Racer Giri
5th: PCP
6th: Mikata of Justice
7th: +Natural
8th: True Human
9th: Love Power A to Z
NINTH...
THIS IS THE LOWEST RANKING NIZUMA'S EVER GOTTEN... NOT LOOKING TOO GOOD FOR HIM.
YOU KNOW, EVEN IF WE WERE TO BEAT HIM HERE, IT WOULDN'T REALLY FEEL THAT SATISFYING...
OF ALL THESE, I THINK MISS AOKI'S *GOD GIVEN...* IN NEXT WEEK'S ISSUE IS GONNA GIVE US THE HARDEST TIME.
TRUE.
HIRAMARU'S STORYBOARDS LOOKED PRETTY GOOD TOO, FROM WHAT I SAW.
...

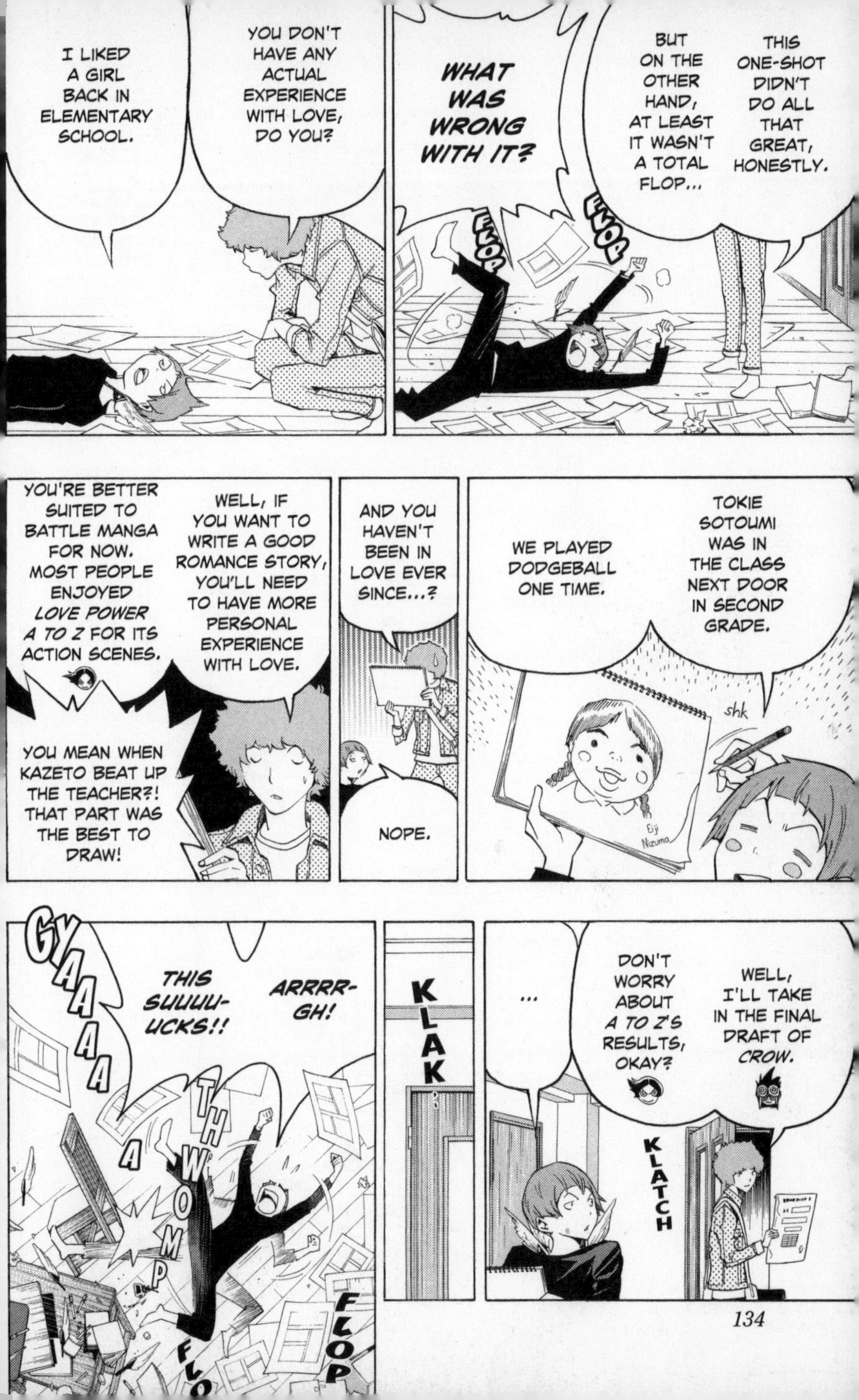
THIS ONE-SHOT DIDN'T DO ALL THAT GREAT, HONESTLY.
BUT ON THE OTHER HAND, AT LEAST IT WASN'T A TOTAL FLOP...
FLOP
FLOP
WHAT WAS WRONG WITH IT?
YOU DON'T HAVE ANY ACTUAL EXPERIENCE WITH LOVE, DO YOU?
I LIKED A GIRL BACK IN ELEMENTARY SCHOOL.
TOKIE SOTOUMI WAS IN THE CLASS NEXT DOOR IN SECOND GRADE.
WE PLAYED DODGEBALL ONE TIME.
shk
Eiji Nizuma
AND YOU HAVEN'T BEEN IN LOVE EVER SINCE...?
NOPE.
WELL, IF YOU WANT TO WRITE A GOOD ROMANCE STORY, YOU'LL NEED TO HAVE MORE PERSONAL EXPERIENCE WITH LOVE.
YOU'RE BETTER SUITED TO BATTLE MANGA FOR NOW. MOST PEOPLE ENJOYED *LOVE POWER A TO Z* FOR ITS ACTION SCENES.
YOU MEAN WHEN KAZETO BEAT UP THE TEACHER?! THAT PART WAS THE BEST TO DRAW!
WELL, I'LL TAKE IN THE FINAL DRAFT OF *CROW*.
DON'T WORRY ABOUT *A TO Z'S* RESULTS, OKAY?
...
KLATCH
KLAK
ARRRR-GH!
THIS SUUUU-UCKS!!
GYAAAAAA
THWOMP
FLOP
FLO

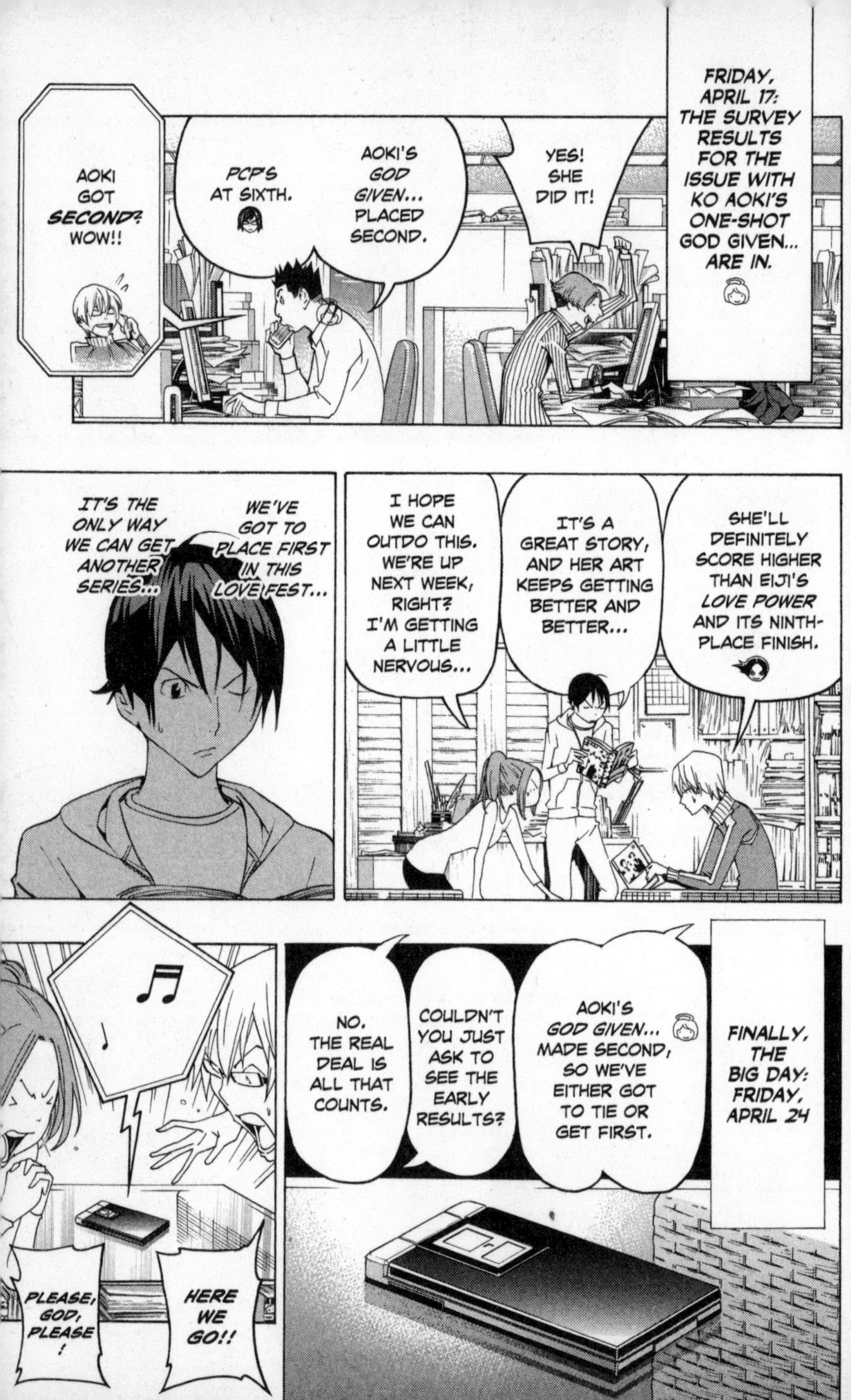
FRIDAY, APRIL 17: THE SURVEY RESULTS FOR THE ISSUE WITH KO AOKI'S ONE-SHOT GOD GIVEN... ARE IN.
YES! SHE DID IT!
AOKI'S GOD GIVEN... PLACED SECOND.
PCP'S AT SIXTH.
AOKI GOT SECOND? WOW!!
SHE'LL DEFINITELY SCORE HIGHER THAN EIJI'S LOVE POWER AND ITS NINTH-PLACE FINISH.
IT'S A GREAT STORY, AND HER ART KEEPS GETTING BETTER AND BETTER...
I HOPE WE CAN OUTDO THIS. WE'RE UP NEXT WEEK, RIGHT? I'M GETTING A LITTLE NERVOUS...
WE'VE GOT TO PLACE FIRST IN THIS LOVE FEST...
IT'S THE ONLY WAY WE CAN GET ANOTHER SERIES...
FINALLY, THE BIG DAY: FRIDAY, APRIL 24
AOKI'S GOD GIVEN... MADE SECOND, SO WE'VE EITHER GOT TO TIE OR GET FIRST.
COULDN'T YOU JUST ASK TO SEE THE EARLY RESULTS?
NO. THE REAL DEAL IS ALL THAT COUNTS.
HERE WE GO!!
PLEASE, GOD, PLEASE!

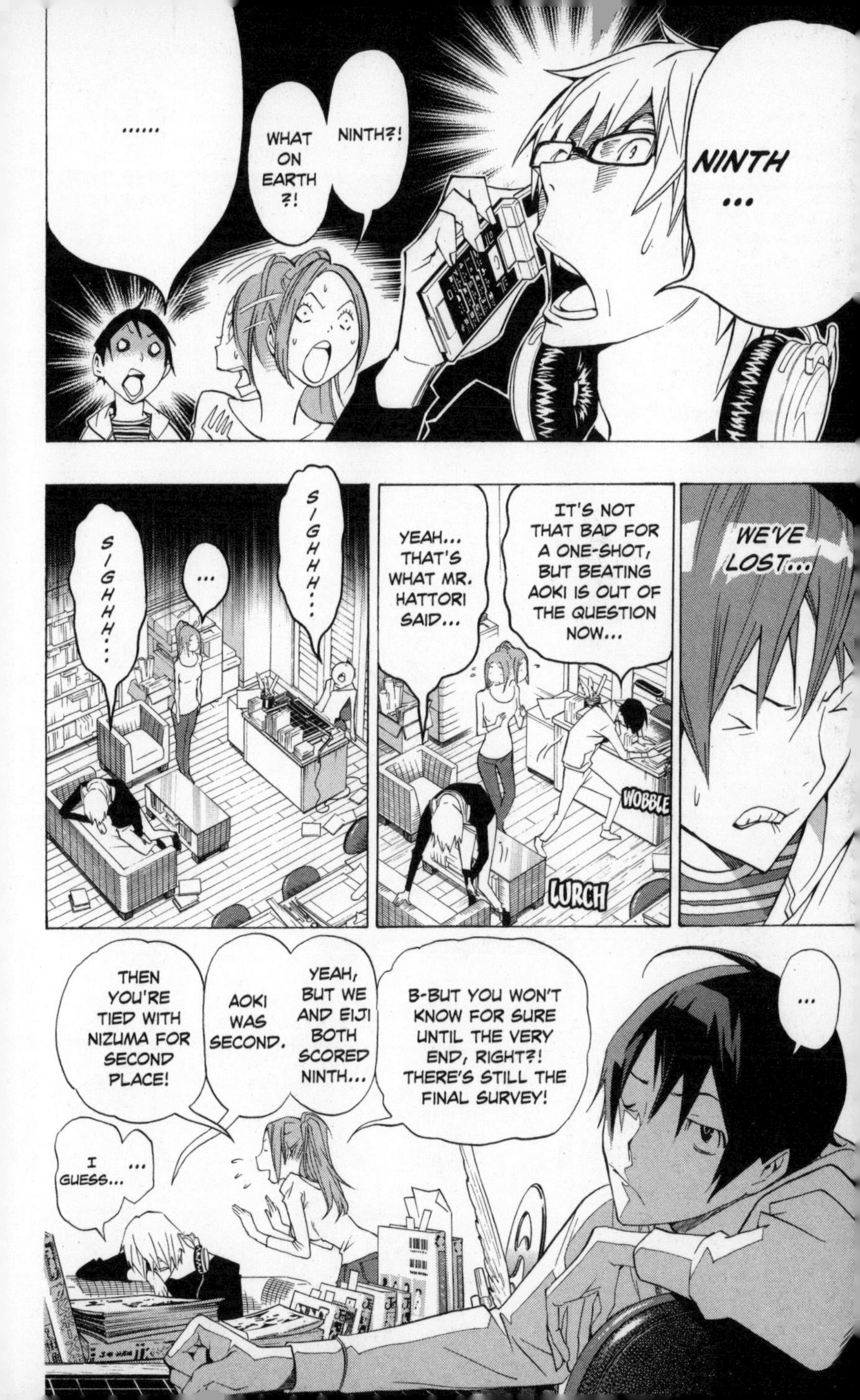
NINTH ...
NINTH?!
WHAT ON EARTH ?!
......
WE'VE LOST...
IT'S NOT THAT BAD FOR A ONE-SHOT, BUT BEATING AOKI IS OUT OF THE QUESTION NOW...
YEAH... THAT'S WHAT MR. HATTORI SAID...
WOBBLE
LURCH
SIGHHH...
...
SIGHHH...
...
B-BUT YOU WON'T KNOW FOR SURE UNTIL THE VERY END, RIGHT?! THERE'S STILL THE FINAL SURVEY!
YEAH, BUT WE AND EIJI BOTH SCORED NINTH...
AOKI WAS SECOND.
THEN YOU'RE TIED WITH NIZUMA FOR SECOND PLACE!
I GUESS... ...

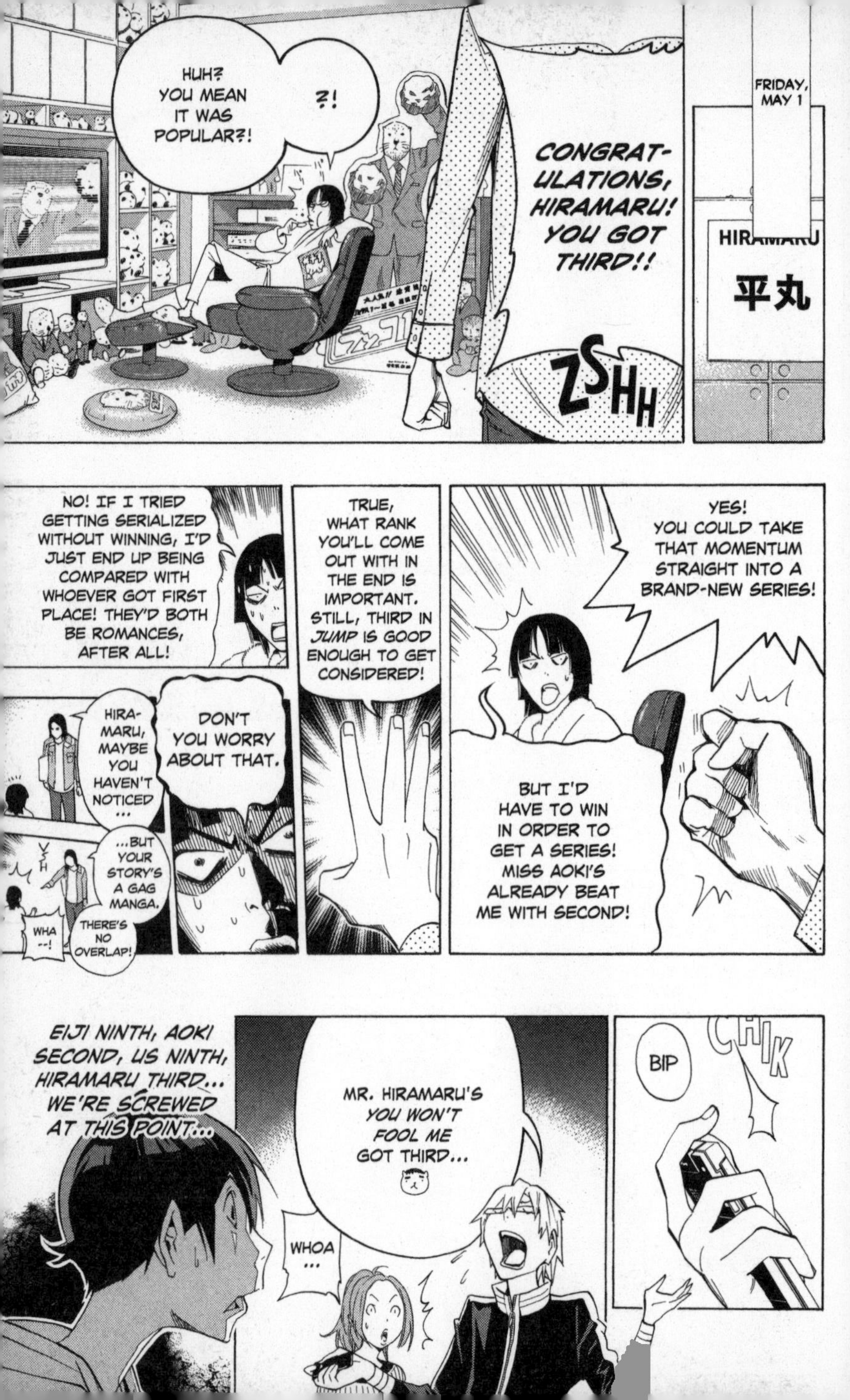
FRIDAY, MAY 1
平丸
CONGRATULATIONS, HIRAMARU! YOU GOT THIRD!!
ZSHH
?!
HUH? YOU MEAN IT WAS POPULAR?!
YES! YOU COULD TAKE THAT MOMENTUM STRAIGHT INTO A BRAND-NEW SERIES!
BUT I'D HAVE TO WIN IN ORDER TO GET A SERIES! MISS AOKI'S ALREADY BEAT ME WITH SECOND!
TRUE, WHAT RANK YOU'LL COME OUT WITH IN THE END IS IMPORTANT. STILL, THIRD IN *JUMP* IS GOOD ENOUGH TO GET CONSIDERED!
NO! IF I TRIED GETTING SERIALIZED WITHOUT WINNING, I'D JUST END UP BEING COMPARED WITH WHOEVER GOT FIRST PLACE! THEY'D BOTH BE ROMANCES, AFTER ALL!
DON'T YOU WORRY ABOUT THAT.
HIRAMARU, MAYBE YOU HAVEN'T NOTICED...
...BUT YOUR STORY'S A GAG MANGA.
THERE'S NO OVERLAP!
WHA--!
CHIK
BIP
MR. HIRAMARU'S GOT THIRD...
YOU WON'T FOOL ME
WHOA...
EIJI NINTH, AOKI SECOND, US NINTH, HIRAMARU THIRD... WE'RE SCREWED AT THIS POINT...

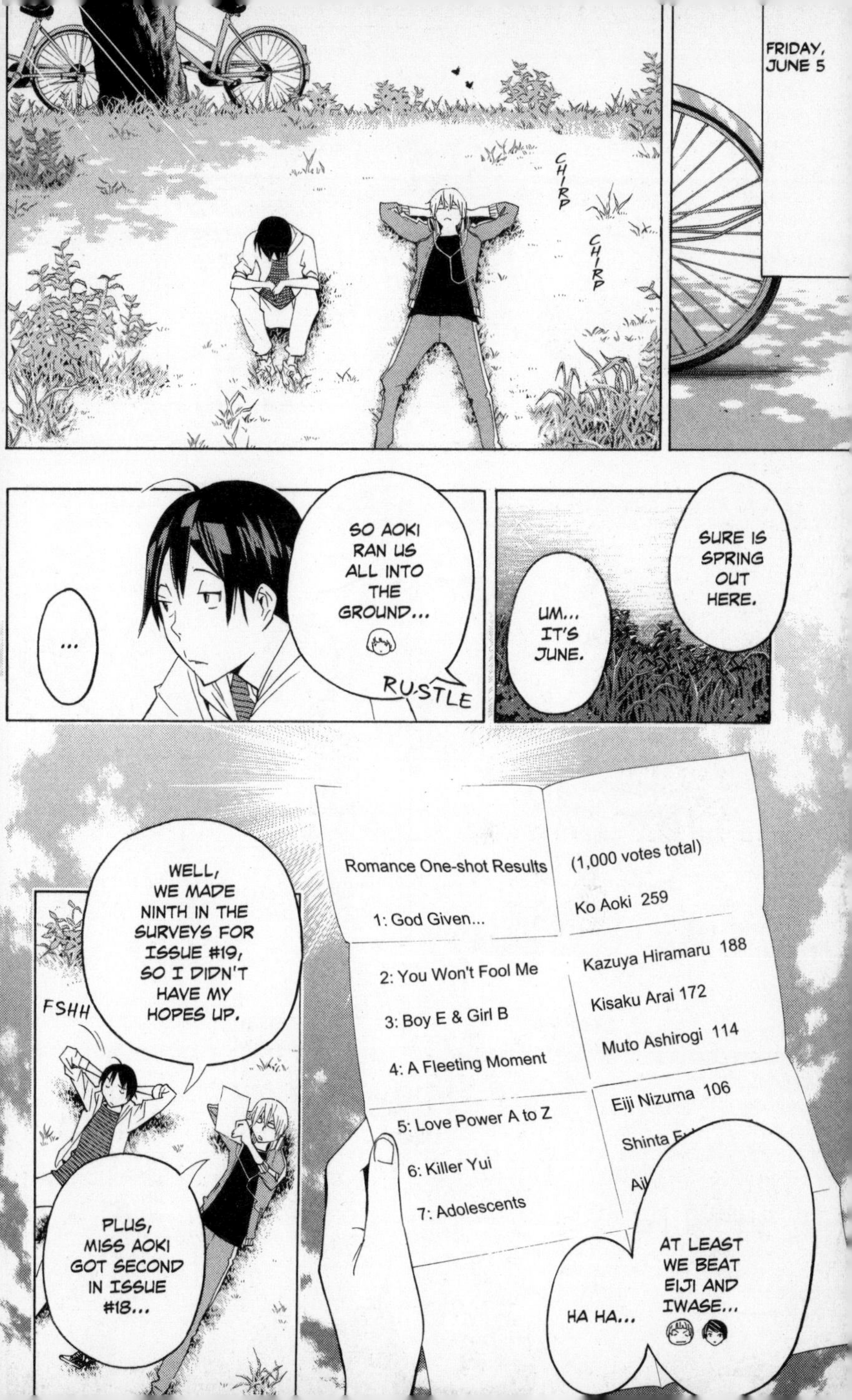
FRIDAY, JUNE 5
CHIRP
CHIRP
SURE IS SPRING OUT HERE.
UM... IT'S JUNE.
SO AOKI RAN US ALL INTO THE GROUND...
RUSTLE
...
Romance One-shot Results
(1,000 votes total)
1: God Given... Ko Aoki 259
2: You Won't Fool Me Kazuya Hiramaru 188
3: Boy E & Girl B Kisaku Arai 172
4: A Fleeting Moment Muto Ashirogi 114
5: Love Power A to Z Eiji Nizuma 106
6: Killer Yui Shinta
7: Adolescents
AT LEAST WE BEAT EIJI AND IWASE...
HA HA...
WELL, WE MADE NINTH IN THE SURVEYS FOR ISSUE #19, SO I DIDN'T HAVE MY HOPES UP.
FSHH
PLUS, MISS AOKI GOT SECOND IN ISSUE #18...

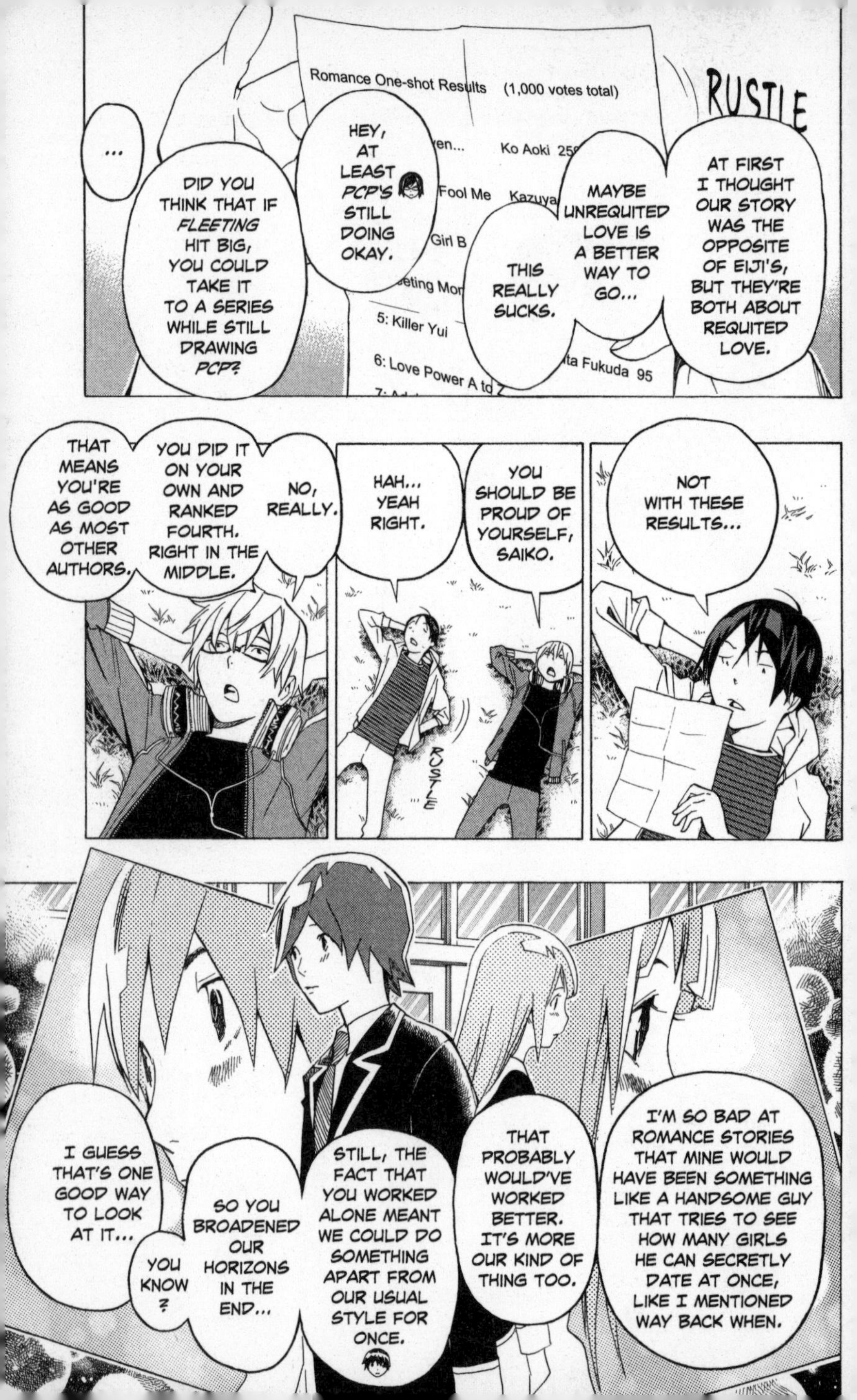
RUSTLE
Romance One-shot Results (1,000 votes total)
Ko Aoki
Fool Me
Girl B
5: Killer Yui
6: Love Power A to
Fukuda 95
AT FIRST I THOUGHT OUR STORY WAS THE OPPOSITE OF EIJI'S, BUT THEY'RE BOTH ABOUT REQUITED LOVE.
MAYBE UNREQUITED LOVE IS A BETTER WAY TO GO...
THIS REALLY SUCKS.
HEY, AT LEAST PCP'S STILL DOING OKAY.
DID YOU THINK THAT IF FLEETING HIT BIG, YOU COULD TAKE IT TO A SERIES WHILE STILL DRAWING PCP?
...
NOT WITH THESE RESULTS...
YOU SHOULD BE PROUD OF YOURSELF, SAIKO.
HAH... YEAH RIGHT.
RUSTLE
NO, REALLY.
YOU DID IT ON YOUR OWN AND RANKED FOURTH. RIGHT IN THE MIDDLE.
THAT MEANS YOU'RE AS GOOD AS MOST OTHER AUTHORS.
I'M SO BAD AT ROMANCE STORIES THAT MINE WOULD HAVE BEEN SOMETHING LIKE A HANDSOME GUY THAT TRIES TO SEE HOW MANY GIRLS HE CAN SECRETLY DATE AT ONCE, LIKE I MENTIONED WAY BACK WHEN.
THAT PROBABLY WOULD'VE WORKED BETTER. IT'S MORE OUR KIND OF THING TOO.
STILL, THE FACT THAT YOU WORKED ALONE MEANT WE COULD DO SOMETHING APART FROM OUR USUAL STYLE FOR ONCE.
SO YOU BROADENED OUR HORIZONS IN THE END...
YOU KNOW?
I GUESS THAT'S ONE GOOD WAY TO LOOK AT IT...

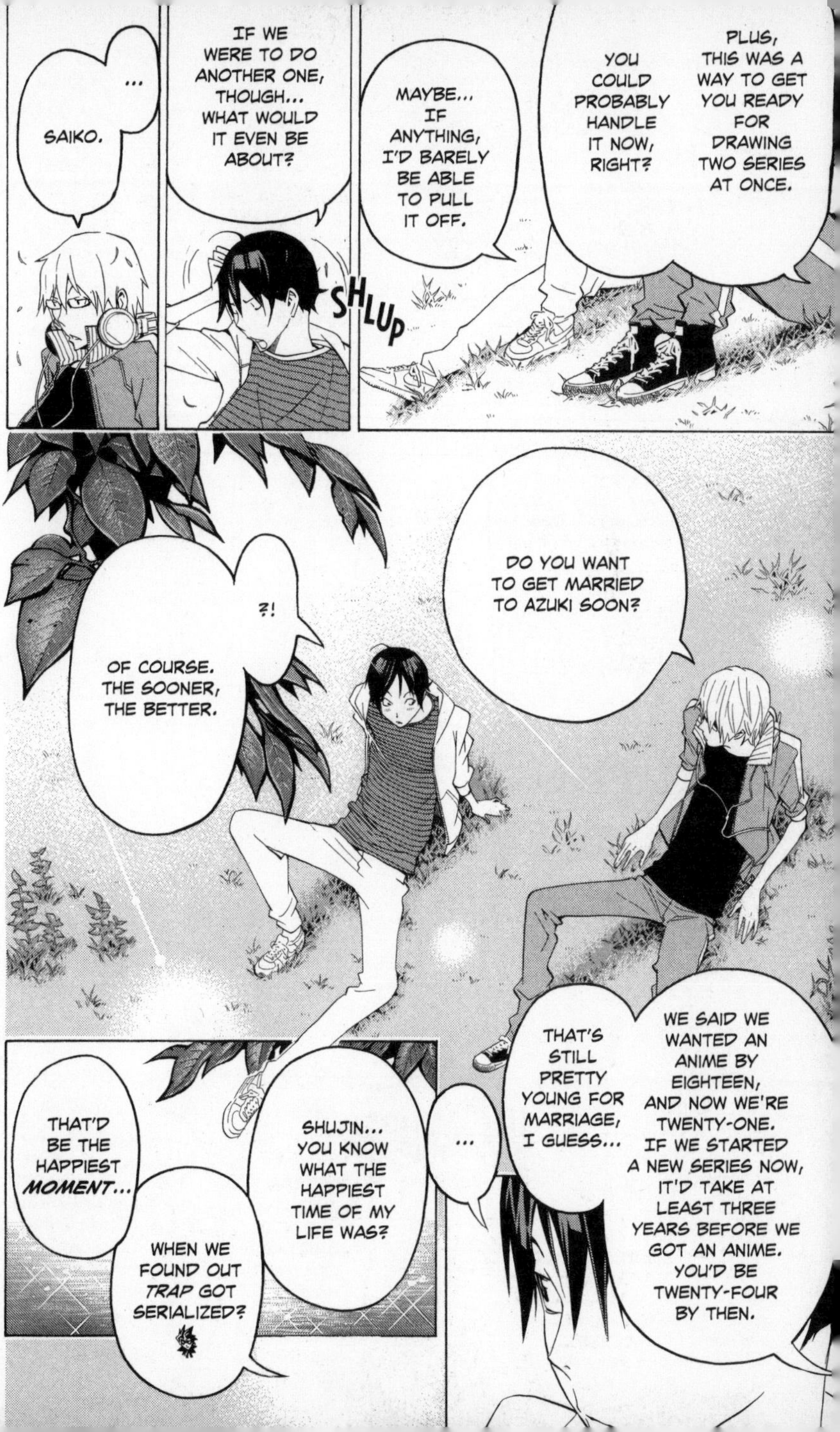
PLUS, THIS WAS A WAY TO GET YOU READY FOR DRAWING TWO SERIES AT ONCE.
YOU COULD PROBABLY HANDLE IT NOW, RIGHT?
MAYBE... IF ANYTHING, I'D BARELY BE ABLE TO PULL IT OFF.
SHLUP
IF WE WERE TO DO ANOTHER ONE, THOUGH... WHAT WOULD IT EVEN BE ABOUT?
...
SAIKO.
DO YOU WANT TO GET MARRIED TO AZUKI SOON?
?!
OF COURSE. THE SOONER, THE BETTER.
WE SAID WE WANTED AN ANIME BY EIGHTEEN, AND NOW WE'RE TWENTY-ONE. IF WE STARTED A NEW SERIES NOW, IT'D TAKE AT LEAST THREE YEARS BEFORE WE GOT AN ANIME. YOU'D BE TWENTY-FOUR BY THEN.
THAT'S STILL PRETTY YOUNG FOR MARRIAGE, I GUESS...
...
SHUJIN... YOU KNOW WHAT THE HAPPIEST TIME OF MY LIFE WAS?
WHEN WE FOUND OUT *TRAP* GOT SERIALIZED?
THAT'D BE THE HAPPIEST ***MOMENT***...

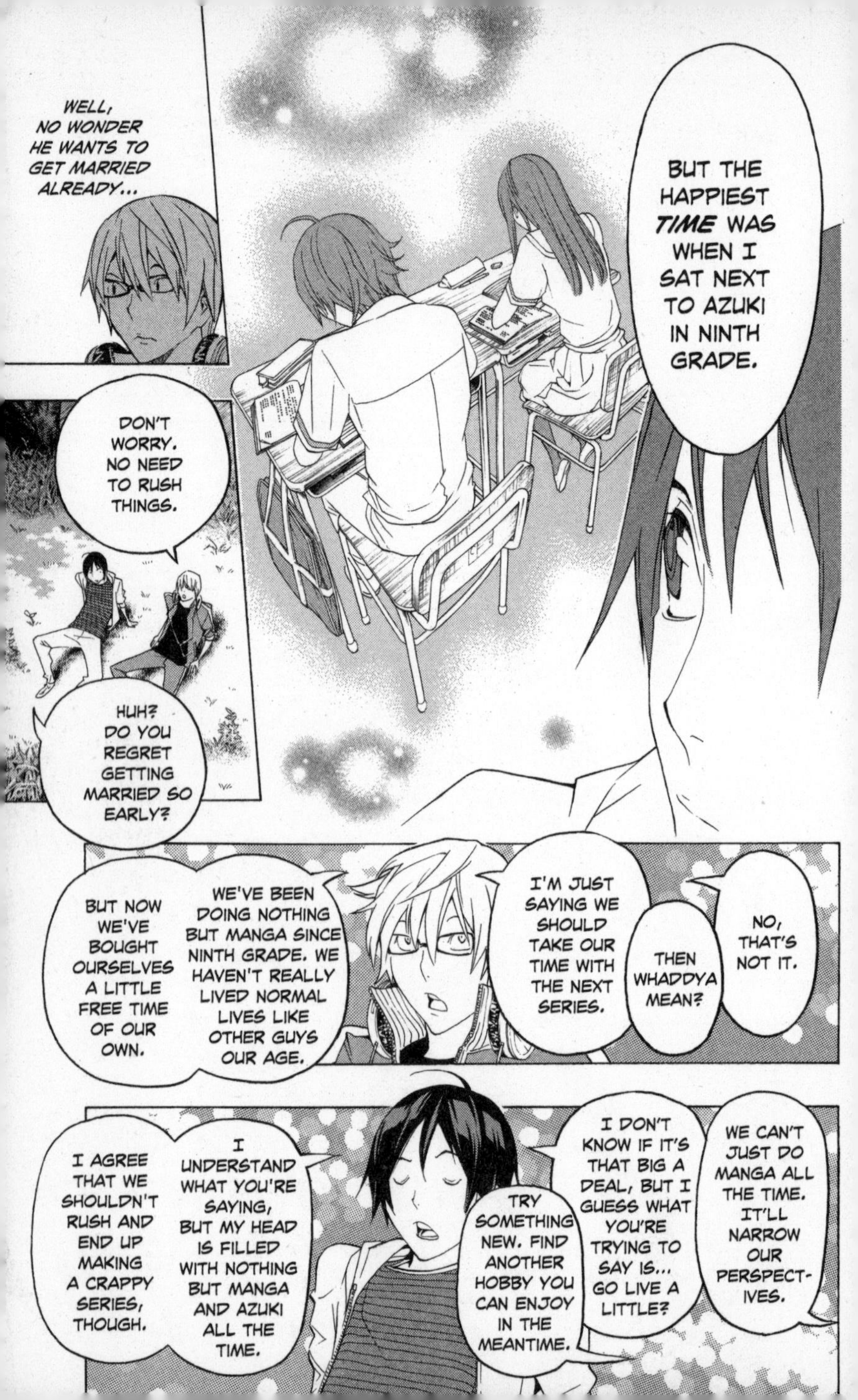
BUT THE HAPPIEST *TIME* WAS WHEN I SAT NEXT TO AZUKI IN NINTH GRADE.
WELL, NO WONDER HE WANTS TO GET MARRIED ALREADY...
DON'T WORRY. NO NEED TO RUSH THINGS.
HUH? DO YOU REGRET GETTING MARRIED SO EARLY?
NO, THAT'S NOT IT.
THEN WHADDYA MEAN?
I'M JUST SAYING WE SHOULD TAKE OUR TIME WITH THE NEXT SERIES.
WE'VE BEEN DOING NOTHING BUT MANGA SINCE NINTH GRADE. WE HAVEN'T REALLY LIVED NORMAL LIVES LIKE OTHER GUYS OUR AGE.
BUT NOW WE'VE BOUGHT OURSELVES A LITTLE FREE TIME OF OUR OWN.
WE CAN'T JUST DO MANGA ALL THE TIME. IT'LL NARROW OUR PERSPECT-IVES.
I DON'T KNOW IF IT'S THAT BIG A DEAL, BUT I GUESS WHAT YOU'RE TRYING TO SAY IS... GO LIVE A LITTLE?
TRY SOMETHING NEW. FIND ANOTHER HOBBY YOU CAN ENJOY IN THE MEANTIME.
I UNDERSTAND WHAT YOU'RE SAYING, BUT MY HEAD IS FILLED WITH NOTHING BUT MANGA AND AZUKI ALL THE TIME.
I AGREE THAT WE SHOULDN'T RUSH AND END UP MAKING A CRAPPY SERIES, THOUGH.

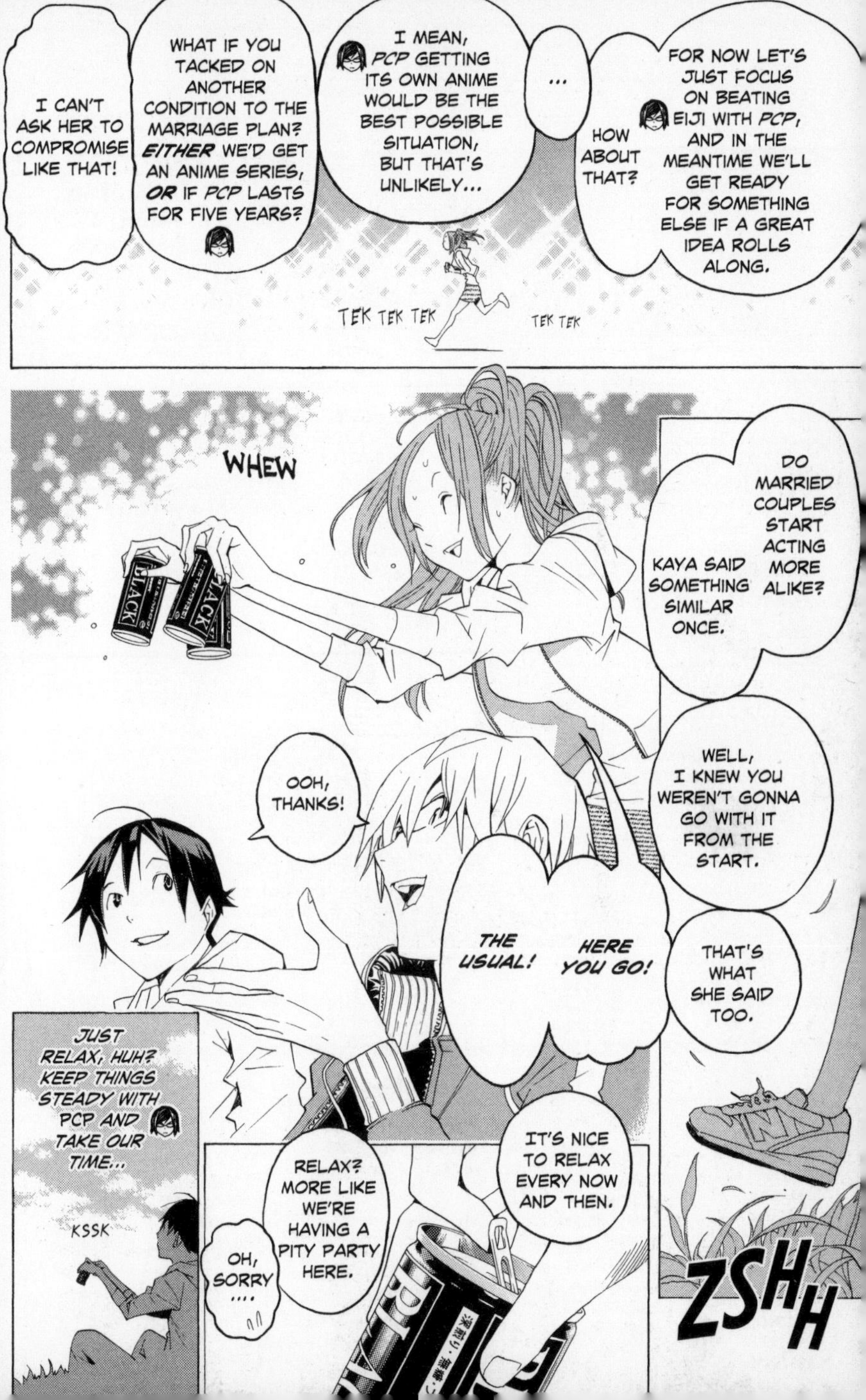

FOR NOW LET'S JUST FOCUS ON BEATING EIJI WITH PCP, AND IN THE MEANTIME WE'LL GET READY FOR SOMETHING ELSE IF A GREAT IDEA ROLLS ALONG.
HOW ABOUT THAT?
...
I MEAN, PCP GETTING ITS OWN ANIME WOULD BE THE BEST POSSIBLE SITUATION, BUT THAT'S UNLIKELY...
WHAT IF YOU TACKED ON ANOTHER CONDITION TO THE MARRIAGE PLAN? EITHER WE'D GET AN ANIME SERIES, OR IF PCP LASTS FOR FIVE YEARS?
I CAN'T ASK HER TO COMPROMISE LIKE THAT!
TEK TEK TEK
TEK TEK
DO MARRIED COUPLES START ACTING MORE ALIKE?
KAYA SAID SOMETHING SIMILAR ONCE.
WELL, I KNEW YOU WEREN'T GONNA GO WITH IT FROM THE START.
THAT'S WHAT SHE SAID TOO.
ZSHH
WHEW
HERE YOU GO!
THE USUAL!
OOH, THANKS!
IT'S NICE TO RELAX EVERY NOW AND THEN.
RELAX? MORE LIKE WE'RE HAVING A PITY PARTY HERE.
OH, SORRY ....
JUST RELAX, HUH? KEEP THINGS STEADY WITH PCP AND TAKE OUR TIME...
KSSK

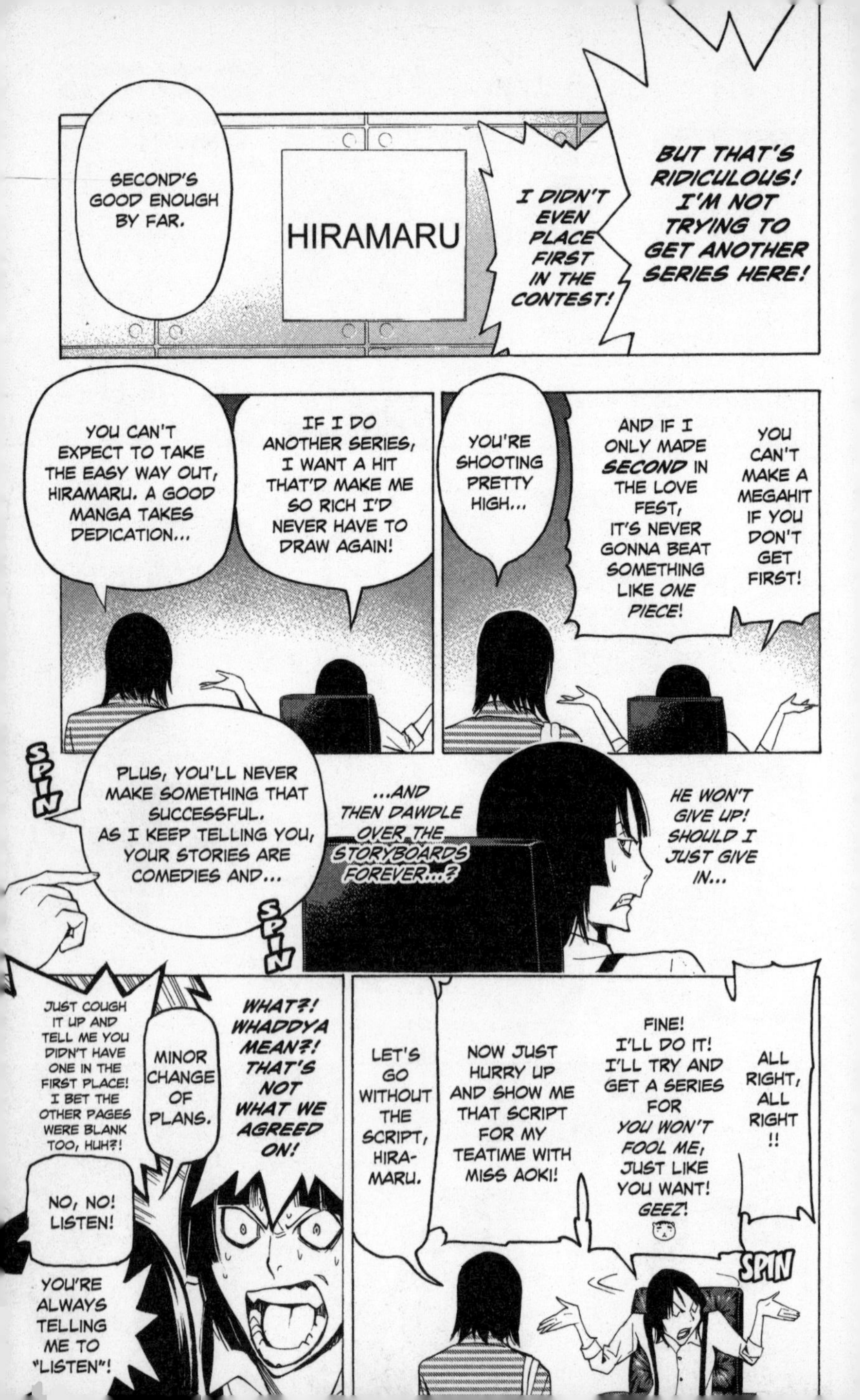
BUT THAT'S RIDICULOUS! I'M NOT TRYING TO GET ANOTHER SERIES HERE!
I DIDN'T EVEN PLACE FIRST IN THE CONTEST!
HIRAMARU
SECOND'S GOOD ENOUGH BY FAR.
YOU CAN'T MAKE A MEGAHIT IF YOU DON'T GET FIRST!
AND IF I ONLY MADE SECOND IN THE LOVE FEST, IT'S NEVER GONNA BEAT SOMETHING LIKE ONE PIECE!
YOU'RE SHOOTING PRETTY HIGH...
IF I DO ANOTHER SERIES, I WANT A HIT THAT'D MAKE ME SO RICH I'D NEVER HAVE TO DRAW AGAIN!
YOU CAN'T EXPECT TO TAKE THE EASY WAY OUT, HIRAMARU. A GOOD MANGA TAKES DEDICATION...
HE WON'T GIVE UP! SHOULD I JUST GIVE IN...
...AND THEN DAWDLE OVER THE STORYBOARDS FOREVER...?
SPIN
PLUS, YOU'LL NEVER MAKE SOMETHING THAT SUCCESSFUL. AS I KEEP TELLING YOU, YOUR STORIES ARE COMEDIES AND...
SPIN
ALL RIGHT, ALL RIGHT!!
FINE! I'LL DO IT! I'LL TRY AND GET A SERIES FOR YOU WON'T FOOL ME, JUST LIKE YOU WANT! GEEZ!
SPIN
NOW JUST HURRY UP AND SHOW ME THAT SCRIPT FOR MY TEATIME WITH MISS AOKI!
LET'S GO WITHOUT THE SCRIPT, HIRA-MARU.
WHAT?! WHADDYA MEAN?! THAT'S NOT WHAT WE AGREED ON!
MINOR CHANGE OF PLANS.
JUST COUGH IT UP AND TELL ME YOU DIDN'T HAVE ONE IN THE FIRST PLACE! I BET THE OTHER PAGES WERE BLANK TOO, HUH?!
NO, NO! LISTEN!
YOU'RE ALWAYS TELLING ME TO "LISTEN"!

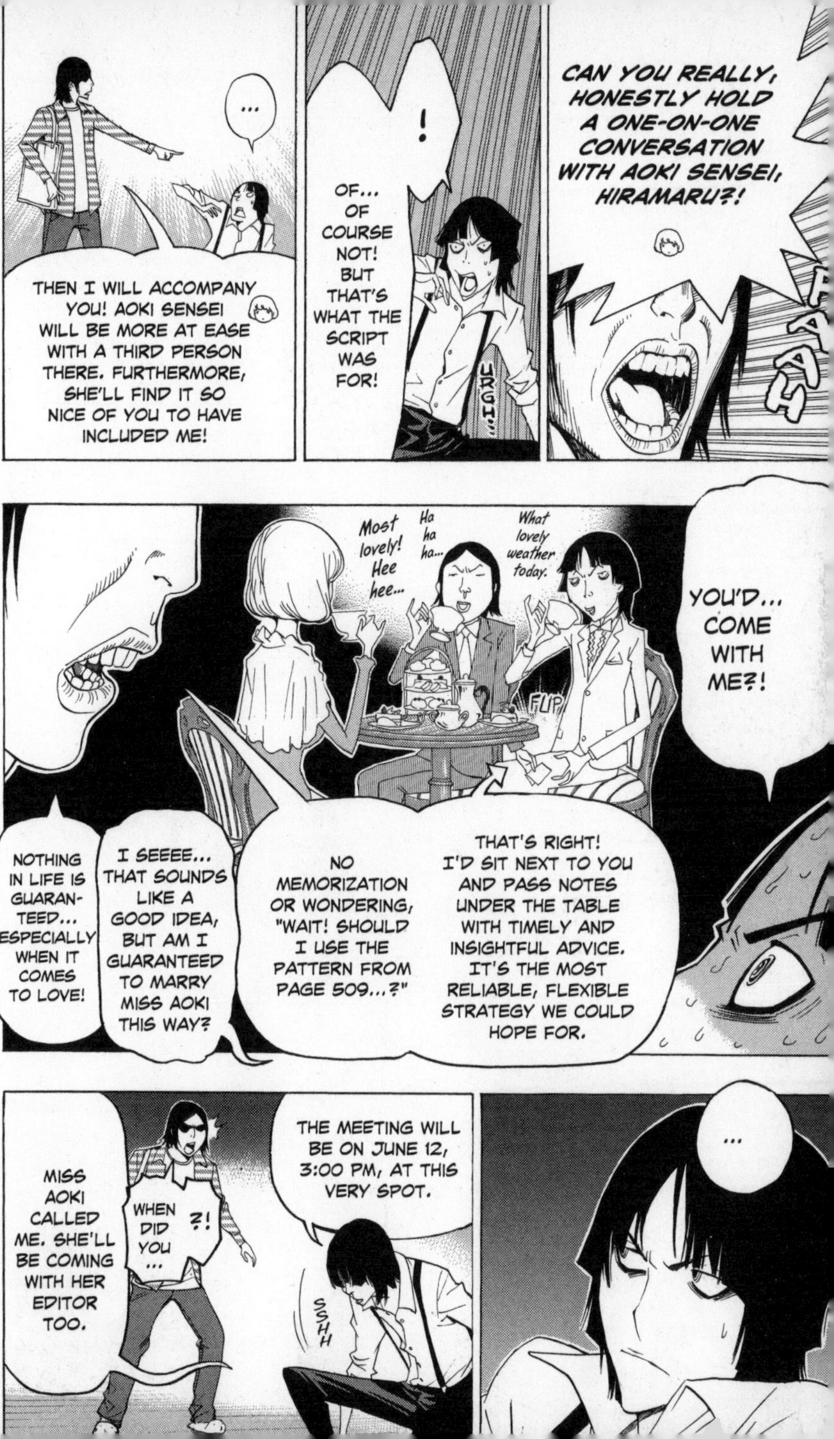
CAN YOU REALLY, HONESTLY HOLD A ONE-ON-ONE CONVERSATION WITH AOKI SENSEI, HIRAMARU?!
!
OF... OF COURSE NOT! BUT THAT'S WHAT THE SCRIPT WAS FOR!
URGH...
...
THEN I WILL ACCOMPANY YOU! AOKI SENSEI WILL BE MORE AT EASE WITH A THIRD PERSON THERE. FURTHERMORE, SHE'LL FIND IT SO NICE OF YOU TO HAVE INCLUDED ME!
YOU'D... COME WITH ME?!
THAT'S RIGHT! I'D SIT NEXT TO YOU AND PASS NOTES UNDER THE TABLE WITH TIMELY AND INSIGHTFUL ADVICE. IT'S THE MOST RELIABLE, FLEXIBLE STRATEGY WE COULD HOPE FOR.
NO MEMORIZATION OR WONDERING, "WAIT! SHOULD I USE THE PATTERN FROM PAGE 509...?"
What lovely weather today.
Ha ha ha...
Most lovely! Hee hee...
FLIP
I SEEEE... THAT SOUNDS LIKE A GOOD IDEA, BUT AM I GUARANTEED TO MARRY MISS AOKI THIS WAY?
NOTHING IN LIFE IS GUARANTEED... ESPECIALLY WHEN IT COMES TO LOVE!
...
THE MEETING WILL BE ON JUNE 12, 3:00 PM, AT THIS VERY SPOT.
SSHH
?!
WHEN DID YOU ...
MISS AOKI CALLED ME. SHE'LL BE COMING WITH HER EDITOR TOO.

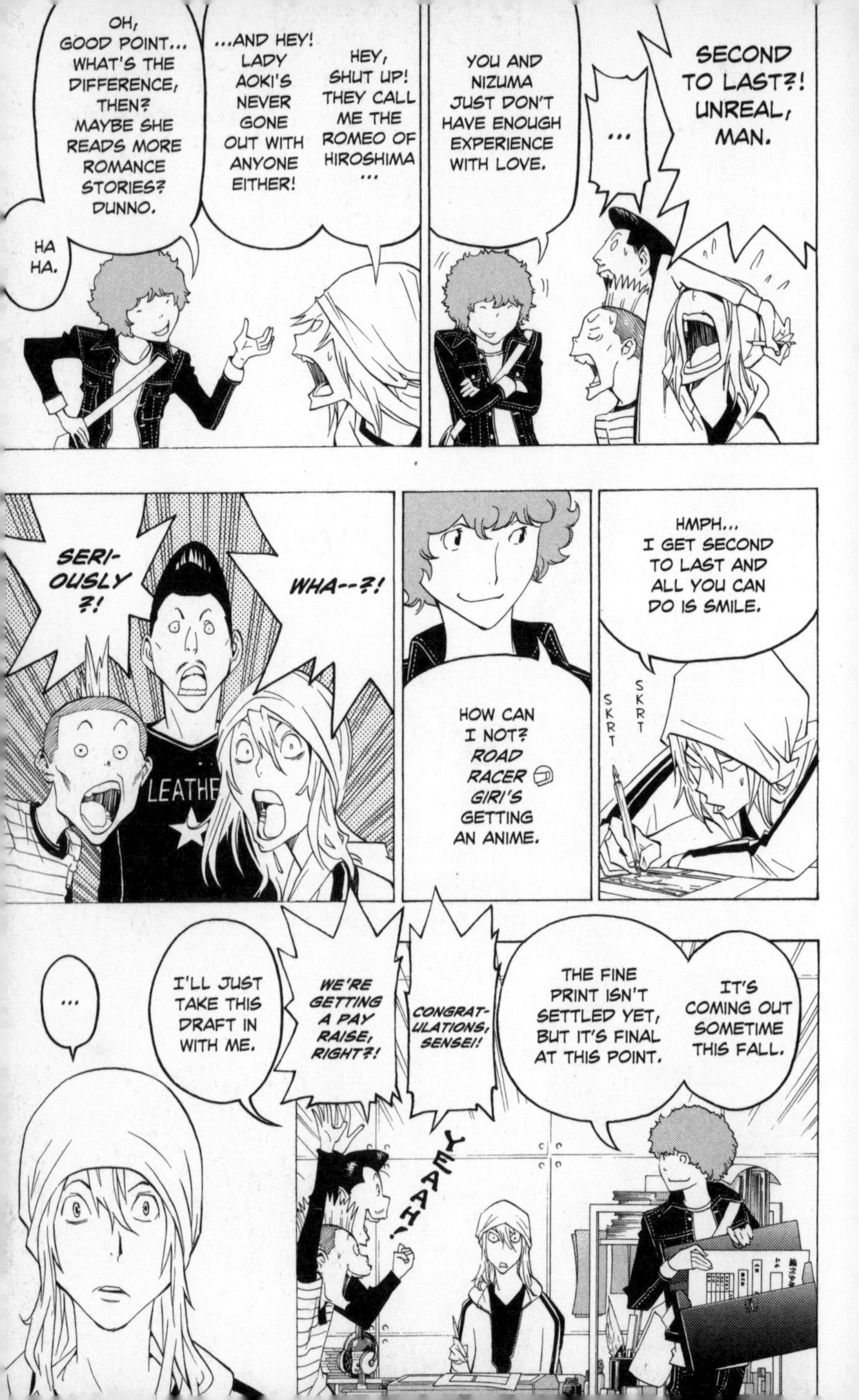
SECOND TO LAST?! UNREAL, MAN.
...
YOU AND NIZUMA JUST DON'T HAVE ENOUGH EXPERIENCE WITH LOVE.
HEY, SHUT UP! THEY CALL ME THE ROMEO OF HIROSHIMA...
...AND HEY! LADY AOKI'S NEVER GONE OUT WITH ANYONE EITHER!
OH, GOOD POINT... WHAT'S THE DIFFERENCE, THEN? MAYBE SHE READS MORE ROMANCE STORIES? DUNNO.
HA HA.
HMPH... I GET SECOND TO LAST AND ALL YOU CAN DO IS SMILE.
SKRT
SKRT
HOW CAN I NOT? *ROAD RACER GIRI'S* GETTING AN ANIME.
WHA--?!
SERI-OUSLY?!
LEATHE
IT'S COMING OUT SOMETIME THIS FALL.
THE FINE PRINT ISN'T SETTLED YET, BUT IT'S FINAL AT THIS POINT.
CONGRAT-ULATIONS, SENSEI!
YEAAH!
WE'RE GETTING A PAY RAISE, RIGHT?!
I'LL JUST TAKE THIS DRAFT IN WITH ME.
...

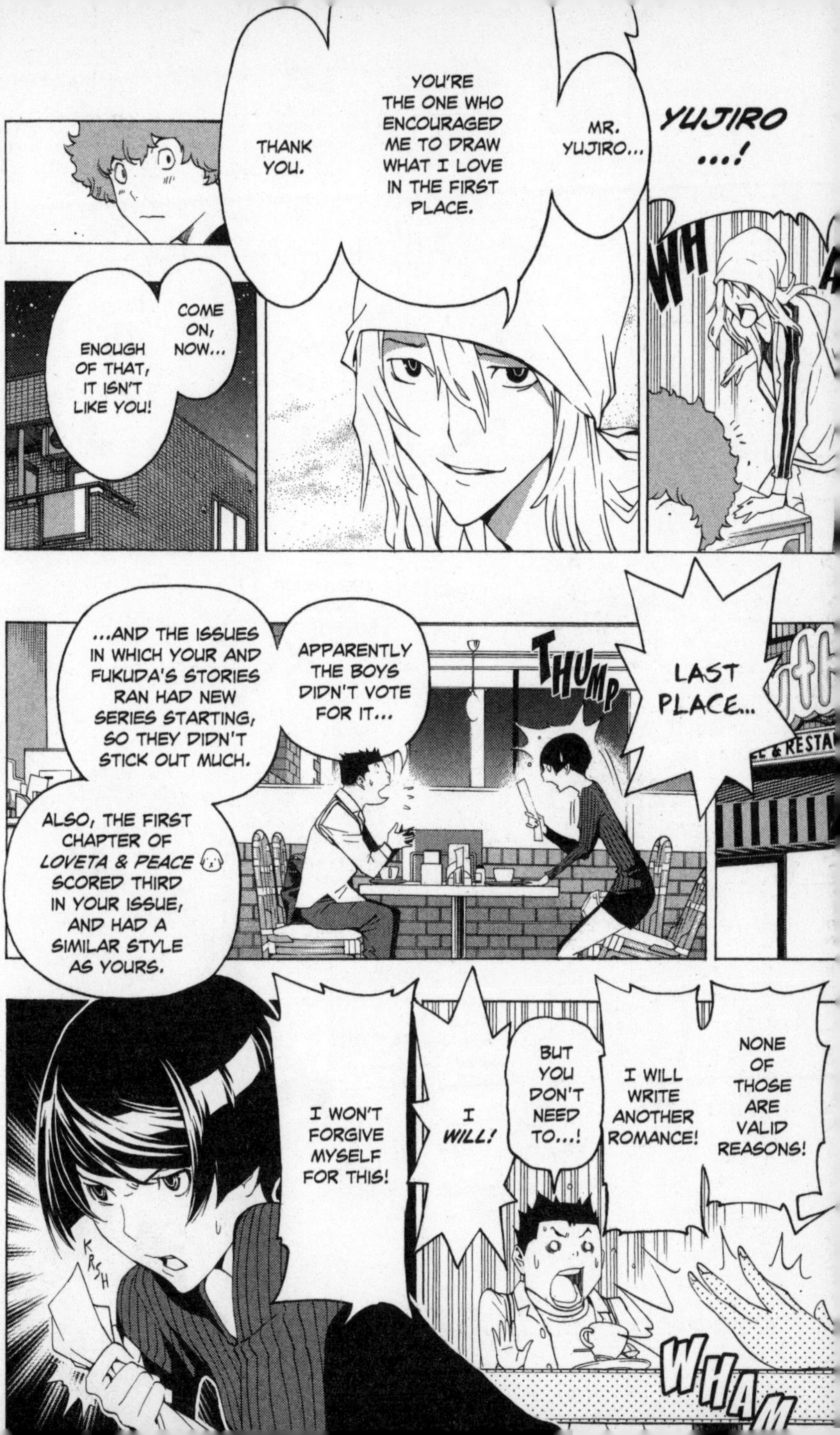

YUJIRO ...!
MR. YUJIRO...
YOU'RE THE ONE WHO ENCOURAGED ME TO DRAW WHAT I LOVE IN THE FIRST PLACE.
THANK YOU.
COME ON, NOW...
ENOUGH OF THAT, IT ISN'T LIKE YOU!
LAST PLACE...
THUMP
APPARENTLY THE BOYS DIDN'T VOTE FOR IT...
...AND THE ISSUES IN WHICH YOUR AND FUKUDA'S STORIES RAN HAD NEW SERIES STARTING, SO THEY DIDN'T STICK OUT MUCH.
ALSO, THE FIRST CHAPTER OF *LOVETA & PEACE* SCORED THIRD IN YOUR ISSUE, AND HAD A SIMILAR STYLE AS YOURS.
NONE OF THOSE ARE VALID REASONS!
WHAM
I WILL WRITE ANOTHER ROMANCE!
BUT YOU DON'T NEED TO...!
I *WILL!*
I WON'T FORGIVE MYSELF FOR THIS!
KRSH

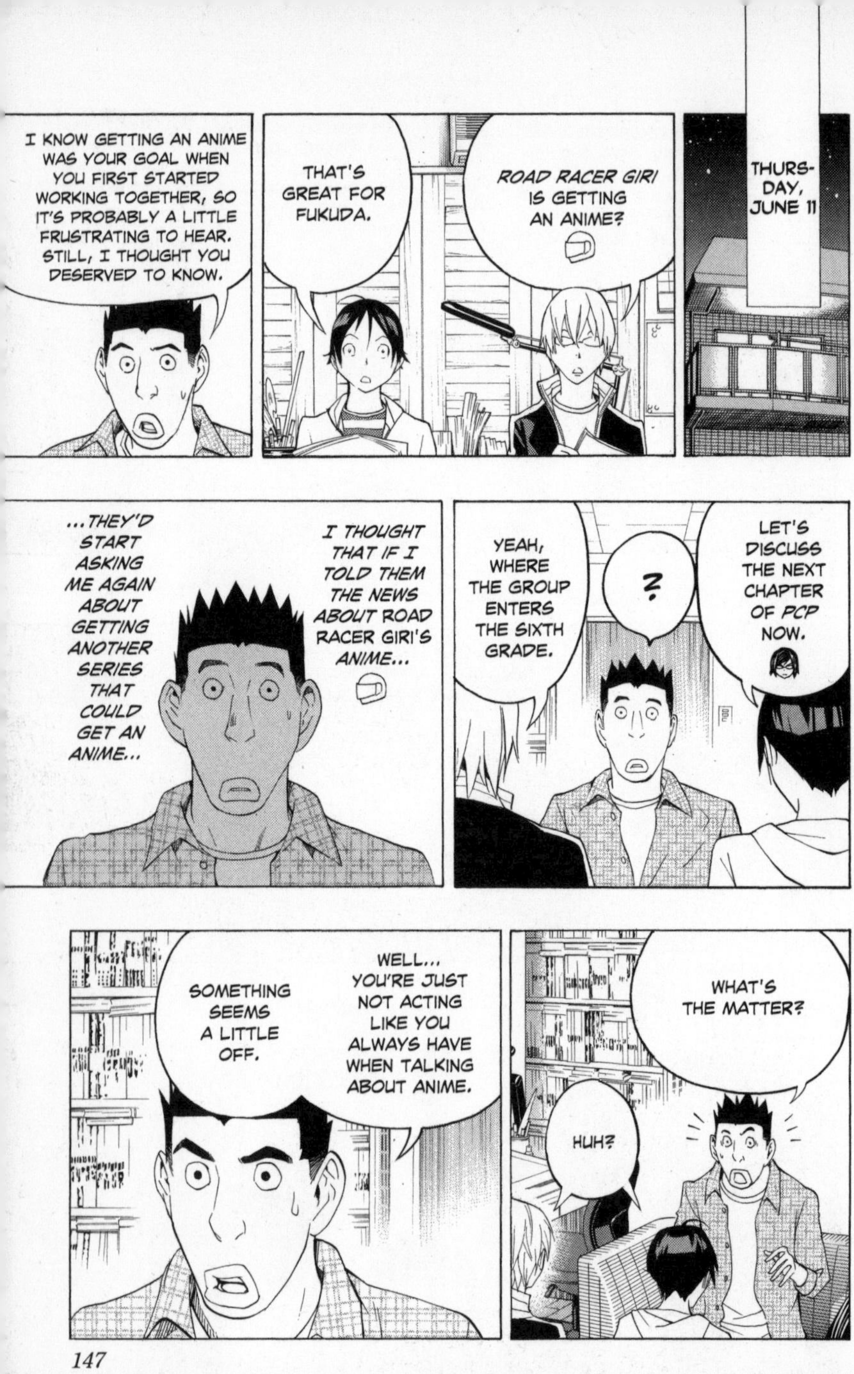
THURS-DAY, JUNE 11
ROAD RACER GIRI IS GETTING AN ANIME?
THAT'S GREAT FOR FUKUDA.
I KNOW GETTING AN ANIME WAS YOUR GOAL WHEN YOU FIRST STARTED WORKING TOGETHER, SO IT'S PROBABLY A LITTLE FRUSTRATING TO HEAR. STILL, I THOUGHT YOU DESERVED TO KNOW.
LET'S DISCUSS THE NEXT CHAPTER OF *PCP* NOW.
?
YEAH, WHERE THE GROUP ENTERS THE SIXTH GRADE.
I THOUGHT THAT IF I TOLD THEM THE NEWS ABOUT ROAD RACER GIRI'S *ANIME...*
...THEY'D START ASKING ME AGAIN ABOUT GETTING ANOTHER SERIES THAT COULD GET AN ANIME...
WHAT'S THE MATTER?
HUH?
WELL... YOU'RE JUST NOT ACTING LIKE YOU ALWAYS HAVE WHEN TALKING ABOUT ANIME.
SOMETHING SEEMS A LITTLE OFF.

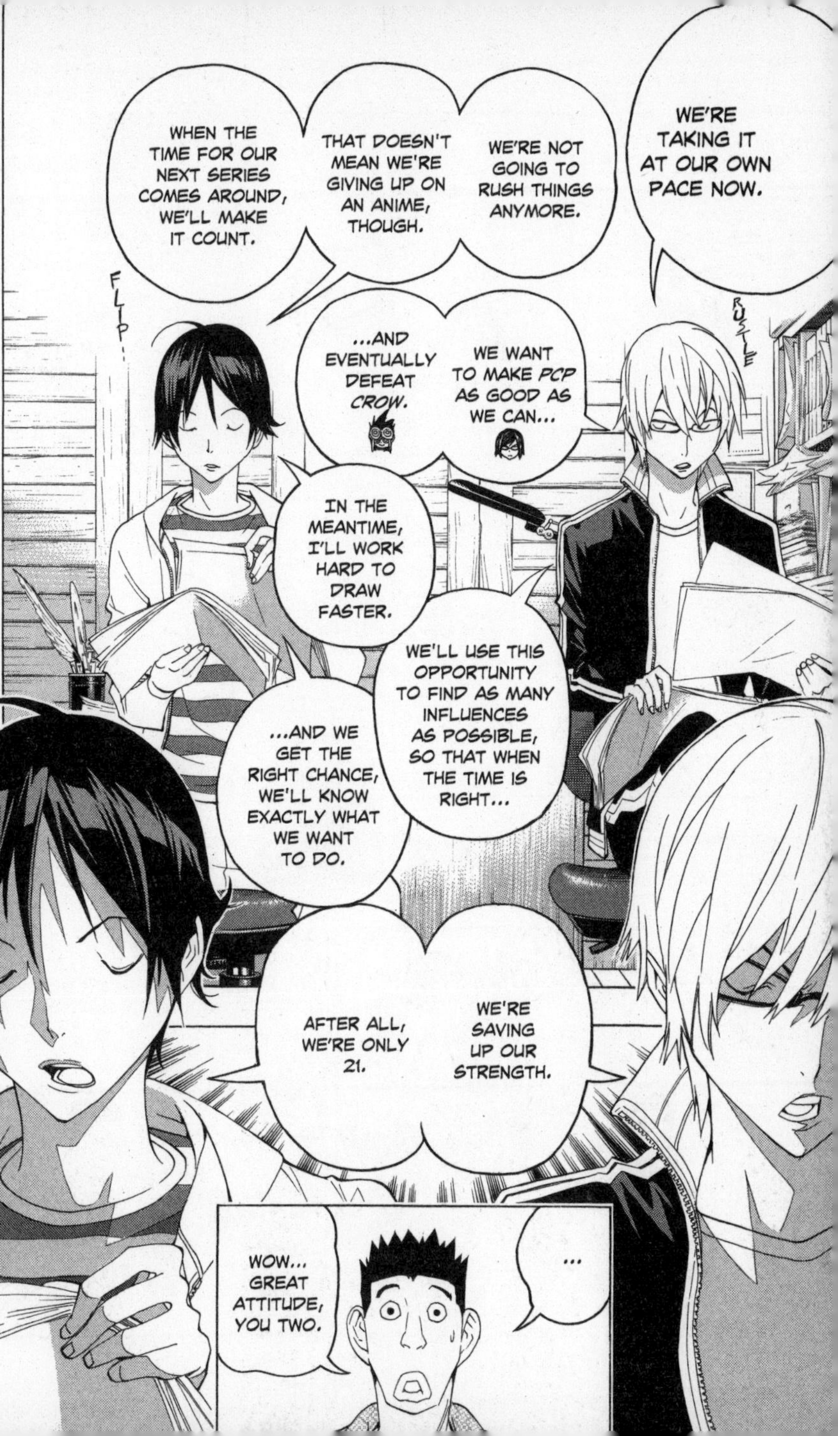
WE'RE TAKING IT AT OUR OWN PACE NOW.
WE'RE NOT GOING TO RUSH THINGS ANYMORE.
THAT DOESN'T MEAN WE'RE GIVING UP ON AN ANIME, THOUGH.
WHEN THE TIME FOR OUR NEXT SERIES COMES AROUND, WE'LL MAKE IT COUNT.
RUSTLE
FLIP...
WE WANT TO MAKE PCP AS GOOD AS WE CAN...
...AND EVENTUALLY DEFEAT CROW.
IN THE MEANTIME, I'LL WORK HARD TO DRAW FASTER.
WE'LL USE THIS OPPORTUNITY TO FIND AS MANY INFLUENCES AS POSSIBLE, SO THAT WHEN THE TIME IS RIGHT...
...AND WE GET THE RIGHT CHANCE, WE'LL KNOW EXACTLY WHAT WE WANT TO DO.
WE'RE SAVING UP OUR STRENGTH.
AFTER ALL, WE'RE ONLY 21.
...
WOW... GREAT ATTITUDE, YOU TWO.

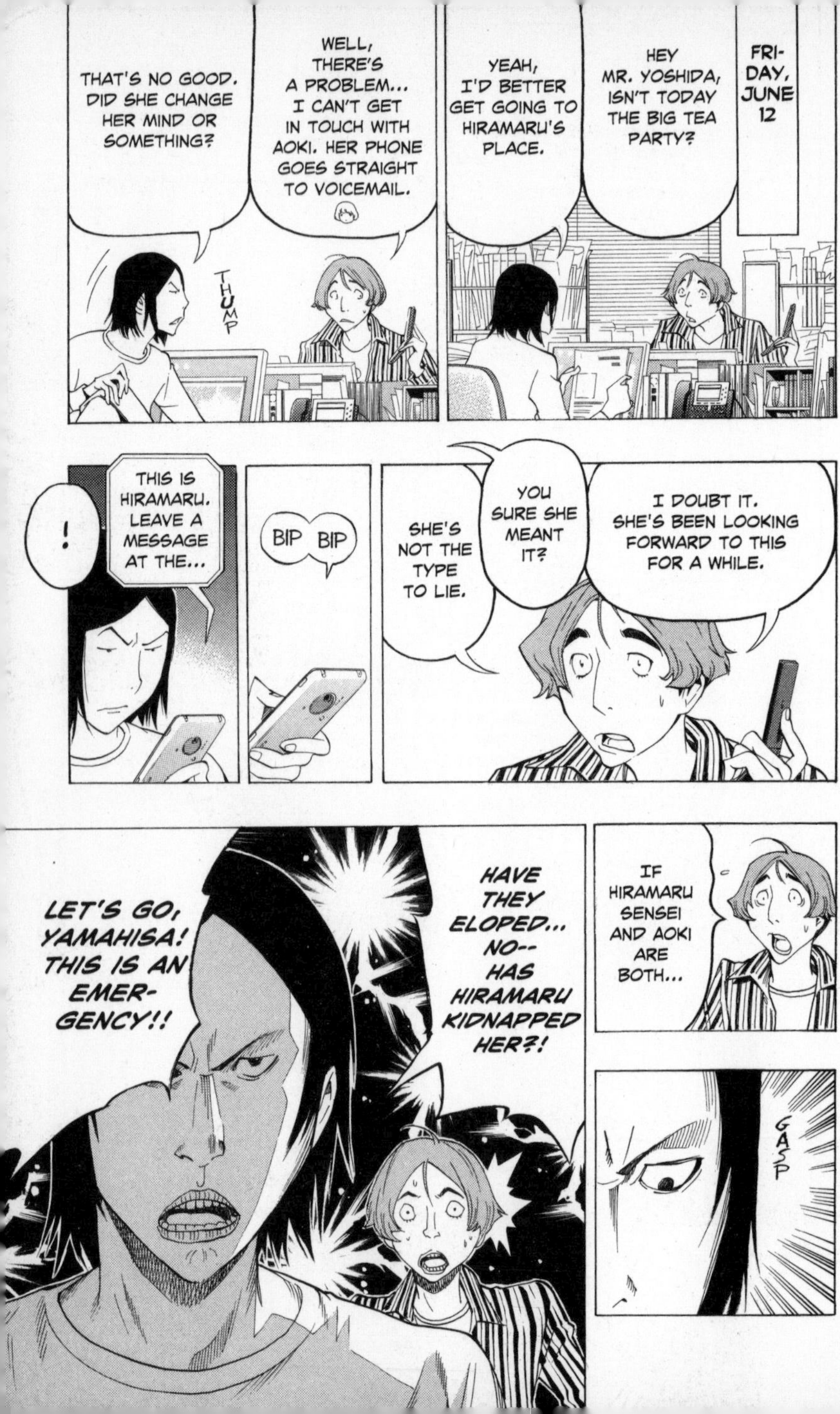
FRIDAY, JUNE 12
HEY MR. YOSHIDA, ISN'T TODAY THE BIG TEA PARTY?
YEAH, I'D BETTER GET GOING TO HIRAMARU'S PLACE.
WELL, THERE'S A PROBLEM... I CAN'T GET IN TOUCH WITH AOKI. HER PHONE GOES STRAIGHT TO VOICEMAIL.
THAT'S NO GOOD. DID SHE CHANGE HER MIND OR SOMETHING?
THUMP
I DOUBT IT. SHE'S BEEN LOOKING FORWARD TO THIS FOR A WHILE.
YOU SURE SHE MEANT IT?
SHE'S NOT THE TYPE TO LIE.
BIP BIP
THIS IS HIRAMARU. LEAVE A MESSAGE AT THE...
!
IF HIRAMARU SENSEI AND AOKI ARE BOTH...
GASP
HAVE THEY ELOPED... NO-- HAS HIRAMARU KIDNAPPED HER?!
LET'S GO, YAMAHISA! THIS IS AN EMERGENCY!!

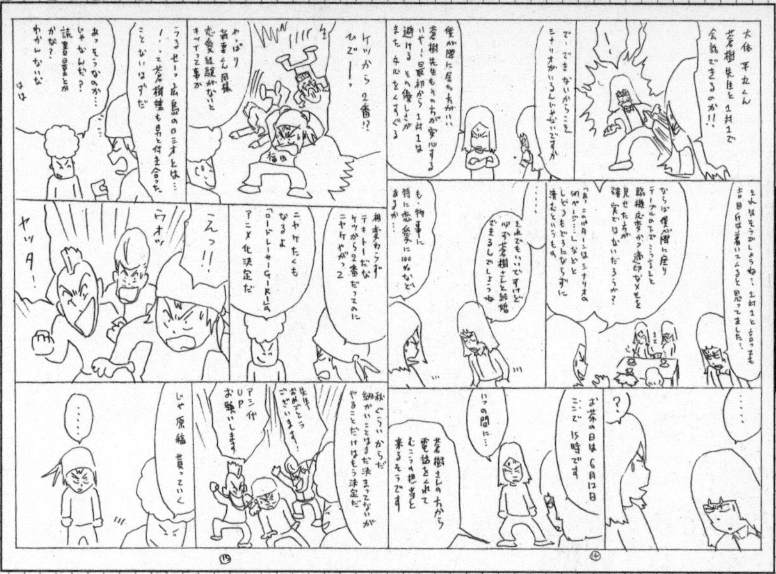

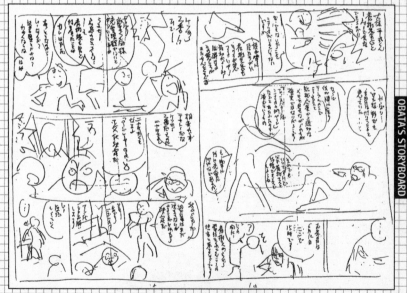

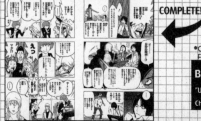

OHBA'S STORYBOARD

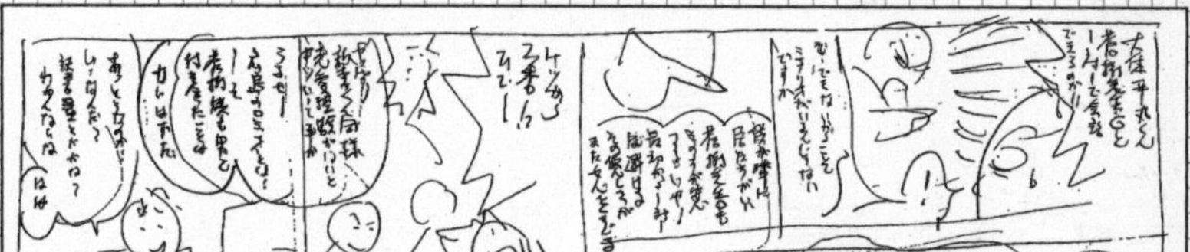

OBATA'S STORYBOARD

COMPLETE!

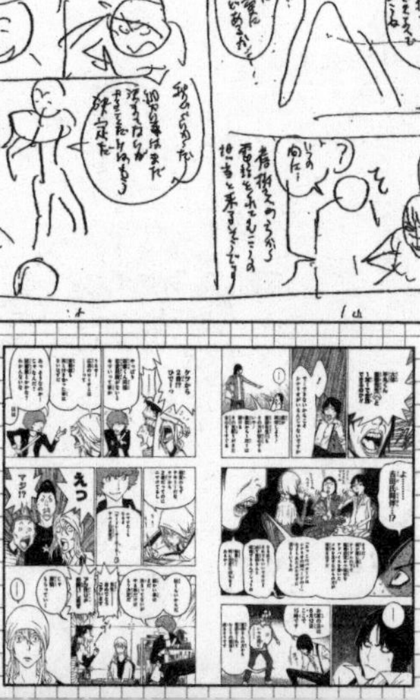

*CREATOR STORYBOARDS AND FINISHED PAGES IN JAPANESE

BAKUMAN。 vol.13

"Until the Final Draft Is Complete"

Chapter 113, pp. 144-145

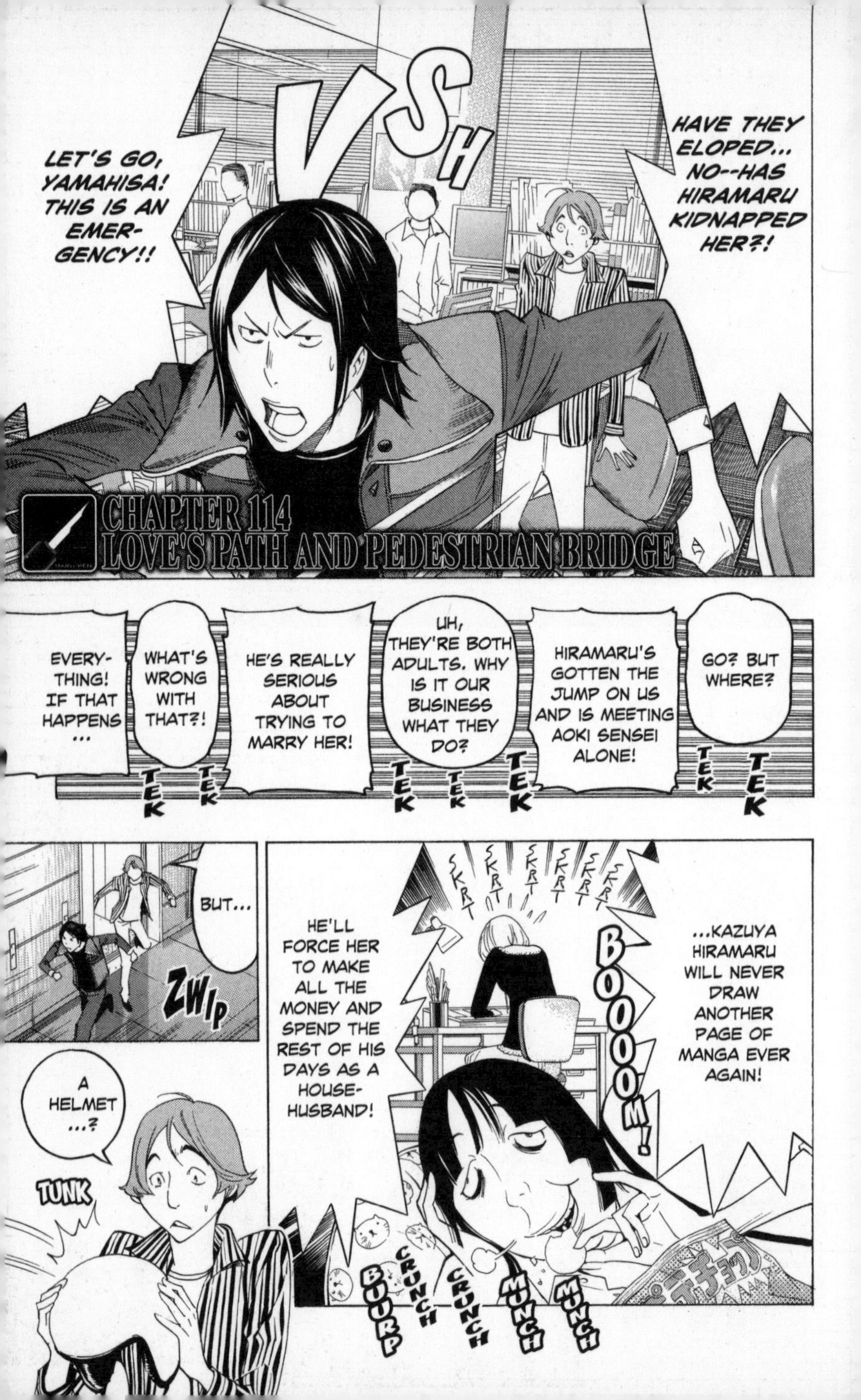
HAVE THEY ELOPED... NO--HAS HIRAMARU KIDNAPPED HER?!
VSH
LET'S GO, YAMAHISA! THIS IS AN EMER-GENCY!!
CHAPTER 114
LOVE'S PATH AND PEDESTRIAN BRIDGE
GO? BUT WHERE?
TEK TEK
HIRAMARU'S GOTTEN THE JUMP ON US AND IS MEETING AOKI SENSEI ALONE!
TEK TEK TEK
UH, THEY'RE BOTH ADULTS. WHY IS IT OUR BUSINESS WHAT THEY DO?
HE'S REALLY SERIOUS ABOUT TRYING TO MARRY HER!
TEK TEK
WHAT'S WRONG WITH THAT?!
EVERY-THING! IF THAT HAPPENS ...
SKRT SKRT SKRT SKRT SKRT SKRT
...KAZUYA HIRAMARU WILL NEVER DRAW ANOTHER PAGE OF MANGA EVER AGAIN!
BOOOOOM!
HE'LL FORCE HER TO MAKE ALL THE MONEY AND SPEND THE REST OF HIS DAYS AS A HOUSE-HUSBAND!
MUNCH MUNCH CRUNCH CRUNCH BUURP
BUT...
ZWIP
A HELMET ...?
TUNK

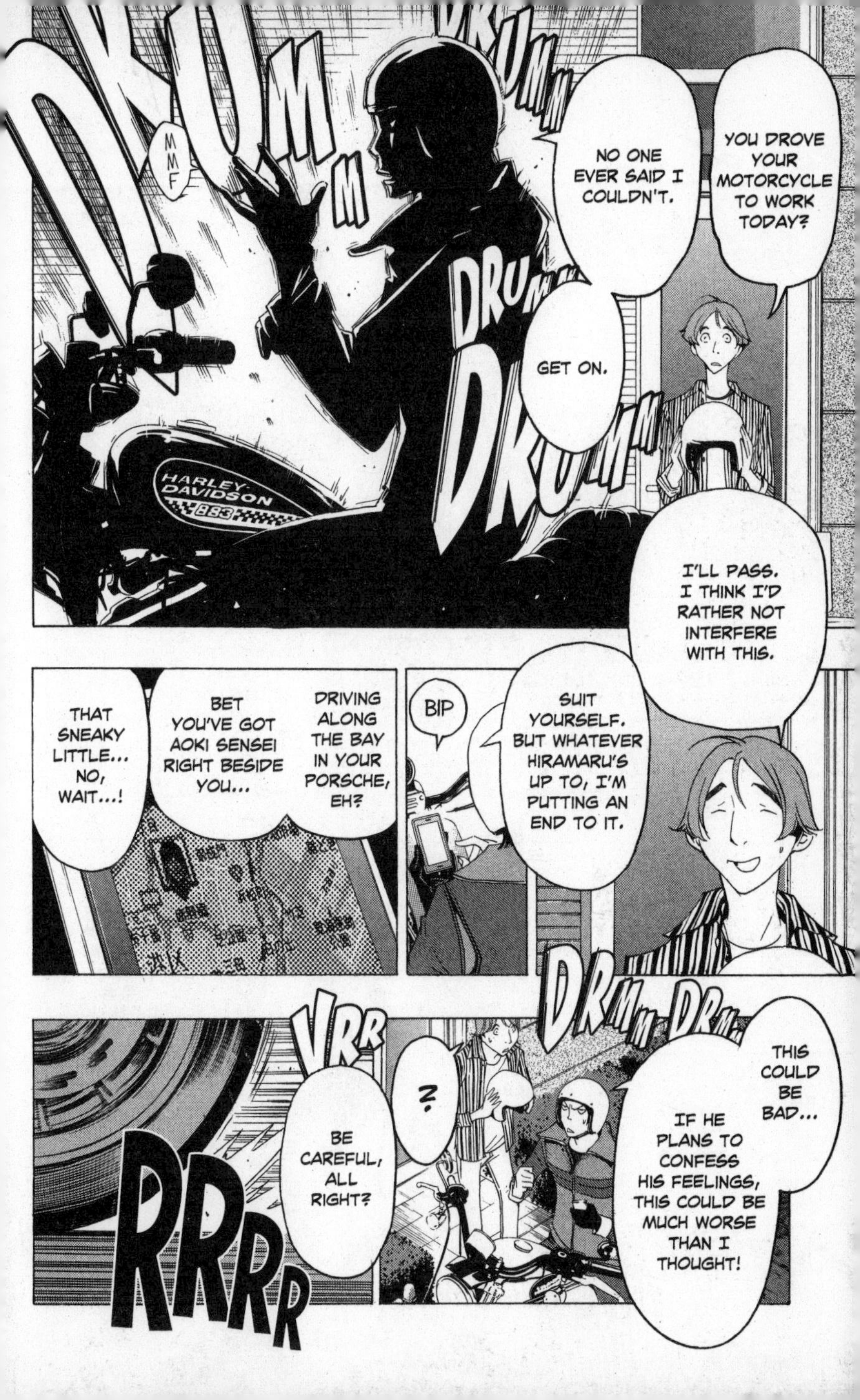
YOU DROVE YOUR MOTORCYCLE TO WORK TODAY?
NO ONE EVER SAID I COULDN'T.
DRUMMM
MMF
HARLEY-DAVIDSON 883
DRUMMM
GET ON.
DRUMMM
I'LL PASS. I THINK I'D RATHER NOT INTERFERE WITH THIS.
SUIT YOURSELF. BUT WHATEVER HIRAMARU'S UP TO, I'M PUTTING AN END TO IT.
BIP
DRIVING ALONG THE BAY IN YOUR PORSCHE, EH?
BET YOU'VE GOT AOKI SENSEI RIGHT BESIDE YOU...
THAT SNEAKY LITTLE... NO, WAIT...!
DRMM DRM
THIS COULD BE BAD...
IF HE PLANS TO CONFESS HIS FEELINGS, THIS COULD BE MUCH WORSE THAN I THOUGHT!
?
BE CAREFUL, ALL RIGHT?
VRR
RRRR

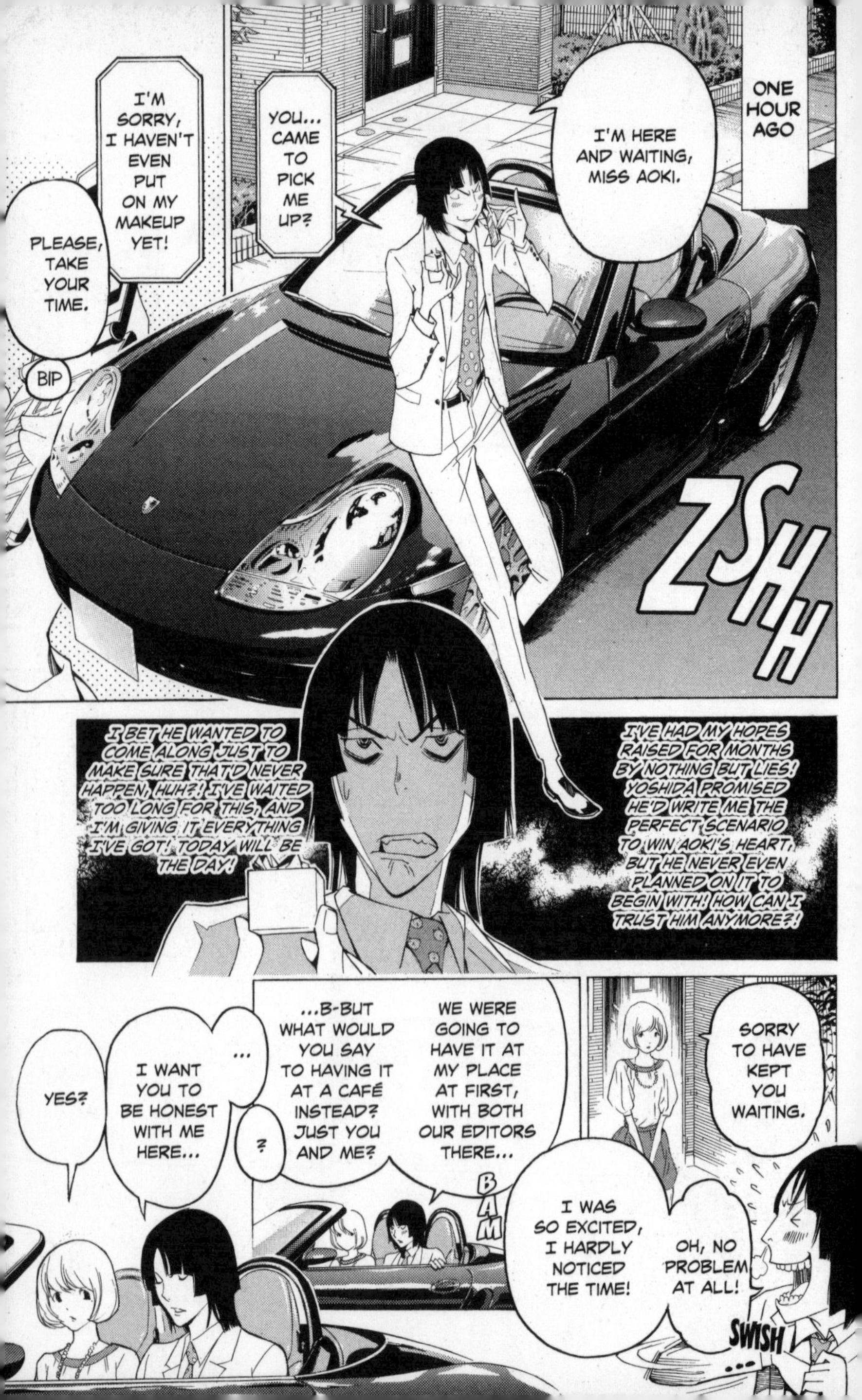
ONE HOUR AGO
I'M HERE AND WAITING, MISS AOKI.
YOU... CAME TO PICK ME UP?
I'M SORRY, I HAVEN'T EVEN PUT ON MY MAKEUP YET!
PLEASE, TAKE YOUR TIME.
BIP
ZSHH
I'VE HAD MY HOPES RAISED FOR MONTHS BY NOTHING BUT LIES! YOSHIDA PROMISED HE'D WRITE ME THE PERFECT SCENARIO TO WIN AOKI'S HEART, BUT HE NEVER EVEN PLANNED ON IT TO BEGIN WITH! HOW CAN I TRUST HIM ANYMORE?!
I BET HE WANTED TO COME ALONG JUST TO MAKE SURE THAT'D NEVER HAPPEN, HUH?! I'VE WAITED TOO LONG FOR THIS, AND I'M GIVING IT EVERYTHING I'VE GOT! TODAY WILL BE THE DAY!
SORRY TO HAVE KEPT YOU WAITING.
OH, NO PROBLEM AT ALL!
I WAS SO EXCITED, I HARDLY NOTICED THE TIME!
SWISH
...
BAM
WE WERE GOING TO HAVE IT AT MY PLACE AT FIRST, WITH BOTH OUR EDITORS THERE...
...B-BUT WHAT WOULD YOU SAY TO HAVING IT AT A CAFÉ INSTEAD? JUST YOU AND ME?
?
...
I WANT YOU TO BE HONEST WITH ME HERE...
YES?

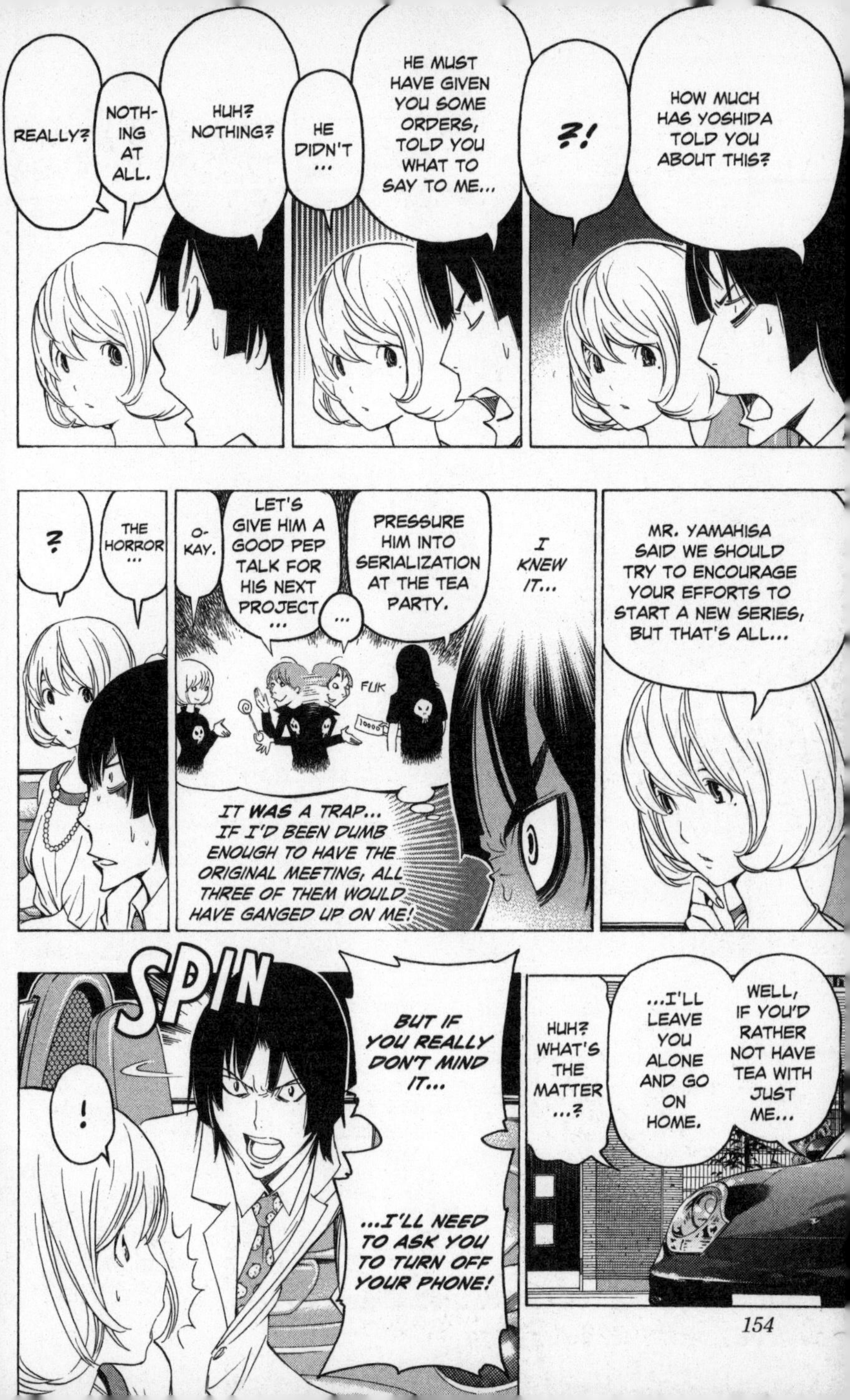
HOW MUCH HAS YOSHIDA TOLD YOU ABOUT THIS?
?!
HE MUST HAVE GIVEN YOU SOME ORDERS, TOLD YOU WHAT TO SAY TO ME...
HE DIDN'T ...
HUH? NOTHING?
NOTHING AT ALL.
REALLY?
MR. YAMAHISA SAID WE SHOULD TRY TO ENCOURAGE YOUR EFFORTS TO START A NEW SERIES, BUT THAT'S ALL...
I KNEW IT...
PRESSURE HIM INTO SERIALIZATION AT THE TEA PARTY.
...
LET'S GIVE HIM A GOOD PEP TALK FOR HIS NEXT PROJECT...
O-KAY.
FUK
IT WAS A TRAP... IF I'D BEEN DUMB ENOUGH TO HAVE THE ORIGINAL MEETING, ALL THREE OF THEM WOULD HAVE GANGED UP ON ME!
THE HORROR...
?
WELL, IF YOU'D RATHER NOT HAVE TEA WITH JUST ME...
...I'LL LEAVE YOU ALONE AND GO ON HOME.
HUH? WHAT'S THE MATTER...?
SPIN
BUT IF YOU REALLY DON'T MIND IT...
...I'LL NEED TO ASK YOU TO TURN OFF YOUR PHONE!
!

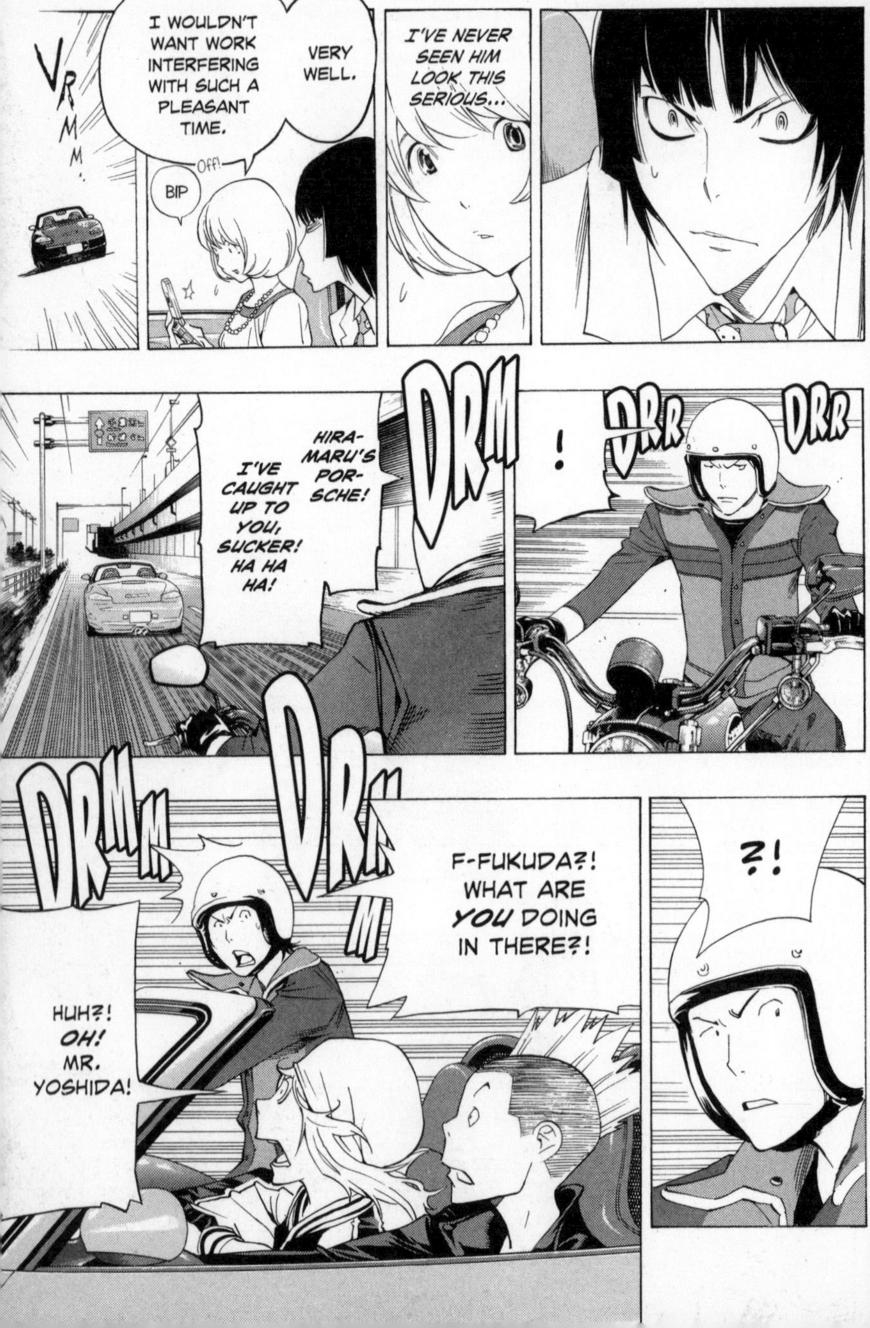
I'VE NEVER SEEN HIM LOOK THIS SERIOUS...
I WOULDN'T WANT WORK INTERFERING WITH SUCH A PLEASANT TIME.
VERY WELL.
Off!
BIP
VRMMM
DRR DRR
!
DRM
HIRA-MARU'S POR-SCHE!
I'VE CAUGHT UP TO YOU, SUCKER! HA HA HA!
?!
DRMM
DRMM
F-FUKUDA?! WHAT ARE YOU DOING IN THERE?!
HUH?! OH! MR. YOSHIDA!

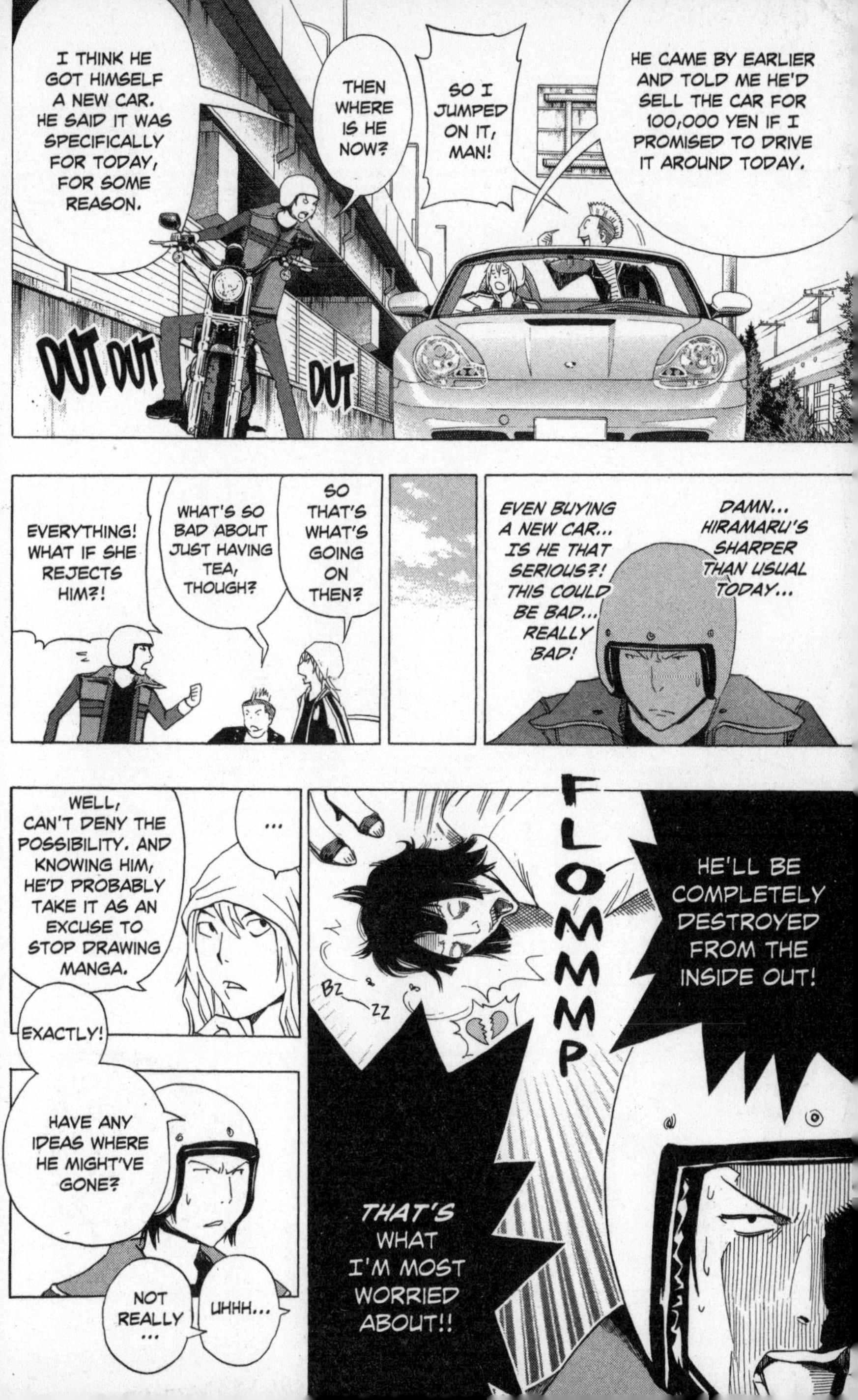
HE CAME BY EARLIER AND TOLD ME HE'D SELL THE CAR FOR 100,000 YEN IF I PROMISED TO DRIVE IT AROUND TODAY.
SO I JUMPED ON IT, MAN!
THEN WHERE IS HE NOW?
I THINK HE GOT HIMSELF A NEW CAR. HE SAID IT WAS SPECIFICALLY FOR TODAY, FOR SOME REASON.
DUT DUT
DUT
DAMN... HIRAMARU'S SHARPER THAN USUAL TODAY...
EVEN BUYING A NEW CAR... IS HE THAT SERIOUS?! THIS COULD BE BAD... REALLY BAD!
SO THAT'S WHAT'S GOING ON THEN?
WHAT'S SO BAD ABOUT JUST HAVING TEA, THOUGH?
EVERYTHING! WHAT IF SHE REJECTS HIM?!
FLOMMMP
HE'LL BE COMPLETELY DESTROYED FROM THE INSIDE OUT!
BZ
ZZ
THAT'S WHAT I'M MOST WORRIED ABOUT!!
...
WELL, CAN'T DENY THE POSSIBILITY. AND KNOWING HIM, HE'D PROBABLY TAKE IT AS AN EXCUSE TO STOP DRAWING MANGA.
EXACTLY!
HAVE ANY IDEAS WHERE HE MIGHT'VE GONE?
UHHH...
NOT REALLY ...

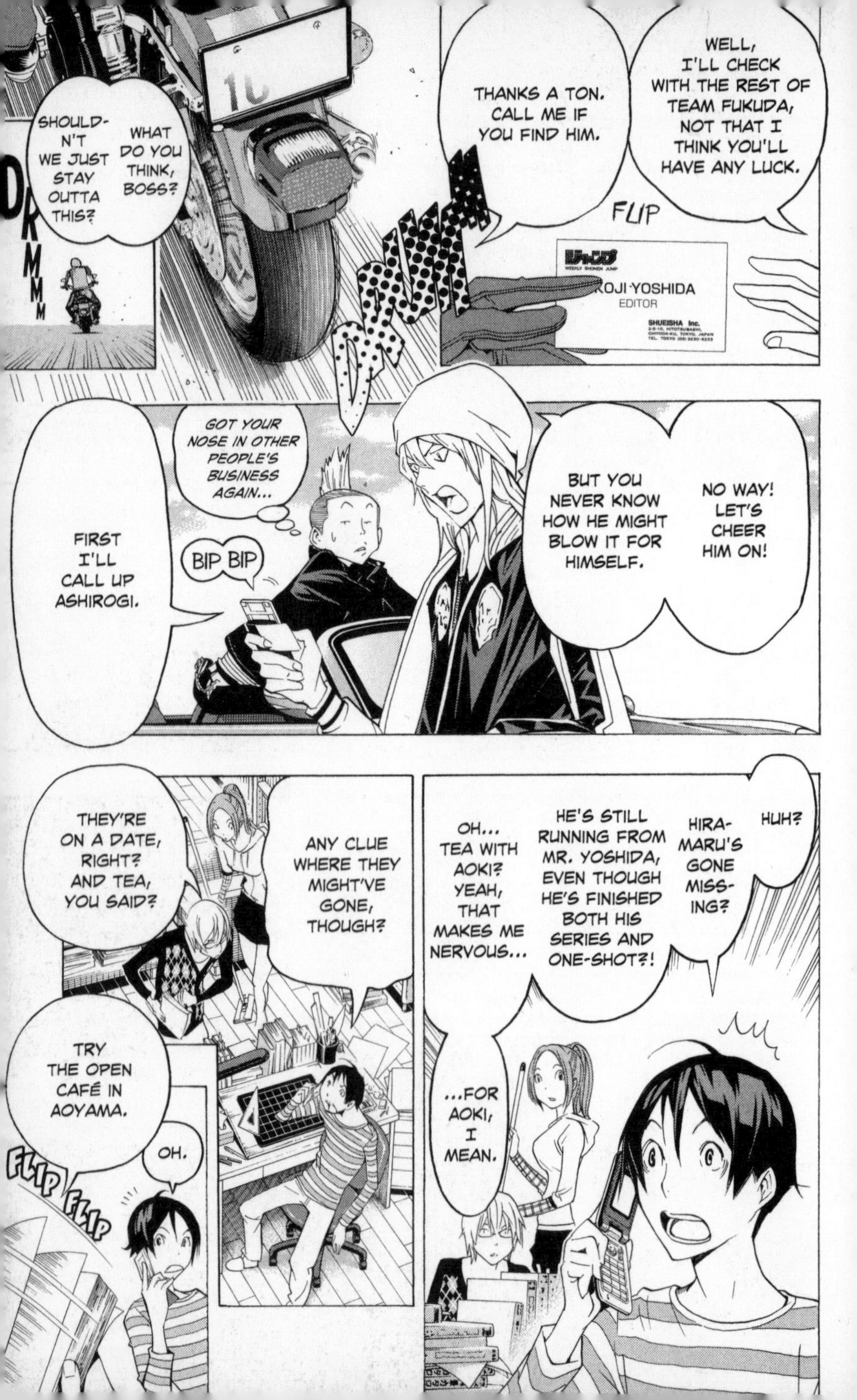
WELL, I'LL CHECK WITH THE REST OF TEAM FUKUDA, NOT THAT I THINK YOU'LL HAVE ANY LUCK.
THANKS A TON. CALL ME IF YOU FIND HIM.
FLIP
WEEKLY SHONEN JUMP
KOJI·YOSHIDA
EDITOR
SHUEISHA Inc.
WHAT DO YOU THINK, BOSS?
SHOULD-N'T WE JUST STAY OUTTA THIS?
DRMMMM
NO WAY! LET'S CHEER HIM ON!
BUT YOU NEVER KNOW HOW HE MIGHT BLOW IT FOR HIMSELF.
GOT YOUR NOSE IN OTHER PEOPLE'S BUSINESS AGAIN...
BIP BIP
FIRST I'LL CALL UP ASHIROGI.
HUH?
HIRA-MARU'S GONE MISS-ING?
HE'S STILL RUNNING FROM MR. YOSHIDA, EVEN THOUGH HE'S FINISHED BOTH HIS SERIES AND ONE-SHOT?!
OH... TEA WITH AOKI? YEAH, THAT MAKES ME NERVOUS...
...FOR AOKI, I MEAN.
ANY CLUE WHERE THEY MIGHT'VE GONE, THOUGH?
THEY'RE ON A DATE, RIGHT? AND TEA, YOU SAID?
TRY THE OPEN CAFÉ IN AOYAMA.
OH.
FLIP FLIP

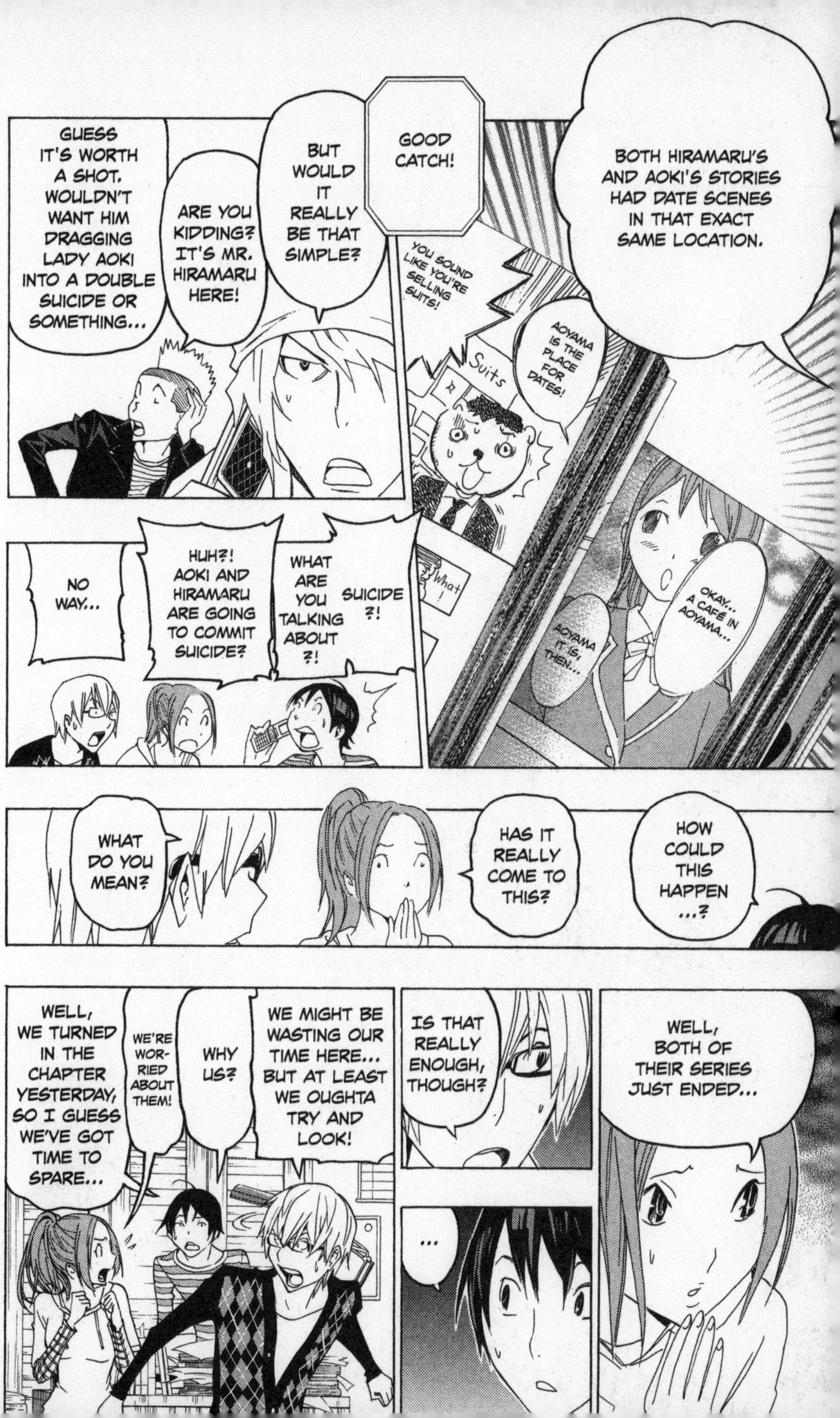
BOTH HIRAMARU'S AND AOKI'S STORIES HAD DATE SCENES IN THAT EXACT SAME LOCATION.
YOU SOUND LIKE YOU'RE SELLING SUITS!
AOYAMA IS THE PLACE FOR DATES!
Suits
What!
OKAY... A CAFÉ IN AOYAMA...
AOYAMA IT IS, THEN...
GOOD CATCH!
BUT WOULD IT REALLY BE THAT SIMPLE?
ARE YOU KIDDING? IT'S MR. HIRAMARU HERE!
GUESS IT'S WORTH A SHOT. WOULDN'T WANT HIM DRAGGING LADY AOKI INTO A DOUBLE SUICIDE OR SOMETHING...
SUICIDE?!
WHAT ARE YOU TALKING ABOUT?!
HUH?! AOKI AND HIRAMARU ARE GOING TO COMMIT SUICIDE?
NO WAY...
HOW COULD THIS HAPPEN...?
HAS IT REALLY COME TO THIS?
WHAT DO YOU MEAN?
WELL, BOTH OF THEIR SERIES JUST ENDED...
IS THAT REALLY ENOUGH, THOUGH?
...
WE MIGHT BE WASTING OUR TIME HERE... BUT AT LEAST WE OUGHTA TRY AND LOOK!
WHY US?
WE'RE WORRIED ABOUT THEM!
WELL, WE TURNED IN THE CHAPTER YESTERDAY, SO I GUESS WE'VE GOT TIME TO SPARE...

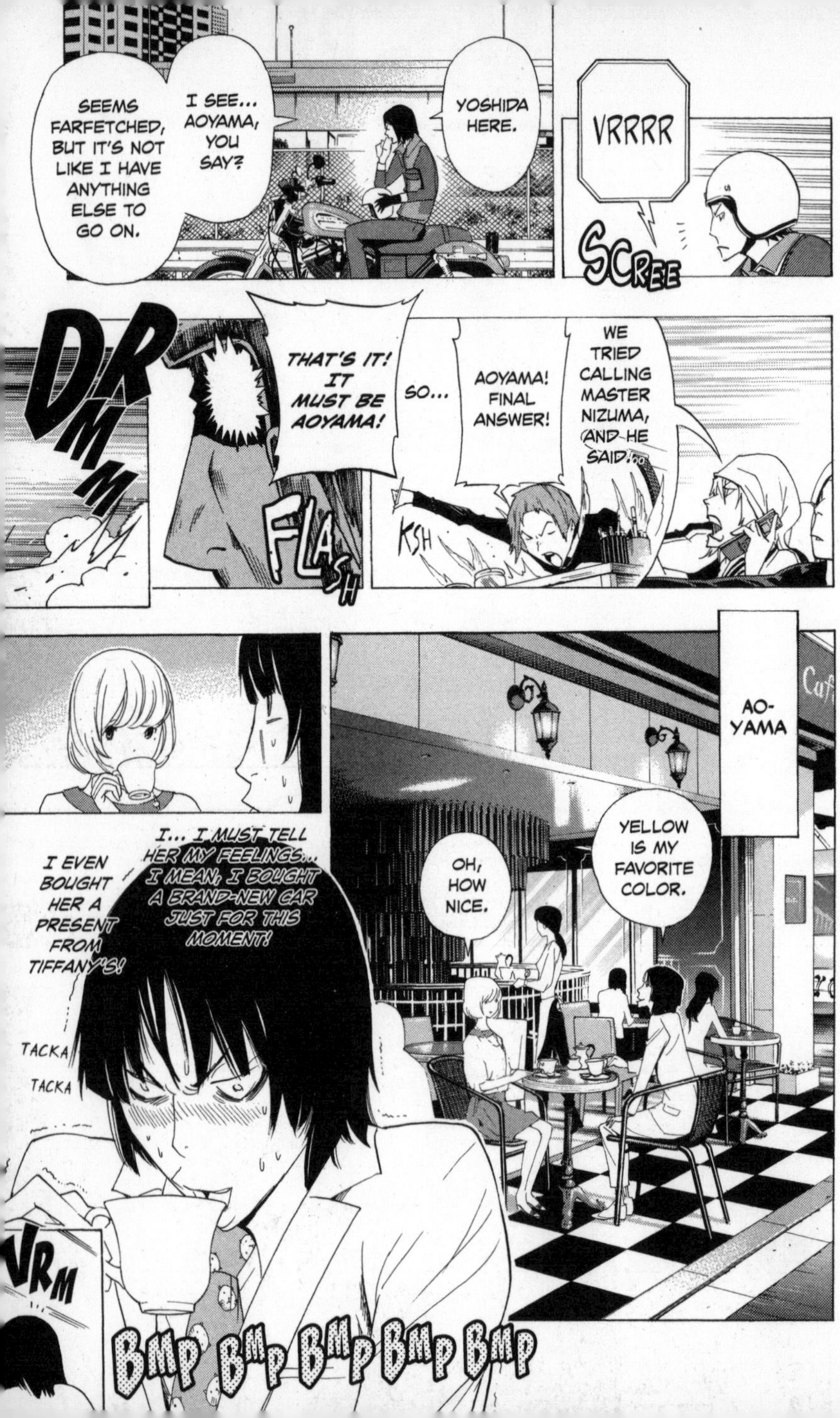
VRRRR
SCREE
YOSHIDA HERE.
I SEE... AOYAMA, YOU SAY?
SEEMS FARFETCHED, BUT IT'S NOT LIKE I HAVE ANYTHING ELSE TO GO ON.
WE TRIED CALLING MASTER NIZUMA, AND HE SAID...
AOYAMA! FINAL ANSWER!
KSH
SO...
THAT'S IT! IT MUST BE AOYAMA!
FLASH
DRMMM
AO-YAMA
YELLOW IS MY FAVORITE COLOR.
OH, HOW NICE.
I... I MUST TELL HER MY FEELINGS... I MEAN, I BOUGHT A BRAND-NEW CAR JUST FOR THIS MOMENT!
I EVEN BOUGHT HER A PRESENT FROM TIFFANY'S!
TACKA
TACKA
VRM
BMP BMP BMP BMP BMP

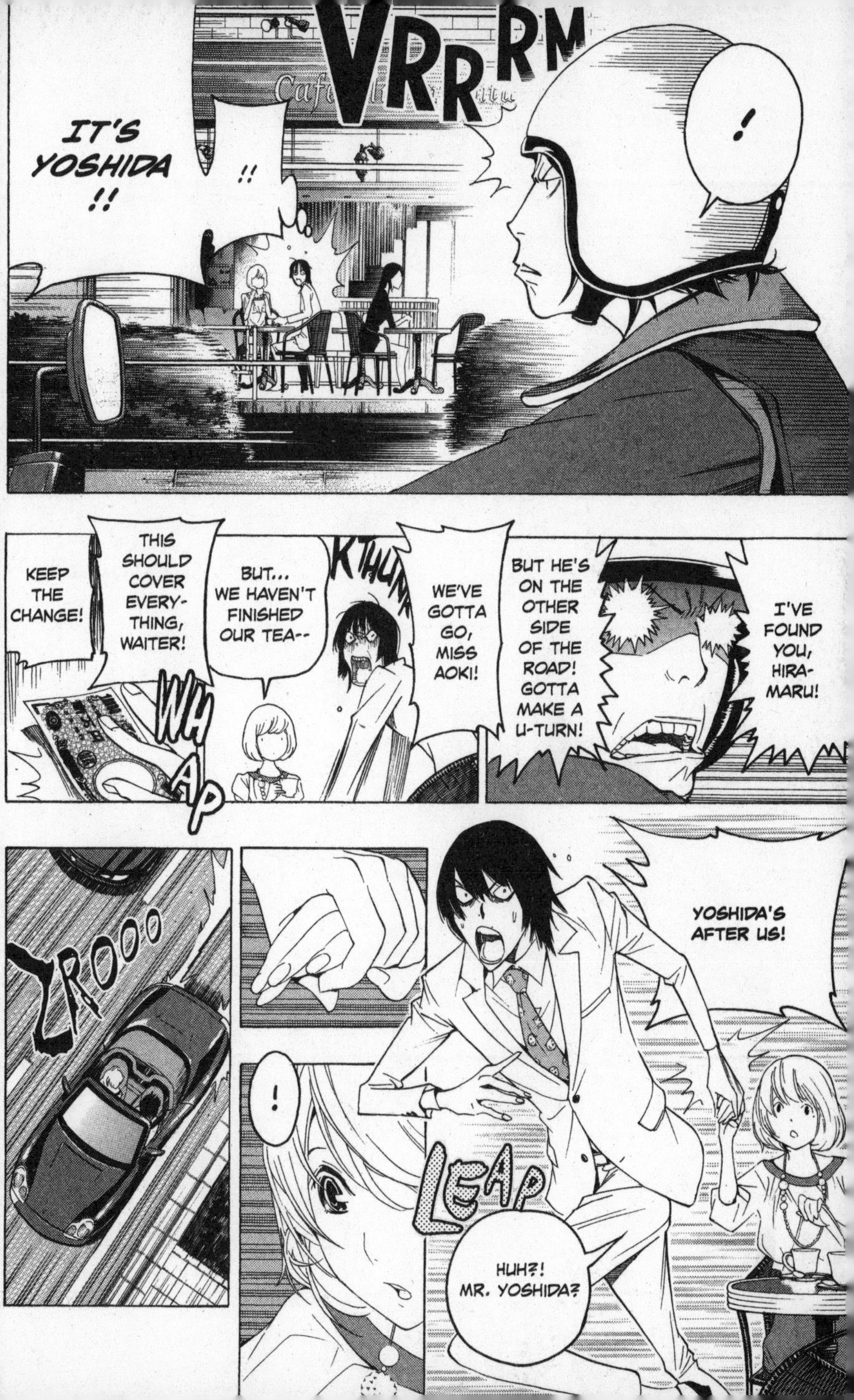
VRRRM
!
!!
IT'S YOSHIDA!!
I'VE FOUND YOU, HIRA-MARU!
BUT HE'S ON THE OTHER SIDE OF THE ROAD! GOTTA MAKE A U-TURN!
WE'VE GOTTA GO, MISS AOKI!
BUT... WE HAVEN'T FINISHED OUR TEA--
THIS SHOULD COVER EVERY-THING, WAITER!
KEEP THE CHANGE!
WHAP
YOSHIDA'S AFTER US!
LEAP
!
HUH?! MR. YOSHIDA?
ZROOO

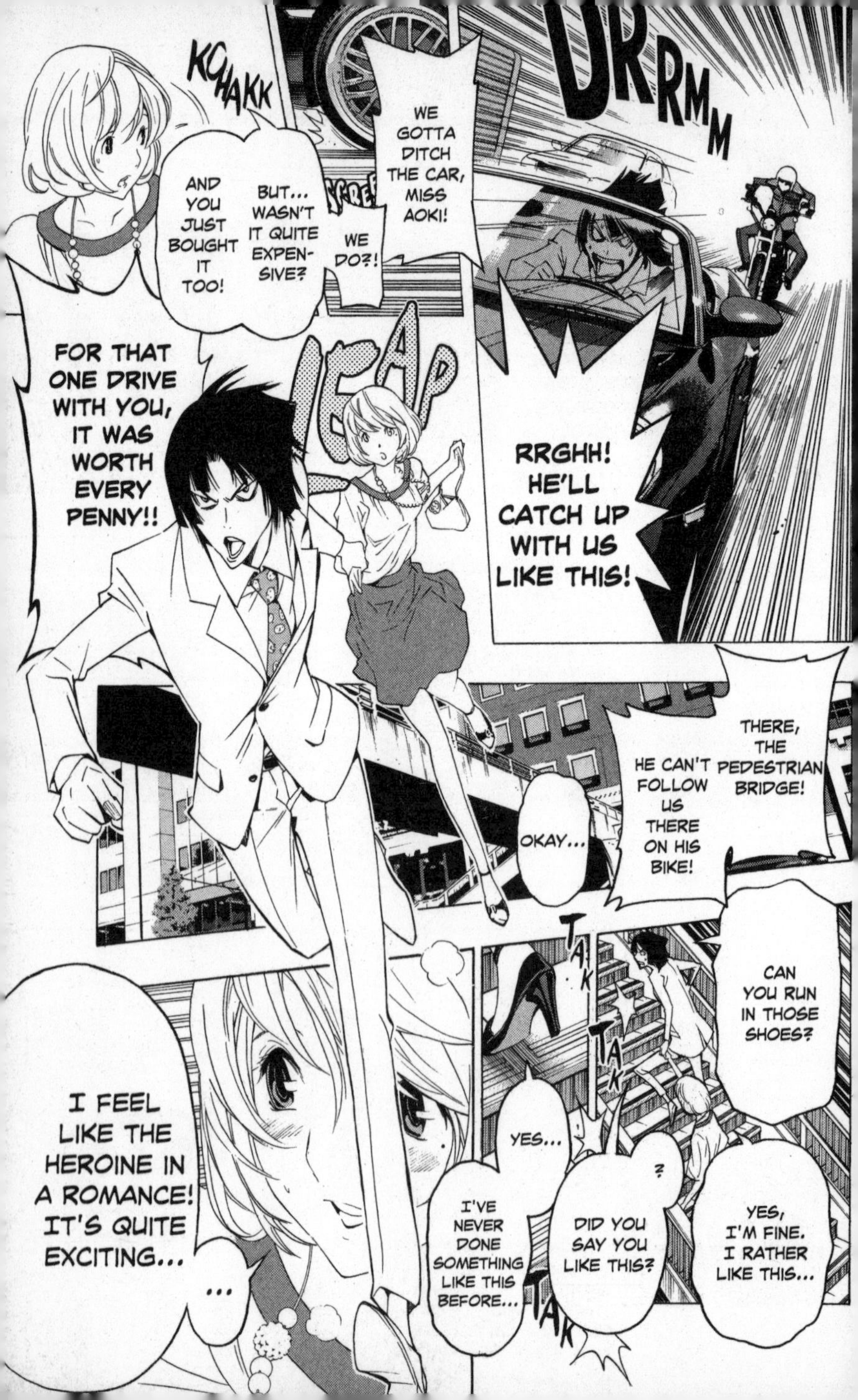
DRRMM
RRGHH! HE'LL CATCH UP WITH US LIKE THIS!
WE GOTTA DITCH THE CAR, MISS AOKI!
SCREE
WE DO?!
BUT... WASN'T IT QUITE EXPENSIVE?
AND YOU JUST BOUGHT IT TOO!
KOHAKK
FOR THAT ONE DRIVE WITH YOU, IT WAS WORTH EVERY PENNY!!
LEAP
THERE, THE PEDESTRIAN BRIDGE!
HE CAN'T FOLLOW US THERE ON HIS BIKE!
OKAY...
CAN YOU RUN IN THOSE SHOES?
TAK
TAK
YES...
YES, I'M FINE. I RATHER LIKE THIS...
?
DID YOU SAY YOU LIKE THIS?
I'VE NEVER DONE SOMETHING LIKE THIS BEFORE...
TAK
I FEEL LIKE THE HEROINE IN A ROMANCE! IT'S QUITE EXCITING...
...

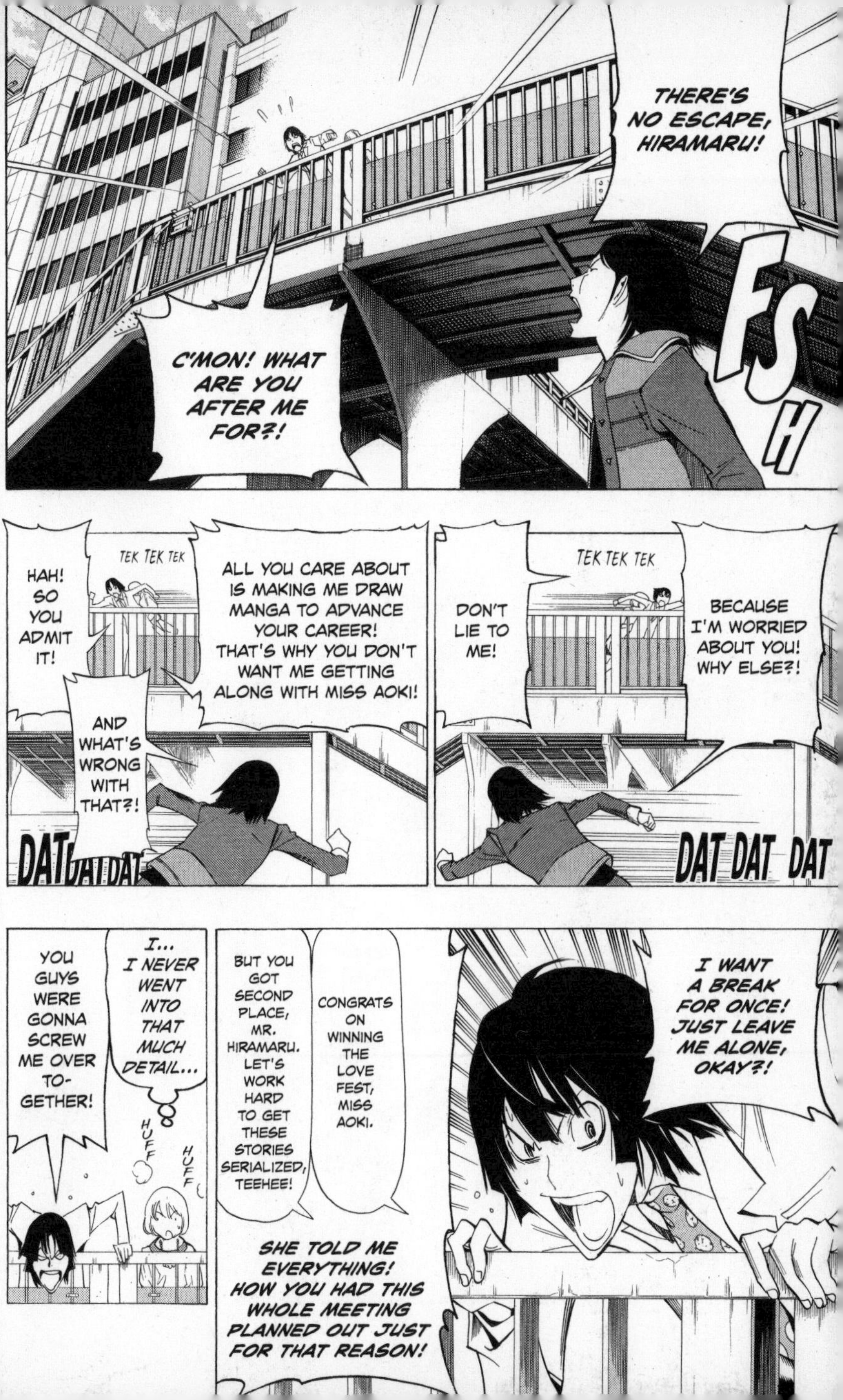
THERE'S NO ESCAPE, HIRAMARU!
FSH
C'MON! WHAT ARE YOU AFTER ME FOR?!
BECAUSE I'M WORRIED ABOUT YOU! WHY ELSE?!
TEK TEK TEK
DON'T LIE TO ME!
DAT DAT DAT
ALL YOU CARE ABOUT IS MAKING ME DRAW MANGA TO ADVANCE YOUR CAREER! THAT'S WHY YOU DON'T WANT ME GETTING ALONG WITH MISS AOKI!
TEK TEK TEK
HAH! SO YOU ADMIT IT!
AND WHAT'S WRONG WITH THAT?!
DAT DAT DAT
I WANT A BREAK FOR ONCE! JUST LEAVE ME ALONE, OKAY?!
CONGRATS ON WINNING THE LOVE FEST, MISS AOKI.
BUT YOU GOT SECOND PLACE, MR. HIRAMARU. LET'S WORK HARD TO GET THESE STORIES SERIALIZED, TEEHEE!
SHE TOLD ME EVERYTHING! HOW YOU HAD THIS WHOLE MEETING PLANNED OUT JUST FOR THAT REASON!
I... I NEVER WENT INTO THAT MUCH DETAIL...
YOU GUYS WERE GONNA SCREW ME OVER TO-GETHER!
HUFF
HUFF

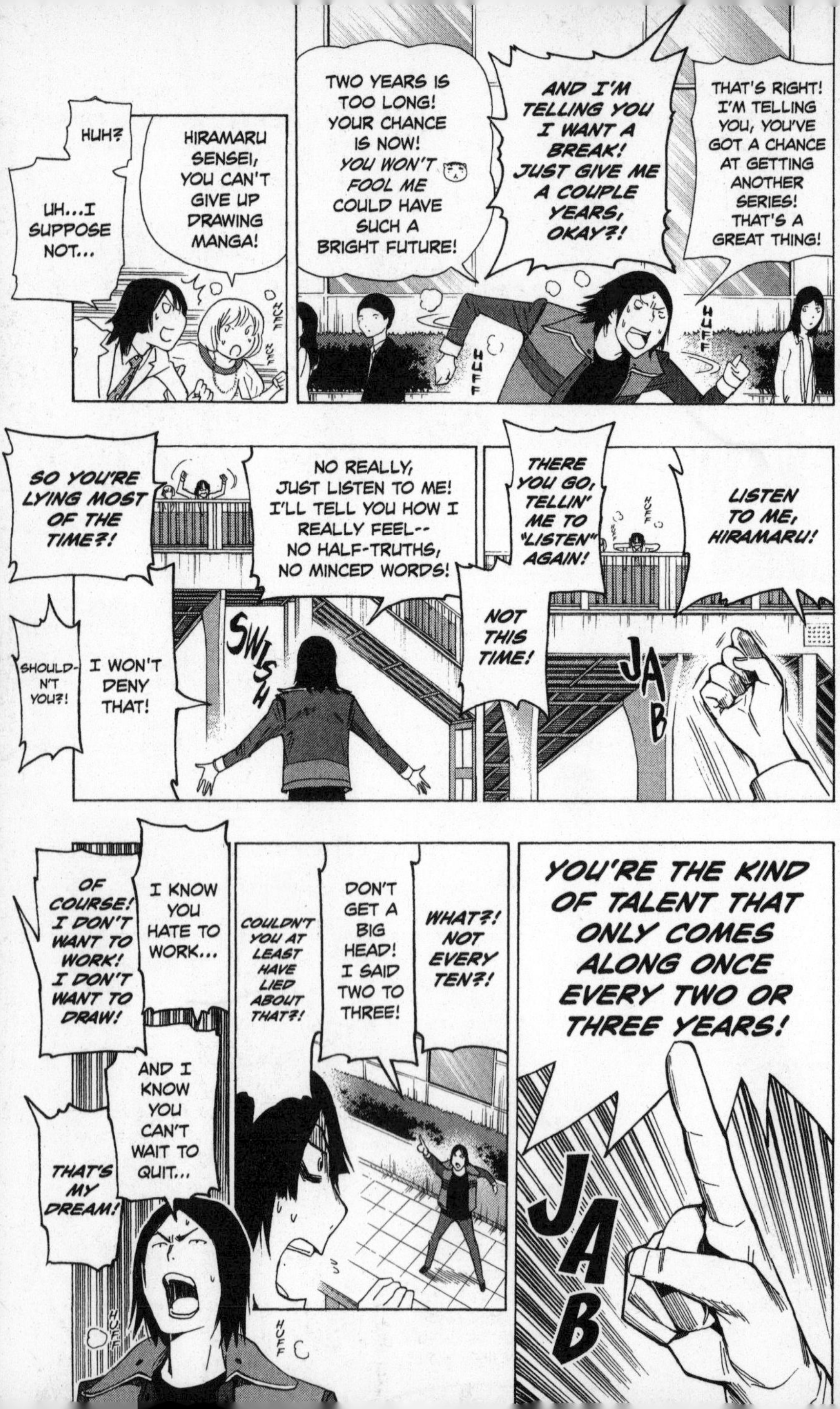
THAT'S RIGHT! I'M TELLING YOU, YOU'VE GOT A CHANCE AT GETTING ANOTHER SERIES! THAT'S A GREAT THING!
HUFF
AND I'M TELLING YOU I WANT A BREAK! JUST GIVE ME A COUPLE YEARS, OKAY?!
HUFF
TWO YEARS IS TOO LONG! YOUR CHANCE IS NOW! YOU WON'T FOOL ME COULD HAVE SUCH A BRIGHT FUTURE!
HIRAMARU SENSEI, YOU CAN'T GIVE UP DRAWING MANGA!
HUH?
UH...I SUPPOSE NOT...
HUFF HUFF
LISTEN TO ME, HIRAMARU!
THERE YOU GO, TELLIN' ME TO "LISTEN" AGAIN!
HUFF HUFF
NOT THIS TIME!
JAB
NO REALLY, JUST LISTEN TO ME! I'LL TELL YOU HOW I REALLY FEEL-- NO HALF-TRUTHS, NO MINCED WORDS!
SWISH
SO YOU'RE LYING MOST OF THE TIME?!
I WON'T DENY THAT!
SHOULD-N'T YOU?!
YOU'RE THE KIND OF TALENT THAT ONLY COMES ALONG ONCE EVERY TWO OR THREE YEARS!
JAB
WHAT?! NOT EVERY TEN?!
DON'T GET A BIG HEAD! I SAID TWO TO THREE!
COULDN'T YOU AT LEAST HAVE LIED ABOUT THAT?!
HUFF
I KNOW YOU HATE TO WORK...
OF COURSE! I DON'T WANT TO WORK! I DON'T WANT TO DRAW!
AND I KNOW YOU CAN'T WAIT TO QUIT...
THAT'S MY DREAM!
HUFF

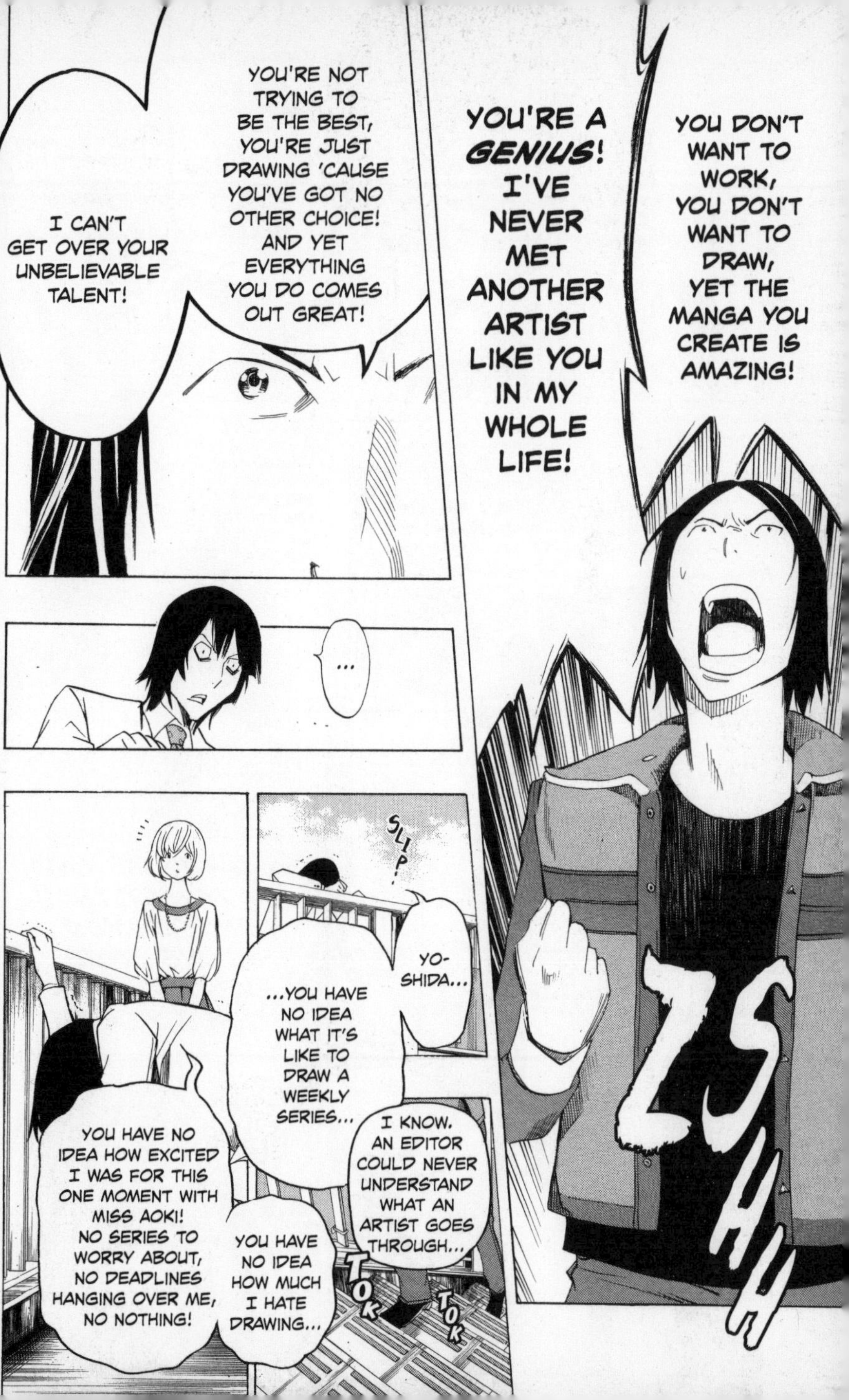
YOU DON'T WANT TO WORK, YOU DON'T WANT TO DRAW, YET THE MANGA YOU CREATE IS AMAZING!
YOU'RE A *GENIUS*! I'VE NEVER MET ANOTHER ARTIST LIKE YOU IN MY WHOLE LIFE!
ZSHHH
YOU'RE NOT TRYING TO BE THE BEST, YOU'RE JUST DRAWING 'CAUSE YOU'VE GOT NO OTHER CHOICE! AND YET EVERYTHING YOU DO COMES OUT GREAT!
I CAN'T GET OVER YOUR UNBELIEVABLE TALENT!
...
SLIP
YO-SHIDA...
...YOU HAVE NO IDEA WHAT IT'S LIKE TO DRAW A WEEKLY SERIES...
I KNOW. AN EDITOR COULD NEVER UNDERSTAND WHAT AN ARTIST GOES THROUGH...
TOK TOK
YOU HAVE NO IDEA HOW MUCH I HATE DRAWING...
YOU HAVE NO IDEA HOW EXCITED I WAS FOR THIS ONE MOMENT WITH MISS AOKI! NO SERIES TO WORRY ABOUT, NO DEADLINES HANGING OVER ME, NO NOTHING!

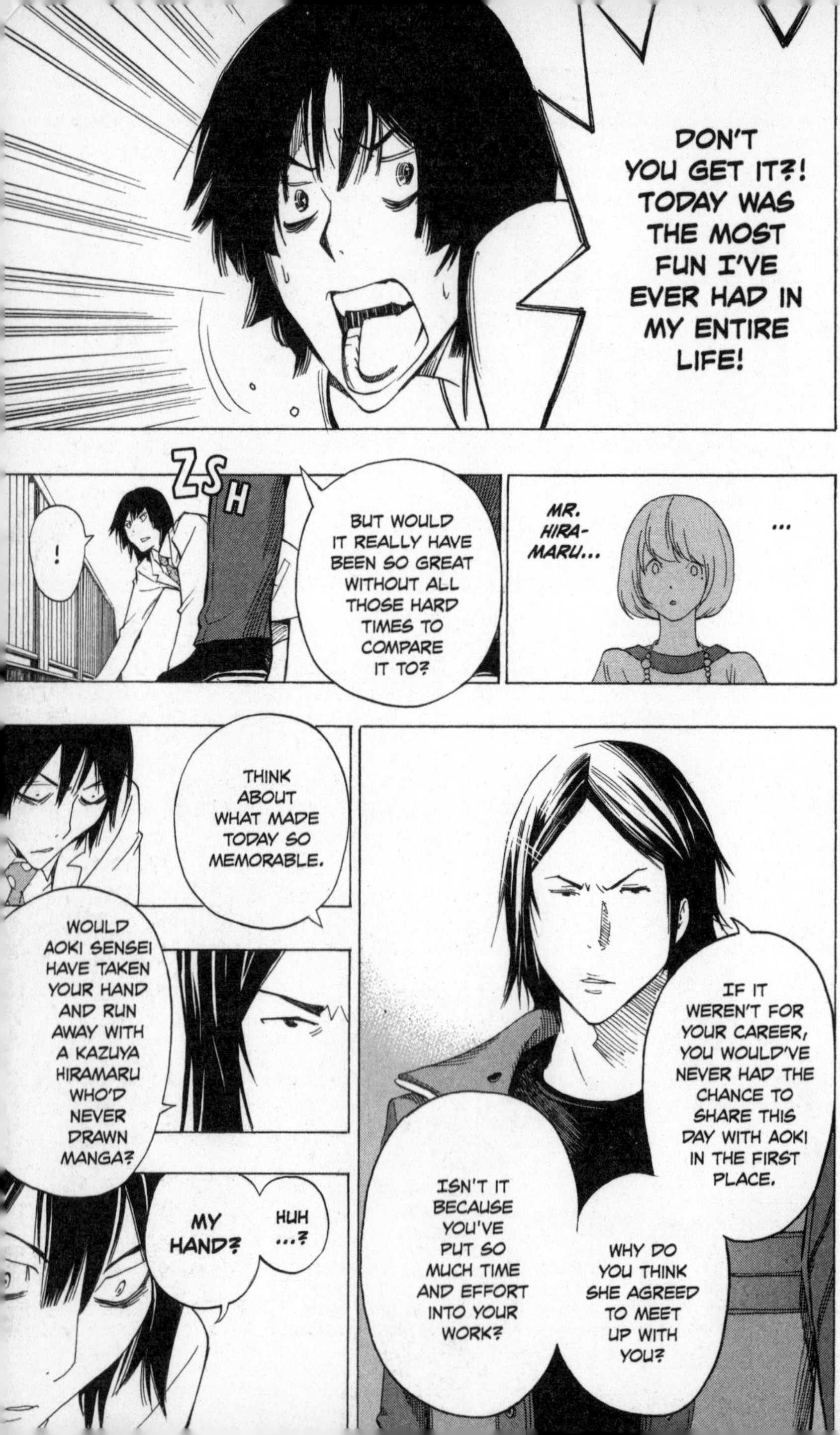
DON'T YOU GET IT?! TODAY WAS THE MOST FUN I'VE EVER HAD IN MY ENTIRE LIFE!
...
MR. HIRA-MARU...
ZSH
BUT WOULD IT REALLY HAVE BEEN SO GREAT WITHOUT ALL THOSE HARD TIMES TO COMPARE IT TO?
!
IF IT WEREN'T FOR YOUR CAREER, YOU WOULD'VE NEVER HAD THE CHANCE TO SHARE THIS DAY WITH AOKI IN THE FIRST PLACE.
WHY DO YOU THINK SHE AGREED TO MEET UP WITH YOU?
ISN'T IT BECAUSE YOU'VE PUT SO MUCH TIME AND EFFORT INTO YOUR WORK?
THINK ABOUT WHAT MADE TODAY SO MEMORABLE.
WOULD AOKI SENSEI HAVE TAKEN YOUR HAND AND RUN AWAY WITH A KAZUYA HIRAMARU WHO'D NEVER DRAWN MANGA?
HUH ...?
MY HAND?

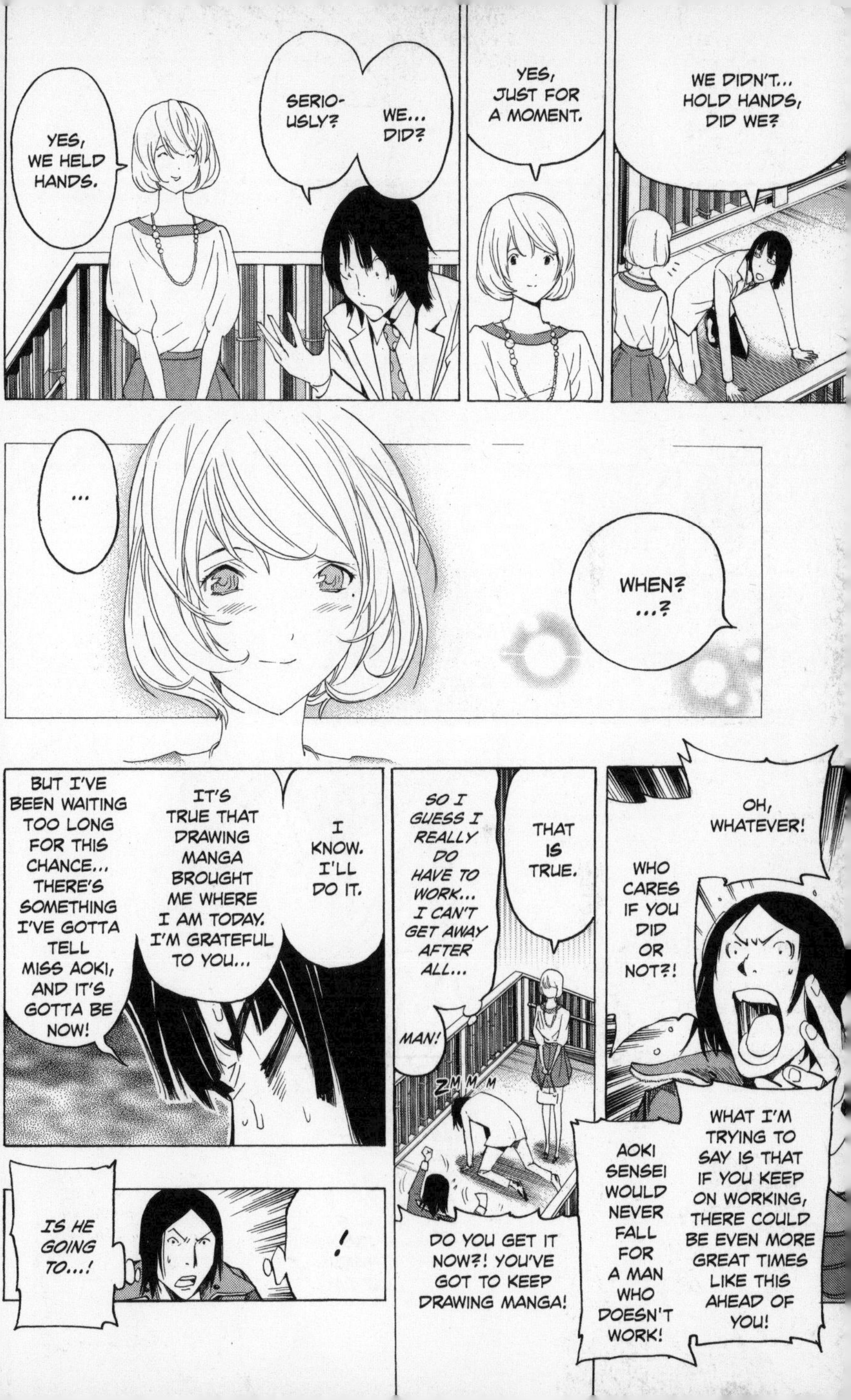
WE DIDN'T... HOLD HANDS, DID WE?
YES, JUST FOR A MOMENT.
WE... DID?
SERIO-USLY?
YES, WE HELD HANDS.
WHEN? ...?
...
OH, WHATEVER!
WHO CARES IF YOU DID OR NOT?!
WHAT I'M TRYING TO SAY IS THAT IF YOU KEEP ON WORKING, THERE COULD BE EVEN MORE GREAT TIMES LIKE THIS AHEAD OF YOU!
AOKI SENSEI WOULD NEVER FALL FOR A MAN WHO DOESN'T WORK!
THAT IS TRUE.
SO I GUESS I REALLY DO HAVE TO WORK... I CAN'T GET AWAY AFTER ALL...
MAN!
ZMMM
DO YOU GET IT NOW?! YOU'VE GOT TO KEEP DRAWING MANGA!
I KNOW. I'LL DO IT.
IT'S TRUE THAT DRAWING MANGA BROUGHT ME WHERE I AM TODAY. I'M GRATEFUL TO YOU...
BUT I'VE BEEN WAITING TOO LONG FOR THIS CHANCE... THERE'S SOMETHING I'VE GOTTA TELL MISS AOKI, AND IT'S GOTTA BE NOW!
!
IS HE GOING TO...!

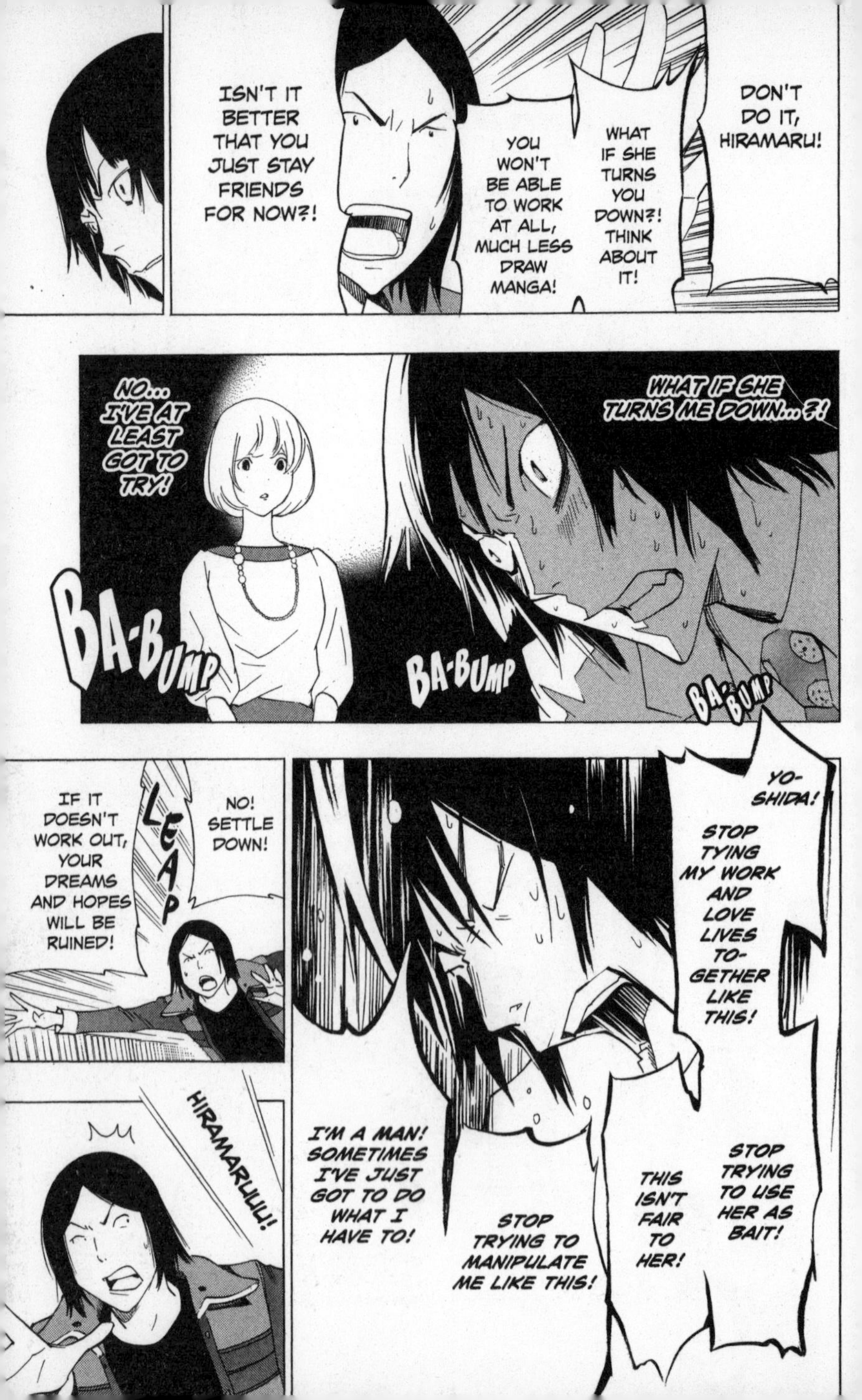
DON'T DO IT, HIRAMARU!
WHAT IF SHE TURNS YOU DOWN?! THINK ABOUT IT!
YOU WON'T BE ABLE TO WORK AT ALL, MUCH LESS DRAW MANGA!
ISN'T IT BETTER THAT YOU JUST STAY FRIENDS FOR NOW?!
WHAT IF SHE TURNS ME DOWN...?!
BA-BUMP
BA-BUMP
BA-BUMP
NO... I'VE AT LEAST GOT TO TRY!
YO-SHIDA!
STOP TYING MY WORK AND LOVE LIVES TO-GETHER LIKE THIS!
STOP TRYING TO USE HER AS BAIT!
THIS ISN'T FAIR TO HER!
STOP TRYING TO MANIPULATE ME LIKE THIS!
I'M A MAN! SOMETIMES I'VE JUST GOT TO DO WHAT I HAVE TO!
NO! SETTLE DOWN!
LEAP
IF IT DOESN'T WORK OUT, YOUR DREAMS AND HOPES WILL BE RUINED!
HIRAMARUUU!

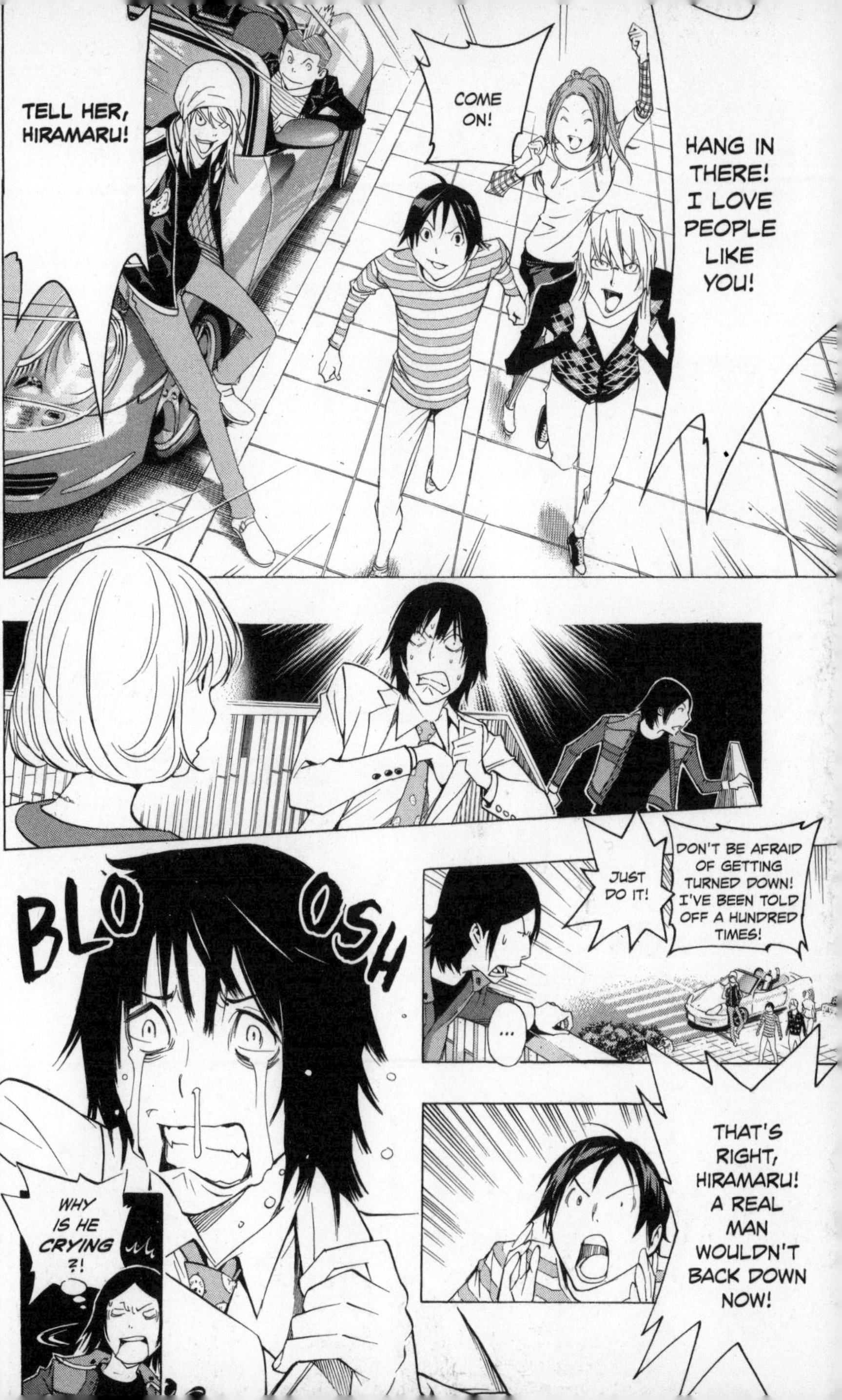
HANG IN THERE! I LOVE PEOPLE LIKE YOU!
COME ON!
TELL HER, HIRAMARU!
DON'T BE AFRAID OF GETTING TURNED DOWN! I'VE BEEN TOLD OFF A HUNDRED TIMES!
JUST DO IT!
...
THAT'S RIGHT, HIRAMARU! A REAL MAN WOULDN'T BACK DOWN NOW!
BLOOSH
WHY IS HE CRYING?!

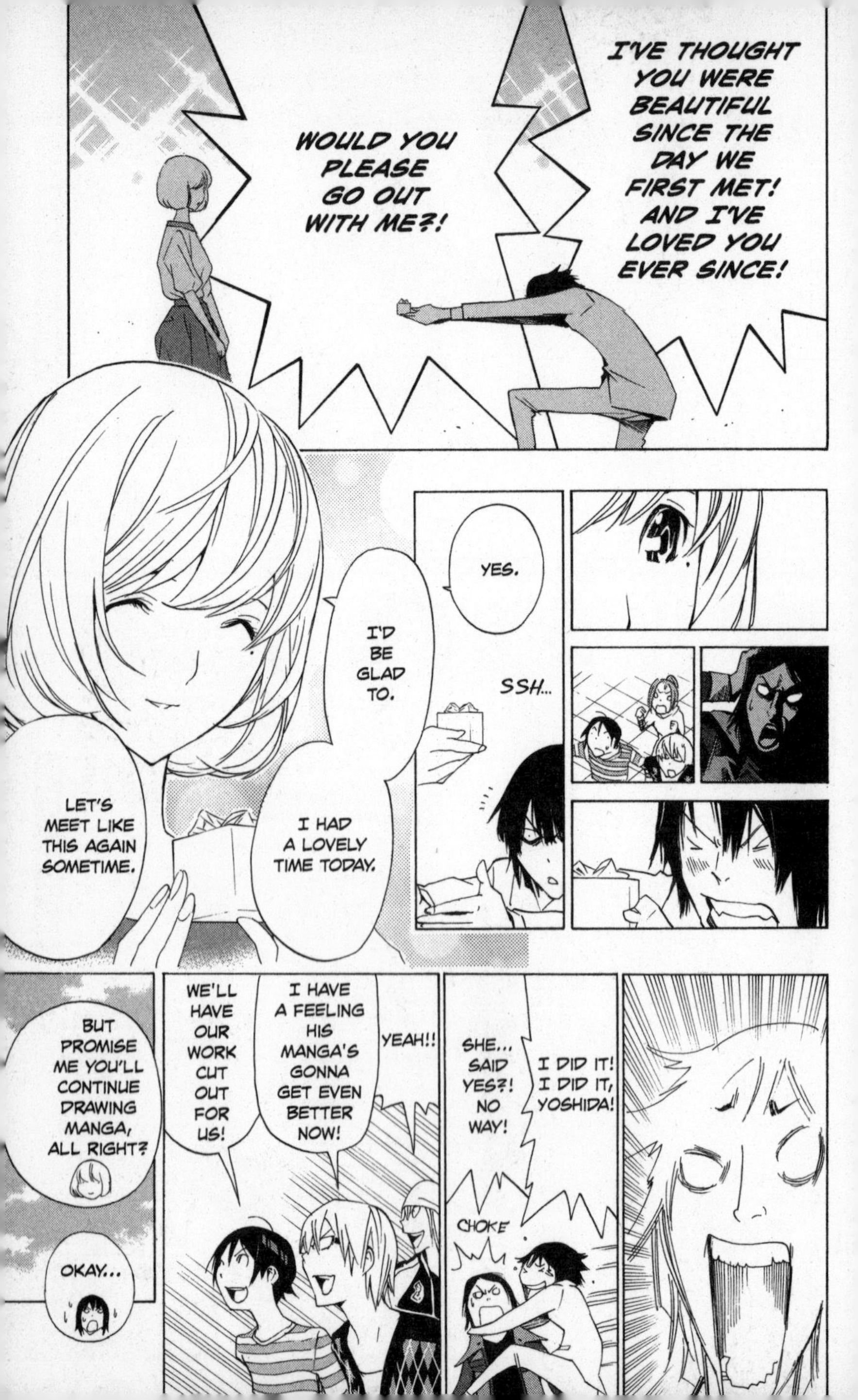
I'VE THOUGHT YOU WERE BEAUTIFUL SINCE THE DAY WE FIRST MET! AND I'VE LOVED YOU EVER SINCE!
WOULD YOU PLEASE GO OUT WITH ME?!
YES.
SSH...
I'D BE GLAD TO.
I HAD A LOVELY TIME TODAY.
LET'S MEET LIKE THIS AGAIN SOMETIME.
I DID IT! I DID IT, YOSHIDA!
SHE... SAID YES?! NO WAY!
CHOKE
YEAH!!
I HAVE A FEELING HIS MANGA'S GONNA GET EVEN BETTER NOW!
WE'LL HAVE OUR WORK CUT OUT FOR US!
BUT PROMISE ME YOU'LL CONTINUE DRAWING MANGA, ALL RIGHT?
OKAY...

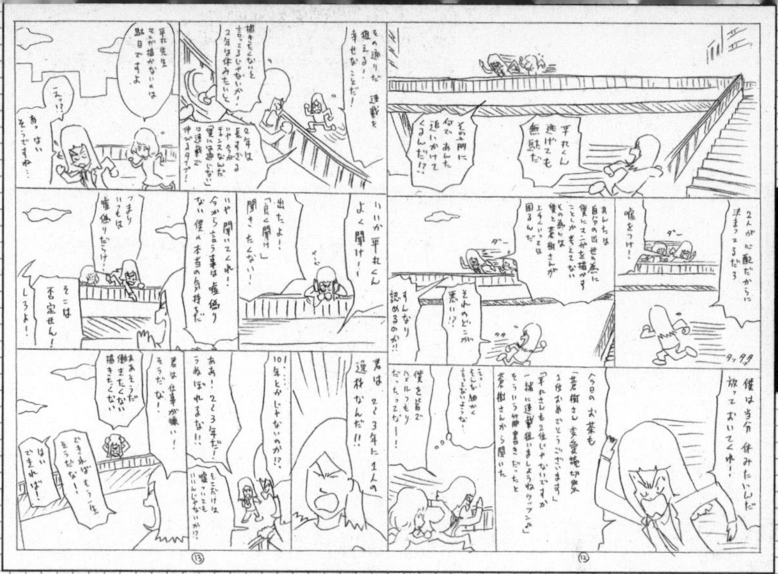

平丸くん 逃げても無駄だ
その前に 何で あんた 追いかけて くるんだ!?
2人が心配だからに決まってるだろ
ダー
嘘をつけ!
タッタタ
あんたは自分の出世の為に僕にマンガを描かすことしか考えてない その為には僕と蒼樹さんが上手くいっては困るんだ
ダー
それのどこが悪い!?
すんなり認めるのか!!
タタ
僕は当分 休みたいんだ 放っておいてくれ!
今日の お茶も 「蒼樹さん 恋愛読切祭1位おめでとうございます」「平丸さんも2位じゃないですか 一緒に連載狙いましょうね ウフフン♪」 そういう筋書きだったと 蒼樹さんから聞いた
えっ… そんな細かく 言ってないような…
僕を皆で ハメるつもり だったってな——!
その通りだ 連載を 狙える! 幸せなことだ!
描きたくないと 言ってるじゃないか! 2年は休みたいと
2年は 長すぎる いや今が チャンスなんだ
平丸先生 マンガ描かないのは 駄目ですよ
えっ!?
あっ はい そうですね…
いいか平丸くん よく聞け!
出たよ! 「良く聞け」 聞きたくない!
いや聞いてくれ! 今から言う事は嘘偽り ない僕の本当の気持ちだ
つまり いつもは 嘘偽りだらけ!
そこは 否定せん!
しろよ!
君は 2〜3年に 1人の 逸材 なんだ!!
10年…とかじゃないのか!?
ああ! 2〜3年だ! うぬぼれるな!!
そこだけは 嘘ついても いいんじゃないか!?
君は仕事が嫌い! そうだな!
まあそうだ 働きたくない 描きたくない
できればもう一生 そうだな!
はい できれば!

OHBA'S STORYBOARD

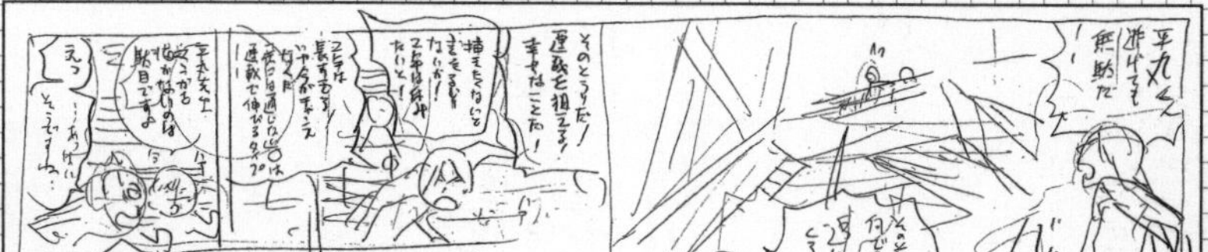

OBATA'S STORYBOARD

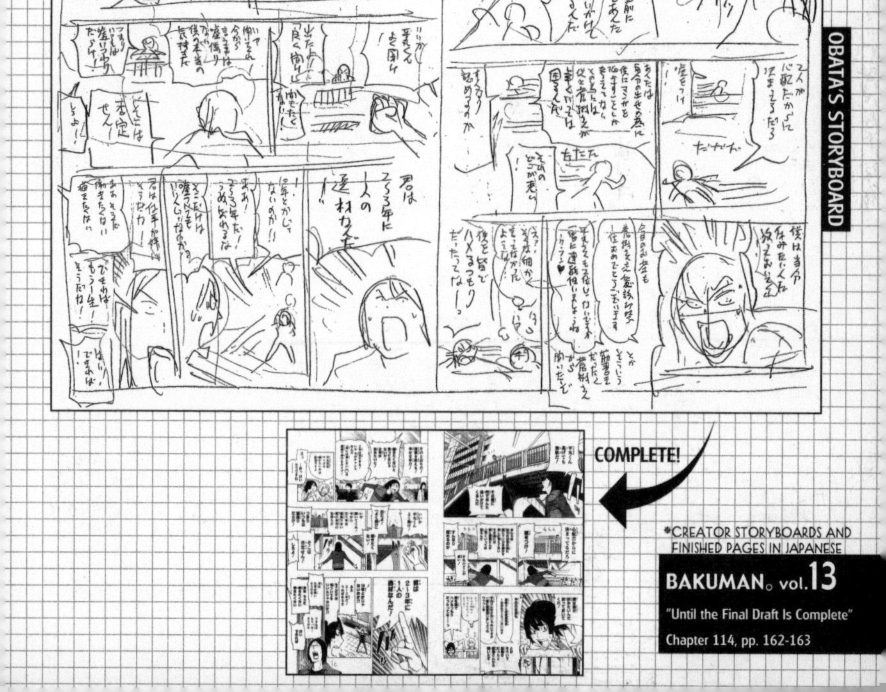

COMPLETE!

*CREATOR STORYBOARDS AND FINISHED PAGES IN JAPANESE

BAKUMAN。 vol.13

"Until the Final Draft Is Complete"

Chapter 114, pp. 162-163

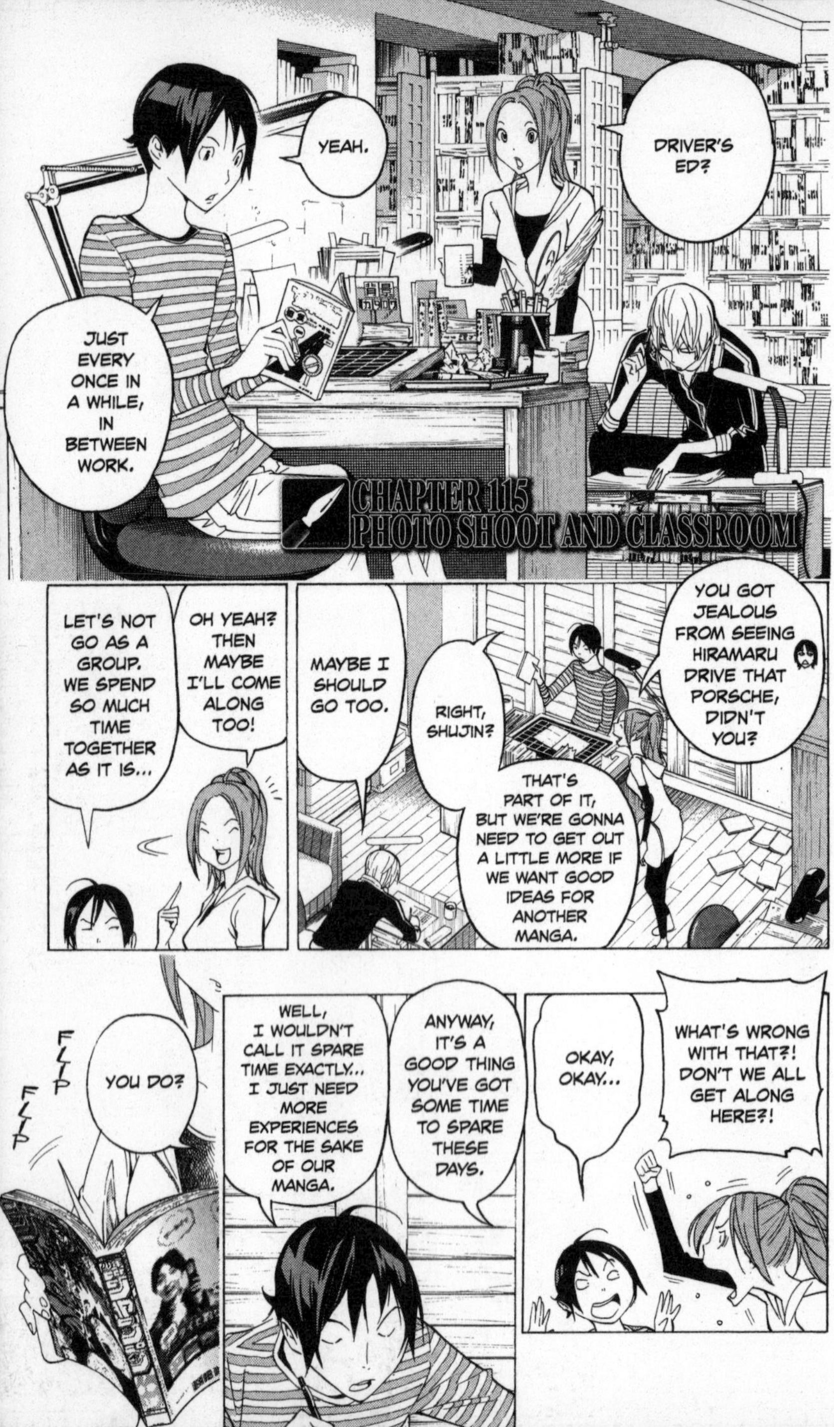
DRIVER'S ED?
YEAH.
JUST EVERY ONCE IN A WHILE, IN BETWEEN WORK.
CHAPTER 115
PHOTO SHOOT AND CLASSROOM
YOU GOT JEALOUS FROM SEEING HIRAMARU DRIVE THAT PORSCHE, DIDN'T YOU?
RIGHT, SHUJIN?
THAT'S PART OF IT, BUT WE'RE GONNA NEED TO GET OUT A LITTLE MORE IF WE WANT GOOD IDEAS FOR ANOTHER MANGA.
MAYBE I SHOULD GO TOO.
OH YEAH? THEN MAYBE I'LL COME ALONG TOO!
LET'S NOT GO AS A GROUP. WE SPEND SO MUCH TIME TOGETHER AS IT IS...
WHAT'S WRONG WITH THAT?! DON'T WE ALL GET ALONG HERE?!
OKAY, OKAY...
ANYWAY, IT'S A GOOD THING YOU'VE GOT SOME TIME TO SPARE THESE DAYS.
WELL, I WOULDN'T CALL IT SPARE TIME EXACTLY... I JUST NEED MORE EXPERIENCES FOR THE SAKE OF OUR MANGA.
YOU DO?
FLIP
FLIP

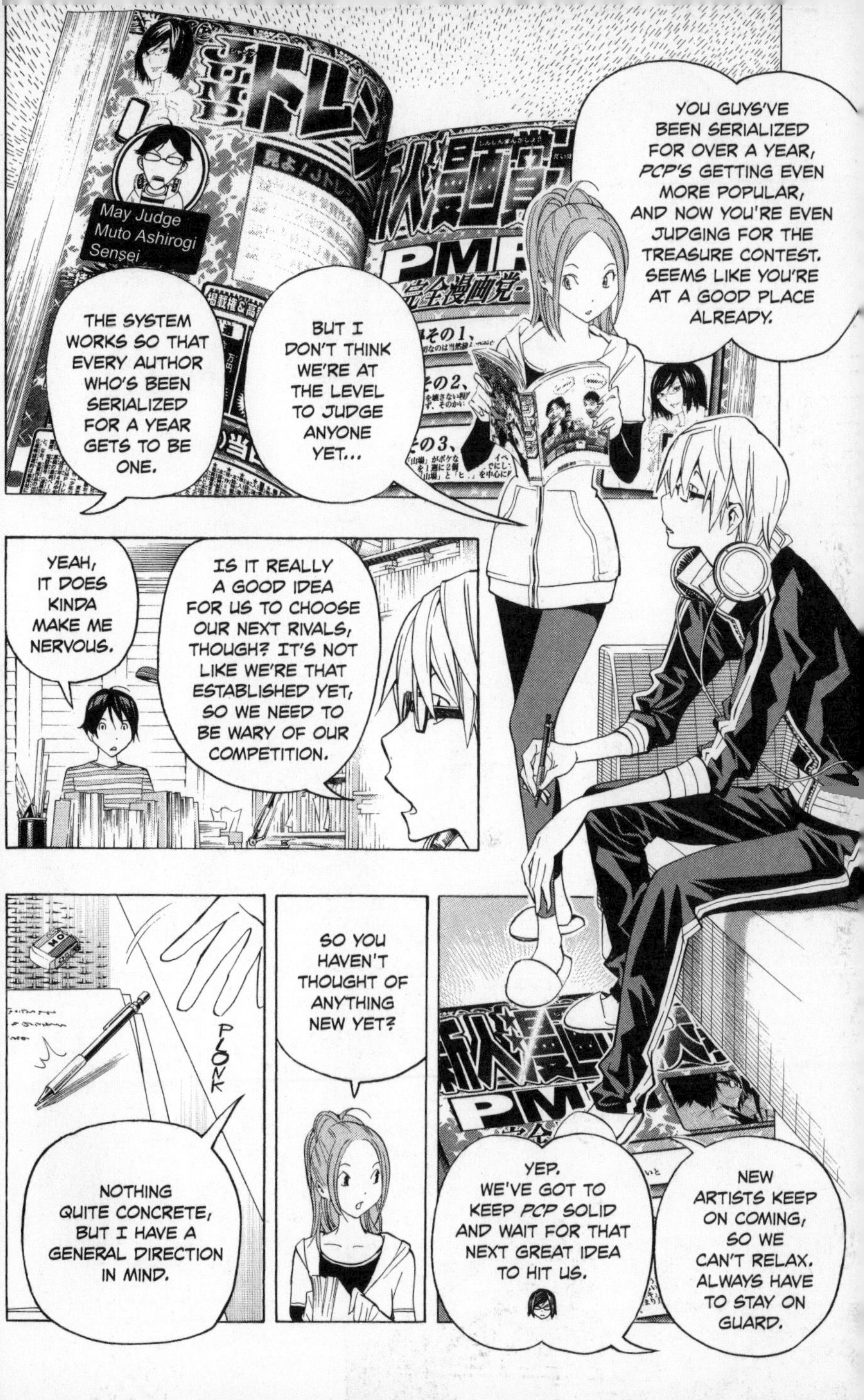
YOU GUYS'VE BEEN SERIALIZED FOR OVER A YEAR, *PCP'S* GETTING EVEN MORE POPULAR, AND NOW YOU'RE EVEN JUDGING FOR THE TREASURE CONTEST. SEEMS LIKE YOU'RE AT A GOOD PLACE ALREADY.
May Judge Muto Ashirogi Sensei
BUT I DON'T THINK WE'RE AT THE LEVEL TO JUDGE ANYONE YET...
THE SYSTEM WORKS SO THAT EVERY AUTHOR WHO'S BEEN SERIALIZED FOR A YEAR GETS TO BE ONE.
IS IT REALLY A GOOD IDEA FOR US TO CHOOSE OUR NEXT RIVALS, THOUGH? IT'S NOT LIKE WE'RE THAT ESTABLISHED YET, SO WE NEED TO BE WARY OF OUR COMPETITION.
YEAH, IT DOES KINDA MAKE ME NERVOUS.
SO YOU HAVEN'T THOUGHT OF ANYTHING NEW YET?
PLONK
NOTHING QUITE CONCRETE, BUT I HAVE A GENERAL DIRECTION IN MIND.
NEW ARTISTS KEEP ON COMING, SO WE CAN'T RELAX. ALWAYS HAVE TO STAY ON GUARD.
YEP. WE'VE GOT TO KEEP *PCP* SOLID AND WAIT FOR THAT NEXT GREAT IDEA TO HIT US.

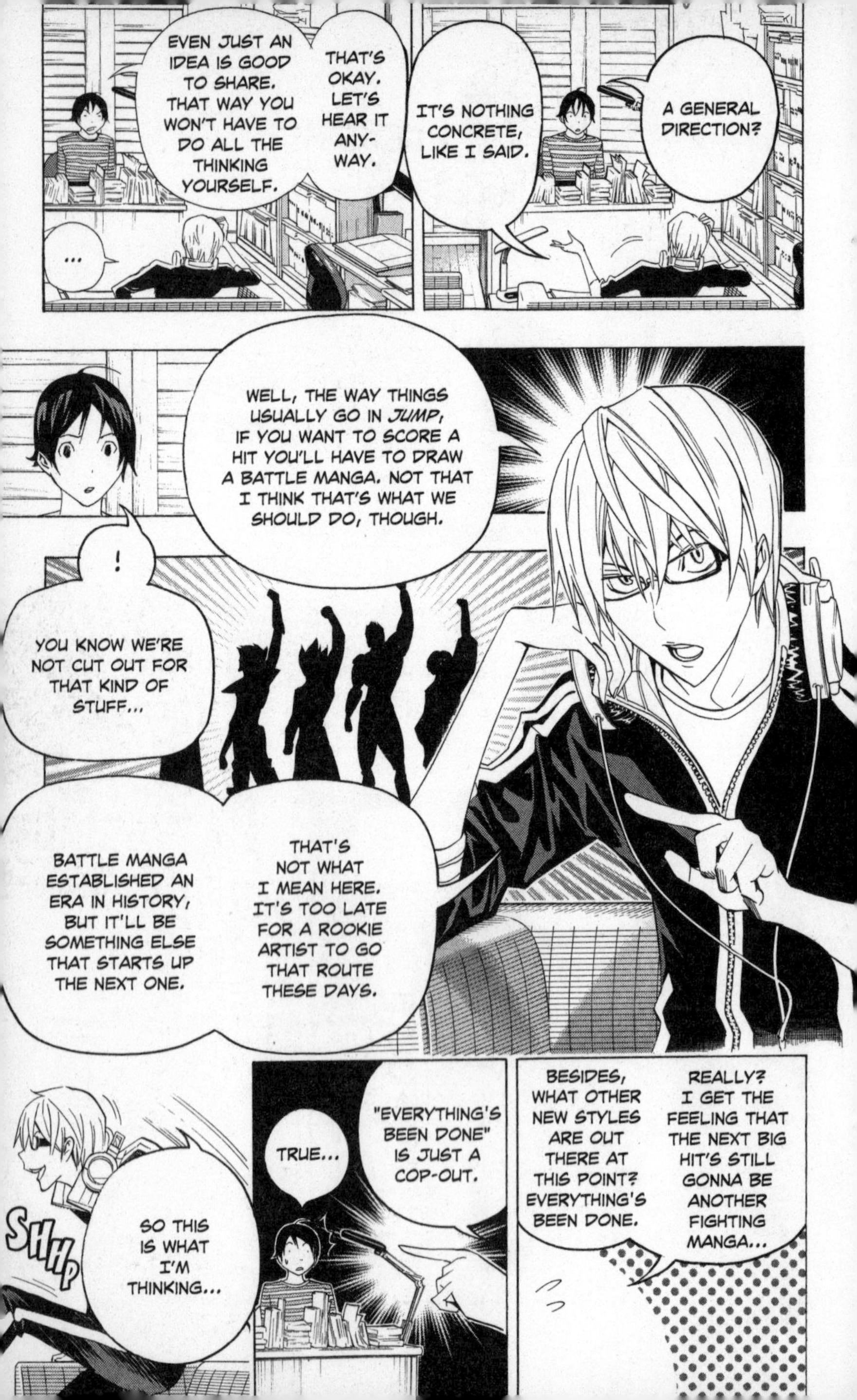
A GENERAL DIRECTION?
IT'S NOTHING CONCRETE, LIKE I SAID.
THAT'S OKAY. LET'S HEAR IT ANYWAY.
EVEN JUST AN IDEA IS GOOD TO SHARE. THAT WAY YOU WON'T HAVE TO DO ALL THE THINKING YOURSELF.
...
WELL, THE WAY THINGS USUALLY GO IN *JUMP*, IF YOU WANT TO SCORE A HIT YOU'LL HAVE TO DRAW A BATTLE MANGA. NOT THAT I THINK THAT'S WHAT WE SHOULD DO, THOUGH.
!
YOU KNOW WE'RE NOT CUT OUT FOR THAT KIND OF STUFF...
THAT'S NOT WHAT I MEAN HERE. IT'S TOO LATE FOR A ROOKIE ARTIST TO GO THAT ROUTE THESE DAYS.
BATTLE MANGA ESTABLISHED AN ERA IN HISTORY, BUT IT'LL BE SOMETHING ELSE THAT STARTS UP THE NEXT ONE.
REALLY? I GET THE FEELING THAT THE NEXT BIG HIT'S STILL GONNA BE ANOTHER FIGHTING MANGA...
BESIDES, WHAT OTHER NEW STYLES ARE OUT THERE AT THIS POINT? EVERYTHING'S BEEN DONE.
"EVERYTHING'S BEEN DONE" IS JUST A COP-OUT.
TRUE...
SHHP
SO THIS IS WHAT I'M THINKING...

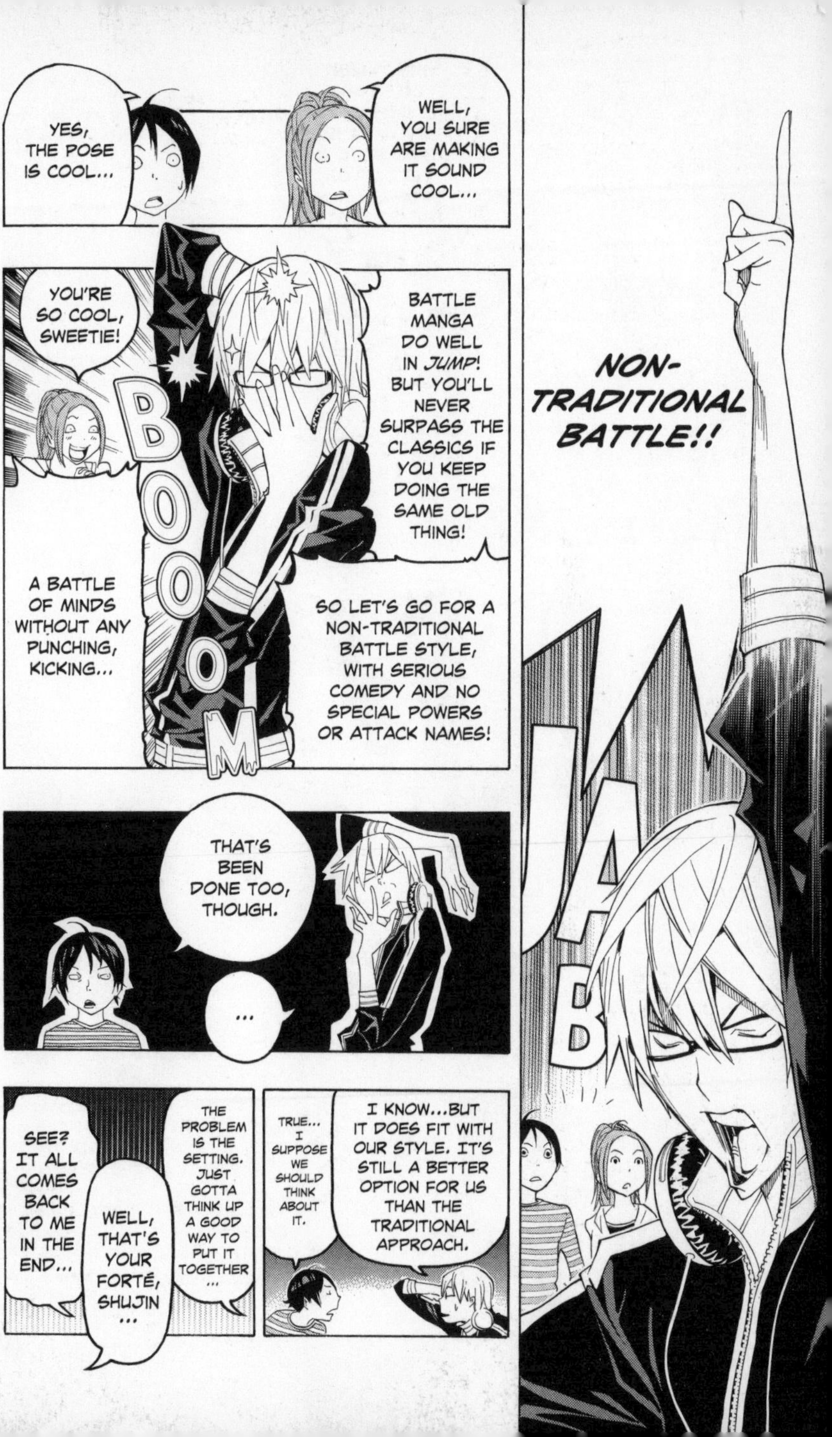
NON-TRADITIONAL BATTLE!!
WELL, YOU SURE ARE MAKING IT SOUND COOL...
YES, THE POSE IS COOL...
BATTLE MANGA DO WELL IN JUMP! BUT YOU'LL NEVER SURPASS THE CLASSICS IF YOU KEEP DOING THE SAME OLD THING!
YOU'RE SO COOL, SWEETIE!
BOOOOM
SO LET'S GO FOR A NON-TRADITIONAL BATTLE STYLE, WITH SERIOUS COMEDY AND NO SPECIAL POWERS OR ATTACK NAMES!
A BATTLE OF MINDS WITHOUT ANY PUNCHING, KICKING...
THAT'S BEEN DONE TOO, THOUGH.
...
I KNOW...BUT IT DOES FIT WITH OUR STYLE. IT'S STILL A BETTER OPTION FOR US THAN THE TRADITIONAL APPROACH.
TRUE... I SUPPOSE WE SHOULD THINK ABOUT IT.
THE PROBLEM IS THE SETTING. JUST GOTTA THINK UP A GOOD WAY TO PUT IT TOGETHER...
SEE? IT ALL COMES BACK TO ME IN THE END...
WELL, THAT'S YOUR FORTÉ, SHUJIN...

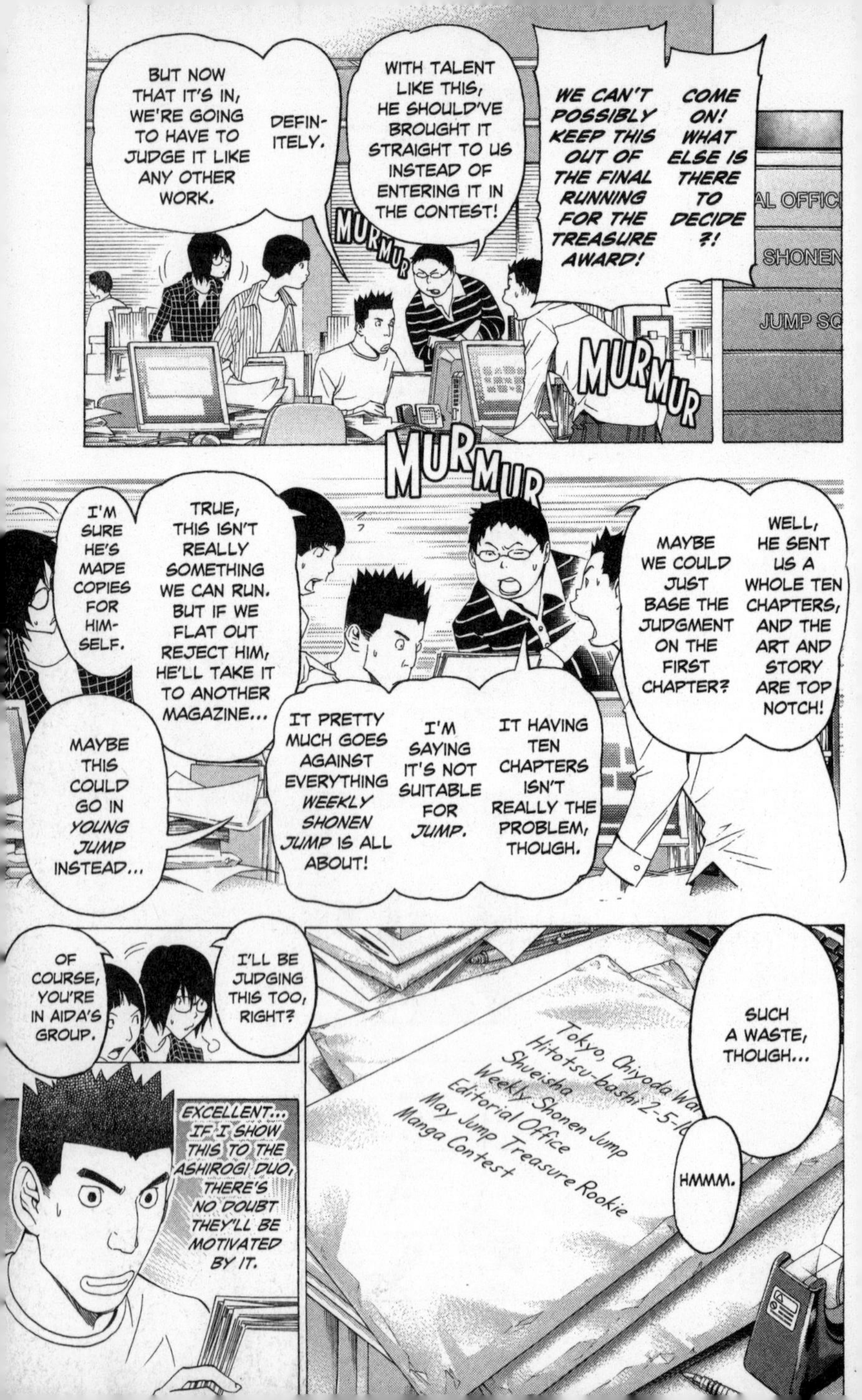
COME ON! WHAT ELSE IS THERE TO DECIDE?!
WE CAN'T POSSIBLY KEEP THIS OUT OF THE FINAL RUNNING FOR THE TREASURE AWARD!
AL OFFIC
SHONEN
JUMP SQ
MURMUR
WITH TALENT LIKE THIS, HE SHOULD'VE BROUGHT IT STRAIGHT TO US INSTEAD OF ENTERING IT IN THE CONTEST!
MURMUR
DEFIN-ITELY.
BUT NOW THAT IT'S IN, WE'RE GOING TO HAVE TO JUDGE IT LIKE ANY OTHER WORK.
MURMUR
WELL, HE SENT US A WHOLE TEN CHAPTERS, AND THE ART AND STORY ARE TOP NOTCH!
MAYBE WE COULD JUST BASE THE JUDGMENT ON THE FIRST CHAPTER?
IT HAVING TEN CHAPTERS ISN'T REALLY THE PROBLEM, THOUGH.
I'M SAYING IT'S NOT SUITABLE FOR *JUMP*.
IT PRETTY MUCH GOES AGAINST EVERYTHING *WEEKLY SHONEN JUMP* IS ALL ABOUT!
TRUE, THIS ISN'T REALLY SOMETHING WE CAN RUN. BUT IF WE FLAT OUT REJECT HIM, HE'LL TAKE IT TO ANOTHER MAGAZINE...
I'M SURE HE'S MADE COPIES FOR HIM-SELF.
MAYBE THIS COULD GO IN *YOUNG JUMP* INSTEAD...
SUCH A WASTE, THOUGH...
HMMM.
Tokyo, Chiyoda Wa
Hitotsu-bashi 2-5-1
Shueisha
Weekly Shonen Jump
Editorial Office
May Jump Treasure Rookie
Manga Contest
I'LL BE JUDGING THIS TOO, RIGHT?
OF COURSE, YOU'RE IN AIDA'S GROUP.
EXCELLENT... IF I SHOW THIS TO THE ASHIROGI DUO, THERE'S NO DOUBT THEY'LL BE MOTIVATED BY IT.

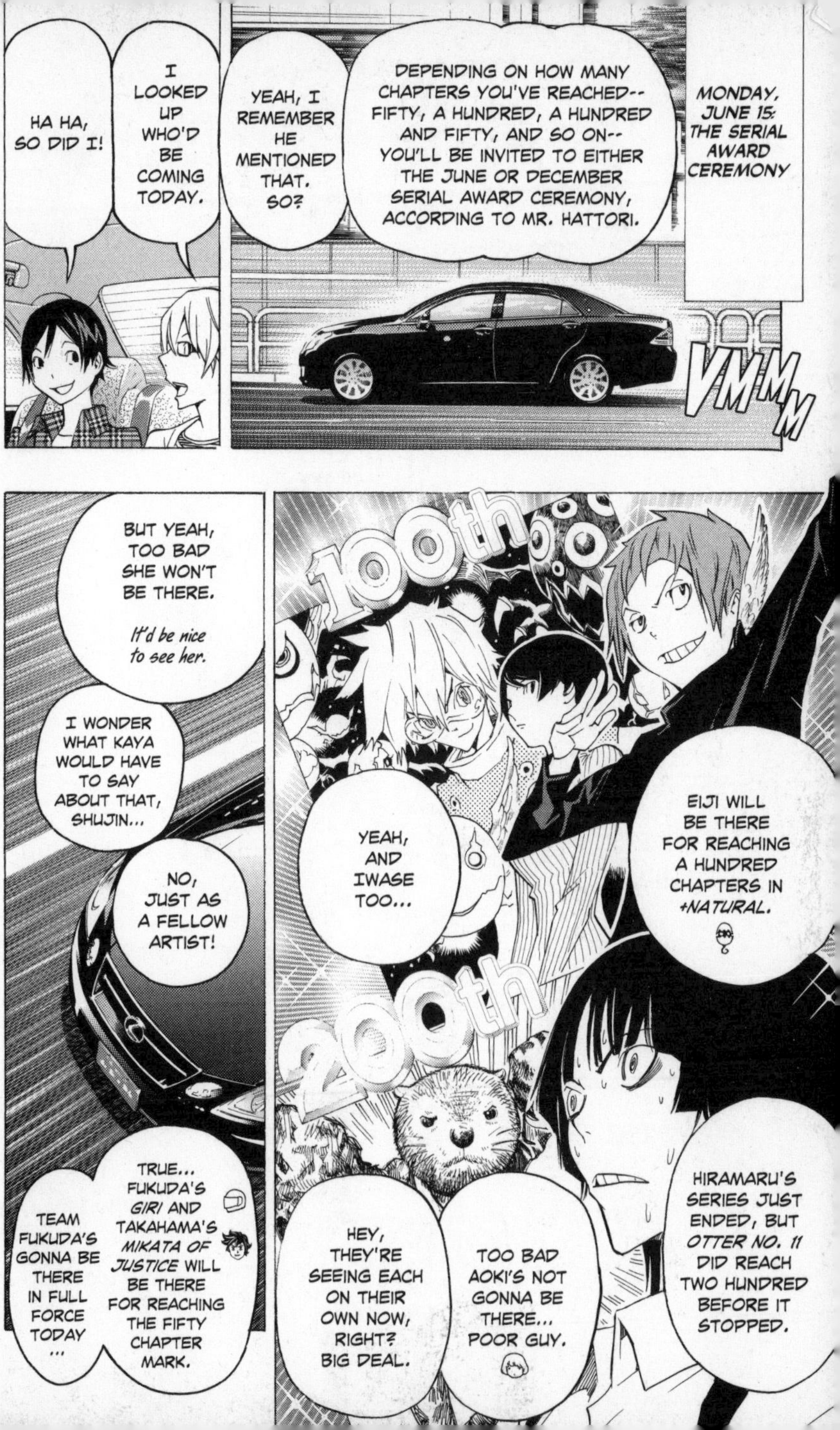
MONDAY, JUNE 15: THE SERIAL AWARD CEREMONY
DEPENDING ON HOW MANY CHAPTERS YOU'VE REACHED-- FIFTY, A HUNDRED, A HUNDRED AND FIFTY, AND SO ON-- YOU'LL BE INVITED TO EITHER THE JUNE OR DECEMBER SERIAL AWARD CEREMONY, ACCORDING TO MR. HATTORI.
VMMMM
YEAH, I REMEMBER HE MENTIONED THAT. SO?
I LOOKED UP WHO'D BE COMING TODAY.
HA HA, SO DID I!
EIJI WILL BE THERE FOR REACHING A HUNDRED CHAPTERS IN +NATURAL.
100th
YEAH, AND IWASE TOO...
200th
HIRAMARU'S SERIES JUST ENDED, BUT OTTER NO. 11 DID REACH TWO HUNDRED BEFORE IT STOPPED.
TOO BAD AOKI'S NOT GONNA BE THERE... POOR GUY.
HEY, THEY'RE SEEING EACH ON THEIR OWN NOW, RIGHT? BIG DEAL.
BUT YEAH, TOO BAD SHE WON'T BE THERE.
It'd be nice to see her.
I WONDER WHAT KAYA WOULD HAVE TO SAY ABOUT THAT, SHUJIN...
NO, JUST AS A FELLOW ARTIST!
TRUE... FUKUDA'S GIRI AND TAKAHAMA'S MIKATA OF JUSTICE WILL BE THERE FOR REACHING THE FIFTY CHAPTER MARK.
TEAM FUKUDA'S GONNA BE THERE IN FULL FORCE TODAY ...

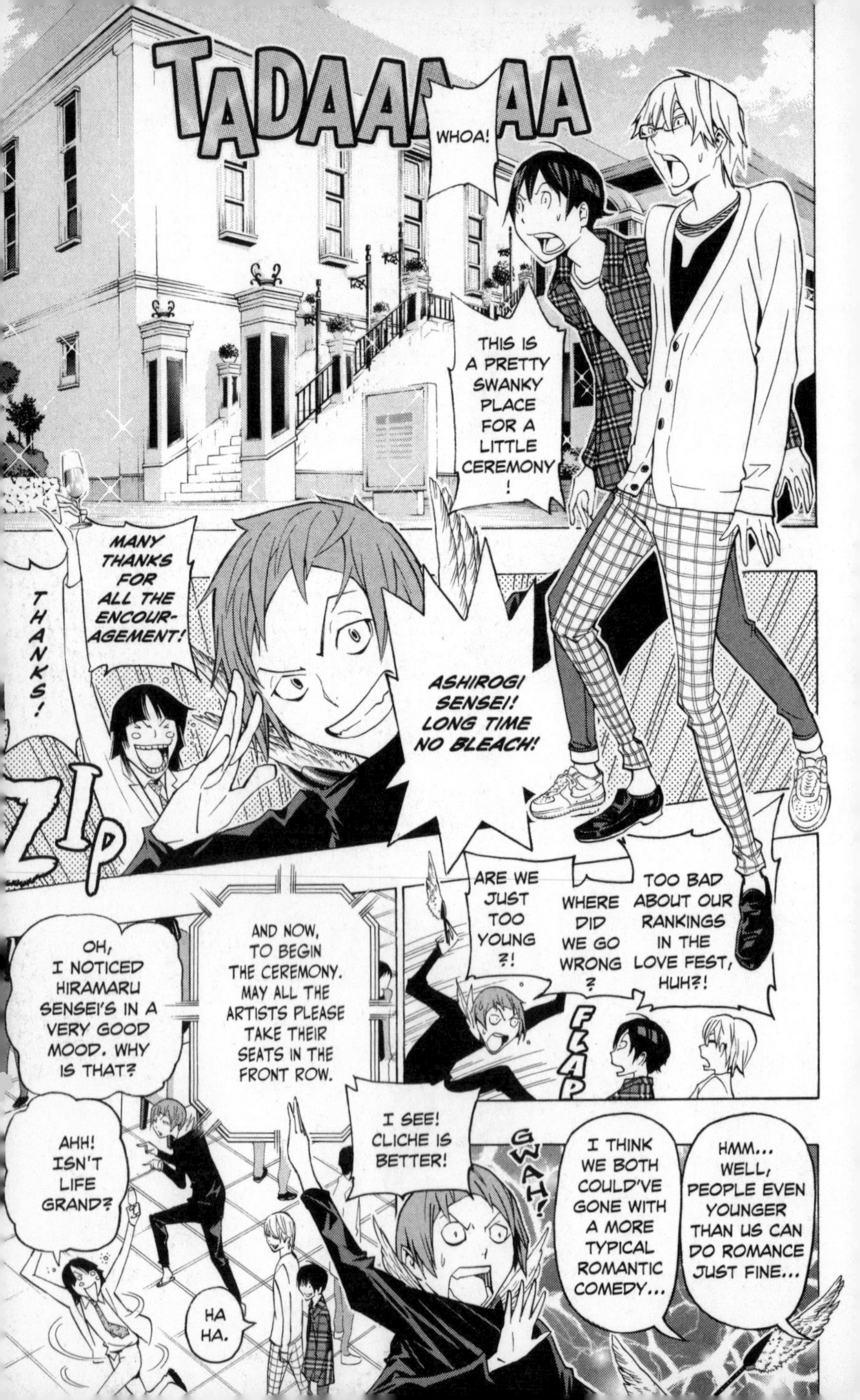
TADAAAAAA
WHOA!
THIS IS A PRETTY SWANKY PLACE FOR A LITTLE CEREMONY!
ASHIROGI SENSEI! LONG TIME NO BLEACH!
MANY THANKS FOR ALL THE ENCOURAGEMENT!
THANKS!
ZIP
TOO BAD ABOUT OUR RANKINGS IN THE LOVE FEST, HUH?!
WHERE DID WE GO WRONG?
ARE WE JUST TOO YOUNG?!
FLAP
AND NOW, TO BEGIN THE CEREMONY. MAY ALL THE ARTISTS PLEASE TAKE THEIR SEATS IN THE FRONT ROW.
OH, I NOTICED HIRAMARU SENSEI'S IN A VERY GOOD MOOD. WHY IS THAT?
HMM... WELL, PEOPLE EVEN YOUNGER THAN US CAN DO ROMANCE JUST FINE...
I THINK WE BOTH COULD'VE GONE WITH A MORE TYPICAL ROMANTIC COMEDY...
GWAH!
I SEE! CLICHE IS BETTER!
AHH! ISN'T LIFE GRAND?
HA HA.

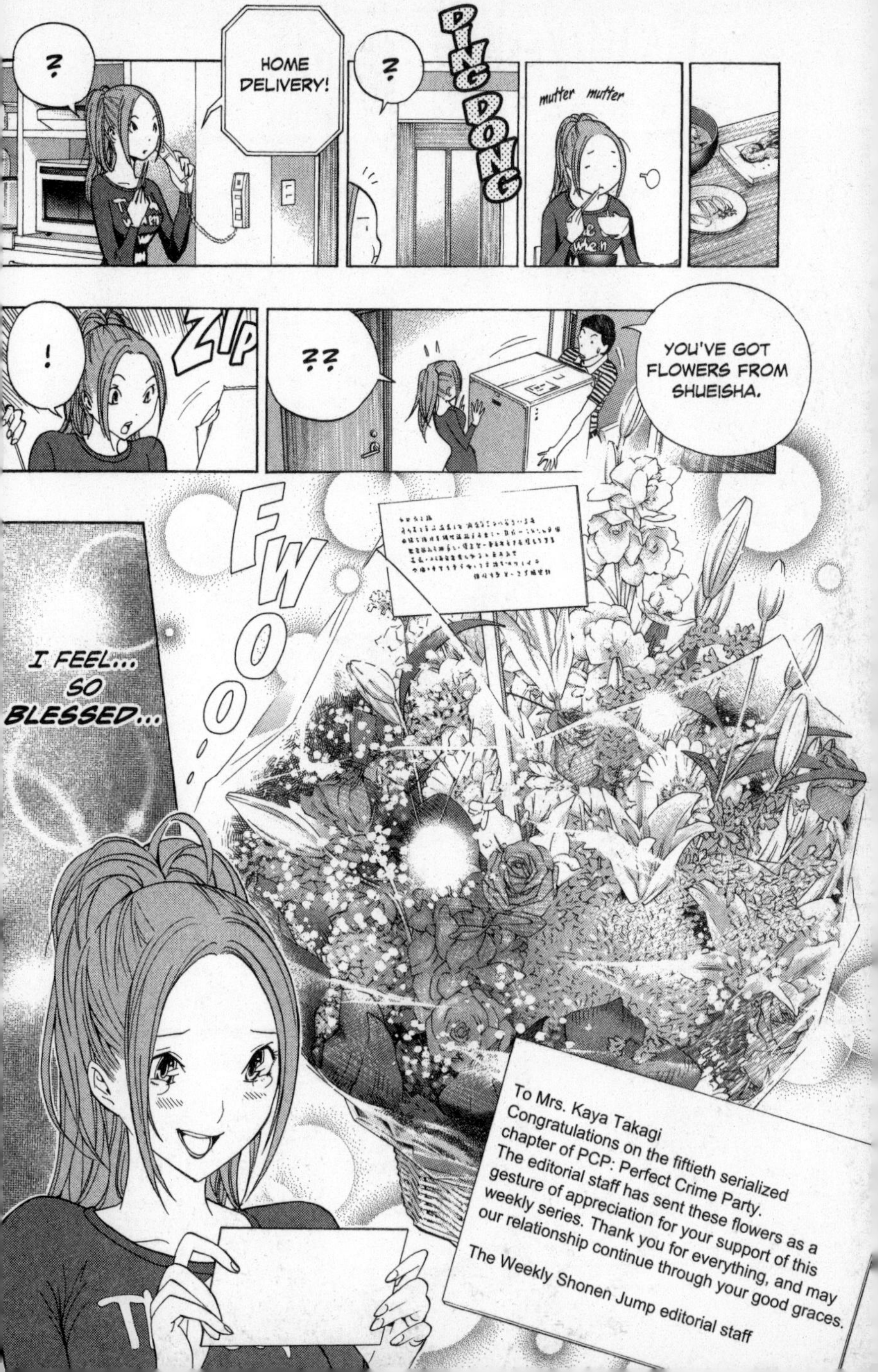
mutter mutter
DING DONG
?
HOME DELIVERY!
?
YOU'VE GOT FLOWERS FROM SHUEISHA.
??
ZIP
!
FWOOO
I FEEL... SO BLESSED...
To Mrs. Kaya Takagi
Congratulations on the fiftieth serialized chapter of PCP: Perfect Crime Party.
The editorial staff has sent these flowers as a gesture of appreciation for your support of this weekly series. Thank you for everything, and may our relationship continue through your good graces.
The Weekly Shonen Jump editorial staff

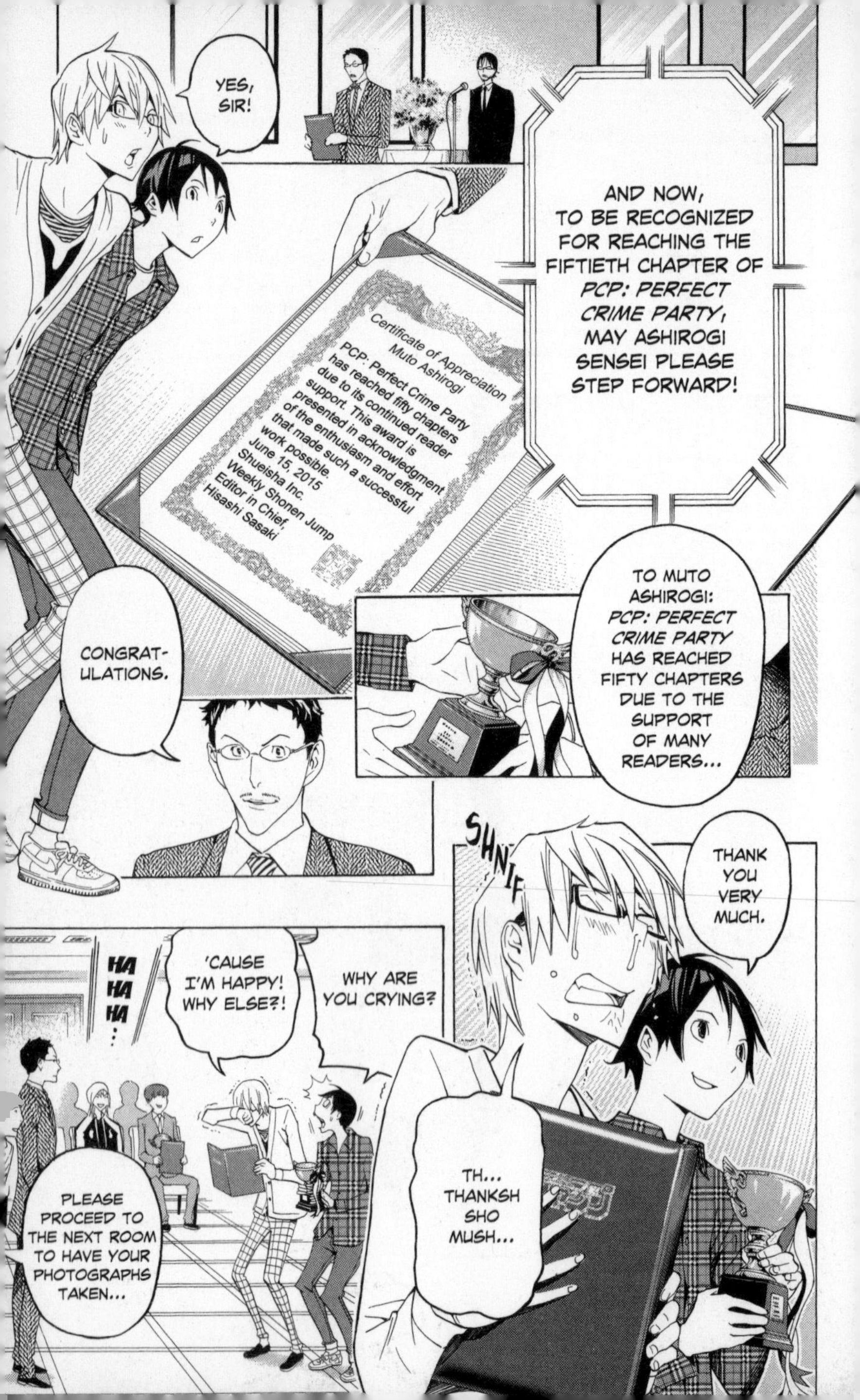
AND NOW, TO BE RECOGNIZED FOR REACHING THE FIFTIETH CHAPTER OF *PCP: PERFECT CRIME PARTY*, MAY ASHIROGI SENSEI PLEASE STEP FORWARD!
YES, SIR!
Certificate of Appreciation
Muto Ashirogi
PCP: Perfect Crime Party has reached fifty chapters due to its continued reader support. This award is presented in acknowledgment of the enthusiasm and effort that made such a successful work possible.
June 15, 2015
Shueisha Inc.
Weekly Shonen Jump
Editor in Chief,
Hisashi Sasaki
TO MUTO ASHIROGI: *PCP: PERFECT CRIME PARTY* HAS REACHED FIFTY CHAPTERS DUE TO THE SUPPORT OF MANY READERS...
CONGRAT-ULATIONS.
SHNIFF
THANK YOU VERY MUCH.
TH... THANKSH SHO MUSH...
WHY ARE YOU CRYING?
'CAUSE I'M HAPPY! WHY ELSE?!
HA HA HA...
PLEASE PROCEED TO THE NEXT ROOM TO HAVE YOUR PHOTOGRAPHS TAKEN...

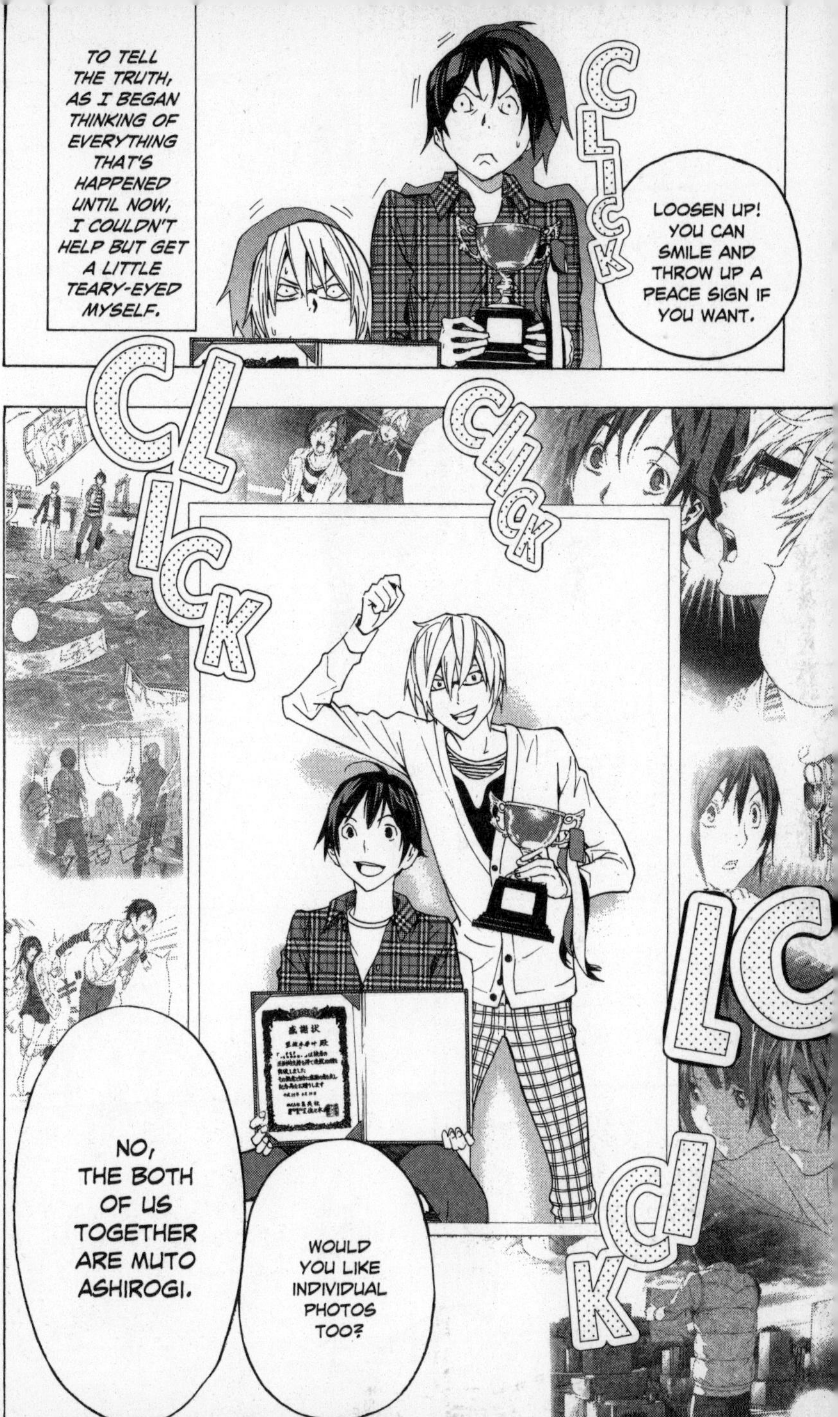
CLICK
LOOSEN UP! YOU CAN SMILE AND THROW UP A PEACE SIGN IF YOU WANT.
TO TELL THE TRUTH, AS I BEGAN THINKING OF EVERYTHING THAT'S HAPPENED UNTIL NOW, I COULDN'T HELP BUT GET A LITTLE TEARY-EYED MYSELF.
CLICK
CLICK
CLICK
CLICK
WOULD YOU LIKE INDIVIDUAL PHOTOS TOO?
NO, THE BOTH OF US TOGETHER ARE MUTO ASHIROGI.

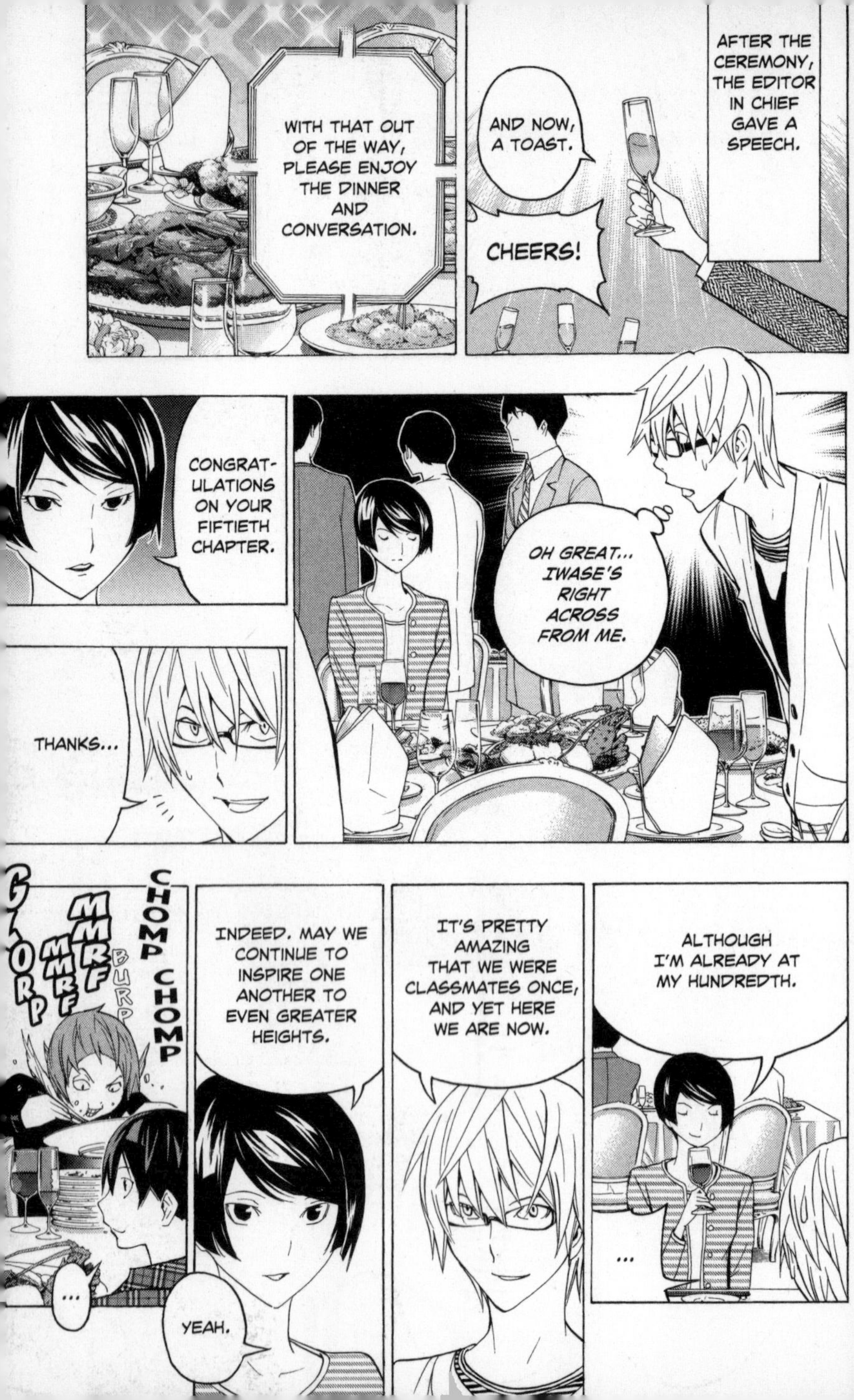
AFTER THE CEREMONY, THE EDITOR IN CHIEF GAVE A SPEECH.
AND NOW, A TOAST.
CHEERS!
WITH THAT OUT OF THE WAY, PLEASE ENJOY THE DINNER AND CONVERSATION.
OH GREAT... IWASE'S RIGHT ACROSS FROM ME.
CONGRAT-ULATIONS ON YOUR FIFTIETH CHAPTER.
THANKS...
ALTHOUGH I'M ALREADY AT MY HUNDREDTH.
...
IT'S PRETTY AMAZING THAT WE WERE CLASSMATES ONCE, AND YET HERE WE ARE NOW.
INDEED. MAY WE CONTINUE TO INSPIRE ONE ANOTHER TO EVEN GREATER HEIGHTS.
YEAH.
CHOMP CHOMP
BURP
MMRF MMRF
GLORP
...

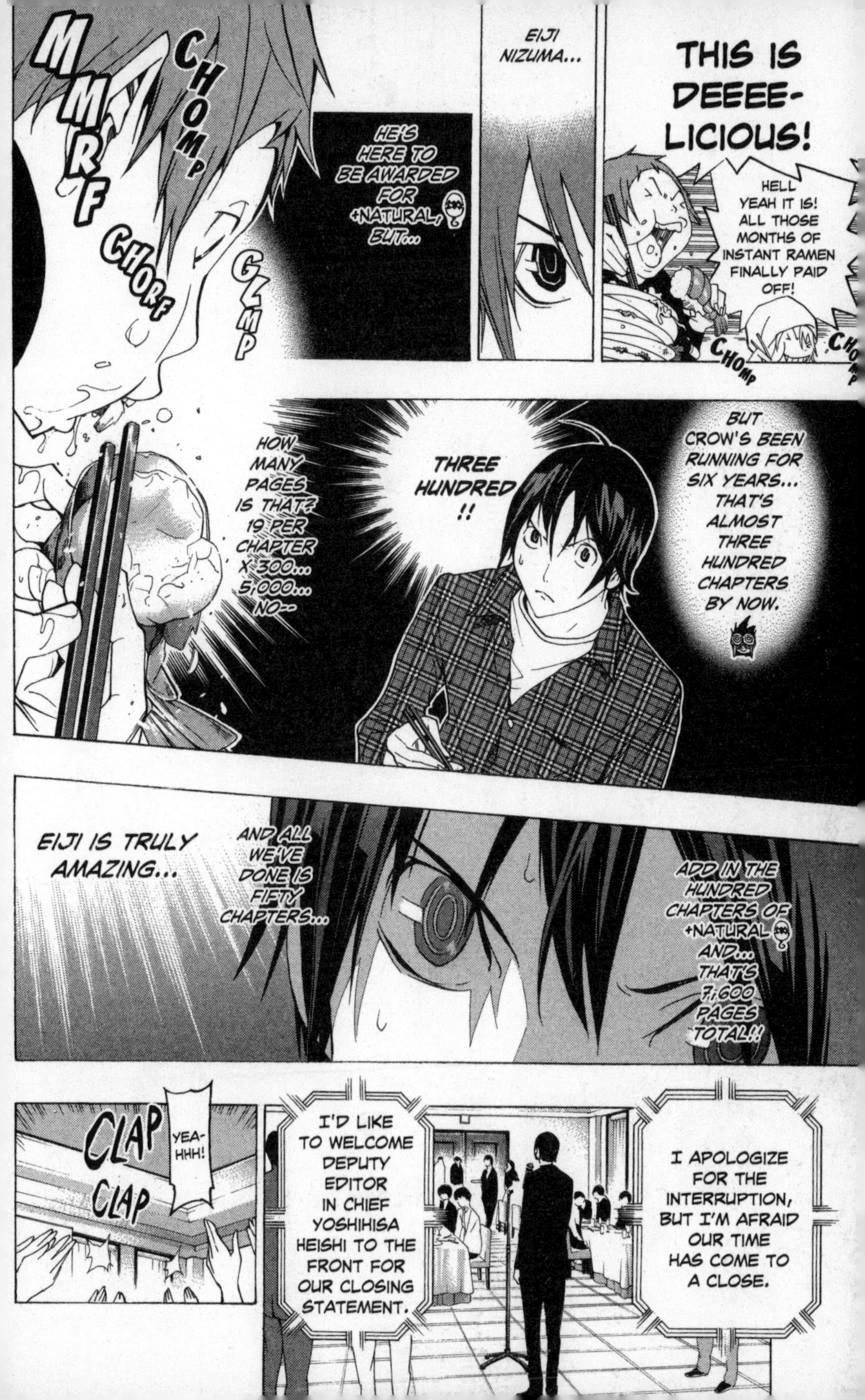
THIS IS DEEEEE-LICIOUS!
HELL YEAH IT IS! ALL THOSE MONTHS OF INSTANT RAMEN FINALLY PAID OFF!
CHOMP
CHOMP
EIJI NIZUMA...
HE'S HERE TO BE AWARDED FOR +NATURAL, BUT...
MMMRF
CHOMP
CHORF
GLMP
BUT CROW'S BEEN RUNNING FOR SIX YEARS... THAT'S ALMOST THREE HUNDRED CHAPTERS BY NOW.
THREE HUNDRED !!
HOW MANY PAGES IS THAT? 19 PER CHAPTER X 300... 5,000... NO--
ADD IN THE HUNDRED CHAPTERS OF +NATURAL AND... THAT'S 7,600 PAGES TOTAL!!
AND ALL WE'VE DONE IS FIFTY CHAPTERS...
EIJI IS TRULY AMAZING...
I APOLOGIZE FOR THE INTERRUPTION, BUT I'M AFRAID OUR TIME HAS COME TO A CLOSE.
I'D LIKE TO WELCOME DEPUTY EDITOR IN CHIEF YOSHIHISA HEISHI TO THE FRONT FOR OUR CLOSING STATEMENT.
YEA-HHH!
CLAP
CLAP

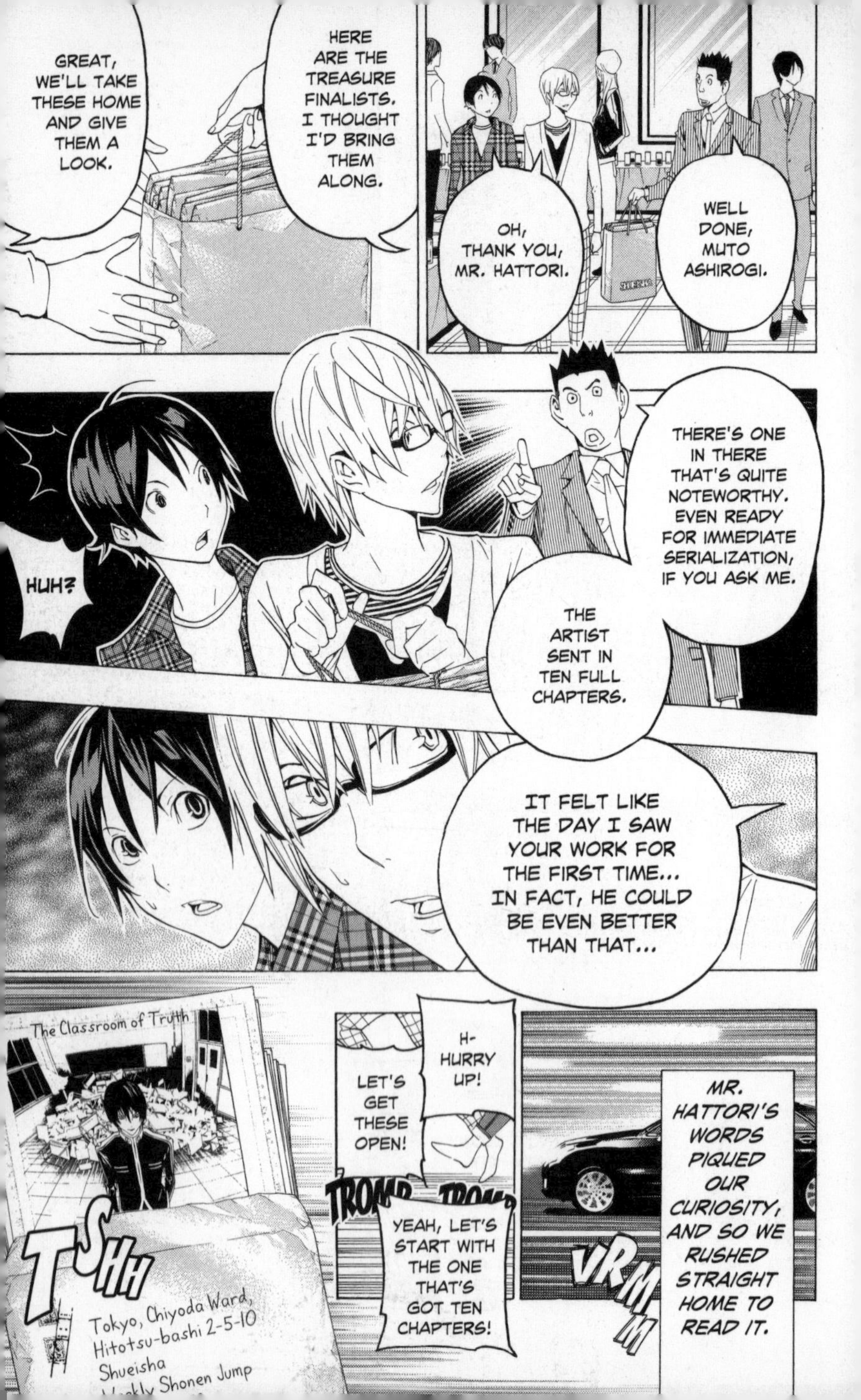
WELL DONE, MUTO ASHIROGI.
OH, THANK YOU, MR. HATTORI.
HERE ARE THE TREASURE FINALISTS. I THOUGHT I'D BRING THEM ALONG.
GREAT, WE'LL TAKE THESE HOME AND GIVE THEM A LOOK.
THERE'S ONE IN THERE THAT'S QUITE NOTEWORTHY. EVEN READY FOR IMMEDIATE SERIALIZATION, IF YOU ASK ME.
HUH?
THE ARTIST SENT IN TEN FULL CHAPTERS.
IT FELT LIKE THE DAY I SAW YOUR WORK FOR THE FIRST TIME... IN FACT, HE COULD BE EVEN BETTER THAN THAT...
MR. HATTORI'S WORDS PIQUED OUR CURIOSITY, AND SO WE RUSHED STRAIGHT HOME TO READ IT.
VRMM
H-HURRY UP!
LET'S GET THESE OPEN!
TROMP TROMP
YEAH, LET'S START WITH THE ONE THAT'S GOT TEN CHAPTERS!
The Classroom of Truth
TSHH
Tokyo, Chiyoda Ward, Hitotsu-bashi 2-5-10
Shueisha

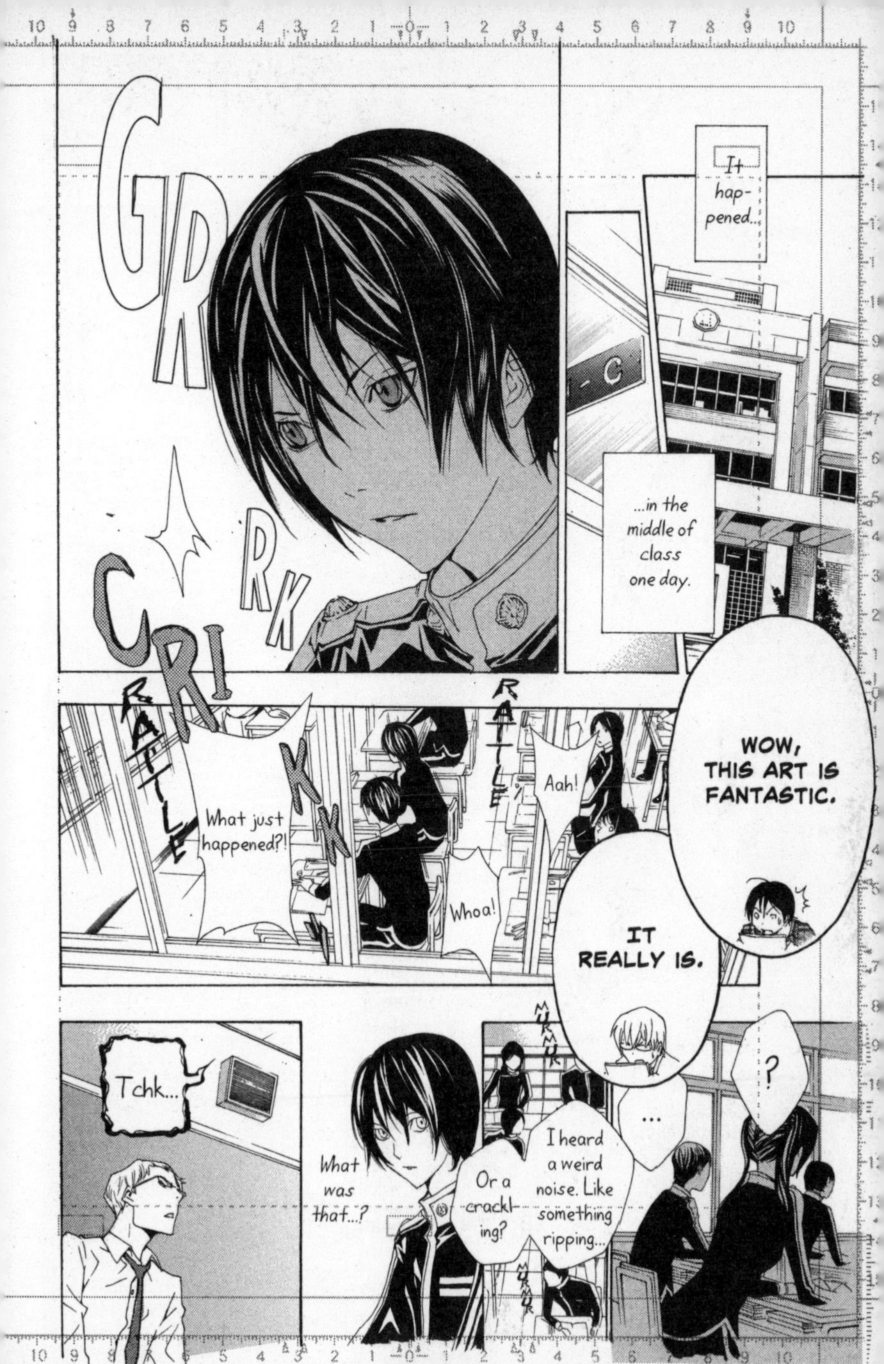
It happened...
...in the middle of class one day.
GRRK
CRIK
WOW, THIS ART IS FANTASTIC.
IT REALLY IS.
RATTLE
Aah!
Whoa!
RATTLE
What just happened?!
?
...
I heard a weird noise. Like something ripping...
Or a crackl-ing?
MURMUR
MURMUR
What was that...?
Tchk...
タイトル
名前
ページ
FOR THE BEST CREATIVE WORK YOU NEED THE BEST MATERIALS & EQUIPMENT.

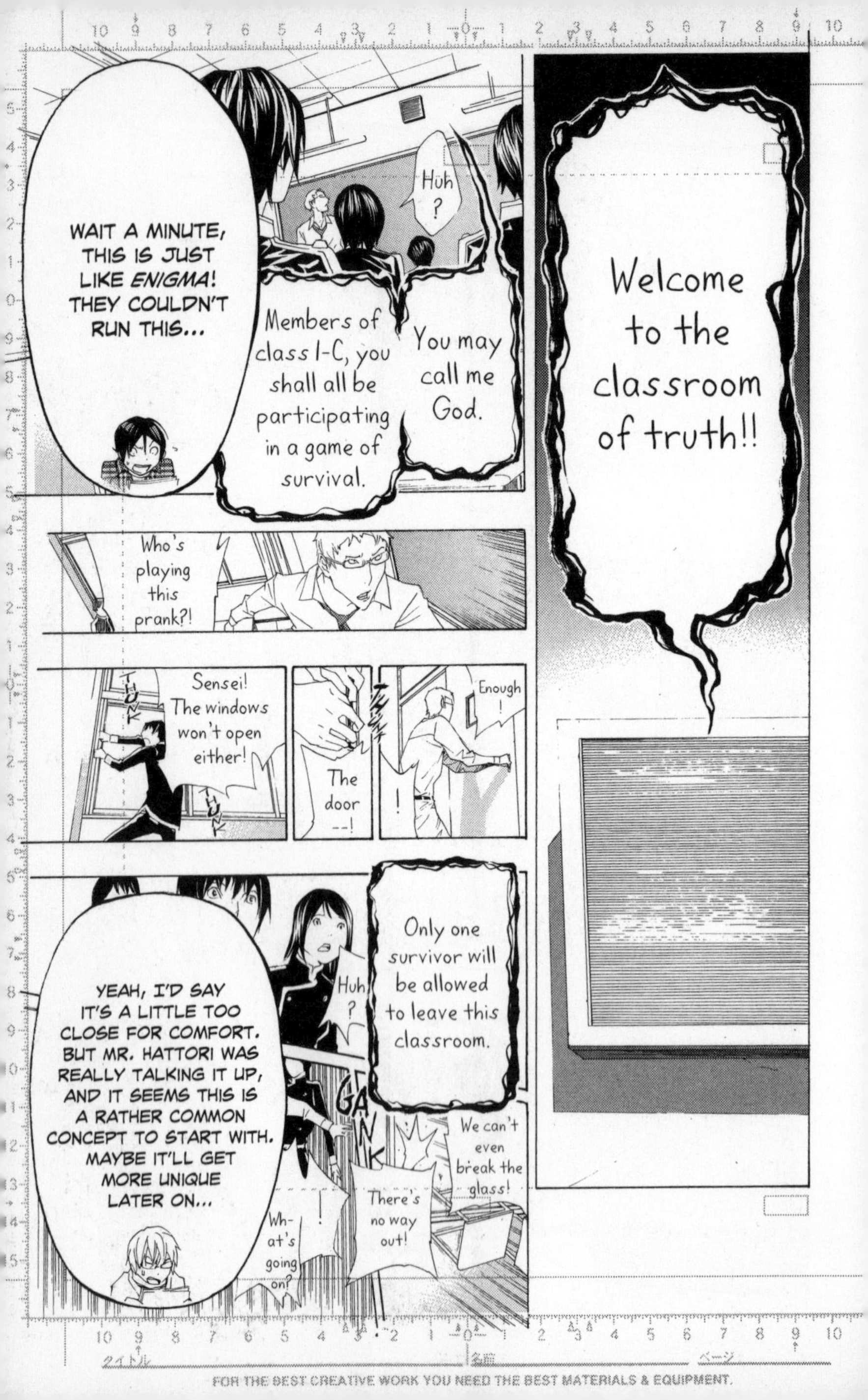
Welcome to the classroom of truth!!
Huh?
You may call me God.
Members of class 1-C, you shall all be participating in a game of survival.
WAIT A MINUTE, THIS IS JUST LIKE *ENIGMA*! THEY COULDN'T RUN THIS...
Who's playing this prank?!
Enough!
!
The door --!
THUNK
Sensei! The windows won't open either!
THUNK
Only one survivor will be allowed to leave this classroom.
Huh?
We can't even break the glass!
There's no way out!
GANK
!
Wh-at's going on?
YEAH, I'D SAY IT'S A LITTLE TOO CLOSE FOR COMFORT. BUT MR. HATTORI WAS REALLY TALKING IT UP, AND IT SEEMS THIS IS A RATHER COMMON CONCEPT TO START WITH. MAYBE IT'LL GET MORE UNIQUE LATER ON...
FOR THE BEST CREATIVE WORK YOU NEED THE BEST MATERIALS & EQUIPMENT.

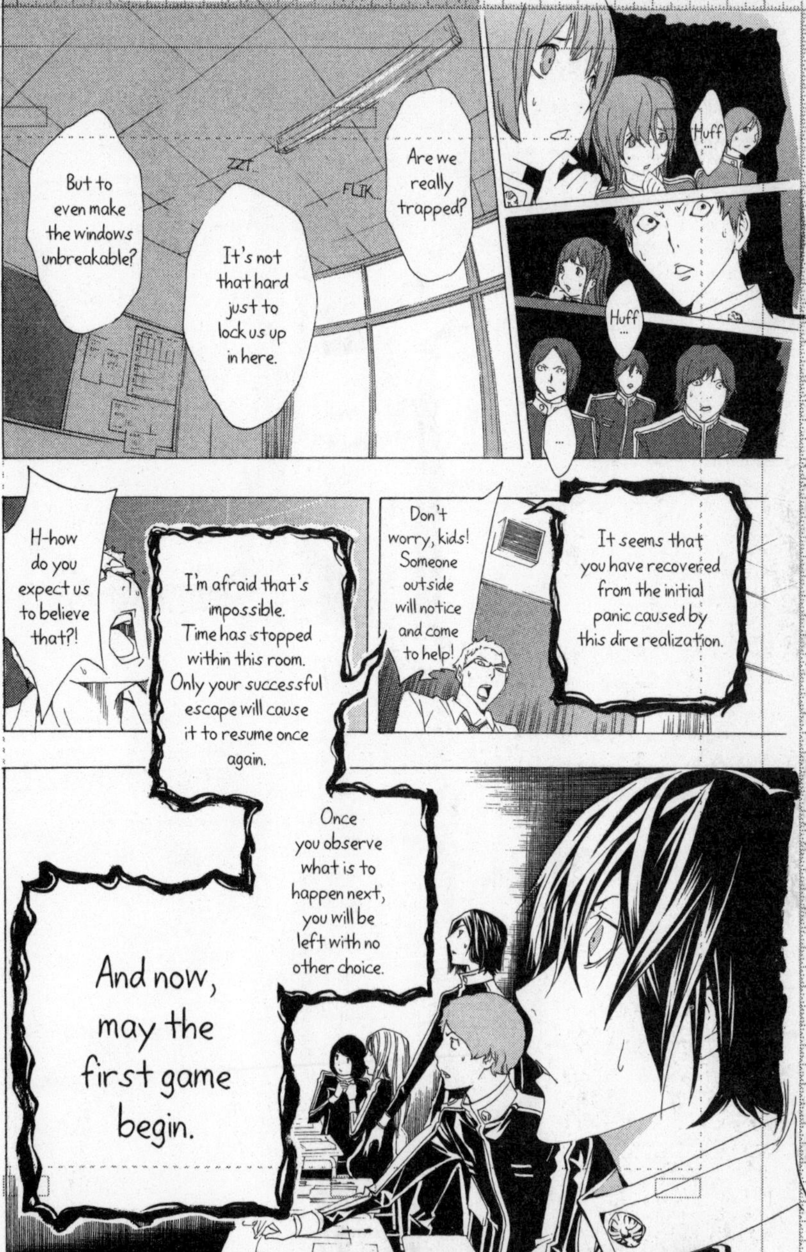
Huff...
Huff...
...
Are we really trapped?
FLIK...
ZZT...
It's not that hard just to lock us up in here.
But to even make the windows unbreakable?
It seems that you have recovered from the initial panic caused by this dire realization.
Don't worry, kids! Someone outside will notice and come to help!
H-how do you expect us to believe that?!
I'm afraid that's impossible. Time has stopped within this room. Only your successful escape will cause it to resume once again.
Once you observe what is to happen next, you will be left with no other choice.
And now, may the first game begin.

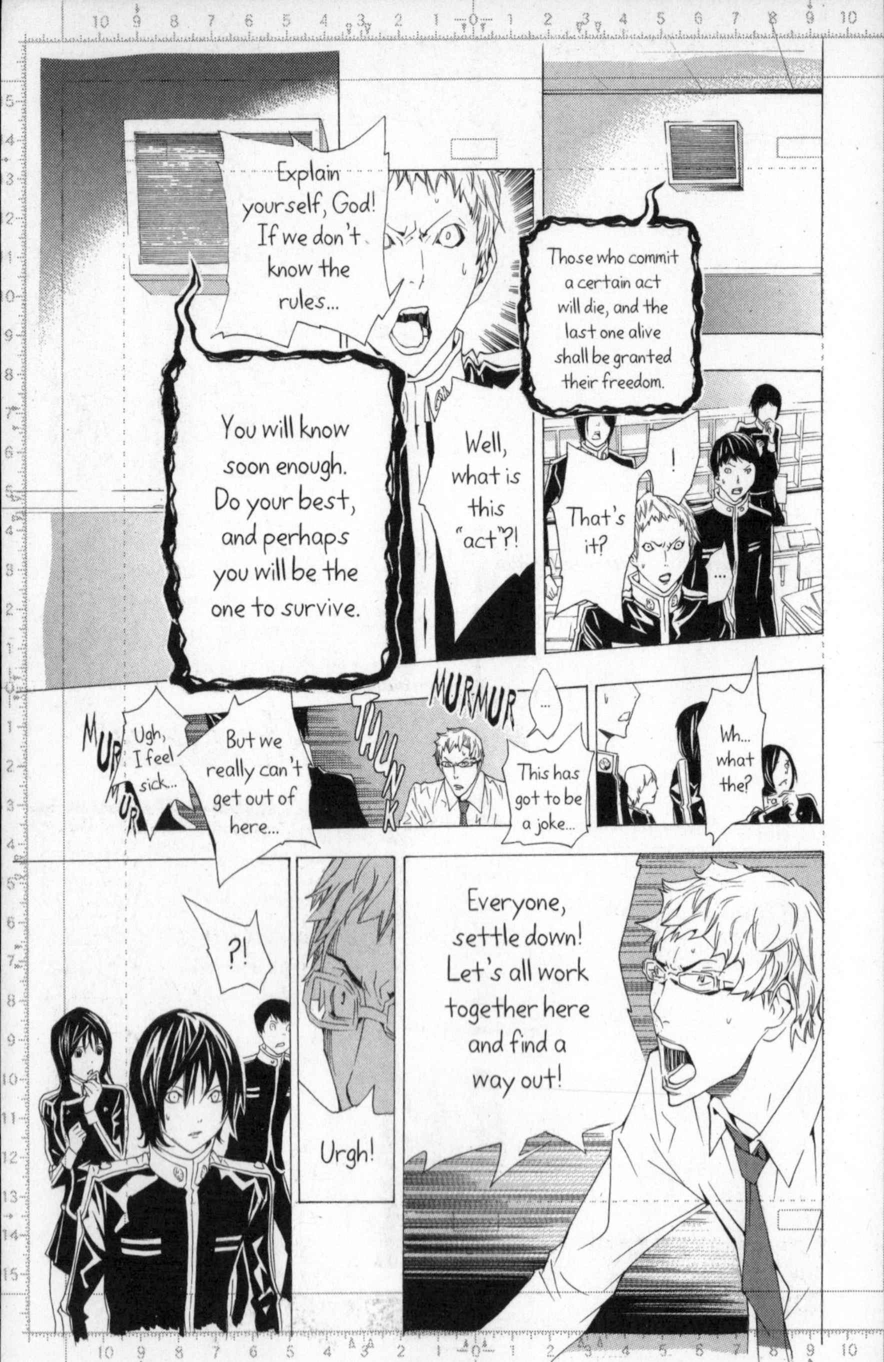
Explain yourself, God! If we don't know the rules...
Those who commit a certain act will die, and the last one alive shall be granted their freedom.
Well, what is this "act"?!
You will know soon enough. Do your best, and perhaps you will be the one to survive.
!
That's it?
...
Wh... what the?
...
MURMUR
This has got to be a joke...
THUNK
But we really can't get out of here...
Ugh, I feel sick...
MURMURMUR
Everyone, settle down! Let's all work together here and find a way out!
Urgh!
?!
FOR THE BEST CREATIVE WORK YOU NEED THE BEST MATERIALS & EQUIPMENT.

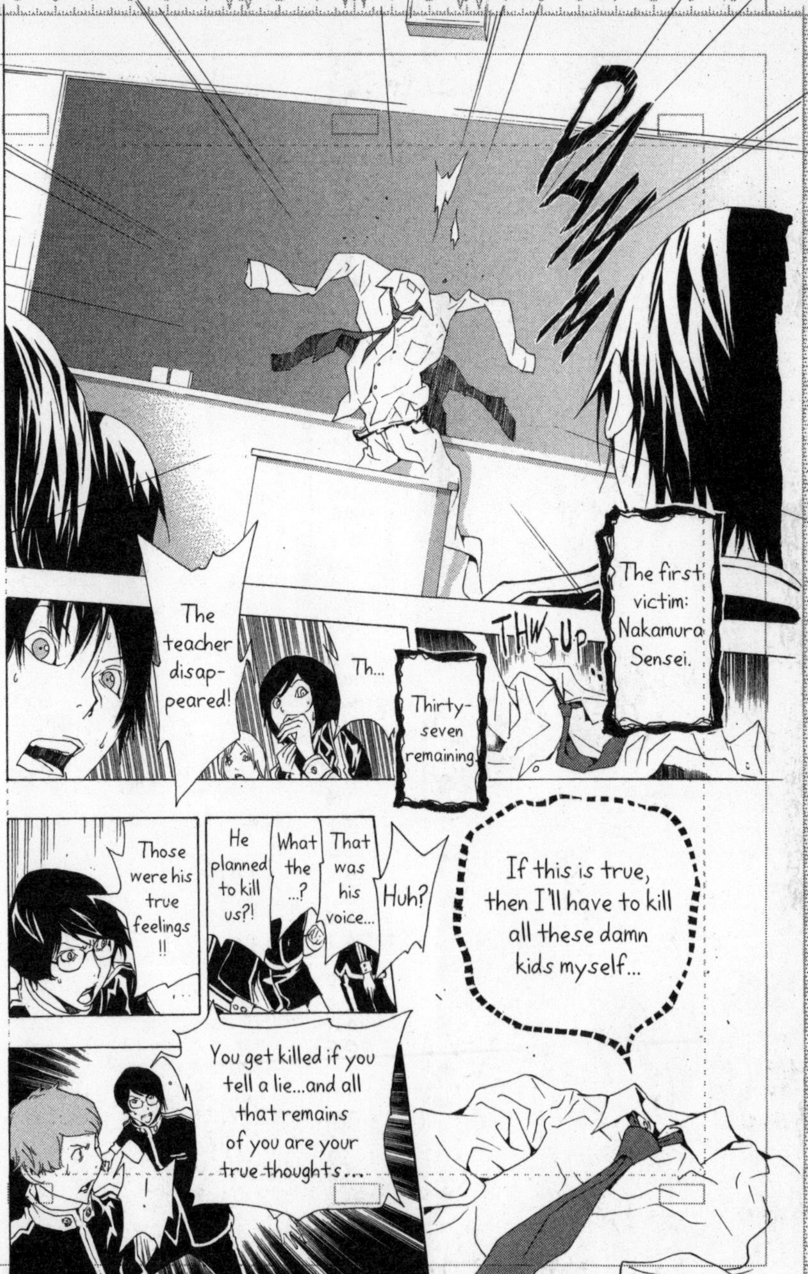
DAMM
The first victim: Nakamura Sensei.
THW-UP..
Thirty-seven remaining.
Th...
The teacher disappeared!
If this is true, then I'll have to kill all these damn kids myself...
Huh?
That was his voice...
What the ...?
He planned to kill us?!
Those were his true feelings!!
...
You get killed if you tell a lie...and all that remains of you are your true thoughts...
!

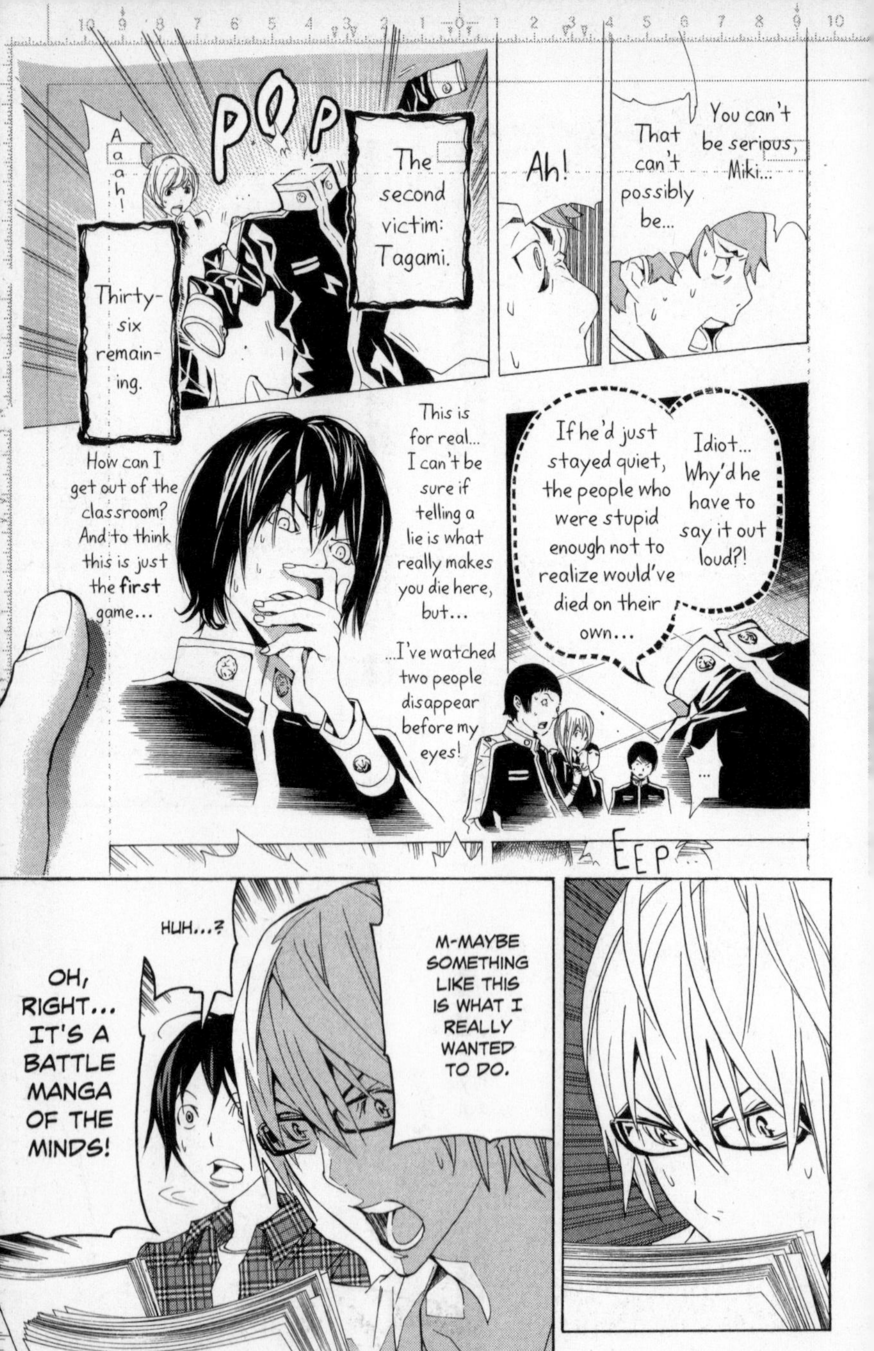
You can't be serious, Miki...
That can't possibly be...
Ah!
POP
The second victim: Tagami.
...
Aaah!
Thirty-six remaining.
Idiot... Why'd he have to say it out loud?!
If he'd just stayed quiet, the people who were stupid enough not to realize would've died on their own...
...
This is for real... I can't be sure if telling a lie is what really makes you die here, but...
...I've watched two people disappear before my eyes!
How can I get out of the classroom? And to think this is just the first game...
EEP
M-MAYBE SOMETHING LIKE THIS IS WHAT I REALLY WANTED TO DO.
HUH...?
OH, RIGHT... IT'S A BATTLE MANGA OF THE MINDS!

13 Fans and Love at First Sight (END)

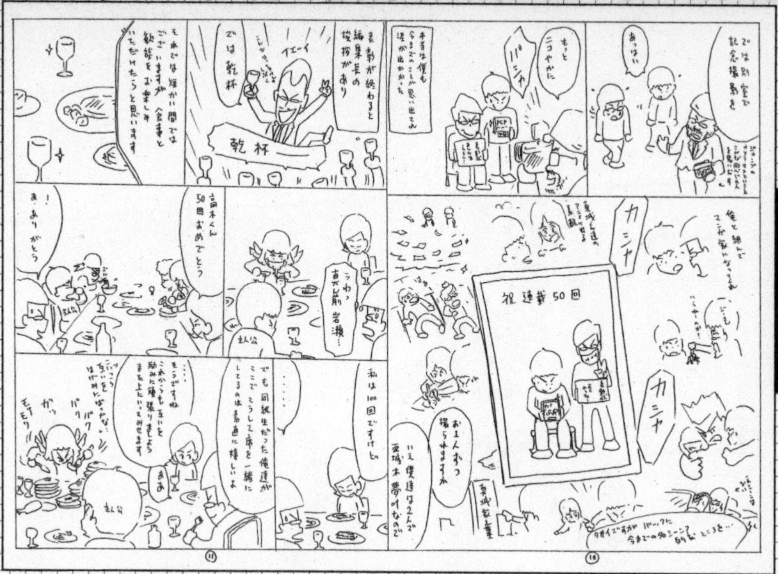

OHBA'S STORYBOARD

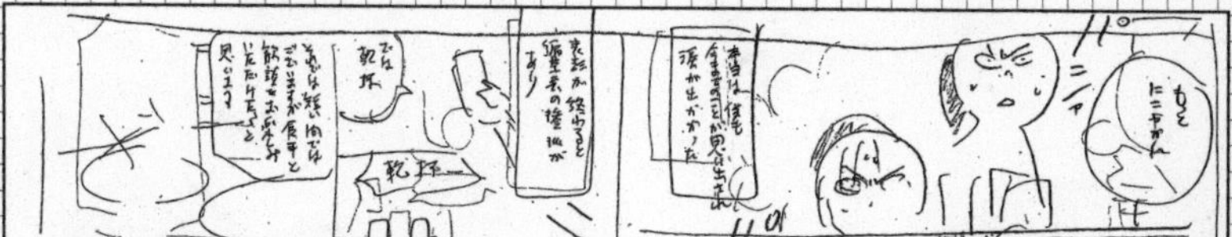

OBATA'S STORYBOARD

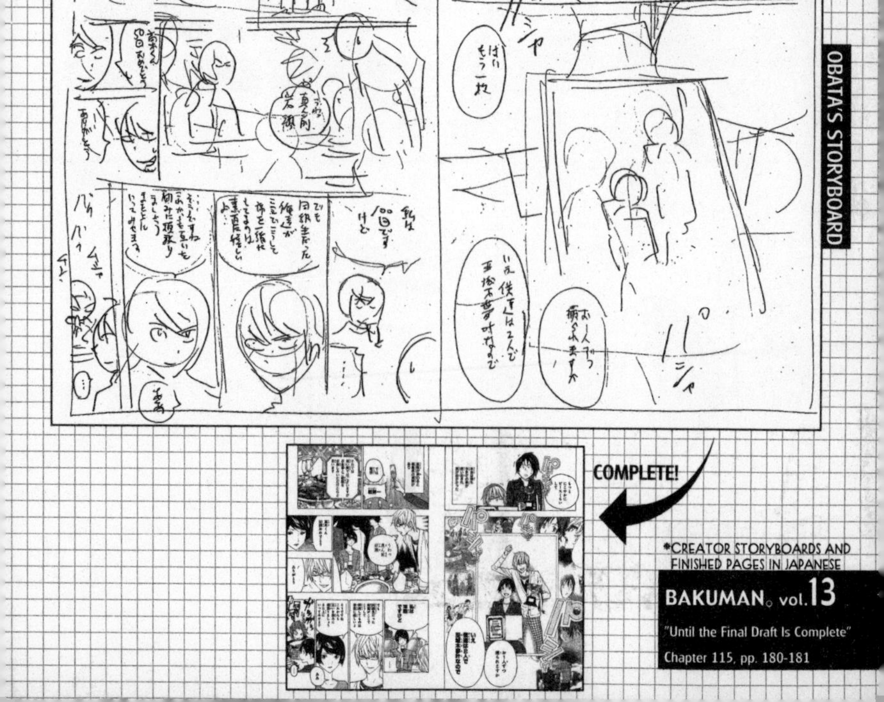

COMPLETE!

*CREATOR STORYBOARDS AND FINISHED PAGES IN JAPANESE

BAKUMAN。vol.13

"Until the Final Draft Is Complete"

Chapter 115, pp. 180-181

BAKUMAN。

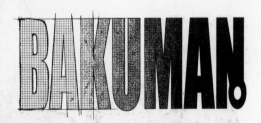

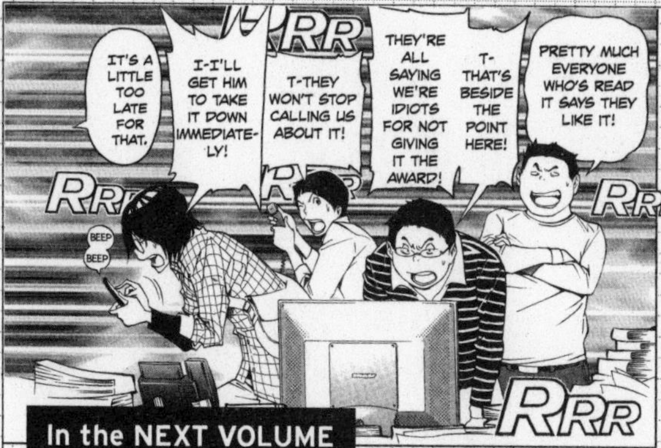
RRR
PRETTY MUCH EVERYONE WHO'S READ IT SAYS THEY LIKE IT!
T- THAT'S BESIDE THE POINT HERE!
THEY'RE ALL SAYING WE'RE IDIOTS FOR NOT GIVING IT THE AWARD!
T-THEY WON'T STOP CALLING US ABOUT IT!
I-I'LL GET HIM TO TAKE IT DOWN IMMEDIATE-LY!
IT'S A LITTLE TOO LATE FOR THAT.
RRR
RRR
RRR
BEEP
BEEP
RRR

In the NEXT VOLUME

As Moritaka and Akito continue reading *The Classroom of Truth*, they notice that the creator has a connection to them! But who is this mysterious newcomer and what is the dark secret to his success? And what trouble will Hiramaru get into when he starts working as Ko Aoki's assistant?!

Available September 2012